AF694987

International Debt Statistics 2022

International Debt Statistics 2022

WORLD BANK GROUP

© 2021 International Bank for Reconstruction and Development / The World Bank
1818 H Street NW, Washington, DC 20433
Telephone: 202-473-1000; Internet: www.worldbank.org

Some rights reserved.

1 2 3 4 24 23 22 21

This work is a product of the staff of The World Bank with external contributions. The findings, interpretations, and conclusions expressed in this work do not necessarily reflect the views of The World Bank, its Board of Executive Directors, or the governments they represent. The World Bank does not guarantee the accuracy, completeness, or currency of the data included in this work and does not assume responsibility for any errors, omissions, or discrepancies in the information, or liability with respect to the use of or failure to use the information, methods, processes, or conclusions set forth. The boundaries, colors, denominations, and other information shown on any map in this work do not imply any judgment on the part of The World Bank concerning the legal status of any territory or the endorsement or acceptance of such boundaries.

Nothing herein shall constitute or be construed or considered to be a limitation upon or waiver of the privileges and immunities of The World Bank, all of which are specifically reserved.

Rights and Permissions

This work is available under the Creative Commons Attribution 3.0 IGO license (CC BY 3.0 IGO) http://creativecommons.org/licenses/by/3.0/igo. Under the Creative Commons Attribution license, you are free to copy, distribute, transmit, and adapt this work, including for commercial purposes, under the following conditions:

Attribution—Please cite the work as follows: World Bank. 2021. *International Debt Statistics 2022*. Washington, DC: World Bank. doi:10.1596/978-1-4648-1800-4. License: Creative Commons Attribution CC BY 3.0 IGO.

Translations—If you create a translation of this work, please add the following disclaimer along with the attribution: *This translation was not created by The World Bank and should not be considered an official World Bank translation. The World Bank shall not be liable for any content or error in this translation.*

Adaptations—If you create an adaptation of this work, please add the following disclaimer along with the attribution: *This is an adaptation of an original work by The World Bank. Views and opinions expressed in the adaptation are the sole responsibility of the author or authors of the adaptation and are not endorsed by The World Bank.*

Third-party content—The World Bank does not necessarily own each component of the content contained within the work. The World Bank therefore does not warrant that the use of any third-party-owned individual component or part contained in the work will not infringe on the rights of those third parties. The risk of claims resulting from such infringement rests solely with you. If you wish to re-use a component of the work, it is your responsibility to determine whether permission is needed for that re-use and to obtain permission from the copyright owner. Examples of components can include, but are not limited to, tables, figures, or images.

All queries on rights and licenses should be addressed to World Bank Publications, The World Bank Group, 1818 H Street NW, Washington, DC 20433, USA; fax: 202-522-2625; e-mail: pubrights@worldbank.org.

ISBN (paper): 978-1-4648-1800-4
ISBN (electronic): 978-1-4648-1801-1
DOI: 10.1596/978-1-4648-1800-4

Cover design: Jomo Tariku, World Bank Group.

The Library of Congress Control Number has been requested.

Table of Contents

Foreword

The COVID-19 pandemic brought unprecedented challenges to low- and middle-income countries. Even prior to the onset of the crisis, rising public debt levels and heightened debt vulnerabilities were already a concern in many countries. These vulnerabilities increased dramatically in 2020. The crisis drove up financing needs and thereby public borrowing, while weakening individual countries' economic fundamentals and capacity to service and repay public debt. The risk now is that too many countries will emerge from the COVID-19 crisis with a large debt overhang that could take years to manage.

The external debt stock of low- and middle-income countries in 2020 rose, on average, 5.6 percent to $8.7 trillion. However, for many countries the increase was in double digits. The external debt stock of countries eligible for the Group of Twenty (G-20) Debt Service Suspension Initiative (DSSI) rose, on average, 12 percent to $860 billion and in some of them by 20 percent or more. For most countries the rise in external indebtedness was not matched by the growth of gross national income and exports.

A large-scale shift in the approach to debt transparency is needed to help countries assess and manage their external debt risks and work toward sustainable debt levels and terms. This is particularly urgent given the scheduled expiration of the DSSI at the end of 2021. The World Bank has long played a leading role in the compilation and dissemination of external debt statistics. *International Debt Statistics*, the World Bank's flagship publication on external debt data, is the most important source of verifiable information on the external debt of low- and middle-income countries and offers a unique dataset that can shape the solutions that will be needed in the coming years.

International Debt Statistics 2022 raises the bar on debt transparency. The 2020 dataset has been expanded to provide more detailed and disaggregated data on external debt than ever before. The data now break down each borrowing country's external debt stock into the amounts owed to each official and private creditor, the currency composition, and the financial terms of the loans extended. In addition, for DSSI-eligible countries, the dataset includes the debt service deferred in 2020 by each bilateral creditor and the projected monthly debt-service payments that will be owed on this debt. More importantly, the borrower classification now presents the Central Bank as a separate borrower entity. Beginning with 2020, the data increasingly reflect external borrowing by state-owned enterprises, and most 2020 data are actual, not estimated, transactions.

The transparency of data on debt must evolve to keep pace with an ever-changing creditor landscape and with new and increasingly complex debt-like instruments and data requirements. We are working hard to be able to capture all debt instruments, including external borrowing by state-owned enterprises, Central Bank deposits, and currency swaps. We are also collecting information on loan guarantees and collateral arrangements.

Reliable and comprehensive debt data are the cornerstone of good development outcomes. Borrowing allows governments and growing private sectors to mobilize the resources they need to invest in innovation, health systems, education, and infrastructure and build durable economic recoveries. Debt transparency invites new investment and helps safeguard long-term sustainability. The World Bank is committed to working with governments and partners to achieve that outcome—by continually improving debt data coverage, quality, timeliness, and transparency.

David Malpass
President
World Bank Group

Acknowledgments

This volume was prepared by the Debt Statistics Team of the Development Data Group (DECDG) at the World Bank, led by Evis Rucaj and comprising Parul Agarwal, Arturo Albarran-Cortes, Arzu Aytekin Balibek, Kifaye Didem Bayar, Daniella Kathyuska Bolanos-Misas, Allen Charles Church Jr., Wendy Ven-dee Huang, Malvina Pollock, Rubena Sukaj, Tin Yu To, Rasiel Vellos, and Bedri Zymeri. The overview of current developments was prepared by the Debt Statistics Team; Aart Kraay, Director of Development Policy and Deputy Chief Economist, Development Economics (DEC), and the MTI Global Macro and Debt team at the World Bank provided valuable feedback on the overview section; and the final statistics were reviewed by country economists. The team was assisted by Nancy Kebe. The work was carried out under the management of Nada Hamadeh, Program Manager, and the direction of Haishan Fu, Director, DECDG. Valuable guidance and input was provided by Carmen M. Reinhart, Senior Vice President and Chief Economist of the World Bank Group.

International Debt Statistics electronic products were prepared by a team led by Anna Maria Kojzar and Sebastian Ariel Dolber and comprising Ramgopal Erabelly, Fatih Dogan, Rajesh Kumar Danda, Gangadhar Simhani, Surya Anandan, Vijayakumar Juttu Mohan, and Palani Devi Somasundaram. The cover was designed by Jomo Tariku. Jewel McFadden, acquisitions editor; Michael Harrup, production editor; and Orlando Mota, print coordinator, for the World Bank's formal publishing program coordinated the publication and dissemination of the book.

PART I
Overview

Overview

The world economy is still reeling from the once-in-a-generation crisis, the COVID-19 pandemic, that hit every part of the globe in 2020 and brought economic activity to a grinding halt. Governments around the world responded rapidly to stem both the health and economic contagion with fiscal and monetary stimulus packages. Hopes for a quick recovery were dashed when the second wave of the pandemic hit the world's major economies in October 2020. World gross domestic product (GDP) fell by an estimated 4.3 percent in 2020—the sharpest contraction of output since the Great Depression. Developed economies were most severely impacted by the pandemic, and output is estimated to have shrunk by 5.6 percent in 2020. Low- and middle-income countries experienced a relatively less severe contraction, with output estimated to have contracted by 2.5 percent in 2020. There were, however, significant differences in the size of the shock among low- and middle-income countries, with those in Latin America and the Caribbean hardest hit. Countries in East Asia and the Pacific fared better, and their output is estimated to have expanded by 1 percent in 2020, thanks to China's robust recovery.

Against this unprecedented and uncertain backdrop, the development in debt stocks and financial flows to low- and middle-income countries in 2020 was a story of highs and lows. Rapid intervention and extraordinary support from multilateral institutions, led by the World Bank and the International Monetary Fund (IMF), raised net inflows from multilateral creditors to $117 billion, the highest level in a decade. The Debt Service Suspension Initiative (DSSI) was launched by Group of Twenty (G-20) countries in April 2020 to assist the poorest and most vulnerable low- and middle-income countries in managing the adverse impacts of the COVID-19 pandemic. It offered 73 International Development Association (IDA)-eligible and least developed countries a temporary suspension of debt-service payments owed to official bilateral creditors. The suspension period was originally set for payments falling due from May 1 to December 31, 2020, but was subsequently extended to end-December 2021. Bond issues from low- and middle-income countries were at a record high of $457 billion in 2020, but issuance from China accounted for nearly half of this amount. Market borrowers in Sub-Saharan Africa were priced out of the bond market for much of the year, and investor retreat from domestic markets in many low- and middle-income countries' biggest borrowers led to large-scale capital flight and shrank debt inflows. Net debt inflows rose 9 percent to $435 billion, but the 26 percent increase in inflows to China masked a marginal, 1 percent increase in debt inflows to other low- and middle-income countries.

Many developing countries entered 2020 in a vulnerable position, with public external debt already at elevated levels. Fiscal support to mitigate the impacts of COVID-19 pushed debt levels in some countries to record highs. The external debt stock of low- and middle-income countries rose, on average 5.3 percent in 2020, about the same pace as the two prior years. Prior to the onset of the COVID-19 pandemic, rising public debt levels and heightened debt vulnerabilities were already a cause for concern in many of the world's poorest IDA borrowers, and these have been further exacerbated. In 2020, the external debt stock of IDA DSSI-eligible countries rose, on average, 12 percent in 2020, and for nine of these countries it rose 20 percent or more. The rise in external indebtedness was not matched by gross national income (GNI) and exports growth. Low- and middle-income countries external debt-to-GNI ratio rose to 29 percent in 2020 from 27 percent in 2019, and the debt-to-export ratio increased to 123 percent from 106 percent in 2019. The worsening of debt indicators was widespread across all geographic regions.

Equity inflows to low- and middle-income countries fell 15 percent in 2020 to $473 billion.

The pandemic had a significant impact on foreign direct investment (FDI) flows. Lockdowns around the world slowed existing investment projects, and the prospect of a global recession deterred investors and led multinational entities to reassess the viability of new projects. Developed countries suffered the largest contraction, but the downturn was global. FDI inflows to low- and middle-income countries combined fell, on average, 14 percent in 2020 to $435 billion, the lowest level in a decade. For low- and middle-income countries, excluding China, FDI fell 23 percent in 2020. Investors in portfolio equity continued to favor China and India in 2020, but overall portfolio equity inflows fell 19 percent from the 2019 level.

International Debt Statistics is the World Bank's flagship publication on external debt data instituted in response to the first global oil crisis of 1973 and now in its 48th consecutive year of publication. This edition provides disaggregated information on public and publicly guaranteed debt stocks and flows by creditor country, including official bilateral creditors and multilateral institution entities. The World Bank has long played a lead role in the compilation and dissemination of external debt statistics and the enhancement and expansion of debt data coverage to meet institutional needs, and the needs of policy makers, analysts, and the broader international community. The task of managing COVID-19-related debt vulnerabilities and crises gave rise to new demands for more granular data regarding the volume and terms of amounts borrowed and lent. For this reason, the DSSI, launched by the G-20 in April 2020 and implemented with the assistance of the World Bank and the IMF, set a standard for greater debt data transparency by member countries of the World Bank and the IMF, as borrowers and as lenders.

This year's publication raises the bar on debt transparency. The 2020 dataset has been expanded to provide more detailed and disaggregated data on external debt than ever before. It now includes information on average lending terms by creditor country (commitment amounts, maturity, grace period, interest rate, and grant element) and the currency composition of debt stock. For DSSI-eligible countries the dataset has expanded to include debt service deferred in 2020 by each bilateral creditor and the projected monthly debt-service payments owed to bilateral creditors in 2021. The borrower classification now shows Central Bank debt, including new debt instruments. A new debt statistics website has also been launched to provide a user-friendly one-stop shop, with enhanced data query capabilities for access to the IDS dataset and other debt statistics.

International Debt Statistics 2022 presents comprehensive stock and flow data for 123 low- and middle-income countries that report to the World Bank Debtor Reporting System (DRS) and a summary overview of the key elements driving outcomes in 2020 debt stocks and financial flows. The headline numbers mask divergent trends because of the dominance of the largest economies. This is particularly so for China, where the volumes of financial flows and external debt stock are not large relative to the size of the domestic economy but are significant in relation to those of other low- and middle-income countries. To assist in the interpretation of the data, the overview looks behind the headline numbers and analyzes recent developments and trends at the regional and country level as well as for the subgroup of DSSI-eligible countries.

Key Messages of the 2020 Data Are as Follows:

- Net financial (debt and equity) flows to low- and middle-income countries fell for the second consecutive year in 2020 to $909 million. Net debt inflows rose 9 percent to $435 billion ($400 in 2019), but net equity inflows fell 15 percent to $473 billion ($554 billion in 2019). FDI inflows fell 14 percent to $435 billion, the lowest level in a decade, and portfolio equity inflows fell 19 percent to $39 billion.
    - Over half of net financial flows (debt and equity) to low- and middle-income countries in 2020 were accounted for by China, the largest recipient. Net financial flows to China rose 33 percent in 2020 to $466 billion. Net debt inflows to China rose 62 percent to $233 billion ($144 billion in 2019), and net equity inflows rose 12 percent to $233 billion ($207 billion in 2019).

  - Net financial (debt and equity) inflows to low- and middle-income countries excluding China fell 26 percent in 2020 to $443 billion ($602 billion in 2019). Net debt inflows fell 21 percent to $202 billion ($256 billion in 2019), and net equity inflows fell 31 percent to $240 billion ($346 billion in 2019).
- Low- and middle-income countries' combined external debt stocks at end-2020 were $8.7 trillion. They rose 5.3 percent in 2020, an annual rate of increase comparable to that in 2018 and 2019. Long-term public and publicly guaranteed external debt rose 10 percent in 2020 to $3.7 trillion, equivalent to 43 percent of total external debt stock. Long-term private non-guaranteed debt rose 3 percent to $2.8 trillion. Short-term debt was unchanged at $2.2 trillion.
- The external debt stock of DSSI-eligible countries rose 12 percent in 2020 to $860 billion ($770 billion in 2019). Long-term public and publicly guaranteed debt rose 14 percent to $618 billion ($541 billion in 2019). Debt owed to multilateral creditors, including the IMF, rose 22 percent to $295 billion ($243 billion in 2019), equivalent to 48 percent of public and publicly guaranteed debt stock at end-2020.
- Net debt inflows to low- and middle-income countries rose 9 percent in 2020 to $435 billion ($400 billion in 2019). Long-term debt inflows rose 13 percent to $419 billion ($372 billion in 2019). Short-term debt inflows fell 43 percent in 2020 to $16 billion ($28 billion in 2019).
  - Net debt inflows to low- and middle-income countries excluding China fell 21 percent to $202 billion ($256 billion in 2019). Net long-term debt inflows rose by 1 percent to $217 billion ($215 billion in 2019). Short-term debt contracted to an outflow of $15 billion ($41 billion inflow in 2019).
- Net debt inflows of external public debt to DSSI-eligible countries rose 25 percent in 2020 to $71 billion, the highest level of the decade. Net inflows from multilateral creditors, including the IMF, were $42 billion, and net inflows from bilateral creditors were $10 billion.
- Bondholders and multilateral institutions accounted for 95 percent of long-term debt inflows to low- and middle-income countries in 2020.
  - Net inflows from bondholders were $280 million in 2020, 10 percent higher than the comparable 2019 figure, and equivalent to two-thirds of 2020 long-term debt inflows. Bondholders accounted for 91 percent of long-term debt inflows to China and, on average, for 44 percent of long-term debt inflows to other low- and middle-income countries.
  - Net debt inflows from multilateral creditors doubled in 2020 to $117 billion, equivalent to 90 percent of inflows from official creditors. Inflows from multilateral creditors accounted for, on average, two thirds of long-term debt inflows to low- and middle-income countries in 2020, excluding China. Net inflows from the World Bank (International Bank for Reconstruction and Development [IBRD] and IDA) rose 42 percent in 2020 to $27 billion.
- New bond issuance by the 123 low- and middle-income countries reporting to the DRS reached an all-time high of $457 billion in 2020, 14 percent higher than 2019 ($400 million). China accounted for close to half (48 percent) of bonds issued in 2020.
- In low- and middle-income countries, excluding China, the ratio of debt to GNI rose to an average of 42 percent in 2020 (37 percent in 2019) and the debt-to-export ratio increased to an average of 154 percent (126 percent in 2019). The worsening of debt indicators was widespread and impacted countries in all geographic regions.
- For DSSI-eligible countries debt indicators worsened significantly over the past decade. In 2020, only 44 percent of DSSI-eligible countries had a debt-to-GNI ratio at or below 60 percent and in 7 percent of DSSI-eligible countries it exceeded 100 percent. In 2020, 21 percent of DSSI eligible countries had a debt-to-export ratio over 250 percent.

Table O.1 Aggregate Net Financial Flows to Low- and Middle-income Countries, 2011–20
US$ (billion)

	2011	2012	2013	2014	2015	2016	2017	2018	2019	2020
Net financial flows, debt and equity	1,324.9	1,223.8	1,457.7	1,136.3	207.6	721.0	1,289.9	1,108.2	953.8	908.6
Percent of GNI (%)	5.7	5.0	5.6	4.2	0.8	2.8	4.5	3.7	3.1	3.0
Net debt inflows	717.2	587.7	814.8	539.8	-316.1	208.4	755.4	574.5	400.1	435.4
Long-term	405.0	468.5	447.6	394.7	171.6	243.3	433.4	352.4	372.3	419.4
Official creditors	39.1	34.3	30.7	47.8	49.2	62.3	56.2	81.3	64.0	128.6
World Bank (IBRD and IDA)	6.4	12.0	14.1	15.1	17.6	13.5	13.1	14.7	19.1	27.2
IMF	0.5	-8.4	-17.7	-7.2	4.8	5.0	3.6	30.9	21.6	46.5
Private creditors	365.9	434.2	416.8	346.9	122.4	181.0	377.2	271.1	308.3	290.8
Bonds	150.5	225.7	172.7	174.8	74.9	120.1	289.1	203.6	255.2	280.1
Banks and other private	215.4	208.6	244.2	172.1	47.5	60.9	88.1	67.5	53.1	10.7
Short-term	312.2	119.1	367.2	145.1	-487.7	-34.9	322.0	222.2	27.8	16.0
Net equity flows	607.6	636.1	642.9	596.5	523.6	512.6	534.5	533.6	553.7	473.2
Net foreign direct investment inflows	603.8	538.8	572.8	512.7	502.4	467.9	467.7	496.5	505.7	434.5
Net portfolio equity inflows	3.8	97.4	70.1	83.8	21.2	44.7	66.7	37.2	48.0	38.7
Change in reserves (– = increase)	-457.4	-284.1	-523.3	96.9	607.1	274.9	-313.5	84.1	-189.3	-330.4
Memorandum item										
Workers' remittances	337.2	362.8	384.0	414.8	416.9	408.0	444.2	481.9	501.7	499.5

Sources: World Bank Debtor Reporting System, International Monetary Fund, and Bank for International Settlements.

Aggregate Financial Flows to Low- and Middle-Income Countries

Financial flows to low- and middle-income countries fell for the second consecutive year in 2020. Aggregate net financial flows, debt and equity combined, totaled $909 billion in 2020, 5 percent lower than the comparable figure for 2019. Measured relative to borrower countries' GNI, aggregate financial flows were equivalent to 3 percent, on par with 2019 but short of the 5.7 percent of GNI in 2011. The decline in net financial flows was the outcome of a 9 percent rise in net debt inflows (gross disbursements of new financing minus principal payments) to $435 billion from $400 billion in 2019, and a 15 percent contraction in net equity inflows. Foreign direct investment inflows, long considered the most resilient and least volatile component of financial flows, fell 14 percent in 2020 to $434 billion, their lowest level in a decade. Portfolio equity inflows dropped 19 percent to $39 billion.

China accounted for over half of the combined aggregate net inflows to low- and middle-income countries in 2020. Aggregate financial flows to China rose 33 percent in 2020 to $466 billion, equivalent to 51 percent of aggregate financial flows to all low- and middle-income countries. Inflows to China were driven by a 62 percent increase in net debt inflows to $233 billion, from $144 billion in 2019, and a 12 percent rise in net equity inflows also to $233 billion (see box O.1). This was in sharp contrast to aggregate net financial flows to other low- and middle-income countries, which fell 26 percent in 2020 to $443 billion, from $602 billion in 2019. The decline was due to a 21 percent contraction in debt inflows and a steeper 31 percent fall in net equity inflows. Within net equity flows, FDI fell 23 percent and portfolio equity flows were negative with an outflow of $24 billion compared to a small, $3 billon inflow in 2019.

Aside from China, the downturn in aggregate financial flows to the largest borrowers was much sharper than to other low- and middle-income countries. Aggregate financial flows to low- and middle-income countries' nine largest borrowers, excluding China (defined on the basis of end-2020 external debt stock), fell to $151 billion in 2020, close to half the comparable figure for 2019.[1] This reflected a near total collapse in net debt inflows, which plummeted from $110 billion in 2019 to $4 billion in 2020 and a 33 percent contraction in net equity inflows. In contrast, other low- and middle-income countries recorded a 7 percent rise in aggregate financial inflows in 2020 to $292 billion underpinned by a 36 percent increase in net debt inflows to $198 billion. However, net equity inflows fell 26 percent, in parallel with those of the nine major borrowers. As a result, net debt inflows accounted for 68 percent of aggregate financial flows to these countries in 2020 as compared to 54 percent in 2019.

[1] The top-10 borrowers, defined as those with the largest end-2020 external debt stock, are Argentina, Brazil, China, India, Indonesia, Mexico, the Russian Federation, South Africa, Thailand, and Turkey.

Figure O.1 Aggregate Net Financial Flows to Low and Middle-Income Countries, Excluding China, 2011–20

US$ (billion)

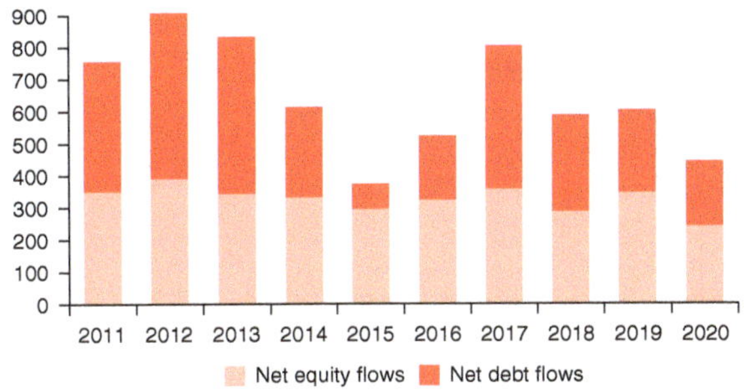

Sources: World Bank Debtor Reporting System, International Monetary Fund, and Bank for International Settlements.

Figure O.2 Aggregate Net Financial Flows to Major Borrowers and Other Low- and Middle-Income Countries, 2019–20

US$ (billion)

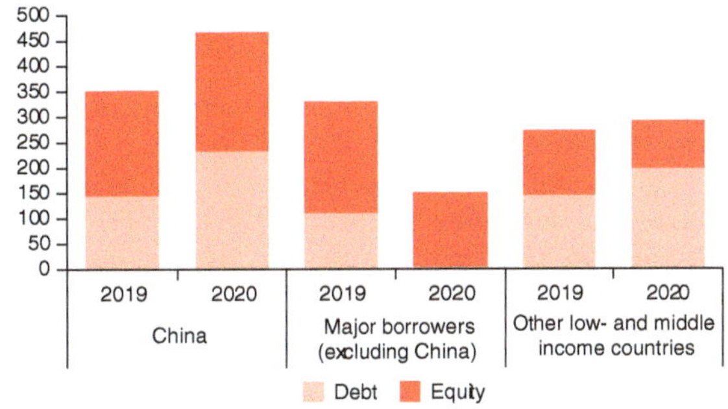

Sources: World Bank Debtor Reporting System and International Monetary Fund.

Box O.1 China: The Largest Borrower and Lender among Low- and Middle-Income Countries

China—A Recipient of External Financial Flows

Over the past decade almost 60 percent of net aggregate financial flows to low- and middle-income countries from external creditors and investors went to China. Over this period China received inflows close to $4 trillion, of which 40 percent were debt-creating flows and 60 percent were foreign direct investment and portfolio equity flows. In 2020, aggregate financial flows to China rose 32 percent to $466 billion, driven by a 62 percent increase in net debt inflows to $233 billion and a 12 percent rise in net equity inflows also to $233 billion.

China's external debt stock rose 11 percent in 2020 to $2.3 trillion, including both domestic and foreign currency–denominated debt, but remained moderate in relation to gross national income at 16 percent. Short-term debt, of which about a third was trade related, accounted for the largest share of China's end-2020 external debt stock, 53 percent at end-2020, down slightly from 57 percent at end-2019. Long-term debt was the fastest-growing component, rising 22 percent in 2020 to $1.1 trillion. The major contributor was the $217 billion in bond issuances by public and private entities in the China Interbank Bond Market (CIBM) purchased by non-residents. This was 65 percent higher than the comparable figure for 2019.

Figure BO.1.1 Aggregate Net Financial Flows to China, 2011–20

US$ (billion)

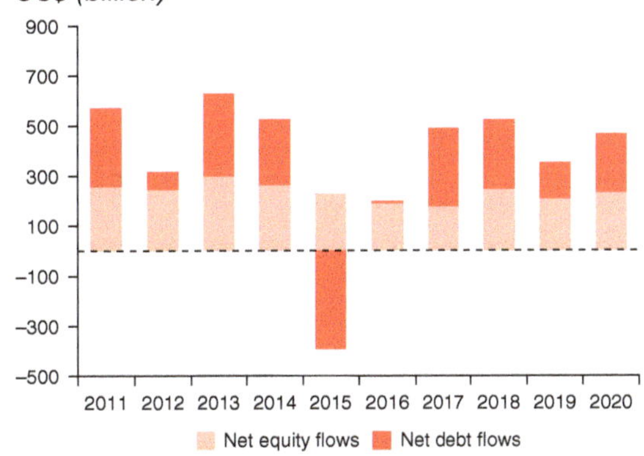

Sources: World Bank Debtor Reporting System, International Monetary Fund, State Administration of Foreign Exchange of the People's Republic of China, and Bank for International Settlements.

The sharp rise in non-resident investors' expansion in the holdings of Chinese renminbi bonds in 2020 reflects not only the economy's early recovery from the COVID-19 pandemic ahead of other major economies, but also China's concerted efforts to liberalize their

Box O.1 China: The Largest Borrower and Lender among Low- and Middle-Income Countries (*Continued*)

financial accounts. Non-resident participation in China's onshore bond market has risen steadily since 2016 when the market was opened to foreign investors. At end-2020, Chinese bonds held by non-residents totaled about $635 billion and accounted for 58 percent of China's long-term external debt.

Since 2016, Chinese authorities have implemented various programs and measures to improve non-resident access to the CIBM. The introduction of the CIBM Direct Access program removed investment quotas or repatriation restrictions for foreign institutional investors. The Bond Connect program, launched in July 2017, gave investors the option of registering and settling trades onshore, easing investor concerns over repatriation and capital account risk since the assets are held and settled offshore. In 2018, repatriation and holding period restrictions were removed. In June 2020, quota restrictions were abolished, and repatriation of fund procedures simplified, while in November 2020, in response to investor feedback on ease of access, the application process was streamlined. Inclusion of renminbi (RMB) bonds in the Bloomberg Barclays Global Aggregate Index and China-A shares in FTSE Russell emerging market index and automated links between the Shanghai, London, and Hong Kong SAR, China markets also encourage and facilitate foreign investors' appetite for access to RMB bonds.

The CIBM, China's domestic bond market to which non-resident have access, has an estimated market value of $12 trillion at end-2020, making it the world's second-largest bond market after the United States, or third if the Eurozone markets are counted together as one. It is regulated by the People's Bank of China and supported by the China Central Depository and Clearing Company Limited. The CIBM has four main segments: (1) ***central government sovereign bonds*** issued in a range of maturities; (2) ***local government bonds*** issued by provincial-level governments to refinance short-term bank loans into longer-term bonds and mostly held by domestic banks; (3) ***policy bank bonds*** issued by the three main development banks, China Development Bank, Agricultural Development Bank of China, and the China Exim-Bank; and (4) ***corporate bonds*** issued by

Figure BO.1.2 Low- and Middle-Income Countries' Debt to China, 2011–20
US$ (billion)

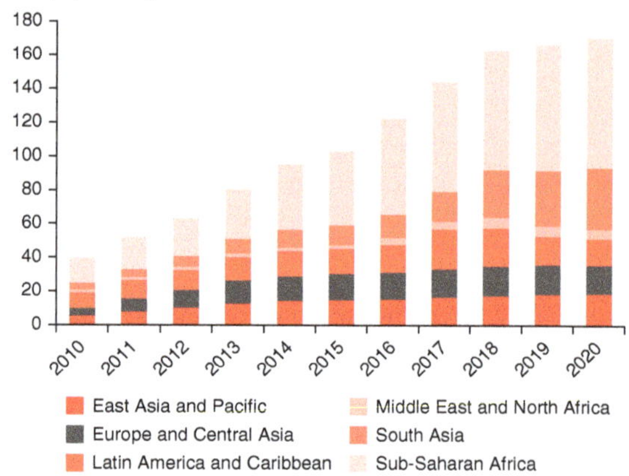

Source: World Bank Debtor Reporting System.

both public and private entities, but primarily by state-owned enterprises including the four major government-owned banks, Agricultural Bank of China, Bank of China, China Construction Bank, and Industrial and Commercial Bank of China. Policy bank and corporate bonds, which together account for 44 percent of the CIBM market value, both support development of the Chinese economy and finance a significant share of China's overseas lending.

China—One of Low- and Middle-Income Countries' Largest Creditors

Over the past two decades China has been one of the world's fastest-growing economies with annual gross domestic product growth averaging over 9 percent, a pace the World Bank describes as "the fastest sustained expansion by a major economy in history." This, combined with China's "Going Global Strategy," initiated in 1999 to foster Chinese investment abroad, has propelled Chinese overseas investment and lending. China has become not only low- and middle-income countries' largest borrower, but also one of the largest creditors.

Low- and middle-income countries' combined debt to China was $170 billion at end-2020,

Box O.1 China: The Largest Borrower and Lender among Low- and Middle-Income Countries (*Continued*)

more than three times the comparable level in 2011. To put this figure in context, low- and middle-income countries' combined obligations to the International Bank for Reconstruction and Development were $204 billion at end-2020 and to the International Development Association $177 billion. Most of the debt owed to China relates to large infrastructure projects and operations in the extractive industries. Countries in Sub-Saharan Africa, led by Angola, have seen one of the sharpest rises in Chinese debt although the pace of accumulation has slowed since 2018. The region accounted for 45 percent of end-2020 obligations to China. In South Asia, debt to China has risen, from $4.7 billion in 2011 to $36.3 billion in 2020, and China is now the largest bilateral creditor to the Maldives, Pakistan, and Sri Lanka.

Regarding measurement and country coverage:

What is measured: The debt referred to above is defined as financing that has been disbursed by China, minus any principal payments made by the borrower. It does not include loan commitments and undisbursed amounts that are much larger. *Country coverage*: Debt owed to China by the Russian Federation and República Bolivariana de Venezuela is not included: these data are not reported to the DRS. Russian debt is reported in aggregate forms; China as a creditor is not identified. *Sectoral coverage*: (1) Public and publicly guaranteed debt. This sector included government, public sector entities, and private sector publicly guaranteed debt. Some DRS reporters do not include borrowing by state-owned enterprises not guaranteed by the government in external public debt data. This exclusion in most instances is related to the national legal framework that governs the coverage, measurement, and monitoring of public debt. The non-reporting of this category lowers the total figures by creditor country breakdown. (2) China lending to private sector not publicly guaranteed or through special purpose vehicles is captured in private non-guaranteed debt. These data are reported to the DRS in aggregate, and creditors cannot be separately identified.

China extends loans to low- and middle-income countries on concessional and non-concessional terms. There are four main types of loans. The first type is concessional loans extended by the government of China at very low interest rates or interest-free, funded from tax revenues. These loans are denominated in renminbi and managed by the China International Development Cooperation Agency. The second type is concessional loans from the Export–Import Bank of China (Chexim) managed by the Preferential Loans Department. There are two types of loans: (1) concessional loans denominated in renminbi funded by the government and (2) US-dollar-denominated "preferential buyers" credits financed from Chexim's own resources. The third, and largest type, is non-concessional loans extended by policy banks, Chexim, the China Development Bank, and the Agricultural Development Bank of China. Policy banks fund their operations through bond issuance in the domestic (CIBM) and international capital markets. Loans from policy banks are denominated in US dollars and have market interest rates and medium-term maturities. The fourth type is loans from Chinese commercial banks and suppliers insured by China's official export credit agency, SINOSURE.

External Debt Stocks in 2020

The combined external debt stocks of low- and middle-income countries rose to $8.7 trillion at end-2020, driven by an increase in long-term debt. The total external debt stock of low- and middle-income countries rose on average 5.3 percent in 2020 to $8.7 trillion. The rate of accumulation in 2020 was comparable to that in 2018 and 2019, but below the annual average increase of 8 percent in external debt stocks from 2011 to 2017. This reflects a much slower accumulation of external private non-guaranteed debt stocks, which averaged 3.3 percent per annum in 2018–2020 compared to 8.6 percent each year from 2011 to 2017. The 2020 increase in external debt stocks resulted from net debt inflows of $435 billion and valuation changes in year-on-year exchange rates in relation to the U.S. dollar (about half the external debt of low- and middle-income countries is denominated in currencies other than the U.S. dollar). Long-term external debt rose 7 percent to $6.5 trillion, equivalent to 75 percent of the total external debt stock, driven by a 10 percent rise in long-term external public and publicly guaranteed debt, including obligations to the IMF, and a much smaller 3 percent increase in long-term non-guaranteed external debt of private sector entities. The short-term debt stock was unchanged at $2.2 trillion at end-2020.

China accounted for over a quarter of the end-2020 external debt stock of low- and middle-income countries. China's external debt stock rose 11 percent in 2020 to $2.3 trillion, propelled by an 18 percent increase in long-term debt. The long-term external debt stock of China's public sector borrowers increased by 30 percent to $415 billion at end-2020 while the external debt stock of private Chinese entities, without any government guarantee, rose 18 percent from the end-2019 level to $688 billion. External short-term debt was $1.2 trillion at end-2020 and only marginally (2.5 percent) higher than the previous end-year level, reflecting the slowdown in trade volumes induced by the global pandemic. However, short-term debt remained by far the most significant component of China's total external debt stock, 53 percent at end-2020, down slightly from 57 percent at end-2019.

China aside, the external debt stocks in 2020 were characterized by a marked divergence between major borrowers and other low- and middle-income countries. The combined external debt stock of low- and middle-income countries, excluding China, rose on average 3.4 percent in 2020 to $6.3 trillion of which the nine major borrowers accounted for 56 percent. Their combined external debt stock was $3.5 trillion at end-2020, relatively unchanged from the prior year. In contrast, the external debt stock of other low- and middle-income countries rose, on average, 9.5 percent to $2.8 trillion. Reasons for the evolution of major borrowers' external debt stocks in 2020 were divergent, but a common factor was contraction in non-resident holdings of domestically issued bonds, including in India, Indonesia, and the Russian Federation. It was also one of the reasons for the 2.5 percent fall in South Africa's long-term public and publicly guaranteed external debt in 2020 in addition to the 19 percent contraction in short-term debt and 21 percent fall in long-term non-guaranteed debt of the private sector. Thailand was the only major borrower to see a significant increase in external debt stock in 2020, 14 percent, driven by a 25 percent increase in short-term debt and 11 percent rise in the long-term non-guaranteed debt of private sector entities through both bond issuance and borrowing from commercial banks.

Looking beyond the major borrowers reveals close convergence in external debt stock accumulation at the regional level in 2020. Viewed from a regional perspective, the external debt stock accumulation of low- and middle-income countries in 2020 appeared divergent, ranging from an average increase of 10 percent for countries in the East Asia and Pacific region to less than 1 percent for countries in the Latin America and the Caribbean region. But top-10 major borrowers dictated these trends: including China they accounted for 68 percent of the end-2020 external debt stocks of low- and middle-income countries. As a result, the picture changes significantly when major borrowers are excluded. For the other 113 low- and middle-income countries included in *International Debt Statistics 2022* aggregates, there was convergence in 2020 in external debt stock accumulation at the regional level. The average rate of external debt stock accumulation remained lowest for countries in Latin America and the Caribbean but averaged 8.4 percent when Argentina, Brazil, and Mexico are excluded. Countries in Sub-Saharan Africa recorded the highest increase in external debt stocks in 2020, on average 10.7 percent. In East Asia and Pacific, Europe and Central Asia, and South Asia, the increase in external debt stock clustered around 9.6 percent, and in the Middle East and North Africa region, it was 8.5 percent.

Figure O.3 External Debt Stocks of Low- and Middle-Income Countries, 2011–20

US$ (billion)

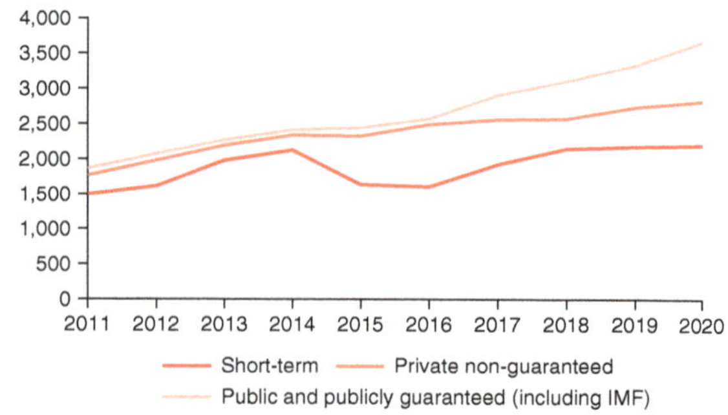

Sources: World Bank Debtor Reporting System and Bank for International Settlements.

Figure O.4 Top-10 Low- and Middle-Income Borrowers, Excluding China, 2019 and 2020
US$ (billion)

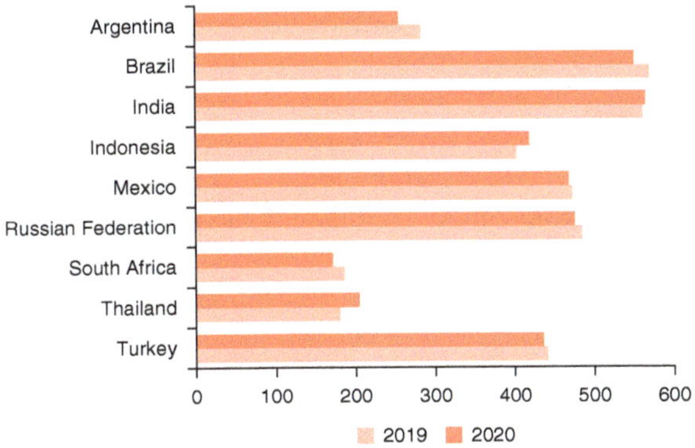

Sources: World Bank Debtor Reporting System and Bank for International Settlements.

Figure O.5 External Debt Stocks by Regions, 2018–20
Percent change

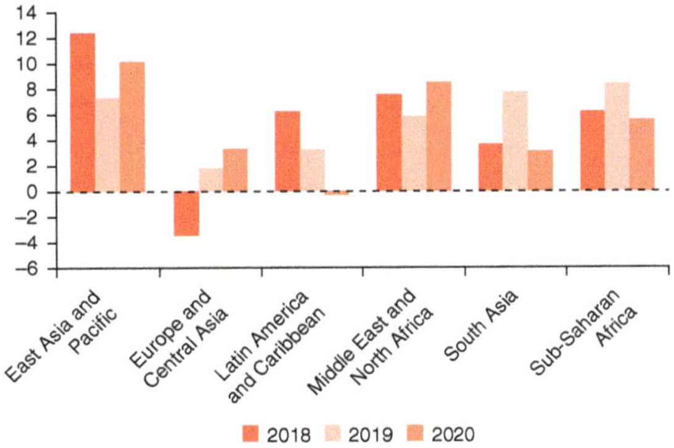

Sources: World Bank Debtor Reporting System and Bank for International Settlements.

Several factors drove the 2020 increase in debt stocks at the regional level, but inflows from bondholders and increased support from multilateral institutions were the most significant. In the East Asia and Pacific region, the 18 percent rise in the external debt stock of the Philippines was driven by the near doubling of inflows from the Asian Development Bank and IBRD and, to a lesser extent, increased Eurobond issuance. Similarly, concessional support from the Asian Development Bank and IDA and increased inflows from bilateral creditors were the main drivers of the 20 percent increase in Myanmar's external debt stock in 2020. In Europe and Central Asia, the external debt stock of Romania rose 20 percent in line with increased Eurobond issuance and $4 billion support from the European Union's temporary Support to Mitigate Unemployment Risks in an Emergency (SURE) program. In Latin America and the Caribbean, the 12 percent rise in external debt stock for Colombia and 14 percent for Peru reflected increased support from IBRD, sovereign Eurobond issues, and for Colombia a $5.2 billion purchase from the IMF. The external debt stock of the two largest borrowers in the Middle East and North Africa region, the Arab Republic of Egypt and Morocco, rose 14 percent and 19 percent, respectively in 2020 driven primarily by sovereign Eurobond issues and for Egypt, a $2.5 billion purchase from the IMF. In South Asia, the external debt stock of Bangladesh rose 19 percent driven by a 32 percent rise in public sector debt owed to bilateral creditors resulting from implementation of large infrastructure projects. For Pakistan, the 8 percent increase in external debt stocks reflected the inflow of budgetary support from official bilateral and multilateral creditors and rollover and new credit lines from commercial banks. In Sub-Saharan Africa, both Ghana and Nigeria recorded a 17 percent increase in external debt stocks driven by purchases from the IMF of $1 billion and $3.4 billion, respectively, plus in Ghana, the $3 billion pre-pandemic Eurobond issue, and for Nigeria, a 16 percent rise in the nonguaranteed debt of the private sector.

Figure O.6 External Debt Stocks by Regions, Excluding 10 Major Borrowers, 2018–20
Percent change

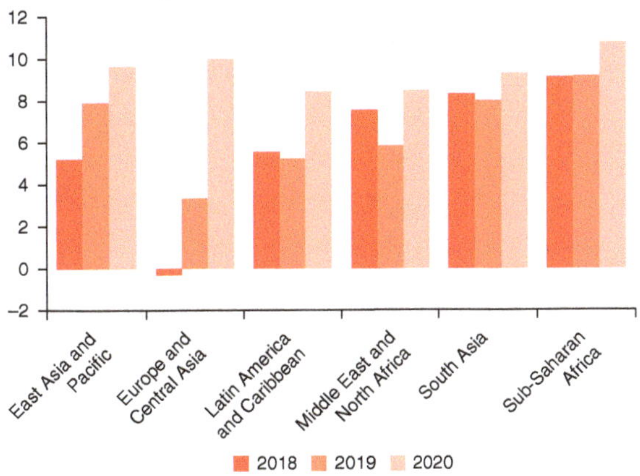

Sources: World Bank Debtor Reporting System and Bank for International Settlements.

External Debt Flows in 2020

China accounted for over half of net debt inflows to low- and middle-income countries in 2020. Net debt inflows to low- and middle-income countries rose 9 percent in 2020 to $435 billion with a 13 percent rise in long-term debt inflows offset by a steep contraction in short-term debt inflows. They fell 43 percent to $16 billion in 2020 from $28 billion in 2019, paralleling the sharp pandemic-induced slowdown in global trade. The volume and trend of 2020 net debt inflows were also dominated and distorted by the precipitous rise in net debt flows to China. They rose 62 percent in 2020 to $233 billion, equivalent to 53 percent of net debt inflows to low- and middle-income countries, propelled by a 28 percent increase in long-term debt inflows and change in direction of short-term flows, to an inflow of $31 billion in 2020 from an outflow of $14 billion in 2019.

The volume and borrower composition of 2020 debt inflows to low- and middle-income countries looks very different when China is excluded. Debt inflows fell 21 percent in 2020 to $202 billion, the lowest level since 2016 primarily because of the reversal of short-term debt flows from an inflow of $41 billion in 2019 to an outflow of $15 billion in 2020. Long-term debt inflows were $217 billion in 2020, almost identical to their prior-year level, but the trajectory of long-term debt inflows of public and publicly guaranteed and private non-guaranteed debt was divergent. Net inflows of long-term public and publicly guaranteed debt rose 24 percent to $210 billion, whereas private non-guaranteed debt inflows dropped to $7 billion, close to one-sixth the level of comparable inflows in 2019. This was equivalent to only 4 percent of net long-term inflows in 2020, compared to 22 percent in 2019 and a far cry from 2011 to 2013 when private non-guaranteed debt accounted for well over half of long-term debt inflows.

Figure O.7 Net Long-Term External Debt Flows by Borrower Composition, Excluding China, 2011–20
US$ (billion)

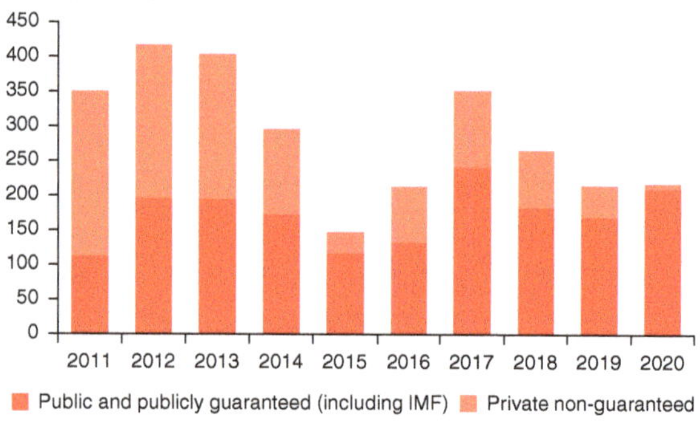

Source: World Bank Debtor Reporting System.

Bondholders and multilateral institutions were the source of over 95 percent of long-term debt inflows to low- and middle-income countries in 2020, including or excluding China. Net inflows from bondholders rose 10 percent in 2020 to $280 billion, of which 66 percent were directed to China. Bondholders' share of net long-term debt inflows to low- and middle-income countries in 2020 was 67 percent, virtually unchanged from 2019. The most significant shift in the creditor composition of debt inflows in 2020 was the surge in inflows from multilateral institutions. They more than doubled in 2020 to $116 billion, raising their share of long-term inflows to 28 percent, from 16 percent in 2019 and offsetting the 80 percent drop in inflows from commercial banks and other private creditors. Inflows from bilateral creditors also rose sharply, 97 percent, in 2020 to $12.4, billion, but as a share of long-term debt inflows they were small, 3 percent. If China is excluded, then net long-term debt inflows to low- and middle-income countries fall to $217 billion, of which 98 percent still come from bondholders and multilateral institutions, but the composition changes. The share of inflows from multilateral institutions rises to 53 percent, and bondholders' share falls to 44 percent with bilateral creditors accounting for the remaining 6 percent. Flows from commercial banks and other private creditors were negative with an outflow of $8.6 billion.

The volume and creditor composition of net long-term debt inflows to public and publicly guaranteed borrowers diverged at the regional level. Countries in Latin America and the Caribbean accounted for the largest share of the $210 billion in net long-term debt inflows to low- and middle-income countries in 2020, followed by Sub-Saharan Africa and Europe and Central Asia. Inflows to Latin America and the Caribbean were $79.6 billion, equivalent to 38 percent of total long-term debt inflows and over double the combined inflows to the Sub-Saharan Africa region, $33 billion, and Europe and Central Asia, $32 billion, equivalent to 16 percent and 15 percent, respectively, of total inflows. Regarding the composition of inflows, 64 percent of inflows to Latin American and Caribbean countries were from bondholders

Figure O.8 Net Long-Term External Debt Flows by Creditor Type, 2011–20
US$ (billion)

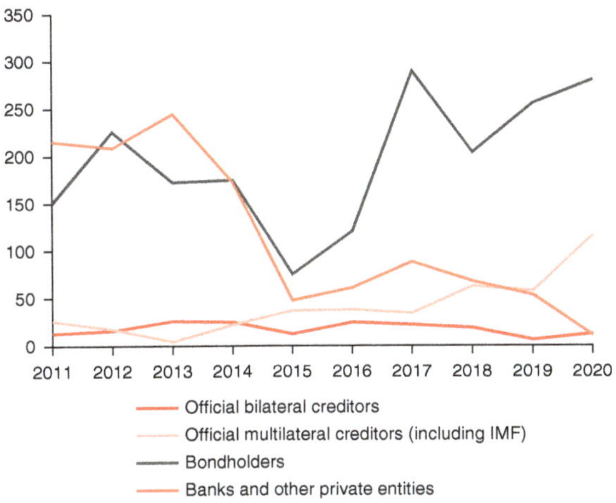

Source: World Bank Debtor Reporting System.

Figure O.9 Net Long-Term External Debt Flows by Creditor Type, Excluding China, 2011–20
US$ (billion)

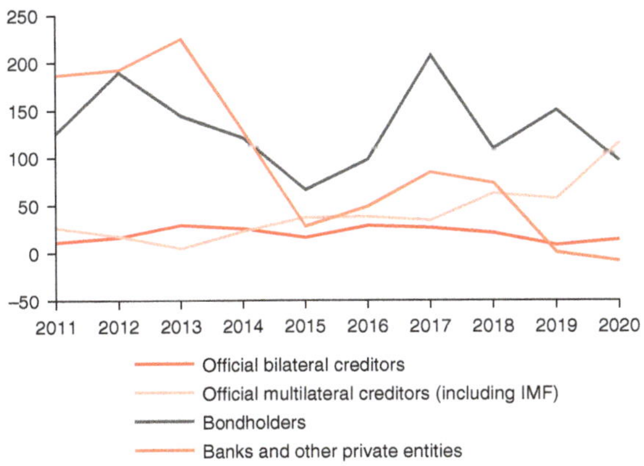

Source: World Bank Debtor Reporting System.

and other private creditors and 37 percent from multilateral institutions, principally the IMF, the Inter-American Development Bank, and the IBRD. Conversely, 92 percent of inflows to Sub-Saharan Africa were from multilateral institutions and the remaining 10 percent from bilateral creditors. In the South Asia region, official bilateral and multilateral creditors accounted for all inflows in 2020 as flows from private creditors to the region were negative.

Net inflows from official creditors doubled in 2020 to \$129 billion, the highest level for a decade driven by the surge in lending from multilateral institutions. Net inflows from official creditors, bilateral and multilateral combined, accounted for 30 percent of 2020 net inflows to low- and middle-income countries from all creditors. In 2019, official creditors' share of net inflows was 16 percent. Inflows from bilateral and multilateral creditors both doubled in 2020 to \$129 billion, but multilateral creditors accounted for the lion's share, 90 percent. Total inflows from multilateral creditors were \$116 billion in 2020 up from \$58 billion in 2019. Inflows from the IMF rose to \$47 billion from \$22 billion in 2019. Inflows from the World Bank (IBRD and IDA) rose to \$27 billion in 2020, 42 percent higher than the comparable figure for 2019. Other multilateral institutions, led by the African Development Bank, the Asian Development Bank, and the Inter-American Development Bank, also ramped up lending in 2020 and tripled collective inflows to \$43 billion in 2020 from \$17 billion in 2019.

Figure O.10 Long-Term Debt Inflows to Public and Publicly Guaranteed Borrowers by Regions, 2020
US$ (billion)

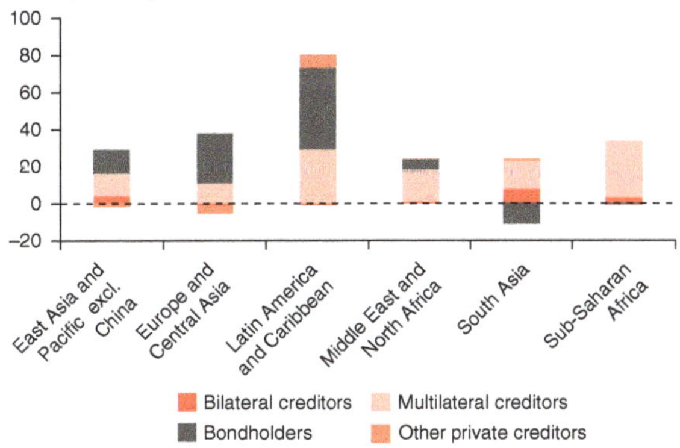

Source: World Bank Debtor Reporting System.

Figure O.11 Net Long-Term Inflows from Official Creditors, 2011–20
US$ (billion)

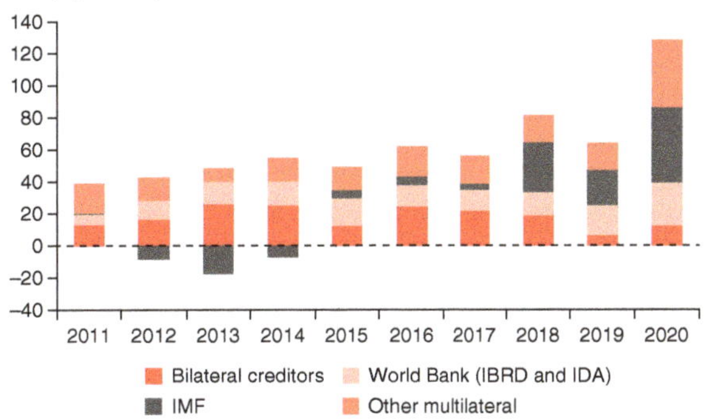

Sources: World Bank Debtor Reporting System and International Monetary Fund.

Box O.2 International Bond Issuance in 2020

Bond issuance by low- and middle-income countries reached an all-time high in 2020, but China accounted for close to half. Bond issuance in international markets by low- and middle-income countries rose to $457 billion in 2020, an increase of 14 percent over the comparable figure for 2019 and surpassing the previous 2017 record high of $400 billion. The driving force was the surge in new issuance by China, which rose 64 percent to $218 billion, equivalent to 48 percent of the combined bonds issued by low- and middle-income countries in 2020.[1] This increase was primarily because of the sharp expansion of non-resident investors' holdings of Chinese renminbi bonds, but 2020 almost marked the first time China issued US-dollar- and euro-denominated bonds in international markets. Issuance by Chinese entities in 2020 was divided equally between public and private sector entities with the former rising 80 percent from the 2019 level to $109 billion and the latter by 52 percent, but also totaling $109 billion.

Bond issuance by low- and middle-income countries, excluding China, fell 11 percent in 2020 to $239 billion. Most of the downturn was accounted for by countries in ***Sub-Saharan Africa***, which fell almost 74 percent in 2020 to $6.5 billion. Several countries in Sub-Saharan Africa, including Angola, Benin, Côte d'Ivoire, Gabon, Ghana Kenya, Nigeria, and South Africa, had signaled an intent to tap international markets in 2020, but only Gabon and Ghana managed to issue bonds prior to the pandemic. After the global lockdown in March 2020, the market effectively closed to Sub-Saharan African borrowers, with investor reluctance in regard to the region heightened by the worsening outlook for growth and public finance caused by the pandemic. The JP Morgan Emerging Market Bond Index (EMBI) Global spread for African issuers spiked to more than 1,000 basis points (bp) in late March, from an average of 469 bp in February, rendering new issuance prohibitively expensive, but fell back to about 600 bp by late November 2020.

In other regions outcomes were mixed. The pandemic complicated access to capital markets for most borrowers at the onset of the pandemic, but access gradually improved after the initial stage of the shock, though there were an unusually high number of credit rating downgrades in 2020, notably in countries rated below investment grade. Downgrades stemmed from worsened macroeconomic outlooks due to the fiscal costs and broader impact of the pandemic.

Bond issuances to countries in ***Latin America and the Caribbean*** rose in 2020, 16 percent, to $104 billion, but little changed in terms of share of issuance by public and private sector entities. Mexico's bond issuance by public and private entities was $43.8 billion in 2020, the same amount as in 2019, and equivalent to 42 percent of the regional issuance in 2020. Peru, one of the countries hardest hit by the pandemic, raised a total of $7 billion in international capital markets in 2020, compared to $750 million in 2019. Sovereign issues from Colombia rose 177 percent to $8.3 billion and doubled in the Dominican Republic to $8.4 billion. Private sector entities in the region issued $26.8 billion in 2020, of which 75 percent was issuance by high-yielding corporates in Brazil and Mexico.

In ***Europe and Central Asia,*** bond issuance fell 8 percent in 2020 with issuance by both public and private sector entities registering a decrease, 7 percent and 12 percent, respectively. The region's three largest issuers, the Russian Federation, Romania, and Turkey, accounted for almost 80 percent of issuance by sovereigns and public sector entities. Issuance by Russia contracted 42 percent due to a drop in non-resident purchases but was largely offset by Romania with significant increases in Eurobond issuance, $13.3 billion in 2020 from $5.6 billion in 2019. Several other sovereigns across the region also issued in international capital markets in 2020 including Albania, Belarus, and Ukraine. Issuance by private sector entities in Russia also fell but was partially offset by the $1.3 billion in issuances by private corporates in Belarus.

The downturn in issuance by countries in the ***Middle East and North Africa*** region in 2020 reflected the economic and financial crisis in Lebanon, which forced the country into its first Eurobond default in April 2020. The 20 percent fall in issuance by countries in the ***East Asia and Pacific*** region, excluding China, was largely attributable to Indonesia. It was one of the first countries to come back to the market after the global lockdown, with the $4.3 billion sovereign Eurobond "pandemic bond" in April 2020. But overall issuance in 2020 fell to $19.2 billion from

[1] Excluding bonds subject to the Argentina, Belize, and Ecuador bond exchanges.

Box O.2 International Bond Issuance in 2020 (*Continued*)

$26.4 billion in 2019 due to a slowdown in non-resident investors' purchases of bonds issued in the domestic market. The fall in bond issuance by India, the only market participant in the ***South Asia*** region in 2020, was also due largely to a fall in non-resident investor purchase of domestic bond issues. In contrast issuance by Indian private sector entities rose 35 percent to $9.7 billion.

Despite the pandemic 2020 saw some innovations in bond issuance and some bond exchanges. Ghana's $3 billion pre-COVID-19 sovereign Eurobond issue in February 2020 was a landmark as the first Sub-Saharan African country's issue of a 20-year bond ($750 million—percent tranche) and Ghana's lowest coupon rate to date, 6.375 percent on the $1.25 billion 6-year tranche. $523 million was used to buy back part of prior bond issues. Mexico's $750 million 7-year 1.350 percent Eurobond in September 2021 was the first sovereign bond linked to the sustainable development objectives of the United Nations. Peru's $4 billion Eurobond issue in November 2020 to help finance costs of the pandemic included a $1 billion "century" tranche with a 3.23 percent coupon repayable in 2121. Côte d'Ivoire's €1 billion 12-year Eurobond issue in November 2020 marked the return of a Debt Service Suspension Initiative (DSSI) participant to the market. Other DSSI-eligible countries to issue bonds in international markets in 2020 (Ghana, Honduras, Mongolia, and Uzbekistan) are not participating in DSSI. Argentina and Ecuador successfully completed bond exchanges in 2020. Ecuador's $17.4 billion exchange had a 98 percent participation rate, extended maturities by an average of 10 years, and substantially reduced coupons. After protracted negotiation, Argentina exchanged about $65 billion with close to 99 percent participation.

Table BO.2.1 Bond Issuance by Low- and Middle-Income Countries, 2019–20
US$ (billion)

	Public issuers		Corporate issuers		All issuers	
	2019	2020	2019	2020	2019	2020
East Asia and Pacific	94.7	135.4	81.8	117.5	176.5	252.9
of which: China	60.7	108.8	71.6	108.7	132.3	217.4
Europe and Central Asia	56.8	53.0	17.9	15.7	74.6	68.7
Latin America and the Caribbean	65.2	78.2	25.2	26.8	90.4	105.0
Middle East and North Africa	13.3	11.1	0.0	0.0	13.3	11.1
South Asia	12.9	3.3	7.2	9.7	20.1	13.0
Sub-Saharan Africa	22.3	5.3	2.3	1.2	24.6	6.5
Low- and middle-income countries	**265.2**	**286.2**	**134.4**	**170.9**	**399.6**	**457.1**

Source: World Bank Debtor Reporting System.

IDA Borrowers Eligible for the DSSI[2]—External Debt Stocks and Flows

The rapid rise in external borrowing by low-income IDA-eligible countries over the past decade and increased share of borrowing on non-concessional terms had raised concerns about debt vulnerabilities prior to the onset of the crisis. These vulnerabilities exacerbated sharply in 2020. Half of IDA countries applying the Low-Income Debt Sustainability Analysis (LIC-DSA) in 2020 were assessed as being at high risk of debt distress or in debt distress, compared to 23 percent in 2013.

The Debt Service Suspension Initiative was launched by G-20 countries in April 2020 to assist the poorest and most vulnerable low- and middle-income countries in managing the adverse

[2] Eligibility for the DSSI is reserved to countries eligible to borrow from IDA at the time the initiative was endorsed in April 2020 and countries on the United Nations list of Least Developed Countries. The following IDA borrowers are not eligible for the DSSI: Eritrea, Sudan, the Syrian Arab Republic, and Zimbabwe.

impacts of the COVID-19 pandemic. It offered 73 IDA-eligible and least developed countries a temporary suspension of debt-service payments owed to official bilateral creditors. The suspension period was originally set for payments falling due from May 1 to December 31, 2020, but was subsequently extended to end-December 2021.

The external debt stock of DSSI-eligible countries accumulated at the same rate as China in 2020 and faster than other low- and middle-income countries. The combined external debt stock of DSSI-eligible countries rose on average 12 percent in 2020 to $860 billion, equivalent on average to 38.8 percent of their combined GNI (measured in nominal terms) and 217.5 percent of export earnings. Long-term public and publicly guaranteed external debt stock, including the use of IMF credit, rose 14 percent in 2020 to $618 billion. Long-term private non-guaranteed external debt and short-term debt increased 6 percent to $176 billion and $65 billion, respectively. The pace at which external debt stocks of DSSI-eligible countries increased in 2020 was comparable to that of China, and end-2020 external debt stocks of DSSI-eligible countries were two and half times higher than the level at the start of the decade.

Debt owed to multilateral creditors increased by 22 percent in 2020 and accounted for almost half of long-term external public debt stocks. The combined long-term external debt stock of public and publicly guaranteed borrowers rose to $618 billion at end-2020, an increase of 14 percent from the 2019 level and 133 percent higher than the comparable figure in 2011. Debt owed to multilateral creditors, including the IMF, rose 22 percent to $295 billion, equivalent to almost half of DSSI-eligible countries' 2020 long-term external public and publicly guaranteed debt stocks. Debt owed to bilateral creditors rose 9 percent to $202 billion, bringing the combined share of debt stocks owed to official creditors to 80 percent. Over the past decade the rise in public and publicly guaranteed external debt of DSSI-eligible countries was accompanied by rapid increase in market-based financing. In 2020, debt owed to private creditors rose 8 percent to $122 billion, but the share of end-2020 long-term external debt stocks declined to 20 percent from 21 percent in 2019.

There was wide divergence in the rate at which external debt accumulated in individual DSSI-eligible countries, including the group's largest borrowers. The combined external debt stock of the 10 largest DSSI-eligible borrowers (Angola, Bangladesh, Ethiopia, Ghana, Kenya, Mongolia, Nigeria, Pakistan, Uzbekistan, and Zambia) was $509 billion at end-2020, 12 percent higher than the comparable figure at end-2019 and equivalent to 59 percent of the external debt obligations of all DSSI-eligible countries combined. They also accounted for 65 percent of the end-2020 private non-guaranteed external debt of DSSI-eligible countries. The rate at which debt accumulated in individual countries varied considerably, from

Figure O.12 External Debt Stock of DSSI-Eligible Countries, 2011–20

US$ (billion)

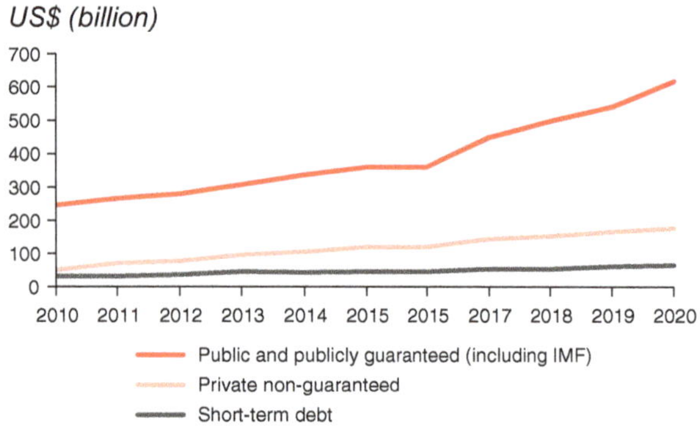

Sources: World Bank Debtor Reporting System and Bank for International Settlements.

Figure O.13 DSSI-Eligible Countries' Long-Term Public and Publicly Guaranteed External Debt by Creditor Type, 2011–20

US$ (billion)

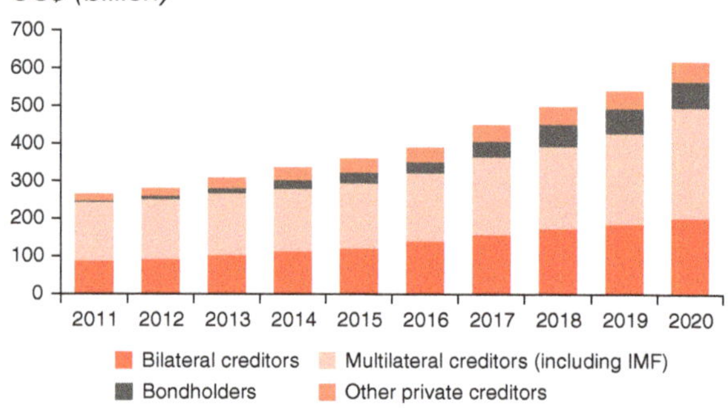

Sources: World Bank Debtor Reporting System and Bank for International Settlements.

Figure O.14 External Debt Stock of Top-10 DSSI-Eligible Borrowers, 2019–20
US$ (billion)

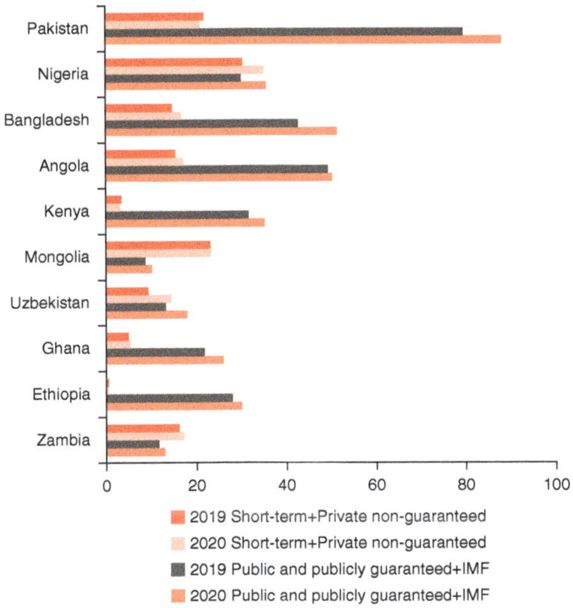

Sources: World Bank Debtor Reporting System and Bank for International Settlements.

Figure O.15 DSSI-Eligible Countries Where Total External Debt Rose 20 Percent or More from 2019 to 2020
Percent change

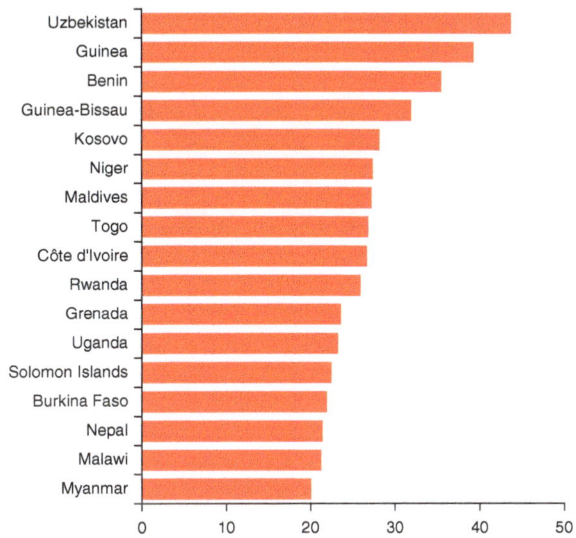

Sources: World Bank Debtor Reporting System and International Monetary Fund.

4 percent in Angola to 19 percent in Bangladesh. Similarly, the public and publicly guaranteed debt for the group as a whole rose 10 percent in 2020 to $356 billion but for individual countries the increase ranged from less than 2 percent for Guyana to 36 percent for Uzbekistan. Countries with more moderate increases in public and publicly guaranteed debt included Ethiopia and Tanzania, 7 percent and 4 percent, respectively, and at the higher end of the range, Bangladesh 20 percent, Mongolia 17 percent, and Ghana 19 percent.

In 17 DSSI-eligible countries external debt stocks increased by 20 percent or more in 2020. DSSI-eligible countries reported an accelerated debt accumulation in 2020, but the factors that drove the increase in external debt are diverse. The group includes two countries classified as IDA-blend and creditworthy for some IBRD financing (Grenada and Uzbekistan), six that have issued Eurobonds in international capital markets (Benin, Côte d'Ivoire, Grenada, Maldives, Rwanda, and Uzbekistan), and six on the fiscal year 2022 (FY22) classified list of fragile states (Burkina Faso, Guinea-Bissau, Kosovo, Myanmar, Niger, and the Solomon Islands). Reasons for the increase varied and included IMF purchases and World Bank disbursements (Côte d'Ivoire, Kosovo, Maldives, Nepal, Togo), inflows from private creditors (Guinea, Togo, Uganda), higher short-term debt inflows (Grenada, Malawi, Uzbekistan), and Eurobond issuance (Côte d'Ivoire, Ghana, Mongolia, Uzbekistan).

Multilateral creditors provided 60 percent of net long-term external debt inflows to DSSI-eligible countries. Net long-term debt inflows to DSSI-eligible countries rose 25 percent in 2020 to $71 billion from $57 billion in 2019 to the highest level of the past decade. This increase was driven by the extraordinary level of support provided to the world's poorest countries by multilateral institutions led by the IMF and the World Bank. Net inflows from multilateral institutions to DSSI-eligible countries rose 74 percent in 2020 to $42 billion, equivalent to 60 percent of 2020 net debt inflows of external public and publicly guaranteed debt from all creditors. The IMF and World Bank combined accounted for

Figure O.16 DSSI-Eligible Countries' Net Long-Term Inflows of Public and Publicly Guaranteed Debt by Creditor Type, 2011–20

US$ (billion)

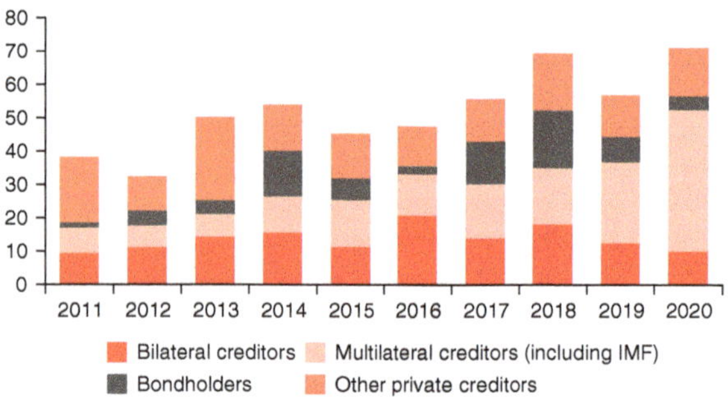

Source: World Bank Debtor Reporting System.

Figure O.17 DSSI-Eligible Countries' Total Debt Service Paid to Creditors, 2020

US$ billion

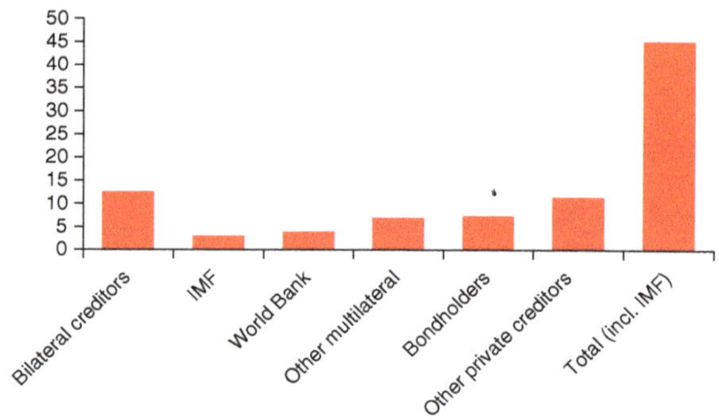

Source: World Bank Debtor Reporting System.

70 percent of the 2020 inflows from multilateral institutions. Inflows from bilateral creditors fell 19 percent to $10 billion, from $12.5 billion in 2019. The inflows from bondholders fell to $4 billion, close to half the 2019 level, and the decrease was due to tightening of market conditions in 2020, which raised borrowing costs and limited market access for most DSSI-eligible countries. Net inflows from other private creditors rose 15 percent in 2020 to $14 billion but were highly concentrated and also reflected rollovers and extension of new credits by commercial bank loans to Pakistan in the context of the IMF program.

In 2020, DSSI-eligible countries expended $45.2 billion to service external public and public guaranteed debt. The combined debt service paid by DSSI-eligible countries in 2020 on external public and publicly guaranteed debt, including the IMF, totaled $45.2 billion, of which principal accounted for $31.1 billion and interest for $14.1 billion. The 2020 debt service comprised $26.4 billion (58 percent) paid to official bilateral and multilateral creditors and $18.8 billion (42 percent) to private creditors, that is, bondholders, commercial banks, and other private entities. Payments to the World Bank and the IMF were $2.9 billion and $3.9 billion, respectively, and together they accounted for 49 percent of 2020 debt service paid to multilateral creditors, followed by the Asian Development Bank (18 percent), Islamic Development Bank (8 percent), and African Development Bank (6 percent). Reforms to the IMF Catastrophe Containment and Relief Fund (CCRT) in March 2020 enabled 29 of the world's poorest countries to receive $488 million in grants to offset 2020 debt-service payments made to the IMF (box O.3).

The DSSI offered 73 IDA-eligible and least developed countries a temporary suspension of debt-service payments owed to official bilateral creditors. As of September 2021, 48 countries were participating in the DSSI. Other eligible countries chose not to participate for various reasons. Countries with market access, like Ghana and Nigeria, had concerns about future access and credit-rating downgrades. For Benin and some small island nations, eligible debt service was negligible or non-existent, and countries like Bangladesh preferred to retain their track record of debt servicing. Under this initiative debt-service payments are deferred and repaid over 4–6 years after a 1-year grace period.

In 2020, DSSI-participating countries paid $30 billion in debt service on external public and publicly guaranteed debt. Of this, $10 billion, equivalent to 30 percent of the total paid, was to bilateral creditors. Participating countries reporting to the World Bank DRS recorded $3.5 billion in debt-service payments due to bilateral creditors in 2020 that had been deferred. This figure includes deferrals agreed with G-20 creditors

Figure O.18 DSSI-Participating Countries: Debt Service Paid and Deferred in 2020

US$ (billion)

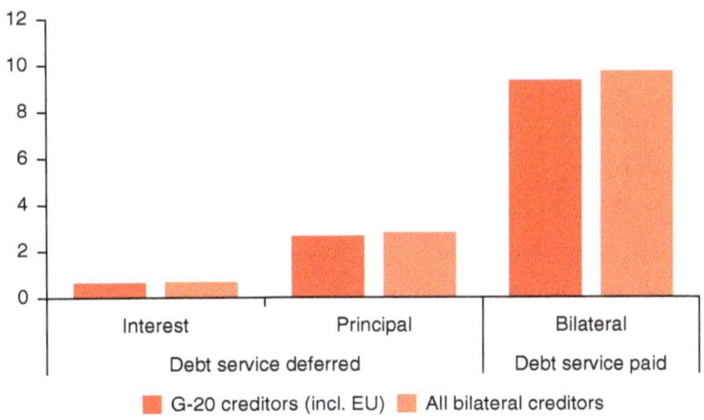

Source: World Bank Debtor Reporting System.

and non-G-20 bilateral creditors, notably Kuwait and the United Arab Emirates, participating in the initiative on comparable terms. Debt service deferred in 2020 included $0.7 billion in deferred interest payments that have been capitalized and added to debt stocks in line with the common term sheet adopted for the initiative, which defines the standstill in payments as net present value neutral. Many DRS reporters signaled that agreements on deferral had been reached with G-20 creditors, that administrative steps to identify precise amounts deferred were still ongoing, and that data reported were preliminary estimates.

With reference to the amount of debt deferred, countries like Kenya did not request participation in the initiative until 2021 and paid all 2020 debt service due to bilateral creditors. Australia and Papua New Guinea agreed on a refinancing operation instead of a deferral, and the estimated $357 million deferral, by Paris Club creditors for the Republic of Yemen is not included. The Republic of Yemen, a country in conflict, did not report to the DRS in 2020.

Box O.3 The IMF Catastrophe and Containment Relief Trust

The International Monetary Fund (IMF) Catastrophe Containment and Relief Trust (CCRT) was created in February 2015, through a transformation of the Post-Catastrophe Debt Relief Trust, to broaden the range of situations covered by IMF disaster assistance to include fast-spreading epidemics. In March 2020, reforms were adopted that enabled the Fund to provide immediate debt-service relief for its poorest and most vulnerable members affected by the COVID-19 pandemic and any future pandemics.

The CCRT provides grants to eligible countries to pay debt service owed to the IMF and free up resources to meet exceptional balance of payments needs created by the disaster. Eligibility for assistance through the CCRT is reserved for countries eligible for concessional borrowing from the IMF Poverty Reduction and Growth Trust and whose per capita income is below the International Development Association's (IDA) operational cutoff (US$1,405 for FY22) or, for small states with a population of less than 1.5 million, per capita income below twice the IDA cutoff (US$2,810 for FY22). Currently 29 countries qualify for assistance from the CCRT. The IMF Executive Board has approved three grant tranches from the CCRT totaling Special Drawing Rights (SDRs) 520 million (US$727 million) covering debt-service payments by eligible countries falling due from April 14, 2020, to October 15, 2021. The CCRT is financed by contributions from bilateral donors including middle-income countries, notably Bulgaria, China, Mexico, and the Philippines.

The data presented in *International Debt Statistics 2022* do not reflect CCRT grants. CCRT assistance to eligible countries *offsets* the cost of debt service falling due during the prescribed period but does not *reduce* debt-service payments to the IMF, which remain due in full on the original due dates. Consistent with this, the data presented in *International Debt Statistics 2022* show total debt service paid to the IMF in 2020. To assist users, Table BO.3.1 separates out debt service paid to the IMF by CCRT-eligible countries in 2020 that was offset by a debt relief grant from the CCRT. Aid statistics such as those compiled by the Organisation for Economic Co-operation and Development will capture both the debt-service payment and the debt relief grant.

Box O.3 The IMF Catastrophe and Containment Relief Fund (*Continued*)

Table BO.3.1 CCRT-Eligible Countries' IMF Debt Service Paid and Offset, 2020
US$ (thousands)

	Debt-Service PRGT Loans	Paid	Paid and Offset
Country	2020	January 1–April 14, 2020	April 15–December 31, 2020
Afghanistan	9,145.0	2,458.6	6,686.4
Benin	25,125.0	5,911.4	19,213.6
Burkina Faso	28,572.0	2,058.3	26,513.7
Burundi	22,025.0	7,793.0	14,232.0
Central African Republic	10,368.6	2,177.7	8,190.9
Chad	2,782.0	0.0	2,782.0
Comoros	2,821.0	434.0	2,387.0
Congo, Dem. Rep.	48,263.0	13,789.4	34,473.6
Djibouti	6,201.0	1,486.9	4,714.1
Ethiopia	16,763.0	0.0	16,763.0
Gambia, The	6,451.0	602.8	5,848.2
Guinea	59,573.0	13,960.8	45,612.2
Guinea-Bissau	3,402.0	0.0	3,402.0
Haiti	15,444.0	4,297.2	11,146.8
Liberia	39,585.0	7,793.3	31,791.7
Madagascar	8,512.0	0.0	8,512.0
Malawi	24,658.0	4,593.9	20,064.1
Mali	23,961.0	3,343.4	20,617.6
Mozambique	28,353.0	0.0	28,353.0
Nepal	8,939.0	0.0	8,939.0
Niger	22,458.0	6,743.9	15,714.1
Rwanda	27,896.0	0.0	27,896.0
São Tomé and Príncipe	500.1	103.0	397.1
Sierra Leone	42,188.0	6,546.1	35,641.9
Solomon Islands	227.0	41.3	185.7
Tajikistan	19,993.3	1,817.2	18,176.1
Tanzania	37,412.0	11,547.1	25,864.9
Togo	11,646.0	3,218.0	8,428.0
Yemen, Rep.	47,027.0	11,637.6	35,389.4
TOTAL	**600,291.0**	**112,397.4**	**487,893.6**

Source: International Monetary Fund.

Debt Indicators 2011–2020

External borrowing to counter the impact of the global pandemic led to a worsening of debt indicators for low- and middle-income countries in 2020. The ratio of external debt to GNI averaged 29 percent at end-2020 compared to an average of 27 percent in 2019. This was the result of a 5.7 percent increase in external stocks and a 3.7 percent fall in GNI. Similarly, an 8.6 percent fall in export earnings raised the ratio of external debt to exports to an average of 123 percent in 2020 from 106 percent in 2019. Moreover, these ratios include China, which accounted for 49 percent of the combined GNI of low- and middle-income countries in 2020 and 42 percent of exports. And China's external debt is low relative to both GNI, 16 percent, and to exports, 79 percent, at end-2020. For low- and middle-income countries, excluding China, the ratio of external debt to GNI rose to an average of 42 percent in 2020, a 4.9 percentage point increase from 2019, and the external debt-to-exports ratio rose to 154 percent, from 126 percent at end-2019. The GNI of low- and middle-income countries, excluding China, fell on average 9 percent in 2020, and exports declined by 15 percent.

All regions were impacted by the worsening of debt indicators in 2020. External debt ratios have deteriorated over the past decade, but this trend was exacerbated by the global pandemic when the pace of external debt accumulation outstripped growth in most low- and middle-income countries. Many also experienced a sharp fall in export earnings. This impact has been felt by both the poorer IDA countries and middle-income market-based borrowers as the rise in debt-to-GNI and debt-to-export ratios in all regions clearly shows. Countries in Sub-Saharan Africa have seen the most pronounced deterioration in debt indicators: the ratio of debt to GNI rose from an average of 23.4 percent in 2011 to 43.7 percent in 2020, and the average debt-to-export ratio tripled over the same period to 212.3 percent in 2020.

As the regional figures show, the ratio of external debt stocks to GNI for borrower countries has risen sharply in the past decade in many low- and middle-income countries. In 2011, 50 percent of all low- and middle-income countries had an external debt-to-GNI ratio at or below 30 percent. By 2020, the picture was very different. The percentage of low- and middle-income countries where the external debt-to-GNI ratio was below 30 percent had fallen to 19 percent. Over the same period the percentage of countries where the debt-to-GNI ratio surpassed 100 percent tripled from 4 percent to 14 percent. Within these parameters, country-specific indicators vary, but in 2020, there were 16 countries (including 2 countries that benefited from Heavily Indebted Poor Countries [HIPC] and Multilateral Debt Relief Initiative [MDRI] debt relief, Mozambique and Zambia) that had a debt-to-GNI ratio above 100 percent.

The ratio of external debt stock to export earnings also increased sharply. At end-2011, 42 percent of low- and middle-income countries had an external debt-to-export ratio at or below 100 percent, as compared to only 15 percent of countries with the comparable ratio in 2020. By 2020, the debt-to-export ratio exceeded 250 percent in 37 percent of countries, a sevenfold

Figure O.19 Countries with 2020 Debt-to-GNI Ratios of 100 Percent or Above
Percent

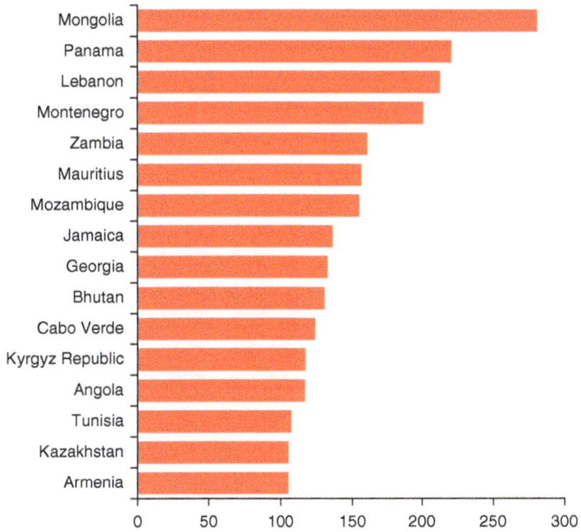

Sources: World Bank Debtor Reporting System and International Monetary Fund.

Table O.2 Debt Ratios to GNI and Exports by Region, 2011, 2019, and 2020
Percent

	Debt-to-GNI			Debt-to-Exports		
	2011	2019	2020	2011	2019	2020
East Asia and Pacific, excluding China	29.0	36.1	40.8	72.4	87.3	105.4
Europe and Central Asia	38.3	46.7	51.9	113.7	124.9	155.8
Latin America and the Caribbean	22.4	40.8	49.0	108.3	160.1	186.4
Middle East and North Africa	14.4	32.5	37.5	50.0	116.5	183.6
South Asia	20.3	22.1	24.4	85.4	116.9	137.0
South Asia, excluding India	27.5	31.2	34.0	153.3	215.9	288.2
Sub-Saharan Africa	23.4	39.6	43.7	70.1	155.6	205.1
Low- and middle-income, excluding China	**26.1**	**36.6**	**41.5**	**92.1**	**126.3**	**153.9**

Sources: World Bank Debtor Reporting System and International Monetary Fund.

Figure O.20 Distribution of Low- and Middle-Income Countries by External Debt-to-GNI Ratio, 2011 and 2020

Number of countries

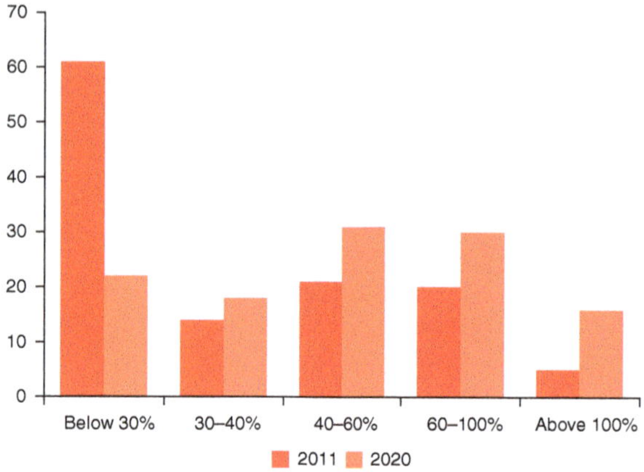

Sources: World Bank Debtor Reporting System and International Monetary Fund.

increase from 2011 when only 5 percent of countries had a ratio that exceeded 250 percent.

For DSSI-eligible countries the increase in external debt stocks in relation to both GNI and exports over the past decade was pronounced. In 2011, 38 DSSI-eligible countries had an external debt-to-GNI ratio at or below 30 percent and in 58 countries it was at or below 60 percent. By 2020, the debt-to-GNI ratio was below 30 percent in only 15 DSSI-eligible countries and at or below 60 percent in 44. Over the same period number of

Figure O.21 Distribution of Low- and Middle-Income Countries by External Debt-to-Exports Ratio, 2011 and 2020

Number of countries

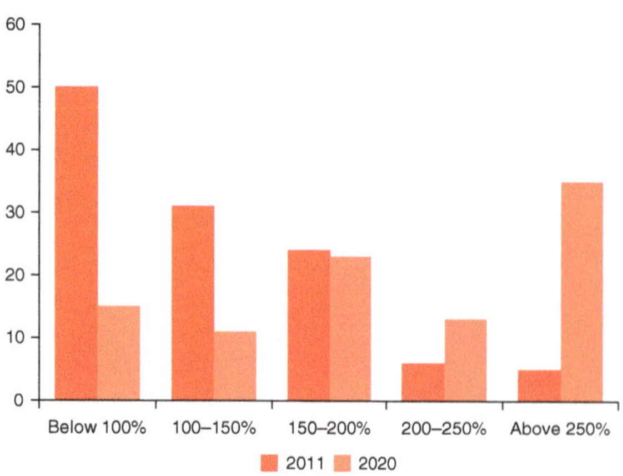

Sources: World Bank Debtor Reporting System and International Monetary Fund.

Figure O.22 Distribution of DSSI-Eligible Countries by External Debt-to-GNI Ratio, 2011 and 2020

Number of countries

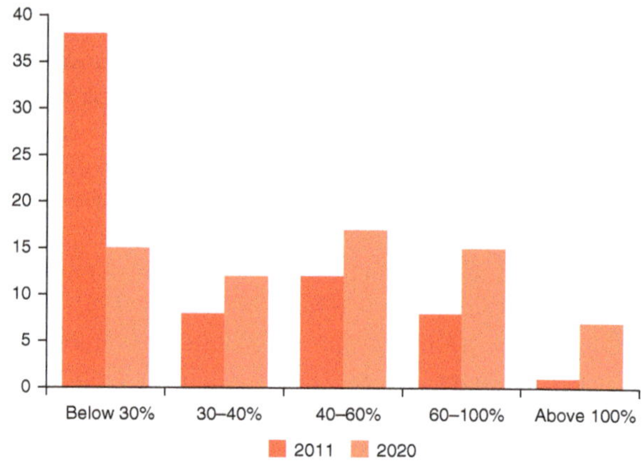

Sources: World Bank Debtor Reporting System and International Monetary Fund.

DSSI-eligible countries with a debt-to-GNI ratio that exceeded 100 percent rose from 1 in 2011 to 7 by 2020.

It was a similar picture for external debt in relation to exports. In 2011, 44 DSSI-eligible countries had an external debt-to-export ratio at or below 150 percent. In contrast only 9 DSSI-eligible countries had a comparable ratio at end-2020. Over the same period the number of DSSI-eligible countries with a debt-to-export ratio above 250 percent quadrupled from 4 in 2011 to 21 in 2020.

Figure O.23 Distribution of DSSI-Eligible Countries by External Debt-to-Exports Ratio, 2011 and 2020

Number of countries

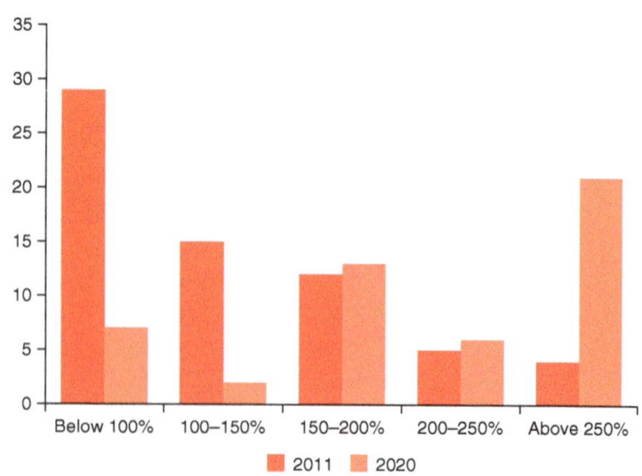

Sources: World Bank Debtor Reporting System and International Monetary Fund.

Box O.4 The Use of the Ratios Debt-to-GDP versus Debt-to-GNI

Gross domestic product (GDP) and gross national income (GNI) measure a country's economic activity, but what they measure differs slightly. For most countries the difference between GDP and GNI is minimal. GDP counts only income received from domestic sources, whereas GNI also includes net primary income received from abroad. GDP is linked to the concept of production, in which value added is generated, while GNI is a concept of income. The difference between the GNI and GDP is equal to the difference of primary income receivable from nonresidents and primary income payable to nonresidents, often described as "net income from abroad."

The World Bank favors the use of GNI for operational purposes. Member countries' relative poverty is measured in relation to GNI per capita, and this measure underpins the annual income classification published by the World Bank: the International Development Association operational cutoff ($1,205 per capita for FY22) and the International Bank for Reconstruction and Development and International Development Association lending terms (interest rate and maturity) for specified borrowers. *International Debt Statistics* follows this convention and provides users with GNI data for each reporting country and the relevant external debt stock and debt service to GNI ratios. The IMF uses the concept of GDP in Article IV consultation reports and Fund programs to measure macroeconomic outcomes. The practice is carried forward to the joint Bank-Fund Debt Sustainability Analysis (DSA), and debt stocks and debt service are measured in relation to GDP.

Equity Flows in 2020

Equity flows in 2020 fell to the lowest level in a decade with both FDI and portfolio equity flows disrupted by the impact of the global pandemic. Net equity inflows to low- and middle-income countries fell 15 percent in 2020 to $473 billion with FDI inflows falling 14 percent to $434 billion and portfolio equity inflows' declining by 19 percent to $39 billion. This was equity inflows' lowest level in a decade, with 2020 inflows 17 percent below the average annual net inflow in 2011–2019 of $571 billion. Net equity inflows are an important element of aggregate financial flows to low- and middle-income countries and have typically accounted for over half of annual aggregate flows (debt and equity combined) and a much higher share in years when debt flows fell sharply or, as in 2015, were negative. Despite the downturn in 2020, equity flows accounted for 52 percent of the combined debt and equity inflows to low- and middle-income countries. Most equity flows are composed of FDI, on average 91 percent per annum since 2011, and only a handful of low- and middle-income countries benefit from portfolio equity flows to any significant degree.

The COVID-19 pandemic had a significant impact on FDI flows in 2020. Lockdowns around the world slowed existing investment projects, and the prospects of a global recession deterred investors and led multinational entities to reassess the viability of new projects. The fall was heavily skewed towards developed economies, but the downturn was global. FDI inflows to low- and middle-income countries combined fell, on average, 14 percent in 2020 to $434 billion, the lowest level in a decade.

Figure O.24 Net Equity Inflows to Low- and Middle-Income Countries, 2011–20

US$ (billion)

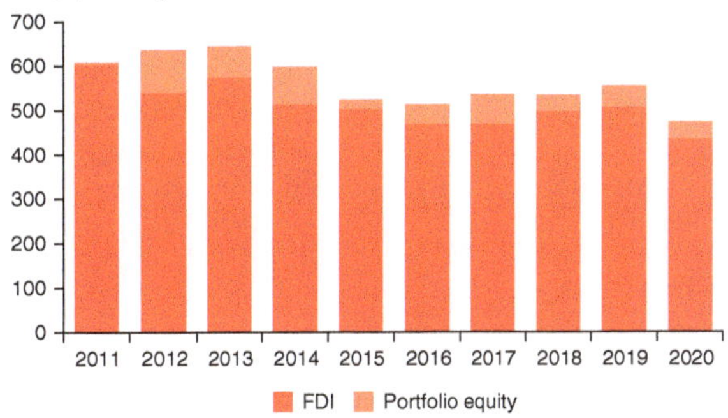

Sources: International Monetary Fund and United Nations Conference on Trade and Development.

In 2020 China and India accounted for more than half of all FDI inflows to low- and middle-income countries. Inflows to China, the world's second-largest FDI recipient after the United States, rose 5 percent in 2020 to $170 billion, raising its share of the combined FDI inflows to low- and middle-income countries to 39 percent, its highest level since 2015. In India, the second-largest FDI recipient among low- and middle-income countries, FDI inflows increased 38 percent to $60 billion, reflecting further relaxation of barriers to foreign investment. Together China and India accounted for 53 percent of FDI inflows to low- and middle-income countries in 2020. In contrast, FDI inflows to other major recipients, Brazil and Russia, fell 36 percent and 56 percent, respectively, from the 2019 level to a combined total of $53 billion. Low- and middle-income countries other than the four largest recipients saw FDI inflows fall on average 27 percent in 2020 to $152 billion with most countries recording a drop in inflows compared to the prior year levels.

The fall in FDI inflows in 2020 at the regional level was uneven. Two regions, South Asia and Sub-Saharan Africa, reported an increase in FDI inflows, 32 percent and 20 percent, respectively, in 2020. In contrast, FDI inflows to countries in Europe and Central Asia fell on average 42 percent to $42.4 billion, the lowest level in two decades. Inflows to countries in Latin America and the Caribbean continued a downward trajectory, falling by one-third from the 2019 level to $84.5 billion with a decline in inflows to all large FDI recipients. In East Asia and Pacific, inflows fell a moderate 4.4 percent, but this reflected a rise in inflows to China. Inflows to other countries in the region fell, on average, 32 percent. In the Middle East and North Africa region, FDI inflows fell on average 16 percent to $14.3 billion, and again the downturn impacted most countries in the region.

Figure O.25 FDI to BRIC and Other Select Low- and Middle-Income Countries, 2011–20

Percent

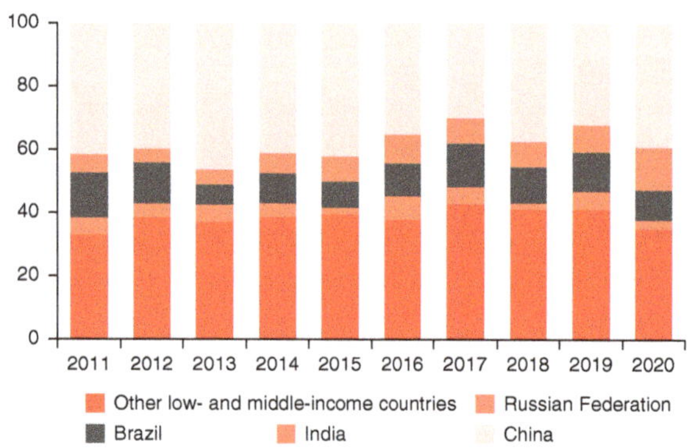

Sources: International Monetary Fund and United Nations Conference on Trade and Development.

FDI inflows to the **East Asia and Pacific region** fell on average 4.4 percent in 2020 to $206 billion, but this was driven by a rise in inflow to China that accounted for 83 percent of FDI inflows to the region in 2020. Inflows to other countries in the region fell, on average, 32.5 percent in 2020 to $36 billion. FDI inflows to **China** increased 5 percent in 2020 to $170 billion. This reflected containment of the pandemic and economic recovery in the second quarter of 2020 and removal of investment barriers. The government expanded the number of industries open to FDI, lifted foreign exchange restrictions in major industries, and widened the options for foreign investment in pilot free trade zones. More than 70 percent of FDI inflows in 2020 were directed at the services sector, notably technology-related industries. Growth in mergers and acquisitions in information and communication technology and pharmaceutical industries also contributed to the increase in FDI. In **Indonesia,** FDI declined by 23 percent, to $19.3 billion, because of a steep fall in investment in manufacturing, and in **Thailand** FDI flows were negative, –$5.6 billion, driven by disinvestment of Tesco (United Kingdom) to a Thai investor group for $10 billion. Among the smaller economies, FDI inflows to the **Lao People's Democratic Republic** rose 28 percent in 2020 to $968 million, because of booming infrastructure investment in projects like the $2.1 billion Sanakham Dam and $5.7 billion Laos-China Railway by Asian, largely Chinese, investors. FDI inflows to **Cambodia** were $3.6 billion, unchanged from 2019. The pandemic slowed investment in the export-oriented garment industry and hospitality sector, but construction projects by Chinese companies, like the 190-km Phnom Penh-Sihanoukville Expressway, remained on schedule. In **Myanmar,** inflows fell 11 percent to $1.8 billion in 2020 due to worsening investor perceptions, a deteriorating business environment, and the impact of the pandemic.

FDI inflows to countries in **Europe and Central Asia** fell, on average, 42 percent in 2020 to $42.4 billion, the lowest level in two decades, and only three countries in the region (Belarus, Bulgaria, and Kosovo) recorded an increase in FDI inflows in 2020. In **Russia,** the region's largest

FDI recipient, net FDI inflows fell 56 percent to $12.6 billion. The introduction of new policies that aimed at diversifying FDI flows were derailed by the pandemic, and investment into high-tech industries also fell sharply. However, despite the downturn in commodity prices, investments into the oil and gas sector held up, accounting for 25 percent of 2020 inflows. Inflows to **Turkey,** the region's second-largest FDI recipient, fell 17 percent to $8.7 billion in 2020, and the downturn would have been steeper, but a rebound in inflows in the second half of the year prevented a steep decline. Major deals included a $200 million investment by Metric Capita (France) in a pharmaceuticals manufacturing unit and Qatar Investment Authority's acquisition of a 10 percent equity stake in a stock exchange operator also valued at $200 million. FDI flows to **Ukraine** plunged 94 percent to $272 million from $4.9 billion in 2019 due to the combined effect of the pandemic, macroeconomic issues and geopolitical tensions, and reduction in reinvested earnings because of uncertainties in the business environment. Inflows to **Belarus** rose 20 percent, to $1.3 billion, in part because the country was very late to adopt anti-pandemic restrictions and large inflows were registered in the first part of the year were in various sectors including the automotive industry (Poland), information technology (United States), furniture manufacture (Germany), logistics (China), and renewable energy (Lithuania). FDI inflows ground to a halt in the second half of the year, with investors deterred by the social unrest following the presidential elections in August 2020.

Countries in the **Latin America and Caribbean region** saw FDI inflows drop by more than one-third in 2020 to $84.5 billion. The severe impact of the pandemic across the region, a sharp fall in export demand, lower prices for commodity exports, and the curtailment of tourism weighed heavily on investment flows to the region. FDI inflows to **Brazil** fell 36 percent in 2020 to $40.5 billion, the lowest level since 2013, despite some sizeable gains from privatization, including the sale by Petrobras of two crude petroleum and natural gas producers to Australian and British investors. In **Peru,** the combination of prolonged lockdowns, economic contraction, and political instability contributed to a 28 percent fall in FDI in 2020 to $4.3 billion from $6 billion in 2019. Large-scale social protests and the downgrade of the country's investment rating weighed heavily on FDI inflows to **Colombia,** which dropped 53 percent to $5.6 billion in 2020 from $11.9 billion in 2019. Investment fell across all sectors but fell the most in oil-related industries. Inflows to **Mexico** fell 27 percent in 2020 to $22.7 billion with about 60 percent of these inflows accounted for by reinvested earnings. New investments were dampened by uncertainties over the authorities' economic agenda and stance on the role of the private sector in key industries. FDI inflows to **Argentina** continued the downward trajectory that began in 2018, falling 42 percent in 2020 to $3.8 billion. The challenging economic environment and prolonged shutdown in the industrial sector had an adverse impact on FDI, with new investment falling 45 percent, reinvested earnings falling 22 percent, and disinvestment by several international companies including Walmart USA, Schlumberger USA, and Danone France who sold their assets to domestic investors. FDI flows to **Panama** turned negative, with outflows of $890 million in 2020 from inflows of $2.4 billion in 2019 despite measures by the government to counter the economic impact of the pandemic. These included the launch of several infrastructure projects and approval of a new investment incentives regime, mainly in the form of tax benefits, targeting multinational companies that carry out operations from Panama and provide manufacturing services.

In the **Middle East and North Africa,** FDI inflows contracted 16 percent in 2020 to $14.3 billion from $16.9 billion in 2019, reflecting a general slowdown in investment across the region. Inflows to **Egypt,** the region's largest recipient, fell 35 percent to $5.9 billion in 2020 despite concerted efforts to promote diversification of FDI, including the agreement to activate a $16 billion Saudi-Egypt investment fund across multiple sectors. Most FDI inflows to Egypt are currently in the oil and gas sector. Inflows to **Tunisia** were down 26 percent from the 2019 level, to $600 million, on account of a steep fall in investments in the service sectors with tourism particularly hard hit. It was a similar story in **Jordan,** where FDI is concentrated in the tourism sector and inflows fell 13 percent in 2020 to $718 million. Inflows to **Algeria** declined 21 percent to $1.1 billion despite the authorities' efforts to diversify FDI by lifting restrictions and the 49 percent cap on foreign ownership. However, these measures should have a positive impact once post-COVID-19 FDI recovers more broadly. **Morocco** was a bright spot, with FDI inflows rising 9 percent in 2020 to $1.5 billion. The country benefited from the established presence of multinational companies in the automotive, aerospace, and textile industries and investment into phosphates, of which it holds the world's largest known reserves. These factors mitigated the impact of the pandemic.

FDI inflows to countries in **South Asia** rose 32 percent in 2020 to $63 billion driven by a surge in FDI inflows to India, which the acute impact of the pandemic there did little to deter. Inflows continued their upward trajectory, rising a further 38 percent to $59.5 billion. The rise in inflows reflected further relaxation of investment barriers, including in the retail and financial sector that began in mid-2019. Inflows in 2020 were also bolstered by $27 billion in mergers and acquisitions, including megadeals like the $5.7 billion acquisition of Jio Platforms by Jaadhu, a subsidiary of Facebook USA, and the $4.6 billion Unilever India merger with GlaxoSmithKline Consumer Healthcare, a subsidiary of GSK United Kingdom. All other countries in the region registered a decline in net FDI inflows of, on average, 25.3 percent from the 2019 level. FDI inflows to **Pakistan** fell moderately to $1.9 billion, 5 percent below the 2019 level, cushioned by continued investment in power generation and the telecom sector from British and Chinese investors. In contrast **Bangladesh,** where FDI is concentrated in export-oriented garment manufacturing, inflows fell 21.4 percent in 2020 to $1 billion as $3 billion worth of export orders, largely from the United States and European Union, were canceled. In the **Maldives,** where FDI is concentrated in tourism and several new hotel complex projects were postponed, the contraction in inflows was severe. They fell 63.6 percent in 2020 to $348 million from $956 million in 2019.

Sub-Saharan Africa was the only other region to record an increase in FDI inflows in 2020. They rose on average 20 percent to $24.3 billion, with many countries recording a rise in inflows in 2020. FDI inflows to **Senegal** rose 39 percent to $1.5 billion due to increased investments in the energy sector and start-up of work on the largest offshore oil and gas project, the SNE Oil Field, being developed by a consortium of Australian and British companies and Petrosen (Senegal). Inflows to the **Republic of the Congo** rose 19 percent to $4.0 billion, propelled by investment in offshore oil fields after a licensing round of available oil blocks in 2019, and in the **Democratic Republic of the Congo** they increased 11 percent to $1.6 billion due to rising demand and increased prices for cobalt used in smartphones and electric car batteries. In **Nigeria,** long-term policies aimed at FDI diversification took effect and inflows rose 9 percent to $930 million from several new investments in the non-oil sector, including a food manufacturing facility in the Lekke Free

Figure O.26 Foreign Direct Investment Inflows by Regions, 2018–20
US$ (billion)

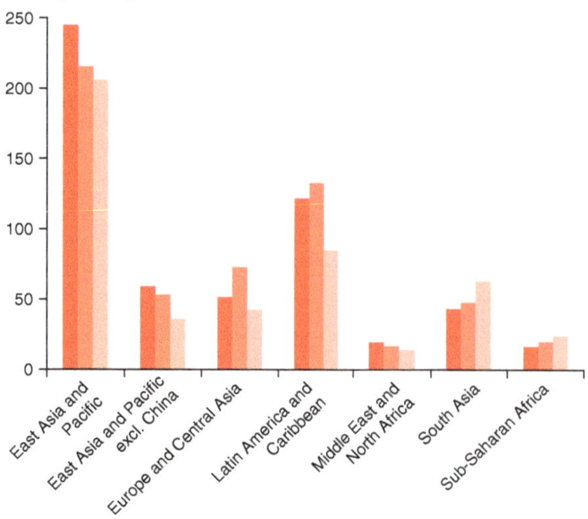

Sources: International Monetary Fund and United Nations Conference on Trade and Development.

Figure O.27 Portfolio Equity Flows to Low- and Middle-Income Countries, 2018–20
US$ (billion)

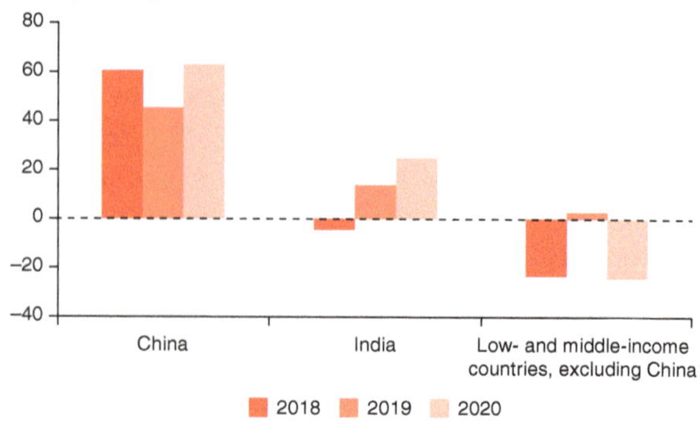

Source: International Monetary Fund.

Trade Zone and development of the Lekke Deep Sea Port by Chinese investors. Inflows to **Togo** jumped 72.3 percent to $639 million largely on account of investment from neighboring countries including $100 million from CimMetal (Burkina Faso) for a construction material plant and $60 million cement plant constructed by Dangote (Nigeria). In **Angola,** a slowdown in repatriation of capital by multinational companies in the oil and gas industry reduced outflows to –$2.0 billion from –$4.7 billion in 2019. In contrast some of the region's large FDI recipients saw inflows fall in 2020. In **Ethiopia,** the largest recipient in Eastern Africa, inflows fell moderately, 6 percent, with continued investment into key sectors like agriculture and manufacturing that offset much of the decline in hospitality and aviation. The government also facilitated FDI for the manufacture of personal protective equipment, and several Chinese companies started production in 2020. In contrast **Ghana,** one of the largest FDI recipients in West Africa and the first country on the continent to impose mobility restrictions, registered a 52 percent decline in FDI inflows in 2020. They fell to $2.0 billion from $3.9 billion in 2019 with manufacturing, services, and the mining sector all recording a downturn.

In common with FDI, portfolio equity inflows to low- and middle-income countries in 2020 centered on China and India. Portfolio equity inflows to low- and middle- income countries fell 19 percent in 2020 to $39 billion from $48 billion in 2019. The total figures mask the sharp divergence in the direction of portfolio equity flows in 2020 at the country level. In 2020, there was significant portfolio equity investment in China and India. Inflows to China rose 39 percent to $63 billion, and those to India increased by 81 percent to $25 billion from $14 billion in 2019. In contrast, other low- and middle-income countries registered combined portfolio equity outflows of $49 billion in 2020. The factors that attracted portfolio equity inflows to China paralleled those that propelled FDI inflows and non-resident investors' purchase of renminbi-denominated bonds, as outlined in box O.1. In India, government initiatives to attract FDI and portfolio equity investors by hosting investor conferences and structural changes to ease business and investment measures have been key factors behind the rise in portfolio equity inflows. They were also boosted by a better-than-expected economic recovery in the second half of 2020 and strong corporate earnings. In addition, the prospects of higher returns fueled a significant shift by non-resident investors from debt to equities in 2020.

Figure O.28 Portfolio Equity Flows to Major Recipients, 2018–20
US$ (billion)

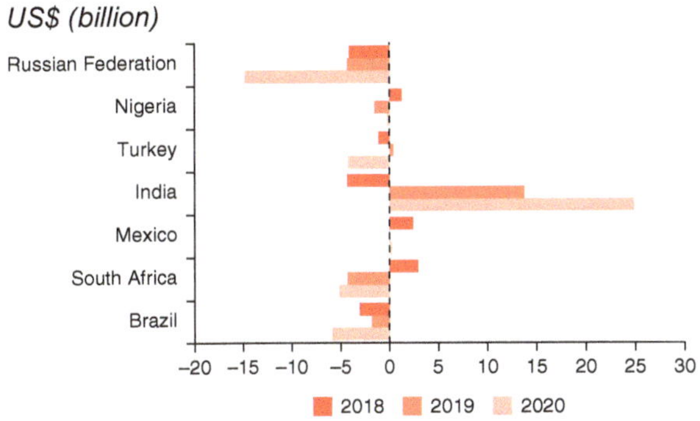

Source: International Monetary Fund.

Supporting Debt Transparency

Comprehensive, transparent public debt data are fundamental to assessing debt sustainability and effective use of borrowed resources. These data are essential for policy makers to make informed borrowing choices, creditors to appropriately price for sovereign risk, and citizens to hold their governments accountable. Yet, despite some improvements, public debt statistics in many low- and middle-income countries still suffer from important gaps in coverage and inadequate levels of transparency. The Debt Management Performance Assessment (DeMPA) conducted by the World Bank for 100 low- and middle-income countries found debt management capacity met the minimum standard for sound debt management in less than half of the dimensions assessed, including debt monitoring and reporting.[3]

Heightened debt vulnerabilities in low- and middle-income countries have been exacerbated by the COVID-19 pandemic. IDA countries have been particularly hard hit, with more than half now in debt distress or at high risk of it. This reflects increased public borrowing in recent years against the backdrop of a changing creditor landscape and multiplicity of non-traditional bilateral

[3] IMF-World Bank G-20 Note on Strengthening Public Debt Transparency, June 2018.

and private creditors and, for some countries, a sharp rise in borrowing in domestic markets. A proliferation of new and complex debt instruments and increased share of non-concessional financing in public debt portfolios has also complicated public debt management processes.

The debt-rescheduling efforts in 2020 and the need for an accurate measure of the impact of and gains from the G-20 DSSI highlighted the importance of debt transparency. Countries that benefit from DSSI are required to use fiscal space created for expenditures related to crisis response, to disclose all public sector debt, and to refrain from contracting new non-concessional debt during the suspension period, other than agreements in the context of DSSI, or in compliance with limits agreed under the IMF Debt Limit Policy or World Bank Sustainable Development Finance Policy.

The World Bank continues to take the lead in disseminating data on DSSI outcomes. *International Debt Statistics 2021* released for the first time a highly disaggregated dataset that provided, for each DSSI participant country, the breakdown of projected debt-service payments to each bilateral creditor and multilateral entity. **One important and ongoing element of the World Bank's focus on debt transparency is to accurately assess DSSI outcomes** and the terms and conditions of other bilateral debt-restructuring arrangements. These data are the essential underpinning of the Bank's multi-pronged program of support for borrowers, which includes not only unprecedented levels of emergency financing, but also implementation of new policies to incentivize sustainable development financing and increased focus on DSAs.

This year, the International Debt Statistics 2022 database further enhances debt transparency by introducing two new datasets. The borrower-creditor matrix is expanded to separately identify the Central Bank in the breakdown of the borrower types. Regarding the creditor breakdown, the average terms of new debt commitments (maturity, interest rate, grace period, and grant element) and the currency composition of debt stock by creditor type and creditor country have been added to the database. This new, disaggregated dataset allows analyses for each borrower-creditor pair, for regions, and for select subgroups. This database sets a new standard for greater debt transparency. It enriches the ways in which external debt data can support analyses and policy making. It confirms the rising importance of the information that allows for the comparison of lending terms extended by bilateral individual creditors, including new bilateral creditors, and by commercial lenders. The data are drawn from the World Bank DRS to which World Bank borrowers (IBRD and IDA) report annually, loan by loan, on stocks and flows for long-term external debt owed by public agencies or private agencies with public guarantees; in aggregate, on long-term external debt owed by the private sector with no public guarantees; and quarterly, loan by loan, on the terms and conditions of new public and publicly guaranteed loan commitments.

The DRS definition of external public debt is holistic. It encompasses all borrowing by (1) central government, state and local government, and municipalities; (2) Central Bank or monetary authority; and (3) public sector entities, irrespective of whether the obligation benefits from a state guarantee. Efforts over time have already closed large gaps in the data on public sector external debt and improved the coverage of borrowing by state-owned enterprises (SOEs). For the 123 countries reporting to the World Bank DRS and for which data are presented in *International Debt Statistics 2022*, 33 percent have full coverage of public sector debt, including the debt of SOEs.

Figure O.29 DRS Reporting Countries—Coverage of Public and Publicly Guaranteed Debt
Number of countries

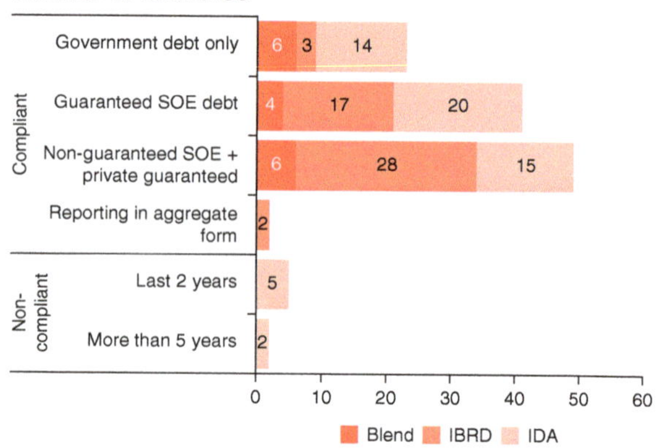

Source: World Bank Debtor Reporting System.

The DRS has a long-standing record for flexibility and capacity to meet new data needs as they arise to support the Bank's institutional requirements and those of the broader international community. Throughout its 60 plus years in operation, the DRS has continuously evolved in response to new data needs. The DRS has adapted to changing borrowing patterns; new and complex lending instruments; and demands for additional, highly detailed debt data, when periodic debt crises erupt, to both support restructuring processes and measure outcomes.

The DRS ongoing agenda prioritizes transparency and closing public sector data and knowledge gaps. Areas of emphasis are (1) an accurate and comprehensive measure of the external obligations of SOEs in all DRS reporting countries; (2) a determination of the extent to which public sector borrowers in low- and middle-income countries have given external creditors collateral or other risk mitigation commitments; and (3) incorporating Central Bank deposits and currency swaps lines into the DRS dataset. Furthering transparency on the external borrowing practices of SOEs is, in many respects, an essential first step in assessing the extent of loan collaterals. SOEs, particularly those in the extractive industries, are likely to account for a large share of collateralized loans. Similarly, a comprehensive measure of Central Bank deposits and foreign currency swap lines, and how they are used in support of public debt management in low- and middle-income countries, will be an important addition to debt data transparency and will help avert "debt surprises." A small number of countries already include information on foreign currency swap lines when reporting to the DRS. However, a preliminary survey of Central Banks in G-20 countries indicates that by mid-2021, a third of low- and middle-income countries had entered into currency swap agreements. Many of these arrangements appear to be precautionary, but a clearer understanding of them would be another important step in debt transparency.

PART II
Aggregate and Country Tables

ALL LOW- AND MIDDLE-INCOME COUNTRIES

(US$ billion, unless otherwise indicated)

	2010	2016	2017	2018	2019	2020
Summary external debt data by debtor type						
Total external debt stocks	**4,360**	**6,658**	**7,386**	**7,828**	**8,246**	**8,687**
Use of IMF credit	148	110	120	148	169	224
Long-term external debt	3,033	4,947	5,343	5,532	5,901	6,268
Public and publicly guaranteed sector	1,581	2,461	2,783	2,960	3,163	3,444
Public sector	1,574	2,457	2,780	2,957	3,160	3,442
of which: General government	1,179	1,779	2,027	2,145	2,334	2,567
Private sector guaranteed by public sector	7	3	3	2	2	2
Private sector not guaranteed	1,452	2,487	2,560	2,573	2,738	2,824
Short-term external debt	1,179	1,601	1,922	2,148	2,177	2,195
Disbursements (long-term)	**648**	**985**	**1,157**	**1,123**	**1,242**	**1,259**
Public and publicly guaranteed sector	290	354	484	481	471	529
Public sector	288	353	483	480	471	529
of which: General government	187	238	317	303	333	359
Private sector guaranteed by public sector	2	0	0	0	0	0
Private sector not guaranteed	359	631	673	642	770	730
Principal repayments (long-term)	**379**	**746**	**727**	**801**	**891**	**886**
Public and publicly guaranteed sector	137	222	210	264	265	273
Public sector	136	221	209	263	265	273
of which: General government	76	114	112	140	130	158
Private sector guaranteed by public sector	1	1	1	1	0	0
Private sector not guaranteed	241	525	517	537	626	613
Interest payments (long-term)	**101**	**174**	**189**	**211**	**231**	**207**
Public and publicly guaranteed sector	47	87	101	109	123	110
Public sector	47	87	101	109	123	110
of which: General government	39	66	76	81	86	77
Private sector guaranteed by public sector	0	0	0	0	0	0
Private sector not guaranteed	54	87	89	102	108	97
Summary external debt stock by creditor type						
Long-term external debt stocks	**3,033**	**4,947**	**5,343**	**5,532**	**5,901**	**6,268**
Public and publicly guaranteed debt from:	1,581	2,461	2,783	2,960	3,163	3,444
Official creditors	828	989	1,075	1,111	1,150	1,266
Multilateral	482	596	649	670	703	792
of which: World Bank	242	293	317	326	344	380
Bilateral	346	393	426	441	447	475
Private creditors	753	1,471	1,709	1,849	2,013	2,178
Bondholders	473	1,038	1,260	1,394	1,563	1,736
Commercial banks and others	281	434	449	455	450	442
Private nonguaranteed debt from:	1,452	2,487	2,560	2,573	2,738	2,824
Bondholders	211	389	471	480	566	677
Commercial banks and others	1,241	2,097	2,089	2,092	2,173	2,147
Use of IMF credit	148	110	120	148	169	224
Net financial inflows						
Net debt inflows						
Use of IMF credit	13	5	4	31	22	47
Long-term	270	238	430	321	351	373
Official creditors	60	57	53	50	42	82
Multilateral	48	33	31	32	36	70
of which: World Bank	22	14	13	15	19	27
Bilateral	12	25	22	19	6	12
Private creditors	210	181	377	271	308	291
Bondholders	101	120	289	204	255	280
Banks and others	109	61	88	68	53	10
Short-term	428	-35	322	222	28	16
Net equity inflows						
Foreign direct investment	529	468	468	496	506	434
Portfolio equity	126	45	67	37	48	39
Debt ratios						
External debt stocks to exports (%)	81	107	104	101	106	123
External debt stocks to GNI (%)	22	26	26	26	27	29
Debt service to exports (%)	10	15	14	14	16	17
Short-term to external debt stocks (%)	27	24	26	27	26	25
Multilateral to external debt stocks (%)	11	9	9	9	9	9
Reserves to external debt stocks (%)	120	83	79	73	72	72
Gross national income (GNI)	19,435	25,993	28,594	30,185	31,018	29,879

EAST ASIA AND PACIFIC

(US$ billion, unless otherwise indicated)

	2010	2016	2017	2018	2019	2020
Summary external debt data by debtor type						
Total external debt stocks	**1,192**	**2,112**	**2,482**	**2,789**	**2,993**	**3,297**
Use of IMF credit	18	16	17	17	17	18
Long-term external debt	558	1,167	1,277	1,400	1,618	1,874
Public and publicly guaranteed sector	318	476	546	641	727	860
Public sector	318	475	546	641	727	860
of which: General government	240	365	404	448	510	596
Private sector guaranteed by public sector	0	0	0	0	0	0
Private sector not guaranteed	240	691	731	759	890	1,014
Short-term external debt	616	930	1,188	1,372	1,359	1,405
Disbursements (long-term)	**116**	**277**	**362**	**407**	**510**	**522**
Public and publicly guaranteed sector	47	60	98	132	130	172
Public sector	47	60	98	132	130	172
of which: General government	29	45	49	65	81	104
Private sector guaranteed by public sector	0	0	0	0	0	0
Private sector not guaranteed	69	217	264	276	381	350
Principal repayments (long-term)	**65**	**216**	**231**	**252**	**309**	**273**
Public and publicly guaranteed sector	29	35	34	34	43	53
Public sector	29	35	34	34	43	53
of which: General government	17	22	15	18	19	27
Private sector guaranteed by public sector	0	0	0	0	0	0
Private sector not guaranteed	36	182	197	218	266	220
Interest payments (long-term)	**16**	**29**	**35**	**47**	**57**	**53**
Public and publicly guaranteed sector	9	12	14	18	22	23
Public sector	9	12	14	18	22	23
of which: General government	7	9	10	13	14	13
Private sector guaranteed by public sector	0	0	0	0	0	0
Private sector not guaranteed	7	17	21	29	35	30
Summary external debt stock by creditor type						
Long-term external debt stocks	**558**	**1,167**	**1,277**	**1,400**	**1,618**	**1,874**
Public and publicly guaranteed debt from:	318	476	546	641	727	860
Official creditors	218	203	208	211	214	234
Multilateral	87	102	107	111	116	130
of which: World Bank	47	55	59	60	62	66
Bilateral	131	101	101	100	98	105
Private creditors	101	273	338	430	513	625
Bondholders	72	223	284	371	449	562
Commercial banks and others	29	50	54	59	64	64
Private nonguaranteed debt from:	240	691	731	759	890	1,014
Bondholders	20	132	183	216	276	371
Commercial banks and others	220	559	548	544	615	643
Use of IMF credit	18	16	17	17	17	18
Net financial inflows						
Net debt inflows						
Use of IMF credit	0	0	0	0	0	1
Long-term	51	60	130	155	201	249
Official creditors	3	0	0	4	3	14
Multilateral	4	4	4	5	5	11
of which: World Bank	3	2	2	2	2	3
Bilateral	-2	-4	-3	-1	-2	3
Private creditors	49	60	130	151	198	234
Bondholders	9	40	111	124	138	204
Banks and others	40	20	19	27	60	30
Short-term	307	-16	259	184	-13	45
Net equity inflows						
Foreign direct investment	265	193	190	245	215	206
Portfolio equity	40	24	35	49	47	48
Debt ratios						
External debt stocks to exports (%)	50	66	69	71	77	85
External debt stocks to GNI (%)	16	16	17	17	18	19
Debt service to exports (%)	5	8	9	9	11	10
Short-term to external debt stocks (%)	52	44	48	49	45	43
Multilateral to external debt stocks (%)	7	5	4	4	4	4
Reserves to external debt stocks (%)	269	163	146	128	122	117
Gross national income (GNI)	7,564	13,170	14,438	16,080	16,685	16,949

EUROPE AND CENTRAL ASIA

(US$ billion, unless otherwise indicated)

	2010	2016	2017	2018	2019	2020
Summary external debt data by debtor type						
Total external debt stocks	**1,265**	**1,540**	**1,610**	**1,556**	**1,584**	**1,636**
Use of IMF credit	62	30	32	30	28	33
Long-term external debt	973	1,292	1,330	1,281	1,292	1,317
Public and publicly guaranteed sector	361	483	543	530	555	601
Public sector	360	482	542	530	555	600
of which: General government	201	279	321	326	364	414
Private sector guaranteed by public sector	1	1	1	0	0	0
Private sector not guaranteed	612	809	787	751	737	716
Short-term external debt	230	218	249	245	263	287
Disbursements (long-term)	**236**	**254**	**274**	**216**	**243**	**257**
Public and publicly guaranteed sector	89	59	94	78	93	102
Public sector	89	59	94	78	93	102
of which: General government	46	36	50	50	65	70
Private sector guaranteed by public sector	1	0	0	0	0	0
Private sector not guaranteed	147	195	179	138	150	155
Principal repayments (long-term)	**175**	**204**	**208**	**244**	**229**	**234**
Public and publicly guaranteed sector	43	68	49	85	65	73
Public sector	43	68	49	85	65	73
of which: General government	17	26	21	39	25	35
Private sector guaranteed by public sector	0	0	0	0	0	0
Private sector not guaranteed	132	136	160	159	164	161
Interest payments (long-term)	**34**	**46**	**46**	**46**	**45**	**46**
Public and publicly guaranteed sector	9	17	18	21	21	22
Public sector	9	17	18	21	21	22
of which: General government	7	10	12	13	13	15
Private sector guaranteed by public sector	0	0	0	0	0	0
Private sector not guaranteed	25	29	27	25	25	24
Summary external debt stock by creditor type						
Long-term external debt stocks	**973**	**1,292**	**1,330**	**1,281**	**1,292**	**1,317**
Public and publicly guaranteed debt from:	361	483	543	530	555	601
Official creditors	110	137	151	149	148	161
Multilateral	75	93	103	100	97	110
of which: World Bank	36	41	45	45	44	47
Bilateral	35	44	49	50	51	51
Private creditors	251	346	391	380	407	439
Bondholders	88	183	220	232	273	308
Commercial banks and others	163	163	172	148	135	132
Private nonguaranteed debt from:	612	809	787	751	737	716
Bondholders	34	67	78	78	88	96
Commercial banks and others	578	742	709	673	649	620
Use of IMF credit	62	30	32	30	28	33
Net financial inflows						
Net debt inflows						
Use of IMF credit	9	1	0	-1	-2	3
Long-term	62	50	65	-28	13	23
Official creditors	18	7	6	2	0	6
Multilateral	14	4	2	0	-2	8
of which: World Bank	3	1	1	1	0	1
Bilateral	4	3	3	2	1	-1
Private creditors	44	43	60	-29	13	17
Bondholders	13	16	38	16	49	31
Banks and others	31	27	22	-45	-36	-14
Short-term	44	-1	30	-5	18	22
Net equity inflows						
Foreign direct investment	66	81	65	51	73	42
Portfolio equity	-1	-1	-5	-7	-4	-19
Debt ratios						
External debt stocks to exports (%)	128	167	147	122	125	156
External debt stocks to GNI (%)	42	53	50	47	47	52
Debt service to exports (%)	22	28	24	24	22	27
Short-term to external debt stocks (%)	18	14	15	16	17	18
Multilateral to external debt stocks (%)	6	6	6	6	6	7
Reserves to external debt stocks (%)	54	36	38	40	43	43
Gross national income (GNI)	3,029	2,892	3,247	3,337	3,395	3,150

LATIN AMERICA AND THE CARIBBEAN

(US$ billion, unless otherwise indicated)

	2010	2016	2017	2018	2019	2020
Summary external debt data by debtor type						
Total external debt stocks	**996**	**1,623**	**1,709**	**1,815**	**1,873**	**1,867**
Use of IMF credit	20	17	17	45	62	79
Long-term external debt	797	1,374	1,453	1,490	1,522	1,548
Public and publicly guaranteed sector	437	769	834	870	885	923
Public sector	433	767	832	869	884	922
of which: General government	337	536	582	610	629	665
Private sector guaranteed by public sector	4	2	2	2	1	1
Private sector not guaranteed	360	605	620	619	636	625
Short-term external debt	180	233	238	280	289	241
Disbursements (long-term)	**185**	**286**	**285**	**274**	**260**	**287**
Public and publicly guaranteed sector	83	132	140	130	107	139
Public sector	82	131	140	130	106	139
of which: General government	56	82	89	86	70	90
Private sector guaranteed by public sector	1	0	0	0	0	0
Private sector not guaranteed	101	154	145	143	154	148
Principal repayments (long-term)	**83**	**201**	**185**	**177**	**228**	**224**
Public and publicly guaranteed sector	39	63	77	75	91	72
Public sector	39	62	76	74	91	72
of which: General government	25	30	44	30	41	40
Private sector guaranteed by public sector	1	1	1	1	0	0
Private sector not guaranteed	44	138	108	102	137	152
Interest payments (long-term)	**35**	**68**	**75**	**75**	**81**	**66**
Public and publicly guaranteed sector	20	40	49	45	51	40
Public sector	20	40	49	45	51	40
of which: General government	16	32	39	35	36	28
Private sector guaranteed by public sector	0	0	0	0	0	0
Private sector not guaranteed	15	28	26	30	30	26
Summary external debt stock by creditor type						
Long-term external debt stocks	**797**	**1,374**	**1,453**	**1,490**	**1,522**	**1,548**
Public and publicly guaranteed debt from:	437	769	834	870	885	923
Official creditors	161	198	208	215	215	232
Multilateral	124	155	159	168	174	191
of which: World Bank	49	58	58	60	62	69
Bilateral	37	43	50	47	41	41
Private creditors	276	570	625	656	670	691
Bondholders	235	436	492	514	526	556
Commercial banks and others	41	135	133	142	144	136
Private nonguaranteed debt from:	360	605	620	619	636	625
Bondholders	134	170	184	161	171	175
Commercial banks and others	226	435	436	458	465	451
Use of IMF credit	20	17	17	45	62	79
Net financial inflows						
Net debt inflows						
Use of IMF credit	1	0	0	29	17	13
Long-term	101	85	100	97	32	63
Official creditors	20	6	9	7	1	15
Multilateral	16	6	3	9	7	16
of which: World Bank	8	2	-1	2	2	7
Bilateral	5	0	6	-2	-6	-1
Private creditors	81	79	91	90	31	47
Bondholders	59	54	73	47	26	47
Banks and others	22	25	17	43	5	0
Short-term	54	-31	9	41	10	-49
Net equity inflows						
Foreign direct investment	122	107	132	121	133	84
Portfolio equity	40	21	20	-2	-3	-6
Debt ratios						
External debt stocks to exports (%)	115	170	159	157	160	186
External debt stocks to GNI (%)	23	38	35	39	41	49
Debt service to exports (%)	14	29	25	23	27	30
Short-term to external debt stocks (%)	18	14	14	15	15	13
Multilateral to external debt stocks (%)	12	10	9	9	9	10
Reserves to external debt stocks (%)	57	46	45	43	40	42
Gross national income (GNI)	4,350	4,323	4,824	4,646	4,589	3,809

MIDDLE EAST AND NORTH AFRICA

(US$ billion, unless otherwise indicated)

	2010	2016	2017	2018	2019	2020
Summary external debt data by debtor type						
Total external debt stocks	**191**	**267**	**300**	**323**	**341**	**370**
Use of IMF credit	8	13	17	18	22	33
Long-term external debt	145	202	230	256	266	277
Public and publicly guaranteed sector	114	157	182	200	215	235
Public sector	113	157	182	199	214	234
of which: General government	91	117	135	148	162	178
Private sector guaranteed by public sector	1	0	0	0	0	0
Private sector not guaranteed	31	44	48	56	51	42
Short-term external debt	38	52	53	49	54	60
Disbursements (long-term)	**22**	**40**	**45**	**50**	**37**	**31**
Public and publicly guaranteed sector	14	28	31	32	29	29
Public sector	13	28	31	32	29	29
of which: General government	11	18	23	22	24	23
Private sector guaranteed by public sector	0	0	0	0	0	0
Private sector not guaranteed	9	12	13	18	8	2
Principal repayments (long-term)	**18**	**24**	**23**	**23**	**25**	**27**
Public and publicly guaranteed sector	10	15	13	12	13	15
Public sector	10	15	13	12	13	15
of which: General government	7	10	9	7	9	11
Private sector guaranteed by public sector	0	0	0	0	0	0
Private sector not guaranteed	8	10	10	11	12	12
Interest payments (long-term)	**6**	**7**	**7**	**9**	**11**	**8**
Public and publicly guaranteed sector	4	5	5	6	8	5
Public sector	4	5	5	6	8	5
of which: General government	3	4	4	5	6	4
Private sector guaranteed by public sector	0	0	0	0	0	0
Private sector not guaranteed	2	2	2	2	3	2
Summary external debt stock by creditor type						
Long-term external debt stocks	**145**	**202**	**230**	**256**	**266**	**277**
Public and publicly guaranteed debt from:	114	157	182	200	215	235
Official creditors	78	102	114	117	121	133
Multilateral	37	49	57	58	62	72
of which: World Bank	12	18	22	24	26	30
Bilateral	42	53	57	58	59	62
Private creditors	36	55	68	83	94	101
Bondholders	27	47	59	70	78	85
Commercial banks and others	9	8	8	13	16	17
Private nonguaranteed debt from:	31	44	48	56	51	42
Bondholders	1	1	0	1	1	1
Commercial banks and others	30	44	48	56	51	42
Use of IMF credit	8	13	17	18	22	33
Net financial inflows						
Net debt inflows						
Use of IMF credit	0	3	3	2	4	11
Long-term	4	16	21	27	12	4
Official creditors	1	13	7	5	5	8
Multilateral	2	7	5	2	4	7
of which: World Bank	1	2	2	2	3	2
Bilateral	-1	6	2	2	1	1
Private creditors	3	2	15	23	7	-4
Bondholders	3	1	11	11	9	6
Banks and others	0	1	3	12	-2	-10
Short-term	5	11	1	-5	5	4
Net equity inflows						
Foreign direct investment	23	19	21	19	17	14
Portfolio equity	2	1	-1	0	1	-2
Debt ratios						
External debt stocks to exports (%)	58	98	96	97	116	184
External debt stocks to GNI (%)	17	22	26	31	33	37
Debt service to exports (%)	7	12	11	10	13	18
Short-term to external debt stocks (%)	20	19	18	15	16	16
Multilateral to external debt stocks (%)	19	18	19	18	18	19
Reserves to external debt stocks (%)	156	84	69	59	51	41
Gross national income (GNI)	1,151	1,236	1,176	1,043	1,050	988

SOUTH ASIA

(US$ billion, unless otherwise indicated)

	2010	2016	2017	2018	2019	2020
Summary external debt data by debtor type						
Total external debt stocks	**410**	**624**	**707**	**733**	**789**	**814**
Use of IMF credit	20	16	17	16	17	20
Long-term external debt	323	501	564	586	636	663
Public and publicly guaranteed sector	189	270	318	330	354	372
Public sector	189	270	318	330	354	372
of which: General government	167	224	273	279	297	314
Private sector guaranteed by public sector	0	0	0	0	0	0
Private sector not guaranteed	134	231	246	256	283	291
Short-term external debt	67	107	126	130	136	131
Disbursements (long-term)	**52**	**59**	**104**	**84**	**103**	**96**
Public and publicly guaranteed sector	31	26	61	43	50	45
Public sector	31	26	61	43	50	45
of which: General government	25	20	54	30	36	36
Private sector guaranteed by public sector	0	0	0	0	0	0
Private sector not guaranteed	22	33	43	41	53	51
Principal repayments (long-term)	**24**	**72**	**48**	**58**	**52**	**77**
Public and publicly guaranteed sector	9	25	20	29	26	34
Public sector	9	25	20	29	26	34
of which: General government	6	16	11	21	17	26
Private sector guaranteed by public sector	0	0	0	0	0	0
Private sector not guaranteed	15	47	28	29	26	43
Interest payments (long-term)	**6**	**12**	**13**	**18**	**18**	**16**
Public and publicly guaranteed sector	3	4	5	6	7	5
Public sector	3	4	5	6	7	5
of which: General government	2	3	4	5	5	5
Private sector guaranteed by public sector	0	0	0	0	0	0
Private sector not guaranteed	4	8	9	12	10	10
Summary external debt stock by creditor type						
Long-term external debt stocks	**323**	**501**	**564**	**586**	**636**	**663**
Public and publicly guaranteed debt from:	189	270	318	330	354	372
Official creditors	156	171	188	203	219	247
Multilateral	101	109	118	121	129	146
of which: World Bank	64	68	72	72	75	82
Bilateral	55	61	70	82	90	101
Private creditors	33	100	130	126	135	125
Bondholders	18	69	101	94	102	91
Commercial banks and others	15	31	29	33	33	34
Private nonguaranteed debt from:	134	231	246	256	283	291
Bondholders	13	10	15	14	19	26
Commercial banks and others	120	220	231	242	263	265
Use of IMF credit	20	16	17	16	17	20
Net financial inflows						
Net debt inflows						
Use of IMF credit	2	1	0	0	1	2
Long-term	29	-13	56	26	51	19
Official creditors	7	8	11	18	16	22
Multilateral	6	4	4	5	8	14
of which: World Bank	3	2	1	2	3	5
Bilateral	2	4	6	12	8	8
Private creditors	21	-22	45	9	35	-2
Bondholders	10	-2	36	-7	13	-5
Banks and others	11	-20	9	16	21	2
Short-term	13	4	19	4	5	-4
Net equity inflows						
Foreign direct investment	31	48	42	43	48	63
Portfolio equity	30	2	6	-5	14	24
Debt ratios						
External debt stocks to exports (%)	96	116	117	110	117	137
External debt stocks to GNI (%)	20	22	21	21	22	24
Debt service to exports (%)	7	16	11	12	11	16
Short-term to external debt stocks (%)	16	17	18	18	17	16
Multilateral to external debt stocks (%)	25	18	17	17	16	18
Reserves to external debt stocks (%)	77	66	66	60	64	78
Gross national income (GNI)	2,048	2,885	3,323	3,412	3,576	3,334

SUB-SAHARAN AFRICA

(US$ billion, unless otherwise indicated)

	2010	2016	2017	2018	2019	2020
Summary external debt data by debtor type						
Total external debt stocks	**305**	**492**	**578**	**613**	**665**	**702**
Use of IMF credit	19	19	21	22	23	41
Long-term external debt	237	411	490	519	567	589
Public and publicly guaranteed sector	161	305	361	389	426	454
Public sector	161	305	361	389	426	454
of which: General government	143	259	312	333	372	400
Private sector guaranteed by public sector	0	0	0	0	0	0
Private sector not guaranteed	76	106	129	130	141	135
Short-term external debt	49	62	67	72	75	72
Disbursements (long-term)	**36**	**69**	**88**	**91**	**88**	**67**
Public and publicly guaranteed sector	26	49	60	65	62	42
Public sector	26	49	60	65	62	42
of which: General government	20	38	52	51	57	36
Private sector guaranteed by public sector	0	0	0	0	..	0
Private sector not guaranteed	10	20	28	27	26	25
Principal repayments (long-term)	**14**	**28**	**31**	**48**	**47**	**52**
Public and publicly guaranteed sector	7	16	17	29	26	26
Public sector	7	16	17	29	26	26
of which: General government	4	10	11	24	19	18
Private sector guaranteed by public sector	0	0	0	0	0	0
Private sector not guaranteed	7	13	13	19	20	26
Interest payments (long-term)	**4**	**13**	**13**	**16**	**20**	**18**
Public and publicly guaranteed sector	3	9	9	12	15	15
Public sector	3	9	9	12	15	15
of which: General government	3	8	8	10	12	12
Private sector guaranteed by public sector	0	..	..	..	0	0
Private sector not guaranteed	1	4	4	4	5	4
Summary external debt stock by creditor type						
Long-term external debt stocks	**237**	**411**	**490**	**519**	**567**	**589**
Public and publicly guaranteed debt from:	161	305	361	389	426	454
Official creditors	106	177	205	215	233	258
Multilateral	59	88	105	111	125	144
of which: World Bank	34	52	61	65	74	86
Bilateral	47	89	100	104	108	115
Private creditors	56	128	156	174	194	195
Bondholders	32	80	104	114	135	135
Commercial banks and others	23	48	53	60	58	60
Private nonguaranteed debt from:	76	106	129	130	141	135
Bondholders	9	10	11	11	11	9
Commercial banks and others	67	96	118	119	129	127
Use of IMF credit	19	19	21	22	23	41
Net financial inflows						
Net debt inflows						
Use of IMF credit	1	0	1	2	1	17
Long-term	23	41	57	43	41	15
Official creditors	10	23	21	15	18	17
Multilateral	6	8	12	10	14	14
of which: World Bank	4	5	6	6	9	9
Bilateral	4	15	8	6	4	3
Private creditors	12	17	37	28	24	-2
Bondholders	6	11	19	13	20	-3
Banks and others	6	7	18	16	4	2
Short-term	5	-2	5	2	2	-2
Net equity inflows						
Foreign direct investment	23	20	18	16	20	24
Portfolio equity	16	-2	12	3	-6	-6
Debt ratios						
External debt stocks to exports (%)	76	148	150	142	156	205
External debt stocks to GNI (%)	24	33	37	38	40	44
Debt service to exports (%)	5	13	12	15	16	22
Short-term to external debt stocks (%)	16	13	12	12	11	10
Multilateral to external debt stocks (%)	19	18	18	18	19	20
Reserves to external debt stocks (%)	51	30	28	27	23	21
Gross national income (GNI)	1,293	1,472	1,558	1,626	1,681	1,605

AFGHANISTAN

(US$ million, unless otherwise indicated)

	2010	2016	2017	2018	2019	2020
Summary external debt data by debtor type						
Total external debt stocks	**2,436**	**2,596**	**2,752**	**2,679**	**2,662**	**3,036**
Use of IMF credit	355	277	285	275	277	629
Long-term external debt	1,976	1,965	1,998	1,970	1,965	1,976
Public and publicly guaranteed sector	1,976	1,950	1,982	1,949	1,944	1,958
Public sector	1,976	1,950	1,982	1,949	1,944	1,958
of which: General government	1,976	1,950	1,982	1,949	1,944	1,958
Private sector guaranteed by public sector	..	..	..	..	..	..
Private sector not guaranteed	..	15	16	22	21	18
Short-term external debt	105	355	470	434	420	431
Disbursements (long-term)	**76**	**12**	**3**	**16**	**29**	**0**
Public and publicly guaranteed sector	76	12	3	16	29	0
Public sector	76	12	3	16	29	0
of which: General government	76	12	3	16	29	0
Private sector guaranteed by public sector	..	..	..	..	..	..
Private sector not guaranteed	..	..	..	..	..	..
Principal repayments (long-term)	**1**	**27**	**27**	**31**	**31**	**26**
Public and publicly guaranteed sector	1	23	23	25	25	22
Public sector	1	23	23	25	25	22
of which: General government	1	23	23	25	25	22
Private sector guaranteed by public sector	..	..	..	..	..	..
Private sector not guaranteed	..	4	4	6	6	5
Interest payments (long-term)	**8**	**8**	**9**	**9**	**9**	**8**
Public and publicly guaranteed sector	8	8	8	8	7	7
Public sector	8	8	8	8	7	7
of which: General government	8	8	8	8	7	7
Private sector guaranteed by public sector	..	..	..	..	..	..
Private sector not guaranteed	..	1	1	1	1	1
Summary external debt stock by creditor type						
Long-term external debt stocks	**1,976**	**1,965**	**1,998**	**1,970**	**1,965**	**1,976**
Public and publicly guaranteed debt from:	1,976	1,950	1,982	1,949	1,944	1,958
Official creditors	1,976	1,950	1,982	1,949	1,944	1,958
Multilateral	1,016	991	1,023	983	955	968
of which: World Bank	406	351	364	348	338	344
Bilateral	959	958	959	965	989	991
Private creditors	0	..	..	..	..	..
Bondholders	..	..	..	..	..	..
Commercial banks and others	0	..	..	..	..	..
Private nonguaranteed debt from:	..	15	16	22	21	18
Bondholders	..	..	..	..	..	..
Commercial banks and others	..	15	16	22	21	18
Use of IMF credit	355	277	285	275	277	629
Net financial inflows						
Net debt inflows						
Use of IMF credit	9	-15	-8	-4	4	329
Long-term	75	-15	-24	-14	-2	-26
Official creditors	75	-11	-19	-8	3	-21
Multilateral	75	-9	-19	-15	-20	-21
of which: World Bank	8	-8	-8	-8	-8	-8
Bilateral	0	-2	0	7	23	-1
Private creditors	..	-4	-4	-6	-6	-5
Bondholders	..	..	..	..	..	..
Banks and others	..	-4	-4	-6	-6	-5
Short-term	37	26	80	-68	-44	-14
Net equity inflows						
Foreign direct investment	191	94	52	119	23	13
Portfolio equity	0	0	0	0	0	0
Debt ratios						
External debt stocks to exports (%)	89	189	189	141	142	177
External debt stocks to GNI (%)	15	14	14	14	14	15
Debt service to exports (%)	0	4	4	3	3	3
Short-term to external debt stocks (%)	4	14	17	16	16	14
Multilateral to external debt stocks (%)	42	38	37	37	36	32
Reserves to external debt stocks (%)	171	249	261	273	279	277
Gross national income (GNI)	15,885	18,197	19,118	18,545	19,598	19,996

ALBANIA

(US$ million, unless otherwise indicated)

	2010	2016	2017	2018	2019	2020
Summary external debt data by debtor type						
Total external debt stocks	**5,437**	**8,516**	**9,801**	**9,876**	**9,557**	**10,859**
Use of IMF credit	129	387	489	470	448	627
Long-term external debt	4,564	6,482	7,421	7,502	8,502	9,562
Public and publicly guaranteed sector	3,210	3,761	4,335	4,559	4,442	5,278
Public sector	3,210	3,761	4,335	4,559	4,442	5,278
of which: General government	2,854	3,489	4,051	4,246	4,160	4,884
Private sector guaranteed by public sector	..	..	..	..	..	..
Private sector not guaranteed	1,354	2,722	3,085	2,942	4,060	4,284
Short-term external debt	743	1,647	1,892	1,904	607	670
Disbursements (long-term)	**866**	**450**	**776**	**1,269**	**457**	**1,311**
Public and publicly guaranteed sector	631	205	421	931	207	1,028
Public sector	631	205	421	931	207	1,028
of which: General government	613	189	420	792	202	922
Private sector guaranteed by public sector	..	..	..	..	..	..
Private sector not guaranteed	235	245	355	338	250	283
Principal repayments (long-term)	**250**	**488**	**407**	**922**	**498**	**948**
Public and publicly guaranteed sector	174	191	222	554	263	537
Public sector	174	191	222	554	263	537
of which: General government	146	160	198	456	234	511
Private sector guaranteed by public sector	..	..	..	..	..	..
Private sector not guaranteed	76	297	185	368	234	410
Interest payments (long-term)	**110**	**95**	**96**	**147**	**122**	**154**
Public and publicly guaranteed sector	66	84	83	120	105	104
Public sector	66	84	83	120	105	104
of which: General government	59	82	80	114	102	99
Private sector guaranteed by public sector	..	..	..	..	..	..
Private sector not guaranteed	44	11	12	28	17	50
Summary external debt stock by creditor type						
Long-term external debt stocks	**4,564**	**6,482**	**7,421**	**7,502**	**8,502**	**9,562**
Public and publicly guaranteed debt from:	3,210	3,761	4,335	4,559	4,442	5,278
Official creditors	2,175	2,532	2,984	3,037	3,004	3,252
Multilateral	1,521	1,890	2,279	2,362	2,338	2,545
of which: World Bank	875	991	1,300	1,301	1,330	1,418
Bilateral	654	642	705	675	666	707
Private creditors	1,035	1,229	1,351	1,522	1,438	2,027
Bondholders	477	611	696	942	925	1,501
Commercial banks and others	558	617	656	580	514	526
Private nonguaranteed debt from:	1,354	2,722	3,085	2,942	4,060	4,284
Bondholders	69	148	192	329	306	284
Commercial banks and others	1,285	2,573	2,894	2,614	3,754	4,000
Use of IMF credit	129	387	489	470	448	627
Net financial inflows						
Net debt inflows						
Use of IMF credit	-12	156	77	-7	-20	155
Long-term	616	-38	369	347	-40	363
Official creditors	111	3	243	137	-1	67
Multilateral	103	-11	240	148	1	69
of which: World Bank	18	2	226	40	44	4
Bilateral	8	14	3	-11	-2	-1
Private creditors	506	-40	126	210	-39	296
Bondholders	444	15	43	340	-20	414
Banks and others	61	-56	83	-130	-19	-118
Short-term	63	61	245	12	-1,297	63
Net equity inflows						
Foreign direct investment	1,052	1,048	1,073	1,271	1,252	1,138
Portfolio equity	7	-15	-12	-3	7	-8
Debt ratios						
External debt stocks to exports (%)	147	219	213	188	181	282
External debt stocks to GNI (%)	46	71	75	65	63	75
Debt service to exports (%)	10	15	11	21	12	30
Short-term to external debt stocks (%)	14	19	19	19	6	6
Multilateral to external debt stocks (%)	28	22	23	24	24	23
Reserves to external debt stocks (%)	45	36	36	39	38	43
Gross national income (GNI)	11,807	12,054	13,054	15,130	15,085	14,541

ALGERIA

(US$ million, unless otherwise indicated)

	2010	2016	2017	2018	2019	2020
Summary external debt data by debtor type						
Total external debt stocks	**7,253**	**5,463**	**5,707**	**5,710**	**5,492**	**5,178**
Use of IMF credit	1,845	1,611	1,706	1,666	1,657	1,726
Long-term external debt	3,630	1,866	1,904	1,725	1,571	1,669
Public and publicly guaranteed sector	2,662	1,653	1,716	1,523	1,398	1,437
Public sector	2,521	1,650	1,713	1,521	1,397	1,436
of which: General government	927	1,247	1,366	1,268	1,205	1,278
Private sector guaranteed by public sector	141	3	3	2	1	0
Private sector not guaranteed	968	214	188	202	173	232
Short-term external debt	1,778	1,986	2,096	2,319	2,264	1,784
Disbursements (long-term)	**42**	**1,032**	**11**	**44**	**33**	**98**
Public and publicly guaranteed sector	40	984	1	0	0	0
Public sector	40	984	1	0	0	0
of which: General government	31	984	0	0	0	0
Private sector guaranteed by public sector	0	0	0	0	0	0
Private sector not guaranteed	2	49	11	44	33	98
Principal repayments (long-term)	**557**	**302**	**176**	**151**	**118**	**118**
Public and publicly guaranteed sector	324	149	140	122	93	77
Public sector	291	149	139	121	92	76
of which: General government	31	44	41	40	36	28
Private sector guaranteed by public sector	33	0	1	1	1	1
Private sector not guaranteed	234	153	36	29	25	41
Interest payments (long-term)	**95**	**22**	**31**	**29**	**25**	**23**
Public and publicly guaranteed sector	64	17	27	26	23	22
Public sector	64	17	27	26	23	22
of which: General government	13	6	20	21	20	20
Private sector guaranteed by public sector	0	0	0	0	0	0
Private sector not guaranteed	31	5	4	3	2	1
Summary external debt stock by creditor type						
Long-term external debt stocks	**3,630**	**1,866**	**1,904**	**1,725**	**1,571**	**1,669**
Public and publicly guaranteed debt from:	2,662	1,653	1,716	1,523	1,398	1,437
Official creditors	1,986	1,580	1,682	1,512	1,393	1,434
Multilateral	10	949	1,079	1,031	1,007	1,095
of which: World Bank	9	1	0	..	..	..
Bilateral	1,976	630	603	481	386	339
Private creditors	676	73	34	11	6	3
Bondholders	..	..	..	..	..	..
Commercial banks and others	676	73	34	11	6	3
Private nonguaranteed debt from:	968	214	188	202	173	232
Bondholders	..	..	..	..	..	..
Commercial banks and others	968	214	188	202	173	232
Use of IMF credit	1,845	1,611	1,706	1,666	1,657	1,726
Net financial inflows						
Net debt inflows						
Use of IMF credit	..	..	..	..	..	..
Long-term	-516	731	-165	-107	-85	-20
Official creditors	-129	880	-97	-99	-88	-74
Multilateral	-2	983	-1	0	0	0
of which: World Bank	-1	0	-1	..	..	..
Bilateral	-126	-103	-96	-99	-88	-74
Private creditors	-387	-149	-68	-8	3	54
Bondholders	..	..	..	..	..	..
Banks and others	-387	-149	-68	-8	3	54
Short-term	286	163	110	223	-55	-481
Net equity inflows						
Foreign direct investment	2,315	1,650	1,231	1,440	1,364	1,073
Portfolio equity	0	..	..	..	..	..
Debt ratios						
External debt stocks to exports (%)	11	16	14	13	14	20
External debt stocks to GNI (%)	5	3	3	3	3	4
Debt service to exports (%)	1	1	1	0	0	1
Short-term to external debt stocks (%)	25	36	37	41	41	34
Multilateral to external debt stocks (%)	0	17	19	18	18	21
Reserves to external debt stocks (%)	2,242	2,094	1,711	1,405	1,152	944
Gross national income (GNI)	160,817	158,469	167,506	170,995	166,956	141,855

ANGOLA

(US$ million, unless otherwise indicated)

	2010	2016	2017	2018	2019	2020
Summary external debt data by debtor type						
Total external debt stocks	**26,796**	**57,827**	**59,176**	**63,218**	**64,446**	**67,287**
Use of IMF credit	1,302	396	389	1,374	1,861	2,992
Long-term external debt	20,926	53,028	55,079	59,012	59,322	57,918
Public and publicly guaranteed sector	15,662	41,423	42,338	47,510	47,286	47,144
Public sector	15,662	41,423	42,338	47,510	47,286	47,144
of which: General government	7,069	23,962	27,668	33,296	34,677	35,047
Private sector guaranteed by public sector	..	..	..	..	..	..
Private sector not guaranteed	5,264	11,604	12,741	11,502	12,036	10,774
Short-term external debt	4,568	4,404	3,708	2,832	3,263	6,377
Disbursements (long-term)	**6,678**	**17,457**	**7,436**	**12,182**	**8,905**	**3,943**
Public and publicly guaranteed sector	4,047	15,190	7,436	12,182	8,105	3,943
Public sector	4,047	15,190	7,436	12,182	8,105	3,943
of which: General government	550	7,142	6,176	9,882	7,105	2,443
Private sector guaranteed by public sector	..	..	..	..	..	..
Private sector not guaranteed	2,632	2,267	..	..	801	..
Principal repayments (long-term)	**2,639**	**8,174**	**7,381**	**8,144**	**8,555**	**5,739**
Public and publicly guaranteed sector	2,113	7,040	6,812	6,905	8,288	4,478
Public sector	2,113	7,040	6,812	6,905	8,288	4,478
of which: General government	534	2,438	2,742	4,154	5,685	2,464
Private sector guaranteed by public sector	..	..	..	..	..	..
Private sector not guaranteed	526	1,134	568	1,239	267	1,261
Interest payments (long-term)	**257**	**2,584**	**1,653**	**2,809**	**2,949**	**2,590**
Public and publicly guaranteed sector	177	2,345	1,337	2,408	2,550	2,408
Public sector	177	2,345	1,337	2,408	2,550	2,408
of which: General government	77	1,862	910	1,627	1,843	1,819
Private sector guaranteed by public sector	..	..	..	..	..	..
Private sector not guaranteed	80	239	315	401	399	182
Summary external debt stock by creditor type						
Long-term external debt stocks	**20,926**	**53,028**	**55,079**	**59,012**	**59,322**	**57,918**
Public and publicly guaranteed debt from:	15,662	41,423	42,338	47,510	47,286	47,144
Official creditors	5,663	22,926	24,212	25,000	22,526	22,237
Multilateral	445	2,018	2,239	2,268	2,847	3,070
of which: World Bank	378	940	1,025	1,042	1,636	1,746
Bilateral	5,218	20,907	21,973	22,732	19,679	19,167
Private creditors	9,999	18,498	18,126	22,510	24,760	24,907
Bondholders	..	2,500	2,500	6,000	8,000	8,000
Commercial banks and others	9,999	15,998	15,626	16,510	16,760	16,907
Private nonguaranteed debt from:	5,264	11,604	12,741	11,502	12,036	10,774
Bondholders	..	..	..	..	..	..
Commercial banks and others	5,264	11,604	12,741	11,502	12,036	10,774
Use of IMF credit	1,302	396	389	1,374	1,861	2,992
Net financial inflows						
Net debt inflows						
Use of IMF credit	524	-124	-30	1,012	495	1,019
Long-term	4,039	9,283	56	4,038	350	-1,796
Official creditors	987	9,372	1,223	799	-2,472	-476
Multilateral	3	432	184	44	585	201
of which: World Bank	-1	26	55	31	600	89
Bilateral	984	8,940	1,038	755	-3,058	-677
Private creditors	3,052	-89	-1,167	3,239	2,823	-1,320
Bondholders	..	0	..	3,500	2,000	0
Banks and others	3,052	-89	-1,167	-261	823	-1,320
Short-term	1,992	-1,645	-685	-863	440	3,112
Net equity inflows						
Foreign direct investment	3,326	-122	-7,293	-7,104	-4,739	-1,980
Portfolio equity	..	0	0	0	0	0
Debt ratios						
External debt stocks to exports (%)	52	202	165	151	180	312
External debt stocks to GNI (%)	35	60	52	68	79	117
Debt service to exports (%)	6	38	26	26	32	39
Short-term to external debt stocks (%)	17	8	6	4	5	9
Multilateral to external debt stocks (%)	2	3	4	4	4	5
Reserves to external debt stocks (%)	73	41	29	24	25	20
Gross national income (GNI)	75,713	95,850	114,618	93,524	81,901	57,403

ARGENTINA

(US$ million, unless otherwise indicated)

	2010	2016	2017	2018	2019	2020
Summary external debt data by debtor type						
Total external debt stocks	**126,642**	**181,639**	**225,925**	**277,827**	**281,724**	**253,760**
Use of IMF credit	3,111	2,716	2,877	30,923	46,924	48,874
Long-term external debt	107,119	137,906	167,542	179,135	167,783	162,279
Public and publicly guaranteed sector	69,184	106,603	128,247	135,603	121,319	119,182
Public sector	69,075	106,603	128,247	135,603	121,297	119,160
of which: General government	66,419	105,887	127,653	135,171	120,792	118,911
Private sector guaranteed by public sector	109	0	0	0	22	22
Private sector not guaranteed	37,934	31,303	39,295	43,531	46,464	43,097
Short-term external debt	16,413	41,017	55,507	67,770	67,016	42,607
Disbursements (long-term)	**6,923**	**55,432**	**61,802**	**66,555**	**25,171**	**23,155**
Public and publicly guaranteed sector	2,623	40,883	41,047	48,369	11,559	12,326
Public sector	2,623	40,883	41,047	48,369	11,537	12,326
of which: General government	2,623	40,784	41,047	48,369	11,351	12,326
Private sector guaranteed by public sector	0	..	..	..	22	0
Private sector not guaranteed	4,300	14,549	20,755	18,186	13,612	10,830
Principal repayments (long-term)	**11,690**	**11,677**	**25,519**	**28,202**	**29,842**	**20,371**
Public and publicly guaranteed sector	6,035	5,363	17,821	15,787	19,296	6,886
Public sector	6,017	5,363	17,821	15,787	19,296	6,886
of which: General government	5,764	5,106	17,723	15,698	19,210	6,642
Private sector guaranteed by public sector	18	..	..	..	..	0
Private sector not guaranteed	5,655	6,313	7,698	12,415	10,546	13,485
Interest payments (long-term)	**3,789**	**13,404**	**13,900**	**13,385**	**11,498**	**5,608**
Public and publicly guaranteed sector	2,700	12,304	12,433	10,996	8,883	2,484
Public sector	2,700	12,304	12,433	10,996	8,883	2,484
of which: General government	2,597	12,270	12,401	10,966	8,855	2,465
Private sector guaranteed by public sector	0	..	..	..	..	0
Private sector not guaranteed	1,089	1,100	1,467	2,389	2,615	3,124
Summary external debt stock by creditor type						
Long-term external debt stocks	**107,119**	**137,906**	**167,542**	**179,135**	**167,783**	**162,279**
Public and publicly guaranteed debt from:	69,184	106,603	128,247	135,603	121,319	119,182
Official creditors	22,849	26,697	28,236	29,040	29,107	30,260
Multilateral	17,016	20,237	21,342	23,005	23,879	25,301
of which: World Bank	5,349	6,048	6,327	6,879	7,128	7,721
Bilateral	5,833	6,460	6,894	6,034	5,228	4,959
Private creditors	46,335	79,906	100,011	106,564	92,212	88,922
Bondholders	44,344	77,532	98,095	105,287	91,240	87,684
Commercial banks and others	1,992	2,374	1,916	1,276	972	1,238
Private nonguaranteed debt from:	37,934	31,303	39,295	43,531	46,464	43,097
Bondholders	7,855	10,505	15,799	15,933	16,417	15,742
Commercial banks and others	30,080	20,798	23,496	27,598	30,047	27,355
Use of IMF credit	3,111	2,716	2,877	30,923	46,924	48,874
Net financial inflows						
Net debt inflows						
Use of IMF credit	..	..	..	28,623	16,166	0
Long-term	-4,767	43,756	36,284	38,353	-4,671	2,784
Official creditors	532	-465	1,358	892	94	982
Multilateral	784	462	1,066	1,669	880	1,426
of which: World Bank	46	198	239	557	249	594
Bilateral	-253	-927	292	-778	-785	-444
Private creditors	-5,298	44,220	34,926	37,461	-4,766	1,802
Bondholders	-2,666	39,697	28,088	33,580	-6,769	3,751
Banks and others	-2,633	4,523	6,838	3,881	2,004	-1,949
Short-term	2,465	-18,073	17,471	12,149	-721	-24,755
Net equity inflows						
Foreign direct investment	7,826	7,992	9,095	10,293	6,496	3,793
Portfolio equity	-71	985	3,013	-508	65	-430
Debt ratios						
External debt stocks to exports (%)	151	245	289	333	327	371
External debt stocks to GNI (%)	31	33	36	56	66	68
Debt service to exports (%)	19	35	52	52	51	41
Short-term to external debt stocks (%)	13	23	25	24	24	17
Multilateral to external debt stocks (%)	13	11	9	8	8	10
Reserves to external debt stocks (%)	39	20	23	23	15	14
Gross national income (GNI)	409,080	545,339	627,248	499,007	427,609	372,835

ARMENIA

(US$ million, unless otherwise indicated)

	2010	2016	2017	2018	2019	2020
Summary external debt data by debtor type						
Total external debt stocks	**6,307**	**9,856**	**10,228**	**10,726**	**11,884**	**13,094**
Use of IMF credit	876	528	530	451	375	646
Long-term external debt	4,775	8,256	8,810	9,141	9,915	10,845
Public and publicly guaranteed sector	2,560	4,472	5,228	5,371	5,652	5,616
Public sector	2,560	4,472	5,228	5,371	5,652	5,616
of which: General government	2,544	4,351	5,015	5,151	5,438	5,385
Private sector guaranteed by public sector	..	..	..	..	..	..
Private sector not guaranteed	2,216	3,784	3,583	3,770	4,262	5,229
Short-term external debt	656	1,072	889	1,134	1,595	1,603
Disbursements (long-term)	**1,734**	**1,855**	**1,501**	**1,678**	**2,377**	**1,827**
Public and publicly guaranteed sector	198	603	677	347	867	129
Public sector	198	603	677	347	867	129
of which: General government	198	575	588	321	854	101
Private sector guaranteed by public sector	..	..	..	..	..	..
Private sector not guaranteed	1,536	1,252	824	1,331	1,510	1,698
Principal repayments (long-term)	**857**	**1,173**	**1,117**	**1,282**	**1,586**	**1,044**
Public and publicly guaranteed sector	24	73	91	138	568	313
Public sector	24	73	91	138	568	313
of which: General government	24	69	85	125	550	291
Private sector guaranteed by public sector	..	..	..	..	..	..
Private sector not guaranteed	833	1,101	1,026	1,144	1,018	731
Interest payments (long-term)	**60**	**224**	**238**	**269**	**362**	**320**
Public and publicly guaranteed sector	35	123	140	162	189	167
Public sector	35	123	140	162	189	167
of which: General government	35	120	136	156	183	161
Private sector guaranteed by public sector	..	..	..	..	..	..
Private sector not guaranteed	25	101	98	107	174	152
Summary external debt stock by creditor type						
Long-term external debt stocks	**4,775**	**8,256**	**8,810**	**9,141**	**9,915**	**10,845**
Public and publicly guaranteed debt from:	2,560	4,472	5,228	5,371	5,652	5,616
Official creditors	2,556	3,423	4,163	4,310	4,496	4,555
Multilateral	1,513	2,824	3,237	3,278	3,352	3,401
of which: World Bank	1,267	1,742	1,810	1,798	1,824	1,830
Bilateral	1,042	599	927	1,032	1,144	1,154
Private creditors	4	1,049	1,064	1,061	1,156	1,061
Bondholders	..	1,000	1,000	1,000	1,098	1,000
Commercial banks and others	4	49	64	61	59	61
Private nonguaranteed debt from:	2,216	3,784	3,583	3,770	4,262	5,229
Bondholders	..	..	..	..	..	300
Commercial banks and others	2,216	3,784	3,583	3,770	4,262	4,929
Use of IMF credit	876	528	530	451	375	646
Net financial inflows						
Net debt inflows						
Use of IMF credit	163	8	-29	-68	-73	247
Long-term	877	681	384	396	792	783
Official creditors	174	522	578	208	204	-84
Multilateral	110	410	301	87	86	-36
of which: World Bank	73	123	5	14	31	-37
Bilateral	65	113	277	122	118	-48
Private creditors	703	159	-193	188	588	867
Bondholders	..	0	0	0	98	202
Banks and others	703	159	-193	188	490	664
Short-term	127	408	-183	245	461	8
Net equity inflows						
Foreign direct investment	361	219	70	302	-23	54
Portfolio equity	7	4	-3	0	-5	1
Debt ratios						
External debt stocks to exports (%)	193	223	188	183	179	310
External debt stocks to GNI (%)	65	91	86	85	85	105
Debt service to exports (%)	30	33	26	28	31	35
Short-term to external debt stocks (%)	10	11	9	11	13	12
Multilateral to external debt stocks (%)	24	29	32	31	28	26
Reserves to external debt stocks (%)	30	22	23	21	24	20
Gross national income (GNI)	9,719	10,791	11,935	12,677	13,901	12,447

AZERBAIJAN

(US$ million, unless otherwise indicated)

	2010	2016	2017	2018	2019	2020
Summary external debt data by debtor type						
Total external debt stocks	**7,251**	**14,590**	**15,301**	**16,211**	**15,840**	**15,812**
Use of IMF credit	282	206	219	214	212	221
Long-term external debt	5,970	12,988	14,407	15,428	15,011	15,139
Public and publicly guaranteed sector	3,812	10,624	12,470	13,956	13,976	14,000
Public sector	3,812	10,624	12,470	13,956	13,976	14,000
of which: General government	2,490	7,339	8,052	7,540	7,776	7,568
Private sector guaranteed by public sector	..	..	..	..	..	..
Private sector not guaranteed	2,158	2,363	1,937	1,471	1,035	1,138
Short-term external debt	999	1,396	675	570	617	452
Disbursements (long-term)	**2,643**	**2,813**	**2,886**	**3,269**	**1,270**	**1,111**
Public and publicly guaranteed sector	729	2,702	2,822	3,250	1,266	584
Public sector	729	2,702	2,822	3,250	1,266	584
of which: General government	569	1,178	1,104	902	767	308
Private sector guaranteed by public sector	..	..	..	..	..	..
Private sector not guaranteed	1,914	111	64	19	4	527
Principal repayments (long-term)	**305**	**1,329**	**1,771**	**2,122**	**1,647**	**1,290**
Public and publicly guaranteed sector	233	735	1,262	1,639	1,201	858
Public sector	233	735	1,262	1,639	1,201	858
of which: General government	72	488	510	1,384	523	571
Private sector guaranteed by public sector	..	..	..	..	..	..
Private sector not guaranteed	72	594	509	483	447	432
Interest payments (long-term)	**78**	**403**	**443**	**538**	**496**	**540**
Public and publicly guaranteed sector	65	259	326	446	429	482
Public sector	65	259	326	446	429	482
of which: General government	39	165	201	252	257	243
Private sector guaranteed by public sector	..	..	..	..	..	..
Private sector not guaranteed	13	144	117	91	66	58
Summary external debt stock by creditor type						
Long-term external debt stocks	**5,970**	**12,988**	**14,407**	**15,428**	**15,011**	**15,139**
Public and publicly guaranteed debt from:	3,812	10,624	12,470	13,956	13,976	14,000
Official creditors	2,646	5,644	6,662	6,885	7,318	7,233
Multilateral	1,758	4,587	5,569	5,789	6,084	5,897
of which: World Bank	1,063	2,203	2,665	2,538	2,395	2,098
Bilateral	888	1,057	1,093	1,096	1,234	1,337
Private creditors	1,166	4,981	5,809	7,071	6,658	6,767
Bondholders	..	3,250	3,750	3,750	3,750	3,750
Commercial banks and others	1,166	1,731	2,059	3,321	2,908	3,017
Private nonguaranteed debt from:	2,158	2,363	1,937	1,471	1,035	1,138
Bondholders	..	..	..	..	..	500
Commercial banks and others	2,158	2,363	1,937	1,471	1,035	638
Use of IMF credit	282	206	219	214	212	221
Net financial inflows						
Net debt inflows						
Use of IMF credit	-15	..	..	..	..	..
Long-term	2,337	1,483	1,115	1,147	-377	-179
Official creditors	325	865	901	246	433	-183
Multilateral	315	891	914	245	302	-220
of which: World Bank	137	122	435	-116	-140	-310
Bilateral	11	-26	-13	0	130	37
Private creditors	2,012	618	214	901	-810	4
Bondholders	..	1,000	500	..	0	500
Banks and others	2,012	-382	-286	901	-810	-496
Short-term	404	-152	-721	-105	47	-165
Net equity inflows						
Foreign direct investment	3,353	4,500	2,867	1,403	1,504	507
Portfolio equity	1	0	0	0	19	75
Debt ratios						
External debt stocks to exports (%)	25	79	72	60	63	93
External debt stocks to GNI (%)	15	41	39	36	34	38
Debt service to exports (%)	1	10	11	10	9	11
Short-term to external debt stocks (%)	14	10	4	4	4	3
Multilateral to external debt stocks (%)	24	31	36	36	38	37
Reserves to external debt stocks (%)	88	40	44	41	44	48
Gross national income (GNI)	49,442	35,395	39,106	44,653	46,113	42,151

BANGLADESH

(US$ million, unless otherwise indicated)

	2010	2016	2017	2018	2019	2020
Summary external debt data by debtor type						
Total external debt stocks	**26,572**	**38,481**	**46,819**	**52,138**	**57,094**	**67,749**
Use of IMF credit	1,403	1,546	1,625	1,536	1,414	2,109
Long-term external debt	22,222	29,099	34,429	41,573	45,943	54,654
Public and publicly guaranteed sector	21,146	26,007	31,034	36,335	41,042	49,029
Public sector	21,146	26,007	31,034	36,335	41,042	49,029
of which: General government	21,145	25,443	30,441	35,778	40,468	48,403
Private sector guaranteed by public sector	..	..	..	..	..	..
Private sector not guaranteed	1,076	3,093	3,395	5,238	4,901	5,625
Short-term external debt	2,947	7,835	10,765	9,029	9,737	10,986
Disbursements (long-term)	**1,355**	**3,259**	**5,521**	**9,690**	**9,181**	**10,050**
Public and publicly guaranteed sector	968	3,079	4,743	6,994	6,068	7,761
Public sector	968	3,079	4,743	6,994	6,068	7,761
of which: General government	968	3,044	4,714	6,978	6,009	7,695
Private sector guaranteed by public sector	..	..	..	..	..	..
Private sector not guaranteed	388	180	778	2,696	3,113	2,289
Principal repayments (long-term)	**821**	**1,325**	**1,468**	**2,033**	**4,689**	**2,873**
Public and publicly guaranteed sector	724	892	993	1,180	1,258	1,309
Public sector	724	892	993	1,180	1,258	1,309
of which: General government	724	892	974	1,142	1,221	1,271
Private sector guaranteed by public sector	..	..	..	..	..	..
Private sector not guaranteed	97	433	475	853	3,431	1,565
Interest payments (long-term)	**203**	**269**	**418**	**485**	**639**	**680**
Public and publicly guaranteed sector	195	228	359	372	487	525
Public sector	195	228	359	372	487	525
of which: General government	195	217	348	361	477	515
Private sector guaranteed by public sector	..	..	..	..	..	..
Private sector not guaranteed	8	40	59	113	152	155
Summary external debt stock by creditor type						
Long-term external debt stocks	**22,222**	**29,099**	**34,429**	**41,573**	**45,943**	**54,654**
Public and publicly guaranteed debt from:	21,146	26,007	31,034	36,335	41,042	49,029
Official creditors	21,129	25,979	31,006	36,312	41,024	49,012
Multilateral	18,463	20,819	23,492	24,944	27,158	30,688
of which: World Bank	10,653	11,890	13,621	14,501	15,788	17,572
Bilateral	2,666	5,161	7,514	11,368	13,866	18,325
Private creditors	16	27	28	23	19	16
Bondholders	..	..	..	..	..	..
Commercial banks and others	16	27	28	23	19	16
Private nonguaranteed debt from:	1,076	3,093	3,395	5,238	4,901	5,625
Bondholders	..	..	..	..	..	..
Commercial banks and others	1,076	3,093	3,395	5,238	4,901	5,625
Use of IMF credit	1,403	1,546	1,625	1,536	1,414	2,109
Net financial inflows						
Net debt inflows						
Use of IMF credit	-45	-19	-13	-52	-114	616
Long-term	534	1,934	4,053	7,656	4,492	7,176
Official creditors	253	2,190	3,753	5,818	4,813	6,456
Multilateral	352	1,390	1,580	1,954	2,350	2,549
of which: World Bank	83	716	1,020	1,219	1,387	1,101
Bilateral	-99	801	2,174	3,864	2,464	3,906
Private creditors	282	-257	299	1,839	-321	721
Bondholders	..	..	..	..	..	..
Banks and others	282	-257	299	1,839	-321	721
Short-term	1,014	1,204	2,930	-1,736	708	1,249
Net equity inflows						
Foreign direct investment	885	2,127	1,477	1,242	1,305	1,026
Portfolio equity	-54	114	258	-33	-70	-355
Debt ratios						
External debt stocks to exports (%)	122	102	119	117	126	174
External debt stocks to GNI (%)	21	16	18	18	18	20
Debt service to exports (%)	5	5	5	6	13	10
Short-term to external debt stocks (%)	11	20	23	17	17	16
Multilateral to external debt stocks (%)	69	54	50	48	48	45
Reserves to external debt stocks (%)	40	83	70	60	56	62
Gross national income (GNI)	124,617	234,168	260,441	286,536	316,899	338,933

BELARUS

(US$ million, unless otherwise indicated)

	2010	2016	2017	2018	2019	2020
Summary external debt data by debtor type						
Total external debt stocks	**28,412**	**37,516**	**39,584**	**38,768**	**40,734**	**42,491**
Use of IMF credit	4,063	496	525	513	510	531
Long-term external debt	12,486	26,398	29,335	28,729	30,026	31,775
Public and publicly guaranteed sector	8,014	18,142	20,988	19,988	19,511	20,270
Public sector	7,995	18,142	20,988	19,988	19,511	20,270
of which: General government	6,554	13,642	16,727	16,894	17,132	18,573
Private sector guaranteed by public sector	19	0	..	..	..	..
Private sector not guaranteed	4,471	8,257	8,346	8,741	10,514	11,505
Short-term external debt	11,864	10,622	9,725	9,526	10,199	10,186
Disbursements (long-term)	**3,810**	**2,615**	**5,811**	**3,743**	**4,106**	**4,994**
Public and publicly guaranteed sector	2,679	2,143	4,349	2,673	1,996	3,533
Public sector	2,679	2,143	4,349	2,673	1,996	3,533
of which: General government	2,562	1,935	4,039	2,367	1,656	3,157
Private sector guaranteed by public sector	..	0	..	..	..	..
Private sector not guaranteed	1,132	472	1,462	1,070	2,111	1,461
Principal repayments (long-term)	**1,265**	**5,014**	**3,030**	**4,130**	**2,900**	**2,881**
Public and publicly guaranteed sector	463	2,314	1,680	3,455	2,563	2,712
Public sector	463	2,277	1,680	3,455	2,563	2,712
of which: General government	116	893	1,029	1,998	1,512	1,630
Private sector guaranteed by public sector	..	37	..	..	..	..
Private sector not guaranteed	802	2,701	1,350	675	338	169
Interest payments (long-term)	**208**	**964**	**1,110**	**1,288**	**1,307**	**1,258**
Public and publicly guaranteed sector	128	745	868	1,022	1,015	892
Public sector	125	743	868	1,022	1,015	892
of which: General government	107	559	688	789	817	765
Private sector guaranteed by public sector	2	2	..	..	..	..
Private sector not guaranteed	80	219	241	265	292	367

	2010	2016	2017	2018	2019	2020
Summary external debt stock by creditor type						
Long-term external debt stocks	**12,486**	**26,398**	**29,335**	**28,729**	**30,026**	**31,775**
Public and publicly guaranteed debt from:	8,014	18,142	20,988	19,988	19,511	20,270
Official creditors	5,729	14,071	15,974	16,495	16,595	16,710
Multilateral	295	3,360	3,942	3,810	3,480	3,595
of which: World Bank	291	725	822	905	948	955
Bilateral	5,434	10,710	12,032	12,685	13,115	13,115
Private creditors	2,286	4,071	5,014	3,493	2,916	3,560
Bondholders	1,019	800	2,200	2,000	2,162	3,521
Commercial banks and others	1,266	3,271	2,814	1,493	755	39
Private nonguaranteed debt from:	4,471	8,257	8,346	8,741	10,514	11,505
Bondholders	..	..	..	..	..	966
Commercial banks and others	4,471	8,257	8,346	8,741	10,514	10,539
Use of IMF credit	4,063	496	525	513	510	531

	2010	2016	2017	2018	2019	2020
Net financial inflows						
Net debt inflows						
Use of IMF credit	668	..	..	..	..	..
Long-term	2,545	-2,400	2,780	-388	1,206	2,112
Official creditors	1,470	914	1,812	727	15	151
Multilateral	34	526	563	-124	-329	82
of which: World Bank	36	83	98	83	39	-10
Bilateral	1,437	387	1,249	851	344	69
Private creditors	1,075	-3,313	968	-1,115	1,191	1,961
Bondholders	1,000	0	1,400	-200	154	2,657
Banks and others	75	-3,313	-432	-915	1,036	-695
Short-term	2,786	-852	-897	-199	672	-8
Net equity inflows						
Foreign direct investment	1,348	1,086	1,068	1,390	1,093	1,307
Portfolio equity	1	0	6	4	7	4

	2010	2016	2017	2018	2019	2020
Debt ratios						
External debt stocks to exports (%)	95	123	106	89	94	112
External debt stocks to GNI (%)	51	82	75	67	65	74
Debt service to exports (%)	6	20	12	13	10	11
Short-term to external debt stocks (%)	42	28	25	25	25	24
Multilateral to external debt stocks (%)	1	9	10	10	9	8
Reserves to external debt stocks (%)	12	9	14	13	17	10
Gross national income (GNI)	56,108	45,508	52,645	57,886	62,540	57,647

BELIZE

(US$ million, unless otherwise indicated)

	2010	2016	2017	2018	2019	2020
Summary external debt data by debtor type						
Total external debt stocks	**1,304**	**1,290**	**1,339**	**1,349**	**1,378**	**1,526**
Use of IMF credit	35	24	25	25	25	26
Long-term external debt	1,262	1,262	1,309	1,320	1,349	1,492
Public and publicly guaranteed sector	1,019	1,177	1,231	1,260	1,286	1,408
Public sector	1,019	1,177	1,231	1,260	1,286	1,408
of which: General government	1,001	1,167	1,215	1,226	1,244	1,363
Private sector guaranteed by public sector	0	..	..	..	..	..
Private sector not guaranteed	243	85	78	61	63	84
Short-term external debt	7	4	5	4	4	8
Disbursements (long-term)	**39**	**69**	**107**	**77**	**79**	**153**
Public and publicly guaranteed sector	32	67	98	71	70	146
Public sector	32	67	98	71	70	146
of which: General government	32	63	91	53	60	141
Private sector guaranteed by public sector	0	..	..	..	..	..
Private sector not guaranteed	7	2	9	6	9	7
Principal repayments (long-term)	**69**	**54**	**57**	**65**	**50**	**45**
Public and publicly guaranteed sector	49	43	44	42	44	43
Public sector	49	43	44	42	44	43
of which: General government	42	42	44	41	41	42
Private sector guaranteed by public sector	0	..	..	..	..	..
Private sector not guaranteed	20	11	12	22	6	2
Interest payments (long-term)	**58**	**48**	**48**	**49**	**54**	**34**
Public and publicly guaranteed sector	47	42	42	43	50	32
Public sector	47	42	42	43	50	32
of which: General government	46	42	41	43	48	30
Private sector guaranteed by public sector	0	..	..	..	..	..
Private sector not guaranteed	11	7	6	6	4	2
Summary external debt stock by creditor type						
Long-term external debt stocks	**1,262**	**1,262**	**1,309**	**1,320**	**1,349**	**1,492**
Public and publicly guaranteed debt from:	1,019	1,177	1,231	1,260	1,286	1,408
Official creditors	425	650	679	706	734	821
Multilateral	254	317	336	348	368	429
of which: World Bank	13	17	16	19	19	28
Bilateral	171	334	344	358	366	392
Private creditors	594	527	552	554	552	587
Bondholders	21	527	527	527	527	563
Commercial banks and others	573	..	25	27	25	24
Private nonguaranteed debt from:	243	85	78	61	63	84
Bondholders	..	..	..	..	..	..
Commercial banks and others	243	85	78	61	63	84
Use of IMF credit	35	24	25	25	25	26
Net financial inflows						
Net debt inflows						
Use of IMF credit	0	..	..	..	..	..
Long-term	-30	14	50	13	28	108
Official creditors	-7	24	28	27	28	87
Multilateral	4	10	18	13	19	61
of which: World Bank	-5	3	0	2	0	9
Bilateral	-11	13	10	14	8	26
Private creditors	-23	-9	22	-14	0	21
Bondholders	..	..	..	..	..	17
Banks and others	-23	-9	22	-14	0	3
Short-term	0	0	0	0	0	0
Net equity inflows						
Foreign direct investment	94	33	32	122	94	76
Portfolio equity	0	..	0	0	0	0
Debt ratios						
External debt stocks to exports (%)	156	132	129	125	124	211
External debt stocks to GNI (%)	105	77	77	78	76	95
Debt service to exports (%)	15	10	10	11	9	11
Short-term to external debt stocks (%)	1	0	0	0	0	1
Multilateral to external debt stocks (%)	19	25	25	26	27	28
Reserves to external debt stocks (%)	17	29	23	22	20	23
Gross national income (GNI)	1,239	1,679	1,733	1,734	1,824	1,605

BENIN

(US$ million, unless otherwise indicated)

	2010	2016	2017	2018	2019	2020
Summary external debt data by debtor type						
Total external debt stocks	**1,596**	**2,258**	**2,794**	**3,586**	**3,878**	**5,250**
Use of IMF credit	146	187	226	245	267	563
Long-term external debt	1,112	2,018	2,506	3,295	3,599	4,405
Public and publicly guaranteed sector	1,112	2,018	2,506	3,295	3,599	4,405
Public sector	1,112	2,018	2,506	3,295	3,599	4,405
of which: General government	1,112	2,018	2,506	3,295	3,599	4,405
Private sector guaranteed by public sector	..	..	..	..	..	..
Private sector not guaranteed	..	..	..	..	..	..
Short-term external debt	339	53	62	46	12	283
Disbursements (long-term)	**175**	**240**	**386**	**1,061**	**761**	**672**
Public and publicly guaranteed sector	175	240	386	1,061	761	672
Public sector	175	240	386	1,061	761	672
of which: General government	175	240	386	1,061	761	672
Private sector guaranteed by public sector	..	..	..	..	..	..
Private sector not guaranteed	..	..	..	..	..	..
Principal repayments (long-term)	**26**	**61**	**54**	**170**	**416**	**145**
Public and publicly guaranteed sector	26	61	54	170	416	145
Public sector	26	61	54	170	416	145
of which: General government	26	61	54	170	416	145
Private sector guaranteed by public sector	..	..	..	..	..	..
Private sector not guaranteed	..	..	..	..	..	..
Interest payments (long-term)	**13**	**28**	**33**	**40**	**77**	**113**
Public and publicly guaranteed sector	13	28	33	40	77	113
Public sector	13	28	33	40	77	113
of which: General government	13	28	33	40	77	113
Private sector guaranteed by public sector	..	..	..	..	..	..
Private sector not guaranteed	..	..	..	..	..	..
Summary external debt stock by creditor type						
Long-term external debt stocks	**1,112**	**2,018**	**2,506**	**3,295**	**3,599**	**4,405**
Public and publicly guaranteed debt from:	1,112	2,018	2,506	3,295	3,599	4,405
Official creditors	1,112	2,018	2,465	2,480	2,535	3,195
Multilateral	937	1,665	2,045	2,028	2,096	2,667
of which: World Bank	383	765	914	984	1,082	1,309
Bilateral	175	353	420	452	439	528
Private creditors	..	0	41	815	1,064	1,210
Bondholders	..	..	..	..	557	614
Commercial banks and others	..	0	41	815	508	597
Private nonguaranteed debt from:	..	..	..	..	..	..
Bondholders	..	..	..	..	..	..
Commercial banks and others	..	..	..	..	..	..
Use of IMF credit	146	187	226	245	267	563
Net financial inflows						
Net debt inflows						
Use of IMF credit	16	-10	28	24	24	275
Long-term	149	180	332	892	345	527
Official creditors	149	180	293	91	82	483
Multilateral	137	166	245	42	88	422
of which: World Bank	78	108	102	93	104	162
Bilateral	12	13	48	49	-6	61
Private creditors	..	..	39	801	263	45
Bondholders	..	..	..	..	555	5
Banks and others	..	..	39	801	-291	39
Short-term	134	-7	9	-15	-1	271
Net equity inflows						
Foreign direct investment	-26	31	44	-14	102	176
Portfolio equity	5	9	18	0	-8	..
Debt ratios						
External debt stocks to exports (%)	93	68	81	91	105	..
External debt stocks to GNI (%)	17	19	22	25	27	34
Debt service to exports (%)	3	3	3	6	14	..
Short-term to external debt stocks (%)	21	2	2	1	0	5
Multilateral to external debt stocks (%)	59	74	73	57	54	51
Reserves to external debt stocks (%)	75	..	..	..	..	..
Gross national income (GNI)	9,482	11,718	12,561	14,106	14,248	15,489

BHUTAN

(US$ million, unless otherwise indicated)

	2010	2016	2017	2018	2019	2020
Summary external debt data by debtor type						
Total external debt stocks	**934.6**	**2,289.7**	**2,607.9**	**2,552.0**	**2,703.8**	**2,869.0**
Use of IMF credit	9.2	8.1	8.5	8.3	8.3	8.6
Long-term external debt	919.4	2,281.5	2,596.4	2,539.3	2,667.7	2,858.9
Public and publicly guaranteed sector	919.4	2,221.2	2,540.8	2,484.2	2,616.3	2,817.5
Public sector	919.4	2,221.2	2,540.8	2,484.2	2,616.3	2,817.5
of which: General government	852.5	2,118.2	2,431.3	2,383.9	2,505.1	2,708.7
Private sector guaranteed by public sector	..	..	..	..	..	..
Private sector not guaranteed	..	60.3	55.6	55.1	51.5	41.4
Short-term external debt	6.0	0.1	3.0	4.3	27.8	1.5
Disbursements (long-term)	**177.8**	**402.0**	**219.8**	**168.1**	**198.4**	**242.3**
Public and publicly guaranteed sector	177.8	365.0	219.8	168.1	197.7	242.3
Public sector	177.8	365.0	219.8	168.1	197.7	242.3
of which: General government	177.8	365.0	219.8	168.1	184.7	242.3
Private sector guaranteed by public sector	..	..	..	..	..	..
Private sector not guaranteed	..	36.9	..	..	0.7	..
Principal repayments (long-term)	**46.6**	**75.4**	**46.3**	**51.3**	**28.4**	**37.6**
Public and publicly guaranteed sector	46.6	41.6	41.6	50.8	23.6	27.1
Public sector	46.6	41.6	41.6	50.8	23.6	27.1
of which: General government	46.6	41.6	41.6	50.8	23.6	27.1
Private sector guaranteed by public sector	..	..	..	..	..	..
Private sector not guaranteed	..	33.8	4.7	0.5	4.9	10.5
Interest payments (long-term)	**40.7**	**35.2**	**36.1**	**35.8**	**32.2**	**20.6**
Public and publicly guaranteed sector	40.7	34.3	33.9	34.0	30.8	19.6
Public sector	40.7	34.3	33.9	34.0	30.8	19.6
of which: General government	37.5	29.1	28.6	28.9	23.4	14.4
Private sector guaranteed by public sector	..	..	..	..	..	..
Private sector not guaranteed	..	1.0	2.2	1.7	1.5	1.0
Summary external debt stock by creditor type						
Long-term external debt stocks	**919.4**	**2,281.5**	**2,596.4**	**2,539.3**	**2,667.7**	**2,858.9**
Public and publicly guaranteed debt from:	919.4	2,221.2	2,540.8	2,484.2	2,616.3	2,817.5
Official creditors	898.5	2,186.0	2,505.5	2,455.0	2,592.0	2,795.9
Multilateral	330.1	460.2	532.5	563.4	646.2	789.4
of which: World Bank	112.3	177.6	219.0	243.7	270.9	337.0
Bilateral	568.5	1,725.8	1,973.0	1,891.6	1,945.8	2,006.5
Private creditors	20.9	35.2	35.3	29.2	24.3	21.7
Bondholders	..	..	..	..	..	..
Commercial banks and others	20.9	35.2	35.3	29.2	24.3	21.7
Private nonguaranteed debt from:	..	60.3	55.6	55.1	51.5	41.4
Bondholders	..	..	..	..	..	..
Commercial banks and others	..	60.3	55.6	55.1	51.5	41.4
Use of IMF credit	9.2	8.1	8.5	8.3	8.3	8.6
Net financial inflows						
Net debt inflows						
Use of IMF credit	..	..	..	..	..	..
Long-term	131.2	326.6	173.5	116.8	170.0	204.6
Official creditors	115.2	327.8	182.6	122.0	178.5	219.6
Multilateral	43.6	1.3	48.1	41.4	85.3	118.4
of which: World Bank	0.4	-0.4	29.7	30.5	28.8	52.0
Bilateral	71.5	326.4	134.5	80.5	93.2	101.2
Private creditors	16.1	-1.2	-9.1	-5.2	-8.6	-15.0
Bondholders	..	..	..	..	..	..
Banks and others	16.1	-1.2	-9.1	-5.2	-8.6	-15.0
Short-term	1.0	0.1	2.9	1.3	23.5	-26.3
Net equity inflows						
Foreign direct investment	20.2	11.5	-0.7	3.3	12.6	-1.1
Portfolio equity	..	0.0	0.0	0.0	0.0	0.0
Debt ratios						
External debt stocks to exports (%)	154.0	343.4	349.4	310.8	331.8	351.5
External debt stocks to GNI (%)	64.0	116.0	116.6	114.6	117.5	130.7
Debt service to exports (%)	14.4	16.6	11.1	10.6	7.6	7.1
Short-term to external debt stocks (%)	0.6	0.0	0.1	0.2	1.0	0.1
Multilateral to external debt stocks (%)	35.3	20.1	20.4	22.1	23.9	27.5
Reserves to external debt stocks (%)	107.2	49.2	46.3	38.7	45.4	52.5
Gross national income (GNI)	1,460.0	1,973.5	2,237.5	2,226.7	2,301.0	2,194.4

BOLIVIA, PLURINATIONAL STATE OF

(US$ million, unless otherwise indicated)

	2010	2016	2017	2018	2019	2020
Summary external debt data by debtor type						
Total external debt stocks	**5,777**	**10,994**	**12,990**	**13,248**	**14,301**	**15,421**
Use of IMF credit	253	221	234	228	227	582
Long-term external debt	5,187	10,299	12,486	12,317	13,437	14,261
Public and publicly guaranteed sector	2,830	7,010	9,151	9,905	11,000	11,878
Public sector	2,829	7,010	9,151	9,905	11,000	11,878
of which: General government	2,563	6,984	9,126	9,884	10,982	11,862
Private sector guaranteed by public sector	1	0	..	..	..	..
Private sector not guaranteed	2,358	3,289	3,336	2,412	2,437	2,383
Short-term external debt	336	475	270	703	637	577
Disbursements (long-term)	**548**	**1,432**	**2,661**	**1,373**	**1,741**	**1,446**
Public and publicly guaranteed sector	518	1,002	2,390	1,198	1,514	1,245
Public sector	517	1,002	2,390	1,198	1,514	1,245
of which: General government	453	1,002	2,390	1,198	1,514	1,245
Private sector guaranteed by public sector	1	..	..	..	..	..
Private sector not guaranteed	30	430	271	176	227	201
Principal repayments (long-term)	**569**	**550**	**688**	**640**	**658**	**764**
Public and publicly guaranteed sector	247	280	331	360	412	458
Public sector	247	280	331	360	412	458
of which: General government	241	276	328	356	409	456
Private sector guaranteed by public sector	0	0	..	..	..	..
Private sector not guaranteed	322	270	357	280	246	306
Interest payments (long-term)	**76**	**211**	**283**	**346**	**400**	**391**
Public and publicly guaranteed sector	54	185	250	316	371	363
Public sector	54	185	250	316	371	363
of which: General government	51	184	250	316	371	363
Private sector guaranteed by public sector	0	0	..	..	..	..
Private sector not guaranteed	22	26	33	30	28	29
Summary external debt stock by creditor type						
Long-term external debt stocks	**5,187**	**10,299**	**12,486**	**12,317**	**13,437**	**14,261**
Public and publicly guaranteed debt from:	2,830	7,010	9,151	9,905	11,000	11,878
Official creditors	2,806	5,999	7,141	7,897	8,959	9,819
Multilateral	2,285	5,282	6,156	6,710	7,467	8,249
of which: World Bank	355	770	830	847	927	1,300
Bilateral	521	717	985	1,187	1,492	1,569
Private creditors	24	1,011	2,010	2,008	2,041	2,060
Bondholders	..	1,000	2,000	2,000	2,000	2,000
Commercial banks and others	24	11	10	8	41	60
Private nonguaranteed debt from:	2,358	3,289	3,336	2,412	2,437	2,383
Bondholders	..	..	..	..	..	..
Commercial banks and others	2,358	3,289	3,336	2,412	2,437	2,383
Use of IMF credit	253	221	234	228	227	582
Net financial inflows						
Net debt inflows						
Use of IMF credit	..	..	..	..	..	334
Long-term	-21	882	1,973	733	1,083	682
Official creditors	338	724	1,060	840	1,070	772
Multilateral	305	661	826	613	756	749
of which: World Bank	44	57	19	37	84	344
Bilateral	33	63	235	227	314	23
Private creditors	-359	159	913	-106	13	-90
Bondholders	..	0	1,000	0	0	0
Banks and others	-359	159	-87	-106	13	-90
Short-term	32	49	-205	433	-66	-60
Net equity inflows						
Foreign direct investment	774	193	706	220	-190	-1,021
Portfolio equity	0	21	30	24	13	-2
Debt ratios						
External debt stocks to exports (%)	83	131	133	126	137	202
External debt stocks to GNI (%)	31	33	36	34	36	43
Debt service to exports (%)	9	9	10	10	10	15
Short-term to external debt stocks (%)	6	4	2	5	4	4
Multilateral to external debt stocks (%)	40	48	47	51	52	53
Reserves to external debt stocks (%)	141	77	65	54	31	17
Gross national income (GNI)	18,761	33,320	36,399	39,312	40,056	36,171

BOSNIA AND HERZEGOVINA

(US$ million, unless otherwise indicated)

	2010	2016	2017	2018	2019	2020
Summary external debt data by debtor type						
Total external debt stocks	**14,289**	**11,631**	**13,029**	**13,254**	**13,231**	**14,263**
Use of IMF credit	769	770	592	466	398	796
Long-term external debt	12,372	10,213	12,151	12,022	12,474	12,993
Public and publicly guaranteed sector	3,733	4,396	4,837	4,919	4,876	5,217
Public sector	3,733	4,396	4,837	4,919	4,876	5,217
of which: General government	3,727	4,029	4,425	4,523	4,531	4,844
Private sector guaranteed by public sector	..	..	..	..	..	..
Private sector not guaranteed	8,638	5,818	7,314	7,103	7,598	7,777
Short-term external debt	1,149	647	286	766	359	474
Disbursements (long-term)	**566**	**1,120**	**2,392**	**1,579**	**1,731**	**1,646**
Public and publicly guaranteed sector	441	399	310	600	409	403
Public sector	441	399	310	600	409	403
of which: General government	441	329	295	559	391	403
Private sector guaranteed by public sector	..	..	..	..	..	..
Private sector not guaranteed	125	721	2,082	978	1,322	1,243
Principal repayments (long-term)	**373**	**952**	**889**	**1,530**	**1,210**	**1,435**
Public and publicly guaranteed sector	145	267	304	340	384	370
Public sector	145	267	304	340	384	370
of which: General government	145	250	286	301	322	368
Private sector guaranteed by public sector	..	..	..	..	..	..
Private sector not guaranteed	227	685	585	1,190	827	1,065
Interest payments (long-term)	**177**	**167**	**231**	**278**	**254**	**217**
Public and publicly guaranteed sector	55	65	63	77	80	82
Public sector	55	65	63	77	80	82
of which: General government	55	62	61	75	77	80
Private sector guaranteed by public sector	..	..	..	..	..	..
Private sector not guaranteed	121	102	167	201	174	135
Summary external debt stock by creditor type						
Long-term external debt stocks	**12,372**	**10,213**	**12,151**	**12,022**	**12,474**	**12,993**
Public and publicly guaranteed debt from:	3,733	4,396	4,837	4,919	4,876	5,217
Official creditors	3,255	4,197	4,668	4,596	4,590	4,938
Multilateral	2,416	3,393	3,765	3,724	3,737	4,035
of which: World Bank	1,626	1,514	1,572	1,610	1,584	1,670
Bilateral	840	804	903	872	853	903
Private creditors	478	198	169	322	286	278
Bondholders	273	98	89	256	231	229
Commercial banks and others	204	100	80	66	55	50
Private nonguaranteed debt from:	8,638	5,818	7,314	7,103	7,598	7,777
Bondholders	..	..	..	..	..	..
Commercial banks and others	8,638	5,818	7,314	7,103	7,598	7,777
Use of IMF credit	769	770	592	466	398	796
Net financial inflows						
Net debt inflows						
Use of IMF credit	237	-6	-218	-114	-66	369
Long-term	194	168	1,503	48	520	211
Official creditors	319	182	59	94	55	64
Multilateral	278	173	27	96	63	69
of which: World Bank	123	0	-36	81	-12	1
Bilateral	41	9	33	-3	-8	-5
Private creditors	-125	-14	1,443	-45	465	147
Bondholders	-25	-21	-21	176	-21	-21
Banks and others	-101	7	1,464	-222	486	168
Short-term	-308	1	-362	481	-407	115
Net equity inflows						
Foreign direct investment	149	281	463	618	344	301
Portfolio equity	0	3	5	-2	1	-1
Debt ratios						
External debt stocks to exports (%)	251	174	163	144	150	198
External debt stocks to GNI (%)	82	69	73	66	66	72
Debt service to exports (%)	10	18	17	22	18	23
Short-term to external debt stocks (%)	8	6	2	6	3	3
Multilateral to external debt stocks (%)	17	29	29	28	28	28
Reserves to external debt stocks (%)	31	43	49	50	53	60
Gross national income (GNI)	17,456	16,937	17,929	20,063	20,190	19,854

BOTSWANA

(US$ million, unless otherwise indicated)

	2010	2016	2017	2018	2019	2020
Summary external debt data by debtor type						
Total external debt stocks	**1,807**	**2,126**	**1,741**	**1,782**	**1,565**	**1,597**
Use of IMF credit	88	77	82	80	79	83
Long-term external debt	1,358	1,670	1,552	1,451	1,346	1,297
Public and publicly guaranteed sector	1,358	1,670	1,552	1,451	1,334	1,278
Public sector	1,358	1,670	1,552	1,451	1,334	1,278
of which: General government	1,350	1,648	1,538	1,447	1,334	1,238
Private sector guaranteed by public sector	..	..	..	..	..	..
Private sector not guaranteed	..	..	..	0	12	19
Short-term external debt	360	379	108	251	139	218
Disbursements (long-term)	**17**	**44**	**12**	**47**	**48**	**90**
Public and publicly guaranteed sector	17	44	12	47	26	74
Public sector	17	44	12	47	26	74
of which: General government	17	44	12	47	26	33
Private sector guaranteed by public sector	..	..	..	..	..	..
Private sector not guaranteed	..	..	..	..	22	16
Principal repayments (long-term)	**58**	**141**	**144**	**144**	**152**	**147**
Public and publicly guaranteed sector	58	141	144	144	141	138
Public sector	58	141	144	144	141	138
of which: General government	54	133	135	135	137	138
Private sector guaranteed by public sector	..	..	..	..	..	..
Private sector not guaranteed	..	..	..	..	10	10
Interest payments (long-term)	**18**	**18**	**29**	**31**	**40**	**32**
Public and publicly guaranteed sector	18	18	29	31	40	31
Public sector	18	18	29	31	40	31
of which: General government	17	18	29	31	40	31
Private sector guaranteed by public sector	..	..	..	..	..	..
Private sector not guaranteed	..	..	..	..	1	1
Summary external debt stock by creditor type						
Long-term external debt stocks	**1,358**	**1,670**	**1,552**	**1,451**	**1,346**	**1,297**
Public and publicly guaranteed debt from:	1,358	1,670	1,552	1,451	1,334	1,278
Official creditors	1,357	1,648	1,538	1,447	1,334	1,278
Multilateral	1,219	1,583	1,476	1,389	1,287	1,242
of which: World Bank	11	159	151	174	172	194
Bilateral	138	65	63	58	47	37
Private creditors	1	22	13	4	0	..
Bondholders	..	..	..	..	..	..
Commercial banks and others	1	22	13	4	0	..
Private nonguaranteed debt from:	..	..	..	0	12	19
Bondholders	..	..	..	..	..	..
Commercial banks and others	..	..	..	0	12	19
Use of IMF credit	88	77	82	80	79	83
Net financial inflows						
Net debt inflows						
Use of IMF credit	..	..	..	..	..	..
Long-term	-41	-97	-132	-97	-104	-57
Official creditors	-40	-88	-123	-88	-111	-63
Multilateral	-27	-81	-118	-84	-100	-51
of which: World Bank	6	27	-7	22	-2	22
Bilateral	-13	-7	-5	-4	-11	-12
Private creditors	-1	-9	-9	-9	8	6
Bondholders	..	..	..	..	..	..
Banks and others	-1	-9	-9	-9	8	6
Short-term	202	-6	-271	143	-112	79
Net equity inflows						
Foreign direct investment	222	68	243	164	-172	-147
Portfolio equity	-64	-123	-47	-47	35	-19
Debt ratios						
External debt stocks to exports (%)	32	25	24	23	24	33
External debt stocks to GNI (%)	15	15	11	10	9	11
Debt service to exports (%)	1	2	2	2	3	4
Short-term to external debt stocks (%)	20	18	6	14	9	14
Multilateral to external debt stocks (%)	67	74	85	78	82	78
Reserves to external debt stocks (%)	436	338	430	374	394	309
Gross national income (GNI)	12,147	14,356	16,039	17,081	16,969	14,524

BRAZIL

(US$ million, unless otherwise indicated)

	2010	2016	2017	2018	2019	2020
Summary external debt data by debtor type						
Total external debt stocks	**352,364**	**543,257**	**543,000**	**557,743**	**568,646**	**549,234**
Use of IMF credit	4,446	3,881	4,112	4,015	3,992	4,158
Long-term external debt	282,426	482,174	486,480	486,883	485,474	476,093
Public and publicly guaranteed sector	97,486	174,683	181,161	190,193	193,737	194,237
Public sector	94,425	172,853	179,675	189,132	192,748	193,325
of which: General government	67,300	71,178	70,026	70,449	74,580	79,414
Private sector guaranteed by public sector	3,061	1,830	1,485	1,061	989	913
Private sector not guaranteed	184,940	307,492	305,320	296,690	291,737	281,856
Short-term external debt	65,492	57,202	52,408	66,844	79,179	68,983
Disbursements (long-term)	**85,379**	**106,247**	**96,730**	**105,057**	**114,547**	**126,736**
Public and publicly guaranteed sector	19,957	19,729	30,315	28,809	23,866	39,466
Public sector	19,063	19,608	30,188	28,675	23,681	39,360
of which: General government	9,155	5,732	7,094	4,655	8,920	8,294
Private sector guaranteed by public sector	894	121	128	134	186	106
Private sector not guaranteed	65,422	86,518	66,415	76,249	90,680	87,270
Principal repayments (long-term)	**32,026**	**94,709**	**75,668**	**74,508**	**123,444**	**109,825**
Public and publicly guaranteed sector	9,628	18,983	23,218	28,431	30,486	23,162
Public sector	9,209	18,238	22,718	27,874	30,234	22,952
of which: General government	7,964	3,809	8,450	3,645	4,661	3,461
Private sector guaranteed by public sector	419	745	500	557	252	210
Private sector not guaranteed	22,398	75,726	52,450	46,077	92,958	86,663
Interest payments (long-term)	**13,157**	**21,605**	**18,467**	**18,681**	**25,701**	**20,348**
Public and publicly guaranteed sector	5,172	5,537	6,696	5,679	11,384	9,057
Public sector	5,081	5,460	6,639	5,630	11,344	9,024
of which: General government	4,255	3,163	3,348	3,186	3,548	4,286
Private sector guaranteed by public sector	91	78	57	49	40	33
Private sector not guaranteed	7,985	16,068	11,771	13,002	14,317	11,292
Summary external debt stock by creditor type						
Long-term external debt stocks	**282,426**	**482,174**	**486,480**	**486,883**	**485,474**	**476,093**
Public and publicly guaranteed debt from:	97,486	174,683	181,161	190,193	193,737	194,237
Official creditors	41,553	41,064	48,327	47,860	43,172	43,946
Multilateral	29,980	32,071	32,678	33,386	33,262	33,712
of which: World Bank	13,523	16,255	16,390	16,213	16,253	15,682
Bilateral	11,573	8,993	15,650	14,474	9,910	10,234
Private creditors	55,933	133,619	132,833	142,333	150,565	150,291
Bondholders	46,806	46,843	44,874	41,979	43,504	47,885
Commercial banks and others	9,127	86,776	87,959	100,355	107,062	102,406
Private nonguaranteed debt from:	184,940	307,492	305,320	296,690	291,737	281,856
Bondholders	83,032	46,930	48,026	32,686	37,553	35,903
Commercial banks and others	101,908	260,562	257,294	264,004	254,184	245,953
Use of IMF credit	4,446	3,881	4,112	4,015	3,992	4,158
Net financial inflows						
Net debt inflows						
Use of IMF credit	..	..	..	..	..	..
Long-term	53,353	11,538	21,062	30,550	-8,897	16,912
Official creditors	8,641	-1,012	7,140	-358	-4,684	500
Multilateral	5,049	427	633	787	-105	516
of which: World Bank	3,512	516	159	-114	43	-569
Bilateral	3,592	-1,439	6,506	-1,144	-4,579	-16
Private creditors	44,712	12,550	13,922	30,907	-4,213	16,412
Bondholders	29,391	-7,710	-643	1,287	-524	3,742
Banks and others	15,321	20,260	14,565	29,620	-3,689	12,670
Short-term	25,706	4,860	-4,798	14,440	12,335	-10,196
Net equity inflows						
Foreign direct investment	68,920	48,854	63,999	57,322	63,631	40,546
Portfolio equity	37,671	11,040	5,674	-3,062	-1,810	-5,926
Debt ratios						
External debt stocks to exports (%)	141	236	197	194	199	212
External debt stocks to GNI (%)	16	31	27	30	31	39
Debt service to exports (%)	18	51	35	33	53	51
Short-term to external debt stocks (%)	19	11	10	12	14	13
Multilateral to external debt stocks (%)	9	6	6	6	6	6
Reserves to external debt stocks (%)	81	67	68	67	62	64
Gross national income (GNI)	2,140,639	1,757,604	2,024,930	1,863,644	1,827,513	1,417,069

BULGARIA

(US$ million, unless otherwise indicated)

	2010	2016	2017	2018	2019	2020
Summary external debt data by debtor type						
Total external debt stocks	**50,697**	**39,994**	**40,989**	**40,103**	**40,501**	**43,347**
Use of IMF credit	941	821	870	850	845	880
Long-term external debt	34,613	30,563	30,583	29,708	29,762	30,592
Public and publicly guaranteed sector	4,845	11,050	11,630	11,506	11,186	11,927
Public sector	4,845	11,050	11,630	11,506	11,186	11,927
of which: General government	4,092	10,171	10,424	10,419	10,195	10,933
Private sector guaranteed by public sector	..	..	..	..	..	..
Private sector not guaranteed	29,768	19,513	18,953	18,202	18,576	18,665
Short-term external debt	15,143	8,609	9,536	9,546	9,895	11,876
Disbursements (long-term)	**1,620**	**7,090**	**5,445**	**5,052**	**4,554**	**4,633**
Public and publicly guaranteed sector	250	2,875	312	917	150	0
Public sector	250	2,875	312	917	150	0
of which: General government	232	2,216	46	892	150	0
Private sector guaranteed by public sector	..	..	..	..	..	..
Private sector not guaranteed	1,370	4,215	5,132	4,135	4,405	4,633
Principal repayments (long-term)	**3,550**	**5,795**	**6,844**	**5,055**	**4,286**	**3,919**
Public and publicly guaranteed sector	268	274	1,355	300	256	266
Public sector	268	274	1,355	300	256	266
of which: General government	186	220	1,294	203	179	185
Private sector guaranteed by public sector	..	..	..	..	..	..
Private sector not guaranteed	3,282	5,521	5,489	4,754	4,029	3,653
Interest payments (long-term)	**609**	**2,170**	**1,713**	**1,388**	**1,180**	**1,020**
Public and publicly guaranteed sector	180	247	304	269	276	279
Public sector	180	247	304	269	276	279
of which: General government	160	237	290	253	261	264
Private sector guaranteed by public sector	..	..	..	..	..	..
Private sector not guaranteed	430	1,923	1,408	1,118	904	741
Summary external debt stock by creditor type						
Long-term external debt stocks	**34,613**	**30,563**	**30,583**	**29,708**	**29,762**	**30,592**
Public and publicly guaranteed debt from:	4,845	11,050	11,630	11,506	11,186	11,927
Official creditors	3,210	3,046	3,664	3,214	3,050	3,041
Multilateral	2,388	2,786	3,339	2,966	2,839	2,854
of which: World Bank	1,338	920	1,148	831	727	701
Bilateral	822	261	325	247	211	187
Private creditors	1,635	8,004	7,967	8,292	8,136	8,886
Bondholders	1,618	7,997	7,960	8,286	8,130	8,881
Commercial banks and others	17	6	7	6	6	6
Private nonguaranteed debt from:	29,768	19,513	18,953	18,202	18,576	18,665
Bondholders	134	1,549	1,686	1,405	1,489	1,465
Commercial banks and others	29,635	17,964	17,267	16,797	17,086	17,200
Use of IMF credit	941	821	870	850	845	880
Net financial inflows						
Net debt inflows						
Use of IMF credit	..	..	..	..	..	..
Long-term	-1,930	1,295	-1,399	-2	268	714
Official creditors	-12	434	31	-92	-107	-265
Multilateral	42	492	-14	-15	-70	-229
of which: World Bank	-70	150	-80	-60	-87	-85
Bilateral	-53	-58	45	-76	-36	-36
Private creditors	-1,919	861	-1,430	89	375	979
Bondholders	..	2,220	-941	560	86	-82
Banks and others	-1,919	-1,359	-488	-471	289	1,062
Short-term	-2,654	-159	897	-113	260	1,789
Net equity inflows						
Foreign direct investment	1,642	1,498	964	1,859	911	1,242
Portfolio equity	-1	-35	-110	49	-91	-165
Debt ratios						
External debt stocks to exports (%)	194	112	99	89	89	108
External debt stocks to GNI (%)	103	77	71	63	60	64
Debt service to exports (%)	16	23	21	15	13	13
Short-term to external debt stocks (%)	30	22	23	24	24	27
Multilateral to external debt stocks (%)	5	7	8	7	7	7
Reserves to external debt stocks (%)	30	59	65	67	64	82
Gross national income (GNI)	49,327	52,130	57,539	64,150	67,446	67,448

BURKINA FASO

(US$ million, unless otherwise indicated)

	2010	2016	2017	2018	2019	2020
Summary external debt data by debtor type						
Total external debt stocks	**2,180**	**2,864**	**3,167**	**3,318**	**3,687**	**4,493**
Use of IMF credit	217	286	284	269	310	466
Long-term external debt	1,963	2,578	2,883	3,049	3,377	4,027
Public and publicly guaranteed sector	1,960	2,570	2,873	3,041	3,372	4,021
Public sector	1,960	2,570	2,873	3,041	3,372	4,021
of which: General government	1,935	2,538	2,841	3,016	3,352	4,002
Private sector guaranteed by public sector	..	..	..	..	..	..
Private sector not guaranteed	3	7	10	7	5	5
Short-term external debt	0	0	0	0	0	0
Disbursements (long-term)	**288**	**265**	**184**	**344**	**463**	**526**
Public and publicly guaranteed sector	286	262	183	344	463	524
Public sector	286	262	183	344	463	524
of which: General government	278	262	183	344	463	524
Private sector guaranteed by public sector	..	..	..	..	..	..
Private sector not guaranteed	1	2	1	..	..	2
Principal repayments (long-term)	**31**	**76**	**84**	**86**	**100**	**100**
Public and publicly guaranteed sector	31	75	83	84	98	98
Public sector	31	75	83	84	98	98
of which: General government	30	70	78	78	93	97
Private sector guaranteed by public sector	..	..	..	..	..	..
Private sector not guaranteed	0	1	1	2	2	2
Interest payments (long-term)	**18**	**32**	**33**	**32**	**32**	**36**
Public and publicly guaranteed sector	18	31	33	32	32	36
Public sector	18	31	33	32	32	36
of which: General government	18	31	32	31	31	36
Private sector guaranteed by public sector	..	..	..	..	..	..
Private sector not guaranteed	0	0	0	1	0	0
Summary external debt stock by creditor type						
Long-term external debt stocks	**1,963**	**2,578**	**2,883**	**3,049**	**3,377**	**4,027**
Public and publicly guaranteed debt from:	1,960	2,570	2,873	3,041	3,372	4,021
Official creditors	1,919	2,552	2,857	3,028	3,360	4,011
Multilateral	1,611	2,196	2,507	2,670	3,008	3,549
of which: World Bank	776	1,171	1,334	1,458	1,673	2,014
Bilateral	308	356	351	358	351	462
Private creditors	41	18	16	14	12	10
Bondholders	..	..	..	..	..	..
Commercial banks and others	41	18	16	14	12	10
Private nonguaranteed debt from:	3	7	10	7	5	5
Bondholders	..	..	..	..	..	..
Commercial banks and others	3	7	10	7	5	5
Use of IMF credit	217	286	284	269	310	466
Net financial inflows						
Net debt inflows						
Use of IMF credit	20	12	-18	-9	42	139
Long-term	257	189	101	258	363	426
Official creditors	241	191	103	262	367	428
Multilateral	230	200	129	246	370	341
of which: World Bank	67	166	78	166	228	230
Bilateral	10	-9	-26	16	-3	87
Private creditors	16	-2	-2	-4	-4	-2
Bondholders	..	..	..	..	..	..
Banks and others	16	-2	-2	-4	-4	-2
Short-term	0	0	0	0	0	0
Net equity inflows						
Foreign direct investment	-32	166	93	242	234	149
Portfolio equity	3	35	28	31	29	..
Debt ratios						
External debt stocks to exports (%)	110	83	81	70	79	..
External debt stocks to GNI (%)	22	23	23	22	24	27
Debt service to exports (%)	3	4	4	3	4	..
Short-term to external debt stocks (%)	0	0	0	0	0	0
Multilateral to external debt stocks (%)	74	77	79	80	82	79
Reserves to external debt stocks (%)	49	..	..	..	..	..
Gross national income (GNI)	9,808	12,262	13,577	15,377	15,326	16,665

BURUNDI

(US$ million, unless otherwise indicated)

	2010	2016	2017	2018	2019	2020
Summary external debt data by debtor type						
Total external debt stocks	**620.9**	**602.8**	**606.8**	**585.0**	**593.9**	**626.0**
Use of IMF credit	223.4	193.6	188.1	166.4	149.1	132.4
Long-term external debt	381.8	408.9	418.5	418.4	444.5	493.3
Public and publicly guaranteed sector	381.8	408.9	418.5	418.4	444.5	493.3
Public sector	381.8	408.9	418.5	418.4	444.5	493.3
of which: General government	380.5	397.6	407.3	407.1	411.0	458.3
Private sector guaranteed by public sector	..	..	..	..	..	..
Private sector not guaranteed	..	..	..	..	..	..
Short-term external debt	15.7	0.3	0.3	0.3	0.3	0.3
Disbursements (long-term)	**31.6**	**19.0**	**5.2**	**14.2**	**45.2**	**48.0**
Public and publicly guaranteed sector	31.6	19.0	5.2	14.2	45.2	48.0
Public sector	31.6	19.0	5.2	14.2	45.2	48.0
of which: General government	31.6	7.8	5.2	14.2	22.8	48.0
Private sector guaranteed by public sector	..	..	..	..	..	..
Private sector not guaranteed	..	..	..	..	..	..
Principal repayments (long-term)	**2.4**	**11.5**	**8.0**	**9.1**	**18.3**	**10.3**
Public and publicly guaranteed sector	2.4	11.5	8.0	9.1	18.3	10.3
Public sector	2.4	11.5	8.0	9.1	18.3	10.3
of which: General government	2.4	11.5	8.0	9.1	18.1	9.8
Private sector guaranteed by public sector	..	..	..	..	..	..
Private sector not guaranteed	..	..	..	..	..	..
Interest payments (long-term)	**1.4**	**3.7**	**2.4**	**3.1**	**4.2**	**3.3**
Public and publicly guaranteed sector	1.4	3.7	2.4	3.1	4.2	3.3
Public sector	1.4	3.7	2.4	3.1	4.2	3.3
of which: General government	1.4	3.7	2.4	3.0	4.1	3.1
Private sector guaranteed by public sector	..	..	..	..	..	..
Private sector not guaranteed	..	..	..	..	..	..
Summary external debt stock by creditor type						
Long-term external debt stocks	**381.8**	**408.9**	**418.5**	**418.4**	**444.5**	**493.3**
Public and publicly guaranteed debt from:	381.8	408.9	418.5	418.4	444.5	493.3
Official creditors	381.8	408.9	418.5	418.4	444.5	493.3
Multilateral	325.1	310.6	319.2	313.7	342.2	353.2
of which: World Bank	162.7	143.0	148.2	141.5	137.5	139.9
Bilateral	56.7	98.3	99.3	104.6	102.2	140.1
Private creditors	..	..	..	..	..	..
Bondholders	..	..	..	..	..	..
Commercial banks and others	..	..	..	..	..	..
Private nonguaranteed debt from:	..	..	..	..	..	..
Bondholders	..	..	..	..	..	..
Commercial banks and others	..	..	..	..	..	..
Use of IMF credit	223.4	193.6	188.1	166.4	149.1	132.4
Net financial inflows						
Net debt inflows						
Use of IMF credit	20.1	-18.0	-16.6	-17.6	-16.2	-22.2
Long-term	29.1	7.5	-2.8	5.1	26.9	37.7
Official creditors	29.1	7.5	-2.8	5.1	26.9	37.7
Multilateral	29.1	9.0	-2.6	-1.1	29.3	0.0
of which: World Bank	17.8	-3.2	-3.2	-3.3	-3.2	-3.2
Bilateral	..	-1.5	-0.2	6.2	-2.4	37.8
Private creditors	..	..	..	..	..	..
Bondholders	..	..	..	..	..	..
Banks and others	..	..	..	..	..	..
Short-term	8.0	0.0	0.0	0.0	0.0	0.0
Net equity inflows						
Foreign direct investment	0.8	0.1	0.3	1.0	1.0	6.1
Portfolio equity	..	..	..	..	..	..
Debt ratios						
External debt stocks to exports (%)	341.4	289.1	213.6	193.8	..	..
External debt stocks to GNI (%)	30.7	20.4	19.2	19.2	19.7	19.1
Debt service to exports (%)	2.4	16.0	9.6	9.9	..	..
Short-term to external debt stocks (%)	2.5	0.0	0.0	0.0	0.0	0.0
Multilateral to external debt stocks (%)	52.4	51.5	52.6	53.6	57.6	56.4
Reserves to external debt stocks (%)	53.3	15.6	15.8	11.4	18.5	14.1
Gross national income (GNI)	2,021.3	2,958.8	3,167.5	3,043.0	3,019.5	3,274.9

CABO VERDE

(US$ million, unless otherwise indicated)

	2010	2016	2017	2018	2019	2020
Summary external debt data by debtor type						
Total external debt stocks	**884.6**	**1,551.7**	**1,790.0**	**1,767.5**	**1,821.2**	**2,069.8**
Use of IMF credit	22.7	12.3	13.1	12.8	12.7	47.3
Long-term external debt	861.9	1,539.4	1,776.9	1,754.7	1,808.5	2,022.4
Public and publicly guaranteed sector	861.9	1,539.4	1,776.9	1,754.7	1,808.5	2,022.4
Public sector	861.9	1,536.3	1,774.0	1,752.1	1,806.5	2,021.4
of which: General government	861.9	1,536.3	1,774.0	1,752.1	1,806.5	2,021.4
Private sector guaranteed by public sector	..	3.1	2.9	2.6	2.0	1.1
Private sector not guaranteed	..	..	..	..	..	..
Short-term external debt	0.0	0.0	0.0	0.0	0.1	0.0
Disbursements (long-term)	**202.7**	**69.5**	**111.8**	**75.2**	**118.4**	**124.2**
Public and publicly guaranteed sector	202.7	69.5	111.8	75.2	118.4	124.2
Public sector	202.7	69.5	111.8	75.2	118.4	124.2
of which: General government	202.7	69.5	111.8	75.2	118.4	124.2
Private sector guaranteed by public sector	..	..	..	..	..	0.0
Private sector not guaranteed	..	..	..	..	..	..
Principal repayments (long-term)	**25.0**	**25.6**	**32.6**	**36.7**	**42.1**	**42.5**
Public and publicly guaranteed sector	25.0	25.6	32.6	36.7	42.1	42.5
Public sector	25.0	25.6	32.2	36.5	41.5	41.5
of which: General government	25.0	25.6	32.2	36.5	41.5	41.5
Private sector guaranteed by public sector	..	..	0.4	0.2	0.6	0.9
Private sector not guaranteed	..	..	..	..	..	..
Interest payments (long-term)	**7.7**	**18.1**	**18.1**	**19.2**	**19.2**	**16.6**
Public and publicly guaranteed sector	7.7	18.1	18.1	19.2	19.2	16.6
Public sector	7.7	18.1	18.1	19.2	19.1	16.4
of which: General government	7.7	18.1	18.1	19.2	19.1	16.4
Private sector guaranteed by public sector	..	..	..	..	0.1	0.2
Private sector not guaranteed	..	..	..	..	..	..
Summary external debt stock by creditor type						
Long-term external debt stocks	**861.9**	**1,539.4**	**1,776.9**	**1,754.7**	**1,808.5**	**2,022.4**
Public and publicly guaranteed debt from:	861.9	1,539.4	1,776.9	1,754.7	1,808.5	2,022.4
Official creditors	777.9	1,077.7	1,238.3	1,240.5	1,301.5	1,464.3
Multilateral	597.6	737.2	811.6	816.9	882.5	1,014.1
of which: World Bank	303.1	344.7	361.7	351.4	406.1	482.1
Bilateral	180.3	340.5	426.7	423.6	419.0	450.1
Private creditors	84.1	461.7	538.6	514.2	507.0	558.2
Bondholders	..	..	..	..	..	..
Commercial banks and others	84.1	461.7	538.6	514.2	507.0	558.2
Private nonguaranteed debt from:	..	..	..	..	..	..
Bondholders	..	..	..	..	..	..
Commercial banks and others	..	..	..	..	..	..
Use of IMF credit	22.7	12.3	13.1	12.8	12.7	47.3
Net financial inflows						
Net debt inflows						
Use of IMF credit	-2.3	..	..	..	..	33.0
Long-term	177.6	43.9	79.2	38.5	76.3	81.7
Official creditors	100.1	27.5	66.7	38.5	73.9	77.6
Multilateral	70.3	20.7	17.0	28.4	74.1	79.1
of which: World Bank	21.7	-2.0	-6.3	-1.0	57.0	55.5
Bilateral	29.9	6.8	49.7	10.1	-0.2	-1.5
Private creditors	77.5	16.4	12.5	..	2.5	4.1
Bondholders	..	..	..	..	..	..
Banks and others	77.5	16.4	12.5	..	2.5	4.1
Short-term	0.0	0.0	0.0	0.0	0.0	0.0
Net equity inflows						
Foreign direct investment	95.3	125.5	120.0	112.5	102.5	74.2
Portfolio equity	0.0	0.0	0.0	0.0	0.0	0.0
Debt ratios						
External debt stocks to exports (%)	137.5	209.7	216.8	177.0	175.2	467.5
External debt stocks to GNI (%)	55.6	96.8	104.8	92.0	93.9	124.3
Debt service to exports (%)	5.4	5.9	6.1	5.6	5.9	13.3
Short-term to external debt stocks (%)	0.0	0.0	0.0	0.0	0.0	0.0
Multilateral to external debt stocks (%)	67.6	47.5	45.3	46.2	48.5	49.0
Reserves to external debt stocks (%)	43.2	36.9	34.5	34.3	40.5	32.6
Gross national income (GNI)	1,591.1	1,603.7	1,708.7	1,920.6	1,939.5	1,665.0

CAMBODIA

(US$ million, unless otherwise indicated)

	2010	2016	2017	2018	2019	2020
Summary external debt data by debtor type						
Total external debt stocks	**4,010**	**10,060**	**11,425**	**13,533**	**15,329**	**17,562**
Use of IMF credit	129	113	120	117	116	121
Long-term external debt	3,502	8,220	9,527	11,050	11,801	13,659
Public and publicly guaranteed sector	3,060	5,831	6,577	6,994	7,562	8,758
Public sector	3,060	5,831	6,577	6,994	7,562	8,758
of which: General government	3,060	5,831	6,577	6,994	7,562	8,758
Private sector guaranteed by public sector	..	..	..	..	..	..
Private sector not guaranteed	442	2,388	2,951	4,056	4,239	4,902
Short-term external debt	379	1,727	1,778	2,366	3,413	3,782
Disbursements (long-term)	**596**	**1,075**	**1,967**	**2,750**	**2,049**	**2,889**
Public and publicly guaranteed sector	348	520	657	716	824	1,212
Public sector	348	520	657	716	824	1,212
of which: General government	348	520	657	716	824	1,212
Private sector guaranteed by public sector	..	..	..	..	..	..
Private sector not guaranteed	248	555	1,310	2,033	1,226	1,677
Principal repayments (long-term)	**33**	**643**	**888**	**1,109**	**1,260**	**1,279**
Public and publicly guaranteed sector	33	114	140	180	218	264
Public sector	33	114	140	180	218	264
of which: General government	33	114	140	180	218	264
Private sector guaranteed by public sector	..	..	..	..	..	..
Private sector not guaranteed	..	529	747	928	1,042	1,014
Interest payments (long-term)	**27**	**83**	**87**	**103**	**139**	**147**
Public and publicly guaranteed sector	26	72	72	85	93	95
Public sector	26	72	72	85	93	95
of which: General government	26	72	72	85	93	95
Private sector guaranteed by public sector	..	..	..	..	..	..
Private sector not guaranteed	1	11	15	17	47	52
Summary external debt stock by creditor type						
Long-term external debt stocks	**3,502**	**8,220**	**9,527**	**11,050**	**11,801**	**13,659**
Public and publicly guaranteed debt from:	3,060	5,831	6,577	6,994	7,562	8,758
Official creditors	3,060	5,831	6,577	6,994	7,562	8,758
Multilateral	1,529	1,735	1,938	1,957	2,102	2,691
of which: World Bank	565	518	550	544	585	685
Bilateral	1,531	4,097	4,639	5,037	5,459	6,066
Private creditors	..	..	..	..	..	..
Bondholders	..	..	..	..	..	..
Commercial banks and others	..	..	..	..	..	..
Private nonguaranteed debt from:	442	2,388	2,951	4,056	4,239	4,902
Bondholders	..	..	..	300	300	650
Commercial banks and others	442	2,388	2,951	3,756	3,939	4,252
Use of IMF credit	129	113	120	117	116	121
Net financial inflows						
Net debt inflows						
Use of IMF credit	..	..	..	..	..	..
Long-term	562	433	1,079	1,641	789	1,610
Official creditors	315	406	517	536	606	947
Multilateral	51	106	98	65	156	502
of which: World Bank	9	-7	1	7	44	73
Bilateral	264	300	419	471	449	445
Private creditors	248	26	562	1,105	183	663
Bondholders	..	..	..	300	..	350
Banks and others	248	26	562	805	183	313
Short-term	149	407	51	588	1,046	369
Net equity inflows						
Foreign direct investment	1,404	2,476	2,788	3,213	3,663	3,625
Portfolio equity	0	0	0	0	0	0
Debt ratios						
External debt stocks to exports (%)	66	69	70	71	70	88
External debt stocks to GNI (%)	37	54	55	59	60	72
Debt service to exports (%)	1	5	6	7	7	7
Short-term to external debt stocks (%)	9	17	16	17	22	22
Multilateral to external debt stocks (%)	38	17	17	14	14	15
Reserves to external debt stocks (%)	81	83	99	99	111	106
Gross national income (GNI)	10,728	18,788	20,800	22,915	25,526	24,281

CAMEROON

(US$ million, unless otherwise indicated)

	2010	2016	2017	2018	2019	2020
Summary external debt data by debtor type						
Total external debt stocks	**3,190**	**7,890**	**10,073**	**10,926**	**12,849**	**13,864**
Use of IMF credit	445	318	602	714	760	1,269
Long-term external debt	2,737	7,310	8,943	9,778	11,712	12,226
Public and publicly guaranteed sector	2,160	6,297	8,018	9,076	10,309	11,460
Public sector	2,160	6,297	8,018	9,076	10,309	11,460
of which: General government	2,157	6,296	8,017	9,075	10,308	11,459
Private sector guaranteed by public sector	..	..	..	..	..	..
Private sector not guaranteed	577	1,012	925	703	1,403	766
Short-term external debt	9	262	528	433	377	369
Disbursements (long-term)	**278**	**1,458**	**1,648**	**1,692**	**2,590**	**1,152**
Public and publicly guaranteed sector	278	1,209	1,588	1,638	1,753	1,126
Public sector	278	1,209	1,588	1,638	1,753	1,126
of which: General government	278	1,209	1,588	1,638	1,753	1,125
Private sector guaranteed by public sector	..	..	..	..	..	..
Private sector not guaranteed	..	249	61	53	837	26
Principal repayments (long-term)	**160**	**550**	**413**	**623**	**762**	**893**
Public and publicly guaranteed sector	122	277	175	372	436	552
Public sector	122	277	175	372	436	552
of which: General government	118	277	175	372	436	551
Private sector guaranteed by public sector	..	..	..	..	..	..
Private sector not guaranteed	38	273	238	250	325	341
Interest payments (long-term)	**42**	**280**	**272**	**405**	**348**	**346**
Public and publicly guaranteed sector	27	168	240	237	235	333
Public sector	27	168	240	237	235	333
of which: General government	27	168	240	237	235	333
Private sector guaranteed by public sector	..	..	..	..	..	..
Private sector not guaranteed	15	112	32	168	112	13
Summary external debt stock by creditor type						
Long-term external debt stocks	**2,737**	**7,310**	**8,943**	**9,778**	**11,712**	**12,226**
Public and publicly guaranteed debt from:	2,160	6,297	8,018	9,076	10,309	11,460
Official creditors	2,140	5,283	6,880	7,799	8,932	10,092
Multilateral	787	1,886	2,448	3,208	3,750	4,423
of which: World Bank	374	897	1,306	1,432	1,733	1,915
Bilateral	1,353	3,396	4,431	4,591	5,183	5,669
Private creditors	20	1,015	1,138	1,277	1,376	1,368
Bondholders	..	750	750	750	750	750
Commercial banks and others	20	265	388	527	626	618
Private nonguaranteed debt from:	577	1,012	925	703	1,403	766
Bondholders	..	..	..	..	..	..
Commercial banks and others	577	1,012	925	703	1,403	766
Use of IMF credit	445	318	602	714	760	1,269
Net financial inflows						
Net debt inflows						
Use of IMF credit	..	-30	258	128	50	461
Long-term	118	908	1,235	1,069	1,828	260
Official creditors	150	896	1,318	1,110	1,210	619
Multilateral	118	247	480	857	581	391
of which: World Bank	75	127	353	165	312	93
Bilateral	32	649	837	254	629	229
Private creditors	-32	12	-82	-41	618	-360
Bondholders	..	..	..	..	..	..
Banks and others	-32	12	-82	-41	618	-360
Short-term	0	-36	262	-95	-62	-27
Net equity inflows						
Foreign direct investment	526	48	219	476	758	488
Portfolio equity	0	0	0	0	0	..
Debt ratios						
External debt stocks to exports (%)	56	122	149	145	161	221
External debt stocks to GNI (%)	12	25	29	29	34	35
Debt service to exports (%)	4	13	11	14	14	20
Short-term to external debt stocks (%)	0	3	5	4	3	3
Multilateral to external debt stocks (%)	25	24	24	29	29	32
Reserves to external debt stocks (%)	114	28	32	32	..	..
Gross national income (GNI)	25,905	32,085	34,348	37,954	38,260	39,217

CENTRAL AFRICAN REPUBLIC

(US$ million, unless otherwise indicated)

	2010	2016	2017	2018	2019	2020
Summary external debt data by debtor type						
Total external debt stocks	**634.3**	**735.4**	**762.8**	**825.0**	**887.6**	**975.7**
Use of IMF credit	172.6	184.6	235.4	279.1	296.5	355.4
Long-term external debt	375.8	462.1	438.6	457.5	458.8	468.8
Public and publicly guaranteed sector	375.8	462.1	438.6	457.5	458.8	468.8
Public sector	375.8	462.1	438.6	457.5	458.8	468.8
of which: General government	357.3	447.7	435.6	454.9	457.1	467.6
Private sector guaranteed by public sector	..	..	..	..	..	..
Private sector not guaranteed	..	..	..	..	..	..
Short-term external debt	85.9	88.7	88.8	88.4	132.3	151.5
Disbursements (long-term)	**35.0**	**12.2**	**14.6**	**66.6**	**22.2**	**26.0**
Public and publicly guaranteed sector	35.0	12.2	14.6	66.6	22.2	26.0
Public sector	35.0	12.2	14.6	66.6	22.2	26.0
of which: General government	35.0	12.2	14.6	66.6	22.2	26.0
Private sector guaranteed by public sector	..	..	..	..	..	..
Private sector not guaranteed	..	..	..	..	..	..
Principal repayments (long-term)	**1.8**	**4.3**	**15.3**	**10.4**	**15.8**	**5.0**
Public and publicly guaranteed sector	1.8	4.3	15.3	10.4	15.8	5.0
Public sector	1.8	4.3	15.3	10.4	15.8	5.0
of which: General government	1.0	4.3	2.7	10.1	15.0	4.5
Private sector guaranteed by public sector	..	..	..	..	..	..
Private sector not guaranteed	..	..	..	..	..	..
Interest payments (long-term)	**1.2**	**1.5**	**7.5**	**2.0**	**2.2**	**1.2**
Public and publicly guaranteed sector	1.2	1.5	7.5	2.0	2.2	1.2
Public sector	1.2	1.5	7.5	2.0	2.2	1.2
of which: General government	1.2	1.5	5.6	2.0	2.2	1.2
Private sector guaranteed by public sector	..	..	..	..	..	..
Private sector not guaranteed	..	..	..	..	..	..
Summary external debt stock by creditor type						
Long-term external debt stocks	**375.8**	**462.1**	**438.6**	**457.5**	**458.8**	**468.8**
Public and publicly guaranteed debt from:	375.8	462.1	438.6	457.5	458.8	468.8
Official creditors	336.6	416.4	392.6	411.6	413.0	422.6
Multilateral	43.1	78.7	96.3	151.1	153.7	176.7
of which: World Bank	13.9	59.9	64.2	98.5	107.0	130.4
Bilateral	293.6	337.7	296.3	260.5	259.2	245.8
Private creditors	39.2	45.7	46.0	45.9	45.9	46.2
Bondholders	..	..	..	..	..	..
Commercial banks and others	39.2	45.7	46.0	45.9	45.9	46.2
Private nonguaranteed debt from:	..	..	..	..	..	..
Bondholders	..	..	..	..	..	..
Commercial banks and others	..	..	..	..	..	..
Use of IMF credit	172.6	184.6	235.4	279.1	296.5	355.4
Net financial inflows						
Net debt inflows						
Use of IMF credit	13.2	15.5	38.8	50.1	19.0	45.1
Long-term	33.1	7.9	-0.6	56.1	6.4	21.0
Official creditors	32.6	7.9	-0.6	56.1	6.4	20.9
Multilateral	5.1	5.6	13.4	58.4	3.4	16.5
of which: World Bank	5.0	3.1	1.1	37.1	9.0	18.4
Bilateral	27.6	2.2	-14.0	-2.3	2.9	4.5
Private creditors	0.5	..	..	..	..	..
Bondholders	..	..	..	..	..	..
Banks and others	0.5	..	..	..	..	..
Short-term	0.0	-2.7	0.6	-0.2	10.3	18.5
Net equity inflows						
Foreign direct investment	61.5	7.3	6.9	18.0	25.6	34.7
Portfolio equity	..	..	..	..	..	..
Debt ratios						
External debt stocks to exports (%)	..	..	..	..	..	..
External debt stocks to GNI (%)	29.5	39.8	35.0	34.6	37.2	39.7
Debt service to exports (%)	..	..	..	..	..	..
Short-term to external debt stocks (%)	13.5	12.1	11.6	10.7	14.9	15.5
Multilateral to external debt stocks (%)	6.8	10.7	12.6	18.3	17.3	18.1
Reserves to external debt stocks (%)	28.6	32.6	47.6	43.9	39.5	..
Gross national income (GNI)	2,152.2	1,847.8	2,177.9	2,386.7	2,386.0	2,456.8

CHAD

(US$ million, unless otherwise indicated)

	2010	2016	2017	2018	2019	2020
Summary external debt data by debtor type						
Total external debt stocks	**2,158**	**2,867**	**3,124**	**3,243**	**3,313**	**3,654**
Use of IMF credit	99	193	254	395	470	678
Long-term external debt	2,049	2,658	2,842	2,817	2,817	2,945
Public and publicly guaranteed sector	2,049	2,658	2,842	2,817	2,817	2,945
Public sector	2,049	2,658	2,842	2,817	2,817	2,945
of which: General government	2,016	2,658	2,842	2,817	2,817	2,945
Private sector guaranteed by public sector	..	..	..	..	..	..
Private sector not guaranteed	..	..	..	..	..	..
Short-term external debt	9	17	28	31	26	31
Disbursements (long-term)	**366**	**151**	**242**	**52**	**42**	**119**
Public and publicly guaranteed sector	366	151	242	52	42	119
Public sector	366	151	242	52	42	119
of which: General government	366	151	242	52	42	119
Private sector guaranteed by public sector	..	..	..	..	..	..
Private sector not guaranteed	..	..	..	..	..	..
Principal repayments (long-term)	**45**	**98**	**128**	**43**	**30**	**61**
Public and publicly guaranteed sector	45	98	128	43	30	61
Public sector	45	98	128	43	30	61
of which: General government	45	98	128	43	30	61
Private sector guaranteed by public sector	..	..	..	..	..	..
Private sector not guaranteed	..	..	..	..	..	..
Interest payments (long-term)	**17**	**53**	**55**	**61**	**59**	**50**
Public and publicly guaranteed sector	17	53	55	61	59	50
Public sector	17	53	55	61	59	50
of which: General government	16	53	55	61	59	50
Private sector guaranteed by public sector	..	..	..	..	..	..
Private sector not guaranteed	..	..	..	..	..	..
Summary external debt stock by creditor type						
Long-term external debt stocks	**2,049**	**2,658**	**2,842**	**2,817**	**2,817**	**2,945**
Public and publicly guaranteed debt from:	2,049	2,658	2,842	2,817	2,817	2,945
Official creditors	2,032	1,286	1,584	1,559	1,559	1,688
Multilateral	1,529	562	687	660	652	692
of which: World Bank	865	180	189	181	176	180
Bilateral	504	724	897	898	907	995
Private creditors	17	1,372	1,258	1,258	1,258	1,258
Bondholders	..	..	..	..	..	..
Commercial banks and others	17	1,372	1,258	1,258	1,258	1,258
Private nonguaranteed debt from:	..	..	..	..	..	..
Bondholders	..	..	..	..	..	..
Commercial banks and others	..	..	..	..	..	..
Use of IMF credit	99	193	254	395	470	678
Net financial inflows						
Net debt inflows						
Use of IMF credit	-11	62	49	149	77	183
Long-term	321	53	114	10	12	58
Official creditors	323	132	228	10	12	59
Multilateral	27	57	84	-9	-2	4
of which: World Bank	-16	-2	-1	-4	-4	-3
Bilateral	296	75	143	18	15	54
Private creditors	-2	-79	-114	..	..	-1
Bondholders	..	..	..	..	..	..
Banks and others	-2	-79	-114	..	..	-1
Short-term	-6	0	0	0	0	0
Net equity inflows						
Foreign direct investment	313	245	363	461	567	558
Portfolio equity	..	..	..	..	..	..
Debt ratios						
External debt stocks to exports (%)	..	..	..	..	..	..
External debt stocks to GNI (%)	21	29	32	29	30	37
Debt service to exports (%)	..	..	..	..	..	..
Short-term to external debt stocks (%)	0	1	1	1	1	1
Multilateral to external debt stocks (%)	71	20	22	20	20	19
Reserves to external debt stocks (%)	29	0	0	5	9	..
Gross national income (GNI)	10,312	9,912	9,870	11,075	11,141	9,948

CHINA

(US$ million, unless otherwise indicated)

	2010	2016	2017	2018	2019	2020
Summary external debt data by debtor type						
Total external debt stocks	**742,756**	**1,413,804**	**1,704,516**	**1,961,528**	**2,114,163**	**2,349,389**
Use of IMF credit	10,764	9,396	9,954	9,721	9,665	10,067
Long-term external debt	219,668	603,012	663,929	732,906	899,185	1,103,090
Public and publicly guaranteed sector	102,293	160,192	196,294	259,689	318,065	414,838
Public sector	102,164	160,144	196,260	259,669	318,058	414,838
of which: General government	59,405	99,109	101,853	126,558	161,780	219,292
Private sector guaranteed by public sector	129	48	34	20	7	0
Private sector not guaranteed	117,375	442,820	467,635	473,217	581,120	688,252
Short-term external debt	512,323	801,396	1,030,633	1,218,901	1,205,312	1,236,232
Disbursements (long-term)	**39,167**	**162,013**	**227,029**	**247,602**	**338,243**	**382,756**
Public and publicly guaranteed sector	12,421	20,639	51,019	79,731	79,493	116,644
Public sector	12,421	20,639	51,019	79,731	79,493	116,644
of which: General government	3,144	10,264	6,482	29,611	38,598	59,200
Private sector guaranteed by public sector	..	0	0	0	0	0
Private sector not guaranteed	26,746	141,374	176,010	167,870	258,750	266,112
Principal repayments (long-term)	**18,784**	**131,319**	**144,688**	**160,496**	**180,605**	**180,784**
Public and publicly guaranteed sector	11,980	16,476	15,447	15,293	20,634	24,179
Public sector	11,967	16,462	15,433	15,279	20,620	24,172
of which: General government	3,154	9,951	3,775	4,779	3,376	3,173
Private sector guaranteed by public sector	14	14	14	14	14	7
Private sector not guaranteed	6,803	114,844	129,241	145,203	159,972	156,605
Interest payments (long-term)	**5,484**	**11,211**	**16,565**	**27,184**	**35,730**	**32,117**
Public and publicly guaranteed sector	1,819	2,035	3,350	6,135	8,670	9,030
Public sector	1,817	2,034	3,349	6,134	8,670	9,030
of which: General government	1,052	754	1,479	2,825	3,387	2,373
Private sector guaranteed by public sector	1	1	1	1	1	0
Private sector not guaranteed	3,665	9,175	13,215	21,049	27,059	23,087
Summary external debt stock by creditor type						
Long-term external debt stocks	**219,668**	**603,012**	**663,929**	**732,906**	**899,185**	**1,103,090**
Public and publicly guaranteed debt from:	102,293	160,192	196,294	259,689	318,065	414,838
Official creditors	75,494	59,894	56,215	54,502	53,840	53,144
Multilateral	35,527	33,430	34,191	34,439	35,427	35,639
of which: World Bank	22,135	16,215	16,356	16,095	16,271	16,236
Bilateral	39,967	26,464	22,025	20,062	18,413	17,506
Private creditors	26,799	100,298	140,079	205,188	264,225	361,693
Bondholders	12,398	69,469	101,554	163,960	214,523	311,239
Commercial banks and others	14,401	30,829	38,524	41,228	49,701	50,454
Private nonguaranteed debt from:	117,375	442,820	467,635	473,217	581,120	688,252
Bondholders	5,561	101,999	152,191	179,902	234,623	323,512
Commercial banks and others	111,814	340,821	315,443	293,314	346,497	364,739
Use of IMF credit	10,764	9,396	9,954	9,721	9,665	10,067
Net financial inflows						
Net debt inflows						
Use of IMF credit	..	..	..	..	..	..
Long-term	20,383	30,694	82,340	87,106	157,638	201,972
Official creditors	-2,277	-3,814	-3,653	-1,702	-698	-1,351
Multilateral	959	31	399	382	1,063	-26
of which: World Bank	-160	-727	-15	-205	205	-83
Bilateral	-3,237	-3,844	-4,052	-2,083	-1,761	-1,325
Private creditors	22,661	34,508	85,993	88,808	158,336	203,323
Bondholders	-1,459	22,273	82,189	94,185	105,319	184,067
Banks and others	24,120	12,234	3,805	-5,377	53,017	19,256
Short-term	271,814	-20,848	229,237	188,268	-13,589	30,920
Net equity inflows						
Foreign direct investment	225,593	164,930	140,569	185,911	162,253	170,022
Portfolio equity	31,110	23,463	36,101	60,411	45,207	62,892
Debt ratios						
External debt stocks to exports (%)	41	58	63	67	73	79
External debt stocks to GNI (%)	12	13	14	14	15	16
Debt service to exports (%)	3	7	8	8	9	9
Short-term to external debt stocks (%)	69	57	60	62	57	53
Multilateral to external debt stocks (%)	5	2	2	2	2	2
Reserves to external debt stocks (%)	386	214	185	158	148	138
Gross national income (GNI)	6,061,092	11,188,325	12,300,722	13,819,938	14,246,121	14,623,681

COLOMBIA

(US$ million, unless otherwise indicated)

	2010	2016	2017	2018	2019	2020
Summary external debt data by debtor type						
Total external debt stocks	**64,432**	**120,659**	**125,769**	**132,965**	**138,625**	**155,172**
Use of IMF credit	1,137	993	1,051	1,027	1,021	6,464
Long-term external debt	55,383	108,386	111,689	117,021	121,969	134,636
Public and publicly guaranteed sector	37,058	73,181	74,191	74,607	74,810	84,826
Public sector	36,555	72,934	73,954	74,383	74,600	84,629
of which: General government	31,631	47,938	51,079	54,323	54,746	61,262
Private sector guaranteed by public sector	503	246	237	224	210	197
Private sector not guaranteed	18,325	35,205	37,498	42,414	47,159	49,810
Short-term external debt	7,912	11,280	13,029	14,918	15,635	14,071
Disbursements (long-term)	**12,970**	**18,508**	**17,291**	**22,912**	**15,786**	**25,161**
Public and publicly guaranteed sector	3,629	6,857	7,074	6,887	5,036	13,105
Public sector	3,559	6,857	7,074	6,887	5,036	13,105
of which: General government	3,426	4,611	5,454	5,712	3,779	8,299
Private sector guaranteed by public sector	71	..	0	0	0	..
Private sector not guaranteed	9,340	11,651	10,217	16,025	10,750	12,056
Principal repayments (long-term)	**6,566**	**10,494**	**16,280**	**17,863**	**12,077**	**15,058**
Public and publicly guaranteed sector	2,318	2,742	6,651	6,754	4,669	3,590
Public sector	2,223	2,733	6,642	6,741	4,656	3,576
of which: General government	1,926	2,058	2,887	2,143	3,260	2,343
Private sector guaranteed by public sector	95	10	10	13	13	13
Private sector not guaranteed	4,248	7,752	9,628	11,109	7,408	11,469
Interest payments (long-term)	**2,839**	**4,820**	**5,480**	**5,875**	**6,401**	**5,991**
Public and publicly guaranteed sector	2,121	3,117	3,528	3,581	3,802	3,478
Public sector	2,112	3,111	3,522	3,574	3,794	3,474
of which: General government	1,812	2,005	2,278	2,257	2,498	2,345
Private sector guaranteed by public sector	10	5	5	7	7	4
Private sector not guaranteed	717	1,703	1,952	2,293	2,600	2,513
Summary external debt stock by creditor type						
Long-term external debt stocks	**55,383**	**108,386**	**111,689**	**117,021**	**121,969**	**134,636**
Public and publicly guaranteed debt from:	37,058	73,181	74,191	74,607	74,810	84,826
Official creditors	16,483	25,125	25,574	27,744	27,775	31,127
Multilateral	15,898	19,918	20,548	22,017	22,692	25,523
of which: World Bank	7,504	9,516	9,520	10,233	10,582	11,989
Bilateral	585	5,206	5,026	5,727	5,083	5,604
Private creditors	20,574	48,056	48,617	46,862	47,035	53,699
Bondholders	17,965	39,601	42,576	40,852	41,581	48,250
Commercial banks and others	2,609	8,456	6,041	6,011	5,454	5,449
Private nonguaranteed debt from:	18,325	35,205	37,498	42,414	47,159	49,810
Bondholders	3,329	9,146	10,206	9,521	10,481	8,954
Commercial banks and others	14,996	26,058	27,292	32,892	36,677	40,856
Use of IMF credit	1,137	993	1,051	1,027	1,021	6,464
Net financial inflows						
Net debt inflows						
Use of IMF credit	..	..	..	..	..	5,224
Long-term	6,404	8,014	1,011	5,049	3,710	10,103
Official creditors	1,137	2,039	152	2,501	169	2,967
Multilateral	1,082	1,861	344	1,683	783	2,594
of which: World Bank	936	945	-279	908	410	1,159
Bilateral	55	178	-192	818	-615	372
Private creditors	5,267	5,976	859	2,547	3,541	7,136
Bondholders	987	1,606	3,820	-2,284	1,715	5,027
Banks and others	4,280	4,369	-2,961	4,831	1,826	2,109
Short-term	3,900	-655	1,749	1,889	718	-1,564
Net equity inflows						
Foreign direct investment	7,065	9,176	12,043	9,931	11,903	5,573
Portfolio equity	1,488	-363	472	-823	-1,232	-454
Debt ratios						
External debt stocks to exports (%)	133	253	230	218	233	357
External debt stocks to GNI (%)	23	43	41	41	44	58
Debt service to exports (%)	20	33	41	40	32	50
Short-term to external debt stocks (%)	12	9	10	11	11	9
Multilateral to external debt stocks (%)	25	17	16	17	16	16
Reserves to external debt stocks (%)	43	38	37	36	37	38
Gross national income (GNI)	276,075	279,763	306,185	325,604	316,299	265,961

COMOROS

(US$ million, unless otherwise indicated)

	2010	2016	2017	2018	2019	2020
Summary external debt data by debtor type						
Total external debt stocks	**278.4**	**180.0**	**186.6**	**245.0**	**265.7**	**300.8**
Use of IMF credit	25.4	26.6	26.1	22.3	30.7	41.9
Long-term external debt	248.5	151.9	159.5	221.4	233.0	257.7
Public and publicly guaranteed sector	248.5	151.9	159.5	221.4	233.0	257.7
Public sector	248.5	151.9	159.5	221.4	233.0	257.7
of which: General government	248.5	151.9	159.5	221.4	233.0	257.7
Private sector guaranteed by public sector	..	..	..	..	..	..
Private sector not guaranteed	..	..	..	..	..	..
Short-term external debt	4.4	1.5	1.1	1.2	1.9	1.2
Disbursements (long-term)	**0.0**	**58.7**	**5.5**	**68.2**	**14.5**	**18.7**
Public and publicly guaranteed sector	0.0	58.7	5.5	68.2	14.5	18.7
Public sector	0.0	58.7	5.5	68.2	14.5	18.7
of which: General government	0.0	58.7	5.5	68.2	14.5	18.7
Private sector guaranteed by public sector	..	..	..	..	..	..
Private sector not guaranteed	..	..	..	..	..	..
Principal repayments (long-term)	**3.1**	**4.4**	**1.9**	**2.0**	**0.3**	**3.3**
Public and publicly guaranteed sector	3.1	4.4	1.9	2.0	0.3	3.3
Public sector	3.1	4.4	1.9	2.0	0.3	3.3
of which: General government	3.1	4.4	1.9	2.0	0.3	3.3
Private sector guaranteed by public sector	..	..	..	..	..	..
Private sector not guaranteed	..	..	..	..	..	..
Interest payments (long-term)	**1.1**	**0.2**	**0.1**	**1.0**	**0.1**	**1.8**
Public and publicly guaranteed sector	1.1	0.2	0.1	1.0	0.1	1.8
Public sector	1.1	0.2	0.1	1.0	0.1	1.8
of which: General government	1.1	0.2	0.1	1.0	0.1	1.8
Private sector guaranteed by public sector	..	..	..	..	..	..
Private sector not guaranteed	..	..	..	..	..	..
Summary external debt stock by creditor type						
Long-term external debt stocks	**248.5**	**151.9**	**159.5**	**221.4**	**233.0**	**257.7**
Public and publicly guaranteed debt from:	248.5	151.9	159.5	221.4	233.0	257.7
Official creditors	248.5	151.9	159.5	221.4	233.0	257.7
Multilateral	201.6	53.2	54.2	54.0	68.0	76.7
of which: World Bank	115.5	12.9	13.3	12.7	12.3	16.7
Bilateral	46.9	98.7	105.2	167.4	165.0	181.0
Private creditors	..	..	..	..	..	0.0
Bondholders	..	..	..	..	..	..
Commercial banks and others	..	..	..	..	..	0.0
Private nonguaranteed debt from:	..	..	..	..	..	..
Bondholders	..	..	..	..	..	..
Commercial banks and others	..	..	..	..	..	..
Use of IMF credit	25.4	26.6	26.1	22.3	30.7	41.9
Net financial inflows						
Net debt inflows						
Use of IMF credit	2.4	-1.8	-2.0	-3.2	8.5	9.6
Long-term	-3.1	54.3	3.6	66.2	14.2	15.4
Official creditors	-3.1	54.3	3.6	66.2	14.2	15.4
Multilateral	-3.1	-3.1	-0.3	0.3	14.1	6.0
of which: World Bank	-1.7	-0.3	-0.3	-0.3	-0.3	3.5
Bilateral	..	57.4	3.9	65.9	0.1	9.4
Private creditors	..	..	..	..	..	0.0
Bondholders	..	..	..	..	..	..
Banks and others	..	..	..	..	..	0.0
Short-term	0.0	0.0	0.0	0.0	0.0	0.0
Net equity inflows						
Foreign direct investment	8.4	3.6	3.9	5.7	3.7	8.6
Portfolio equity	0.0	..	..	..	..	..
Debt ratios						
External debt stocks to exports (%)	306.7	155.4	137.2	154.9	175.9	385.1
External debt stocks to GNI (%)	30.7	17.7	17.2	20.7	22.7	24.5
Debt service to exports (%)	4.7	5.5	3.0	3.9	2.9	10.4
Short-term to external debt stocks (%)	1.6	0.8	0.6	0.5	0.7	0.4
Multilateral to external debt stocks (%)	72.4	29.6	29.1	22.0	25.6	25.5
Reserves to external debt stocks (%)	52.2	88.2	111.0	81.0	75.7	97.5
Gross national income (GNI)	907.1	1,018.2	1,083.4	1,185.4	1,171.0	1,227.3

CONGO, DEMOCRATIC REPUBLIC OF

(US$ million, unless otherwise indicated)

	2010	2016	2017	2018	2019	2020
Summary external debt data by debtor type						
Total external debt stocks	**6,137**	**5,022**	**5,084**	**4,956**	**5,618**	**6,137**
Use of IMF credit	1,110	989	954	839	1,130	1,511
Long-term external debt	4,592	3,817	4,004	4,023	4,279	4,496
Public and publicly guaranteed sector	4,592	3,817	4,004	4,023	4,279	4,496
Public sector	4,592	3,817	4,004	4,023	4,279	4,496
of which: General government	4,361	3,817	4,004	4,023	4,279	4,496
Private sector guaranteed by public sector	..	..	..	..	..	..
Private sector not guaranteed	..	..	..	..	..	..
Short-term external debt	435	215	126	94	209	131
Disbursements (long-term)	**78**	**65**	**348**	**233**	**480**	**277**
Public and publicly guaranteed sector	78	65	348	233	480	277
Public sector	78	65	348	233	480	277
of which: General government	78	65	348	233	480	277
Private sector guaranteed by public sector	..	..	..	..	..	..
Private sector not guaranteed	..	..	..	..	..	..
Principal repayments (long-term)	**89**	**271**	**182**	**180**	**184**	**160**
Public and publicly guaranteed sector	89	271	182	180	184	160
Public sector	89	271	182	180	184	160
of which: General government	77	271	182	180	184	160
Private sector guaranteed by public sector	..	..	..	..	..	..
Private sector not guaranteed	..	..	..	..	..	..
Interest payments (long-term)	**124**	**132**	**119**	**98**	**824**	**110**
Public and publicly guaranteed sector	124	132	119	98	824	110
Public sector	124	132	119	98	824	110
of which: General government	120	132	119	98	824	110
Private sector guaranteed by public sector	..	..	..	..	..	..
Private sector not guaranteed	..	..	..	..	..	..
Summary external debt stock by creditor type						
Long-term external debt stocks	**4,592**	**3,817**	**4,004**	**4,023**	**4,279**	**4,496**
Public and publicly guaranteed debt from:	4,592	3,817	4,004	4,023	4,279	4,496
Official creditors	4,514	3,816	4,003	3,993	4,177	4,361
Multilateral	2,585	1,724	1,995	2,037	2,122	2,290
of which: World Bank	849	827	942	1,098	1,288	1,521
Bilateral	1,929	2,091	2,008	1,956	2,055	2,071
Private creditors	77	2	1	30	102	135
Bondholders	..	..	..	..	..	..
Commercial banks and others	77	2	1	30	102	135
Private nonguaranteed debt from:	..	..	..	..	..	..
Bondholders	..	..	..	..	..	..
Commercial banks and others	..	..	..	..	..	..
Use of IMF credit	1,110	989	954	839	1,130	1,511
Net financial inflows						
Net debt inflows						
Use of IMF credit	19	-78	-92	-94	295	323
Long-term	-11	-206	166	53	296	116
Official creditors	-27	-197	166	37	224	83
Multilateral	1	-126	182	73	93	92
of which: World Bank	17	11	65	180	195	178
Bilateral	-27	-71	-16	-36	130	-8
Private creditors	16	-9	-1	16	72	33
Bondholders	..	..	..	..	..	..
Banks and others	16	-9	-1	16	72	33
Short-term	38	15	9	-33	116	-78
Net equity inflows						
Foreign direct investment	2,736	1,205	1,340	1,617	1,478	1,647
Portfolio equity	..	0	-10	-7	-30	-6
Debt ratios						
External debt stocks to exports (%)	69	42	44	31	37	43
External debt stocks to GNI (%)	30	14	14	11	11	13
Debt service to exports (%)	3	4	3	2	7	2
Short-term to external debt stocks (%)	7	4	2	2	4	2
Multilateral to external debt stocks (%)	42	34	39	41	38	37
Reserves to external debt stocks (%)	21	14	14	13	21	12
Gross national income (GNI)	20,655	36,345	36,946	45,550	48,962	48,596

CONGO, REPUBLIC OF

(US$ million, unless otherwise indicated)

	2010	2016	2017	2018	2019	2020
Summary external debt data by debtor type						
Total external debt stocks	**2,947**	**4,090**	**4,614**	**4,224**	**5,175**	**5,149**
Use of IMF credit	150	116	120	115	157	162
Long-term external debt	2,601	3,788	4,221	3,842	4,795	4,713
Public and publicly guaranteed sector	2,601	3,788	4,221	3,842	4,795	4,707
Public sector	2,601	3,788	4,221	3,842	4,795	4,707
of which: General government	2,601	3,788	4,221	3,842	4,795	4,707
Private sector guaranteed by public sector	..	..	..	..	..	..
Private sector not guaranteed	..	..	..	..	..	6
Short-term external debt	197	187	273	266	223	274
Disbursements (long-term)	**874**	**344**	**693**	**115**	**1,332**	**187**
Public and publicly guaranteed sector	874	344	693	115	1,332	181
Public sector	874	344	693	115	1,332	181
of which: General government	835	344	693	115	1,332	181
Private sector guaranteed by public sector	..	..	..	..	..	..
Private sector not guaranteed	..	..	..	..	..	6
Principal repayments (long-term)	**124**	**271**	**304**	**355**	**414**	**560**
Public and publicly guaranteed sector	124	271	304	355	414	560
Public sector	124	271	304	355	414	560
of which: General government	124	271	304	355	414	560
Private sector guaranteed by public sector	..	..	..	..	..	..
Private sector not guaranteed	..	..	..	..	..	..
Interest payments (long-term)	**28**	**35**	**35**	**78**	**86**	**95**
Public and publicly guaranteed sector	28	35	35	78	86	95
Public sector	28	35	35	78	86	95
of which: General government	28	35	35	78	86	95
Private sector guaranteed by public sector	..	..	..	..	..	..
Private sector not guaranteed	..	..	..	..	..	0
Summary external debt stock by creditor type						
Long-term external debt stocks	**2,601**	**3,788**	**4,221**	**3,842**	**4,795**	**4,713**
Public and publicly guaranteed debt from:	2,601	3,788	4,221	3,842	4,795	4,707
Official creditors	1,174	2,655	3,273	3,023	4,075	3,920
Multilateral	209	259	687	675	894	1,002
of which: World Bank	84	122	153	192	243	342
Bilateral	965	2,396	2,586	2,348	3,181	2,918
Private creditors	1,426	1,133	948	820	720	787
Bondholders	454	377	350	322	295	268
Commercial banks and others	973	756	598	497	425	519
Private nonguaranteed debt from:	..	..	..	..	..	6
Bondholders	..	..	..	..	..	..
Commercial banks and others	..	..	..	..	..	6
Use of IMF credit	150	116	120	115	157	162
Net financial inflows						
Net debt inflows						
Use of IMF credit	2	-4	-2	-2	43	-1
Long-term	750	73	389	-240	918	-373
Official creditors	443	178	517	-99	1,018	-248
Multilateral	12	51	407	-2	223	58
of which: World Bank	2	16	23	43	53	87
Bilateral	431	127	110	-98	795	-306
Private creditors	307	-105	-127	-140	-100	-125
Bondholders	0	-23	-27	-27	-27	-27
Banks and others	307	-82	-100	-113	-73	-98
Short-term	-40	-266	135	-63	-47	54
Net equity inflows						
Foreign direct investment	670	-232	4,417	4,315	3,366	4,016
Portfolio equity	0	..	..	..	..	..
Debt ratios						
External debt stocks to exports (%)	33	89	..	..	..	..
External debt stocks to GNI (%)	24	42	48	36	52	55
Debt service to exports (%)	2	7	..	..	..	..
Short-term to external debt stocks (%)	7	5	6	6	4	5
Multilateral to external debt stocks (%)	7	6	15	16	17	19
Reserves to external debt stocks (%)	151	17	8	10	19	..
Gross national income (GNI)	12,210	9,768	9,551	11,623	9,961	9,313

COSTA RICA

(US$ million, unless otherwise indicated)

	2010	2016	2017	2018	2019	2020
Summary external debt data by debtor type						
Total external debt stocks	**8,154**	**25,563**	**25,616**	**28,369**	**29,801**	**31,288**
Use of IMF credit	241	210	223	218	216	757
Long-term external debt	5,482	22,797	22,855	24,782	26,829	26,589
Public and publicly guaranteed sector	3,822	11,054	11,037	11,941	13,392	12,570
Public sector	3,822	11,054	11,037	11,941	13,392	12,570
of which: General government	2,772	6,142	6,264	6,581	8,457	8,464
Private sector guaranteed by public sector	..	..	..	..	..	..
Private sector not guaranteed	1,660	11,744	11,817	12,841	13,437	14,019
Short-term external debt	2,431	2,555	2,538	3,370	2,755	3,942
Disbursements (long-term)	**1,455**	**3,991**	**1,985**	**4,418**	**3,569**	**1,873**
Public and publicly guaranteed sector	928	1,351	599	1,701	2,486	498
Public sector	928	1,351	599	1,701	2,486	498
of which: General government	596	434	248	449	2,006	383
Private sector guaranteed by public sector	..	..	..	..	..	..
Private sector not guaranteed	528	2,640	1,386	2,716	1,083	1,375
Principal repayments (long-term)	**617**	**1,721**	**1,797**	**2,024**	**1,959**	**2,139**
Public and publicly guaranteed sector	342	444	485	897	1,073	1,325
Public sector	342	444	485	897	1,073	1,325
of which: General government	146	134	135	127	131	381
Private sector guaranteed by public sector	..	..	..	..	..	..
Private sector not guaranteed	275	1,277	1,312	1,127	886	814
Interest payments (long-term)	**313**	**1,055**	**1,109**	**1,261**	**1,123**	**767**
Public and publicly guaranteed sector	213	601	638	687	674	310
Public sector	213	601	638	687	674	310
of which: General government	161	356	364	368	375	176
Private sector guaranteed by public sector	..	..	..	..	..	..
Private sector not guaranteed	100	454	471	574	448	457
Summary external debt stock by creditor type						
Long-term external debt stocks	**5,482**	**22,797**	**22,855**	**24,782**	**26,829**	**26,589**
Public and publicly guaranteed debt from:	3,822	11,054	11,037	11,941	13,392	12,570
Official creditors	2,196	3,176	3,230	4,662	4,910	4,918
Multilateral	1,767	2,751	2,777	4,199	4,443	4,456
of which: World Bank	570	736	788	903	955	1,021
Bilateral	430	426	453	464	466	462
Private creditors	1,626	7,877	7,807	7,278	8,482	7,652
Bondholders	1,310	6,251	6,250	6,250	7,600	6,983
Commercial banks and others	316	1,626	1,557	1,028	882	670
Private nonguaranteed debt from:	1,660	11,744	11,817	12,841	13,437	14,019
Bondholders	..	1,850	2,150	2,100	2,100	2,100
Commercial banks and others	1,660	9,894	9,667	10,741	11,337	11,919
Use of IMF credit	241	210	223	218	216	757
Net financial inflows						
Net debt inflows						
Use of IMF credit	..	..	..	..	..	515
Long-term	839	2,270	188	2,394	1,610	-266
Official creditors	590	519	184	1,333	209	2
Multilateral	579	414	171	1,321	208	29
of which: World Bank	512	135	52	115	52	71
Bilateral	11	105	13	12	1	-26
Private creditors	249	1,751	3	1,061	1,401	-268
Bondholders	0	1,001	299	-50	1,350	-617
Banks and others	249	750	-296	1,111	50	349
Short-term	188	-49	-16	831	-614	1,186
Net equity inflows						
Foreign direct investment	1,508	1,468	2,352	2,221	2,145	1,592
Portfolio equity	8	42	53	54	55	57
Debt ratios						
External debt stocks to exports (%)	64	134	129	129	131	155
External debt stocks to GNI (%)	22	45	45	48	49	54
Debt service to exports (%)	8	15	15	16	14	15
Short-term to external debt stocks (%)	30	10	10	12	9	13
Multilateral to external debt stocks (%)	22	11	11	15	15	14
Reserves to external debt stocks (%)	57	30	28	26	30	23
Gross national income (GNI)	36,450	56,365	57,353	59,010	60,212	58,036

CÔTE D'IVOIRE

(US$ million, unless otherwise indicated)

	2010	2016	2017	2018	2019	2020
Summary external debt data by debtor type						
Total external debt stocks	**11,703**	**11,457**	**13,449**	**16,185**	**19,816**	**25,073**
Use of IMF credit	861	1,495	1,738	1,814	1,915	3,047
Long-term external debt	10,431	9,693	11,683	14,233	17,012	20,967
Public and publicly guaranteed sector	9,413	8,369	10,445	13,221	15,733	19,976
Public sector	9,413	8,369	10,445	13,221	15,733	19,976
of which: General government	9,412	8,369	10,445	12,673	15,182	19,014
Private sector guaranteed by public sector	..	..	..	..	..	..
Private sector not guaranteed	1,018	1,324	1,238	1,011	1,279	991
Short-term external debt	411	269	28	138	890	1,059
Disbursements (long-term)	**599**	**1,237**	**3,232**	**3,867**	**5,080**	**4,307**
Public and publicly guaranteed sector	244	897	3,091	3,747	4,508	4,307
Public sector	244	897	3,091	3,747	4,508	4,307
of which: General government	244	897	3,091	3,182	4,495	3,938
Private sector guaranteed by public sector	..	..	..	..	..	..
Private sector not guaranteed	355	341	141	120	572	..
Principal repayments (long-term)	**623**	**1,096**	**1,730**	**1,036**	**2,247**	**1,536**
Public and publicly guaranteed sector	438	726	1,418	702	1,946	1,225
Public sector	438	726	1,418	702	1,946	1,225
of which: General government	438	726	1,418	702	1,946	1,189
Private sector guaranteed by public sector	..	..	..	..	..	..
Private sector not guaranteed	185	370	312	334	302	311
Interest payments (long-term)	**114**	**402**	**399**	**453**	**556**	**699**
Public and publicly guaranteed sector	58	315	329	407	518	671
Public sector	58	315	329	407	518	671
of which: General government	58	315	329	406	517	642
Private sector guaranteed by public sector	..	..	..	..	..	..
Private sector not guaranteed	56	87	70	47	38	28
Summary external debt stock by creditor type						
Long-term external debt stocks	**10,431**	**9,693**	**11,683**	**14,233**	**17,012**	**20,967**
Public and publicly guaranteed debt from:	9,413	8,369	10,445	13,221	15,733	19,976
Official creditors	9,301	4,108	5,007	5,187	5,957	7,925
Multilateral	2,373	1,021	1,582	2,011	2,592	3,972
of which: World Bank	1,763	522	781	883	1,204	1,882
Bilateral	6,928	3,087	3,425	3,176	3,364	3,953
Private creditors	112	4,261	5,438	8,034	9,776	12,051
Bondholders	0	4,219	5,398	7,230	7,589	8,532
Commercial banks and others	112	43	40	804	2,187	3,519
Private nonguaranteed debt from:	1,018	1,324	1,238	1,011	1,279	991
Bondholders	..	..	..	..	..	..
Commercial banks and others	1,018	1,324	1,238	1,011	1,279	991
Use of IMF credit	861	1,495	1,738	1,814	1,915	3,047
Net financial inflows						
Net debt inflows						
Use of IMF credit	44	33	150	119	111	1,019
Long-term	-25	142	1,502	2,831	2,832	2,771
Official creditors	-220	43	540	328	765	1,552
Multilateral	17	152	450	497	513	1,095
of which: World Bank	-26	140	205	132	236	536
Bilateral	-237	-109	90	-169	252	457
Private creditors	196	99	962	2,503	2,067	1,219
Bondholders	..	136	1,136	1,928	404	478
Banks and others	196	-38	-173	575	1,663	741
Short-term	20	269	-241	110	752	169
Net equity inflows						
Foreign direct investment	371	531	644	590	618	509
Portfolio equity	2	8	24	15	12	..
Debt ratios						
External debt stocks to exports (%)	91	95	102	120	140	..
External debt stocks to GNI (%)	49	24	27	29	35	42
Debt service to exports (%)	6	13	17	12	21	..
Short-term to external debt stocks (%)	4	2	0	1	4	4
Multilateral to external debt stocks (%)	20	9	12	12	13	16
Reserves to external debt stocks (%)	31	..	..	..	..	..
Gross national income (GNI)	23,996	46,888	50,052	55,809	56,976	59,585

DJIBOUTI

(US$ million, unless otherwise indicated)

	2010	2016	2017	2018	2019	2020
Summary external debt data by debtor type						
Total external debt stocks	**768.5**	**1,702.2**	**2,267.0**	**2,321.4**	**2,552.6**	**2,678.7**
Use of IMF credit	35.5	45.8	44.0	36.7	31.6	72.3
Long-term external debt	611.6	1,602.8	1,944.9	2,045.0	2,145.5	2,353.5
Public and publicly guaranteed sector	611.6	1,602.8	1,944.9	2,045.0	2,145.5	2,353.5
Public sector	611.6	1,602.8	1,944.9	2,045.0	2,145.5	2,353.5
of which: General government	501.8	713.6	914.3	963.6	1,036.0	1,097.5
Private sector guaranteed by public sector	..	..	..	..	..	..
Private sector not guaranteed	..	..	..	..	..	..
Short-term external debt	121.5	53.7	278.1	239.6	375.4	252.9
Disbursements (long-term)	**35.2**	**473.2**	**335.9**	**140.7**	**136.3**	**213.7**
Public and publicly guaranteed sector	35.2	473.2	335.9	140.7	136.3	213.7
Public sector	35.2	473.2	335.9	140.7	136.3	213.7
of which: General government	27.4	244.0	194.6	75.7	94.1	59.5
Private sector guaranteed by public sector	..	..	..	..	..	..
Private sector not guaranteed	..	..	..	..	..	..
Principal repayments (long-term)	**22.4**	**31.0**	**25.1**	**27.2**	**34.7**	**28.3**
Public and publicly guaranteed sector	22.4	31.0	25.1	27.2	34.7	28.3
Public sector	22.4	31.0	25.1	27.2	34.7	28.3
of which: General government	12.6	23.4	18.3	17.4	21.7	15.8
Private sector guaranteed by public sector	..	..	..	..	..	..
Private sector not guaranteed	..	..	..	..	..	..
Interest payments (long-term)	**8.2**	**25.3**	**35.7**	**32.2**	**29.1**	**25.1**
Public and publicly guaranteed sector	8.2	25.3	35.7	32.2	29.1	25.1
Public sector	8.2	25.3	35.7	32.2	29.1	25.1
of which: General government	5.5	6.2	11.9	13.2	16.7	13.0
Private sector guaranteed by public sector	..	..	..	..	..	..
Private sector not guaranteed	..	..	..	..	..	..
Summary external debt stock by creditor type						
Long-term external debt stocks	**611.6**	**1,602.8**	**1,944.9**	**2,045.0**	**2,145.5**	**2,353.5**
Public and publicly guaranteed debt from:	611.6	1,602.8	1,944.9	2,045.0	2,145.5	2,353.5
Official creditors	593.2	1,600.5	1,942.8	2,042.9	2,143.4	2,351.4
Multilateral	406.1	493.3	535.4	572.5	633.7	682.4
of which: World Bank	154.7	127.9	143.6	152.2	161.3	191.3
Bilateral	187.1	1,107.2	1,407.4	1,470.4	1,509.7	1,669.0
Private creditors	18.4	2.3	2.1	2.1	2.1	2.1
Bondholders	..	..	..	..	..	..
Commercial banks and others	18.4	2.3	2.1	2.1	2.1	2.1
Private nonguaranteed debt from:	..	..	..	..	..	..
Bondholders	..	..	..	..	..	..
Commercial banks and others	..	..	..	..	..	..
Use of IMF credit	35.5	45.8	44.0	36.7	31.6	72.3
Net financial inflows						
Net debt inflows						
Use of IMF credit	-3.3	-1.9	-4.4	-6.3	-4.9	38.1
Long-term	12.8	442.2	310.9	113.5	101.6	185.4
Official creditors	15.2	442.8	311.1	113.5	101.6	185.4
Multilateral	7.7	43.3	23.6	43.9	62.3	35.1
of which: World Bank	-0.8	2.0	7.8	12.1	10.0	22.5
Bilateral	7.5	399.5	287.5	69.6	39.2	150.4
Private creditors	-2.4	-0.7	-0.2	0.0	0.0	0.0
Bondholders	..	..	..	..	..	..
Banks and others	-2.4	-0.7	-0.2	0.0	0.0	0.0
Short-term	3.0	49.1	220.4	-56.0	108.6	-159.5
Net equity inflows						
Foreign direct investment	36.5	160.0	164.9	170.0	175.0	158.2
Portfolio equity	..	0.0	0.0	0.0	0.0	219.5
Debt ratios						
External debt stocks to exports (%)	169.4	62.1	54.1	50.2	48.8	71.3
External debt stocks to GNI (%)	67.1	62.0	78.9	74.6	79.0	81.4
Debt service to exports (%)	7.9	2.1	1.7	1.6	1.5	1.7
Short-term to external debt stocks (%)	15.8	3.2	12.3	10.3	14.7	9.4
Multilateral to external debt stocks (%)	52.8	29.0	23.6	24.7	24.8	25.5
Reserves to external debt stocks (%)	32.4	23.9	24.5	19.6	19.7	25.6
Gross national income (GNI)	1,146.0	2,745.4	2,874.2	3,113.7	3,230.8	3,288.9

DOMINICA

(US$ million, unless otherwise indicated)

	2010	2016	2017	2018	2019	2020
Summary external debt data by debtor type						
Total external debt stocks	**271**	**300**	**300**	**283**	**283**	**329**
Use of IMF credit	30	24	24	22	21	36
Long-term external debt	236	267	264	248	251	276
Public and publicly guaranteed sector	236	267	264	248	251	276
Public sector	236	267	264	248	251	276
of which: General government	214	243	243	229	231	259
Private sector guaranteed by public sector	..	..	..	..	..	..
Private sector not guaranteed	..	..	..	..	..	..
Short-term external debt	6	9	11	13	12	18
Disbursements (long-term)	**30**	**4**	**11**	**5**	**22**	**38**
Public and publicly guaranteed sector	30	4	11	5	22	38
Public sector	30	4	11	5	22	38
of which: General government	30	2	10	4	19	38
Private sector guaranteed by public sector	..	..	..	..	..	..
Private sector not guaranteed	..	..	..	..	..	..
Principal repayments (long-term)	**10**	**18**	**20**	**18**	**19**	**19**
Public and publicly guaranteed sector	10	18	20	18	19	19
Public sector	10	18	20	18	19	19
of which: General government	7	15	15	15	16	17
Private sector guaranteed by public sector	..	..	..	..	..	..
Private sector not guaranteed	..	..	..	..	..	..
Interest payments (long-term)	**5**	**7**	**8**	**9**	**7**	**6**
Public and publicly guaranteed sector	5	7	8	9	7	6
Public sector	5	7	8	9	7	6
of which: General government	4	7	7	8	6	6
Private sector guaranteed by public sector	..	..	..	..	..	..
Private sector not guaranteed	..	..	..	..	..	..
Summary external debt stock by creditor type						
Long-term external debt stocks	**236**	**267**	**264**	**248**	**251**	**276**
Public and publicly guaranteed debt from:	236	267	264	248	251	276
Official creditors	162	209	207	193	183	214
Multilateral	117	127	129	124	122	153
of which: World Bank	28	24	33	34	36	51
Bilateral	45	81	78	69	61	60
Private creditors	74	58	57	55	68	62
Bondholders	57	29	30	30	45	42
Commercial banks and others	16	30	28	26	23	20
Private nonguaranteed debt from:	..	..	..	..	..	..
Bondholders	..	..	..	..	..	..
Commercial banks and others	..	..	..	..	..	..
Use of IMF credit	30	24	24	22	21	36
Net financial inflows						
Net debt inflows						
Use of IMF credit	-1	-2	-1	-2	-1	14
Long-term	20	-14	-9	-13	4	19
Official creditors	20	-12	-8	-11	-9	25
Multilateral	1	-5	0	-4	-2	30
of which: World Bank	0	-1	7	2	2	14
Bilateral	19	-7	-8	-7	-7	-5
Private creditors	0	-2	-1	-2	13	-6
Bondholders	0	0	1	..	15	-3
Banks and others	0	-2	-2	-2	-3	-3
Short-term	0	0	2	2	-2	6
Net equity inflows						
Foreign direct investment	10	42	25	14	60	26
Portfolio equity	..	0	0	0	0	0
Debt ratios						
External debt stocks to exports (%)	151	111	134	164	132	292
External debt stocks to GNI (%)	56	54	57	51	50	68
Debt service to exports (%)	9	10	13	17	12	24
Short-term to external debt stocks (%)	2	3	4	5	4	5
Multilateral to external debt stocks (%)	43	42	43	44	43	47
Reserves to external debt stocks (%)	28	74	71	68	59	54
Gross national income (GNI)	484	555	522	550	565	484

DOMINICAN REPUBLIC

(US$ million, unless otherwise indicated)

	2010	2016	2017	2018	2019	2020
Summary external debt data by debtor type						
Total external debt stocks	**13,499**	**28,291**	**31,156**	**33,564**	**38,396**	**44,468**
Use of IMF credit	1,461	281	297	290	289	988
Long-term external debt	10,283	24,958	28,857	31,086	35,593	41,308
Public and publicly guaranteed sector	9,441	17,186	20,214	23,075	27,238	34,061
Public sector	9,437	17,185	20,213	23,074	27,237	34,061
of which: General government	8,700	17,044	20,124	23,026	27,215	34,043
Private sector guaranteed by public sector	3	1	1	1	0	0
Private sector not guaranteed	843	7,772	8,643	8,011	8,355	7,246
Short-term external debt	1,754	3,053	2,001	2,187	2,515	2,172
Disbursements (long-term)	**2,111**	**3,724**	**5,055**	**4,620**	**5,004**	**9,777**
Public and publicly guaranteed sector	2,111	2,259	3,780	3,651	4,940	9,777
Public sector	2,111	2,259	3,780	3,651	4,940	9,777
of which: General government	2,107	2,259	3,780	3,651	4,940	9,777
Private sector guaranteed by public sector	0	..	0	0	0	..
Private sector not guaranteed	..	1,465	1,275	969	64	..
Principal repayments (long-term)	**799**	**2,075**	**1,961**	**1,422**	**1,846**	**4,620**
Public and publicly guaranteed sector	798	861	808	752	677	2,823
Public sector	798	861	807	752	677	2,823
of which: General government	688	770	748	714	652	2,818
Private sector guaranteed by public sector	1	0	0	0	0	0
Private sector not guaranteed	0	1,214	1,154	670	1,169	1,797
Interest payments (long-term)	**444**	**1,205**	**1,012**	**1,541**	**1,922**	**2,018**
Public and publicly guaranteed sector	336	922	716	1,069	1,395	1,676
Public sector	336	922	716	1,069	1,395	1,676
of which: General government	309	917	713	1,067	1,394	1,676
Private sector guaranteed by public sector	0	0	0	0	0	0
Private sector not guaranteed	108	282	296	472	528	342
Summary external debt stock by creditor type						
Long-term external debt stocks	**10,283**	**24,958**	**28,857**	**31,086**	**35,593**	**41,308**
Public and publicly guaranteed debt from:	9,441	17,186	20,214	23,075	27,238	34,061
Official creditors	6,355	5,818	5,710	5,793	6,069	7,095
Multilateral	3,079	4,439	4,454	4,704	5,092	5,905
of which: World Bank	872	933	923	923	939	1,183
Bilateral	3,276	1,379	1,256	1,089	977	1,190
Private creditors	3,086	11,368	14,504	17,282	21,169	26,966
Bondholders	1,134	9,812	13,200	16,296	20,430	26,359
Commercial banks and others	1,952	1,556	1,304	986	740	608
Private nonguaranteed debt from:	843	7,772	8,643	8,011	8,355	7,246
Bondholders	843	1,945	1,945	1,945	1,395	707
Commercial banks and others	0	5,827	6,698	6,066	6,959	6,539
Use of IMF credit	1,461	281	297	290	289	988
Net financial inflows						
Net debt inflows						
Use of IMF credit	383	-114	..	..	..	665
Long-term	1,312	1,650	3,094	3,197	3,158	5,157
Official creditors	869	157	-124	90	278	1,014
Multilateral	469	291	10	253	388	812
of which: World Bank	116	1	-10	0	16	243
Bilateral	400	-134	-134	-163	-110	201
Private creditors	443	1,493	3,218	3,108	2,880	4,143
Bondholders	645	1,870	3,400	3,108	3,656	5,408
Banks and others	-202	-377	-182	0	-775	-1,264
Short-term	-1	-127	-1,051	186	328	-345
Net equity inflows						
Foreign direct investment	1,470	2,340	3,733	2,677	2,796	2,792
Portfolio equity	0	0	0	0	0	0
Debt ratios						
External debt stocks to exports (%)	106	152	160	162	181	300
External debt stocks to GNI (%)	26	39	41	41	45	59
Debt service to exports (%)	11	19	16	15	18	45
Short-term to external debt stocks (%)	13	11	6	7	7	5
Multilateral to external debt stocks (%)	23	16	14	14	13	13
Reserves to external debt stocks (%)	29	22	22	23	23	24
Gross national income (GNI)	51,932	72,451	76,204	81,863	84,871	74,984

ECUADOR

(US$ million, unless otherwise indicated)

	2010	2016	2017	2018	2019	2020
Summary external debt data by debtor type						
Total external debt stocks	**15,377**	**35,378**	**41,159**	**44,944**	**51,883**	**56,191**
Use of IMF credit	444	739	783	765	2,114	6,781
Long-term external debt	13,869	33,768	39,281	43,102	48,860	48,468
Public and publicly guaranteed sector	8,787	25,571	31,629	35,481	38,394	37,816
Public sector	8,759	25,546	31,606	35,461	38,377	37,801
of which: General government	8,260	24,019	29,446	33,859	37,438	37,079
Private sector guaranteed by public sector	28	25	23	20	18	15
Private sector not guaranteed	5,082	8,196	7,652	7,621	10,465	10,652
Short-term external debt	1,064	871	1,094	1,077	910	942
Disbursements (long-term)	**2,977**	**10,737**	**9,998**	**10,354**	**12,307**	**7,610**
Public and publicly guaranteed sector	2,307	7,326	8,895	7,153	6,875	3,689
Public sector	2,304	7,326	8,895	7,153	6,875	3,689
of which: General government	2,253	6,502	7,859	6,963	6,794	3,497
Private sector guaranteed by public sector	2	..	0	0	0	..
Private sector not guaranteed	670	3,411	1,103	3,201	5,432	3,922
Principal repayments (long-term)	**1,259**	**3,861**	**4,559**	**6,443**	**6,508**	**7,551**
Public and publicly guaranteed sector	636	1,859	2,906	3,202	3,919	3,816
Public sector	636	1,857	2,904	3,200	3,917	3,813
of which: General government	587	1,489	2,496	2,452	3,173	3,402
Private sector guaranteed by public sector	0	2	2	2	2	2
Private sector not guaranteed	623	2,002	1,653	3,241	2,588	3,735
Interest payments (long-term)	**470**	**1,507**	**2,032**	**2,663**	**2,792**	**1,517**
Public and publicly guaranteed sector	331	1,200	1,753	2,238	2,385	1,173
Public sector	330	1,199	1,752	2,237	2,384	1,171
of which: General government	315	1,100	1,641	2,108	2,303	1,128
Private sector guaranteed by public sector	1	1	1	1	1	1
Private sector not guaranteed	139	306	279	425	407	344
Summary external debt stock by creditor type						
Long-term external debt stocks	**13,869**	**33,768**	**39,281**	**43,102**	**48,860**	**48,468**
Public and publicly guaranteed debt from:	8,787	25,571	31,629	35,481	38,394	37,816
Official creditors	7,547	16,742	16,785	17,269	18,117	19,672
Multilateral	5,207	8,202	8,707	9,864	11,079	13,295
of which: World Bank	456	246	399	617	1,251	2,596
Bilateral	2,340	8,540	8,078	7,405	7,038	6,377
Private creditors	1,240	8,830	14,844	18,211	20,278	18,145
Bondholders	1,082	6,114	12,565	15,250	18,307	17,694
Commercial banks and others	159	2,716	2,278	2,961	1,970	451
Private nonguaranteed debt from:	5,082	8,196	7,652	7,621	10,465	10,652
Bondholders	..	..	..	..	..	..
Commercial banks and others	5,082	8,196	7,652	7,621	10,465	10,652
Use of IMF credit	444	739	783	765	2,114	6,781
Net financial inflows						
Net debt inflows						
Use of IMF credit	..	364	0	0	1,353	4,428
Long-term	1,718	6,875	5,439	3,911	5,800	59
Official creditors	1,727	2,637	-11	549	872	1,497
Multilateral	822	649	519	1,181	1,222	2,214
of which: World Bank	-87	-11	153	218	634	1,345
Bilateral	904	1,988	-530	-632	-350	-717
Private creditors	-9	4,238	5,450	3,362	4,928	-1,437
Bondholders	-16	2,717	6,451	2,685	3,057	-77
Banks and others	7	1,522	-1,002	677	1,871	-1,360
Short-term	-304	-206	207	-33	-180	197
Net equity inflows						
Foreign direct investment	478	879	682	702	600	994
Portfolio equity	0	6	4	6	2	1
Debt ratios						
External debt stocks to exports (%)	78	175	181	175	197	251
External debt stocks to GNI (%)	22	36	40	43	49	59
Debt service to exports (%)	9	27	29	36	36	42
Short-term to external debt stocks (%)	7	2	3	2	2	2
Multilateral to external debt stocks (%)	34	23	21	22	21	24
Reserves to external debt stocks (%)	9	11	4	4	4	9
Gross national income (GNI)	68,518	98,125	101,978	104,733	105,080	95,951

EGYPT, ARAB REPUBLIC OF

(US$ million, unless otherwise indicated)

	2010	2016	2017	2018	2019	2020
Summary external debt data by debtor type						
Total external debt stocks	**36,775**	**69,164**	**84,722**	**100,186**	**115,080**	**131,580**
Use of IMF credit	1,384	3,856	7,401	9,220	13,130	20,362
Long-term external debt	32,242	53,362	66,193	80,625	90,665	99,259
Public and publicly guaranteed sector	32,189	53,206	65,787	80,179	90,305	98,857
Public sector	31,825	53,129	65,729	80,153	90,305	98,857
of which: General government	28,267	32,200	42,283	51,239	60,963	67,119
Private sector guaranteed by public sector	364	77	58	26	0	..
Private sector not guaranteed	54	157	406	446	360	402
Short-term external debt	3,149	11,945	11,128	10,341	11,284	11,959
Disbursements (long-term)	**3,616**	**14,675**	**15,850**	**20,287**	**15,322**	**14,797**
Public and publicly guaranteed sector	3,611	14,515	15,552	20,161	15,251	14,604
Public sector	3,609	14,515	15,552	20,161	15,251	14,604
of which: General government	3,302	6,280	11,927	11,302	12,329	10,184
Private sector guaranteed by public sector	2	..	..	..	..	..
Private sector not guaranteed	5	160	298	126	71	193
Principal repayments (long-term)	**2,164**	**5,106**	**4,622**	**5,119**	**4,632**	**8,024**
Public and publicly guaranteed sector	2,139	5,102	4,575	5,032	4,476	7,874
Public sector	2,058	5,071	4,547	5,002	4,451	7,874
of which: General government	1,678	3,987	2,704	1,994	2,115	5,140
Private sector guaranteed by public sector	81	31	27	30	26	..
Private sector not guaranteed	25	3	48	87	156	151
Interest payments (long-term)	**770**	**1,027**	**1,579**	**2,220**	**3,403**	**3,114**
Public and publicly guaranteed sector	769	1,026	1,565	2,204	3,384	3,102
Public sector	755	1,024	1,564	2,203	3,384	3,102
of which: General government	655	785	1,105	1,616	2,223	2,120
Private sector guaranteed by public sector	14	1	1	1	1	..
Private sector not guaranteed	1	2	14	16	19	12
Summary external debt stock by creditor type						
Long-term external debt stocks	**32,242**	**53,362**	**66,193**	**80,625**	**90,665**	**99,259**
Public and publicly guaranteed debt from:	32,189	53,206	65,787	80,179	90,305	98,857
Official creditors	28,004	47,544	52,767	55,970	57,636	62,578
Multilateral	9,293	15,846	18,876	20,119	21,508	25,558
of which: World Bank	3,881	7,114	8,435	9,930	11,250	11,093
Bilateral	18,712	31,698	33,891	35,851	36,128	37,020
Private creditors	4,184	5,662	13,020	24,209	32,669	36,279
Bondholders	3,333	3,600	10,000	15,800	23,273	26,304
Commercial banks and others	851	2,062	3,020	8,409	9,396	9,975
Private nonguaranteed debt from:	54	157	406	446	360	402
Bondholders	..	..	..	..	..	..
Commercial banks and others	54	157	406	446	360	402
Use of IMF credit	1,384	3,856	7,401	9,220	13,130	20,362
Net financial inflows						
Net debt inflows						
Use of IMF credit	..	2,738	3,229	2,029	3,959	6,468
Long-term	1,452	9,570	11,227	15,168	10,690	6,772
Official creditors	-189	10,020	3,772	3,790	1,866	3,675
Multilateral	755	4,304	2,562	1,426	1,454	3,705
of which: World Bank	649	1,545	1,289	1,507	1,321	733
Bilateral	-944	5,716	1,210	2,364	411	-29
Private creditors	1,641	-450	7,455	11,379	8,824	3,097
Bondholders	1,500	-1,250	6,400	5,868	7,887	2,646
Banks and others	141	800	1,055	5,511	937	451
Short-term	588	7,521	-817	-787	943	675
Net equity inflows						
Foreign direct investment	6,386	8,107	7,409	8,141	9,010	5,852
Portfolio equity	1,724	610	224	220	-12	-1,997
Debt ratios						
External debt stocks to exports (%)	74	203	194	191	211	324
External debt stocks to GNI (%)	17	21	37	41	39	37
Debt service to exports (%)	6	20	15	15	16	29
Short-term to external debt stocks (%)	9	17	13	10	10	9
Multilateral to external debt stocks (%)	25	23	22	20	19	19
Reserves to external debt stocks (%)	91	30	39	39	35	26
Gross national income (GNI)	214,619	327,970	231,165	243,433	292,071	351,715

EL SALVADOR

(US$ million, unless otherwise indicated)

	2010	2016	2017	2018	2019	2020
Summary external debt data by debtor type						
Total external debt stocks	**11,496**	**16,567**	**17,179**	**16,725**	**17,379**	**18,334**
Use of IMF credit	252	220	233	228	227	650
Long-term external debt	10,408	13,814	14,903	14,426	14,939	15,813
Public and publicly guaranteed sector	6,839	8,710	9,489	9,505	9,856	10,645
Public sector	6,836	8,710	9,489	9,505	9,856	10,645
of which: General government	6,257	7,965	8,655	8,727	9,063	9,780
Private sector guaranteed by public sector	2	0	0	0	..	..
Private sector not guaranteed	3,569	5,103	5,414	4,921	5,083	5,167
Short-term external debt	836	2,533	2,043	2,070	2,214	1,871
Disbursements (long-term)	**1,455**	**1,029**	**3,513**	**3,211**	**5,283**	**5,297**
Public and publicly guaranteed sector	1,107	410	978	588	1,419	1,378
Public sector	1,107	410	978	588	1,419	1,378
of which: General government	943	130	748	496	1,266	1,191
Private sector guaranteed by public sector	..	..	..	..	..	..
Private sector not guaranteed	348	619	2,535	2,623	3,865	3,918
Principal repayments (long-term)	**605**	**693**	**2,995**	**2,879**	**4,873**	**4,205**
Public and publicly guaranteed sector	456	455	434	436	1,179	421
Public sector	456	455	434	436	1,179	421
of which: General government	242	284	292	290	1,039	304
Private sector guaranteed by public sector	0	0	0	0	..	..
Private sector not guaranteed	149	238	2,561	2,443	3,694	3,785
Interest payments (long-term)	**495**	**660**	**768**	**589**	**684**	**927**
Public and publicly guaranteed sector	380	514	547	589	684	625
Public sector	380	514	547	589	684	625
of which: General government	355	483	511	539	632	577
Private sector guaranteed by public sector	0	0	0	0	..	..
Private sector not guaranteed	115	145	221	..	..	302
Summary external debt stock by creditor type						
Long-term external debt stocks	**10,408**	**13,814**	**14,903**	**14,426**	**14,939**	**15,813**
Public and publicly guaranteed debt from:	6,839	8,710	9,489	9,505	9,856	10,645
Official creditors	4,208	4,229	4,224	4,367	4,396	4,538
Multilateral	3,549	3,804	3,804	3,996	4,049	4,158
of which: World Bank	922	912	906	876	831	786
Bilateral	659	425	420	371	347	381
Private creditors	2,631	4,481	5,265	5,138	5,460	6,107
Bondholders	2,599	4,438	5,238	5,109	5,423	6,072
Commercial banks and others	32	43	27	29	37	35
Private nonguaranteed debt from:	3,569	5,103	5,414	4,921	5,083	5,167
Bondholders	..	38	38	38	12	0
Commercial banks and others	3,569	5,065	5,376	4,883	5,071	5,167
Use of IMF credit	252	220	233	228	227	650
Net financial inflows						
Net debt inflows						
Use of IMF credit	..	..	..	..	..	400
Long-term	850	336	518	331	410	1,092
Official creditors	319	-44	-26	148	30	124
Multilateral	364	-37	-2	194	54	106
of which: World Bank	345	-9	0	-31	-45	-45
Bilateral	-45	-7	-25	-46	-24	18
Private creditors	531	380	544	183	381	967
Bondholders	400	0	589	0	196	838
Banks and others	131	380	-44	183	185	129
Short-term	-27	515	-490	27	143	-342
Net equity inflows						
Foreign direct investment	282	415	844	129	576	21
Portfolio equity	0	0	0	0	0	0
Debt ratios						
External debt stocks to exports (%)	229	237	233	215	211	284
External debt stocks to GNI (%)	64	72	73	68	68	79
Debt service to exports (%)	22	20	52	45	68	80
Short-term to external debt stocks (%)	7	15	12	12	13	10
Multilateral to external debt stocks (%)	31	23	22	24	23	23
Reserves to external debt stocks (%)	22	19	20	21	25	16
Gross national income (GNI)	17,910	22,945	23,592	24,551	25,559	23,325

ERITREA

(US$ million, unless otherwise indicated)

	2010	2016	2017	2018	2019	2020
Summary external debt data by debtor type						
Total external debt stocks	**1,037.3**	**797.3**	**820.8**	**791.2**	**771.7**	**788.5**
Use of IMF credit	23.3	20.4	21.6	21.1	21.0	21.8
Long-term external debt	998.4	750.3	772.0	736.1	718.1	729.4
Public and publicly guaranteed sector	998.4	750.3	772.0	736.1	718.1	729.4
Public sector	998.4	750.3	772.0	736.1	718.1	729.4
of which: General government	998.4	750.3	772.0	736.1	718.1	729.4
Private sector guaranteed by public sector	..	..	..	..	..	..
Private sector not guaranteed	..	..	..	..	..	..
Short-term external debt	15.5	26.6	27.1	34.0	32.7	37.3
Disbursements (long-term)	**8.6**	**9.5**	**6.9**	**4.2**	**4.2**	**2.8**
Public and publicly guaranteed sector	8.6	9.5	6.9	4.2	4.2	2.8
Public sector	8.6	9.5	6.9	4.2	4.2	2.8
of which: General government	8.6	9.5	6.9	4.2	4.2	2.8
Private sector guaranteed by public sector	..	..	..	..	..	..
Private sector not guaranteed	..	..	..	..	..	..
Principal repayments (long-term)	**16.9**	**23.4**	**23.7**	**24.9**	**18.4**	**19.0**
Public and publicly guaranteed sector	16.9	23.4	23.7	24.9	18.4	19.0
Public sector	16.9	23.4	23.7	24.9	18.4	19.0
of which: General government	16.9	23.4	23.7	24.9	18.4	19.0
Private sector guaranteed by public sector	..	..	..	..	..	..
Private sector not guaranteed	..	..	..	..	..	..
Interest payments (long-term)	**10.0**	**3.5**	**3.2**	**3.1**	**2.6**	**2.6**
Public and publicly guaranteed sector	10.0	3.5	3.2	3.1	2.6	2.6
Public sector	10.0	3.5	3.2	3.1	2.6	2.6
of which: General government	10.0	3.5	3.2	3.1	2.6	2.6
Private sector guaranteed by public sector	..	..	..	..	..	..
Private sector not guaranteed	..	..	..	..	..	..
Summary external debt stock by creditor type						
Long-term external debt stocks	**998.4**	**750.3**	**772.0**	**736.1**	**718.1**	**729.4**
Public and publicly guaranteed debt from:	998.4	750.3	772.0	736.1	718.1	729.4
Official creditors	960.5	720.3	738.0	703.6	686.2	694.5
Multilateral	651.4	557.5	587.3	571.6	567.1	587.8
of which: World Bank	467.9	420.0	444.9	434.5	432.0	449.9
Bilateral	309.1	162.8	150.7	132.0	119.0	106.8
Private creditors	38.0	29.9	34.1	32.5	31.9	34.9
Bondholders	..	..	..	..	..	..
Commercial banks and others	38.0	29.9	34.1	32.5	31.9	34.9
Private nonguaranteed debt from:	..	..	..	..	..	..
Bondholders	..	..	..	..	..	..
Commercial banks and others	..	..	..	..	..	..
Use of IMF credit	23.3	20.4	21.6	21.1	21.0	21.8
Net financial inflows						
Net debt inflows						
Use of IMF credit	..	..	..	..	..	..
Long-term	-8.3	-13.8	-16.8	-20.6	-14.2	-16.2
Official creditors	-8.3	-13.8	-16.8	-20.6	-14.2	-16.2
Multilateral	0.1	-1.0	-1.6	-3.8	-1.7	-2.4
of which: World Bank	-0.5	0.0	0.0	0.0	..	0.0
Bilateral	-8.4	-12.8	-15.2	-16.8	-12.5	-13.8
Private creditors	..	0.0	..	..	..	..
Bondholders	..	..	..	..	..	..
Banks and others	..	0.0	..	..	..	..
Short-term	2.0	-45.7	-4.0	4.4	-4.4	0.0
Net equity inflows						
Foreign direct investment	91.0	52.3	55.5	61.0	67.1	73.8
Portfolio equity	..	..	..	..	..	..
Debt ratios						
External debt stocks to exports (%)	..	..	..	..	..	..
External debt stocks to GNI (%)	66.1	..	..	..	..	..
Debt service to exports (%)	..	..	..	..	..	..
Short-term to external debt stocks (%)	1.5	3.3	3.3	4.3	4.2	4.7
Multilateral to external debt stocks (%)	62.8	69.9	71.6	72.2	73.5	74.5
Reserves to external debt stocks (%)	11.0	18.2	17.5	20.6	24.8	..
Gross national income (GNI)	1,569.9	..	..	..	..	..

ESWATINI

(US$ million, unless otherwise indicated)

	2010	2016	2017	2018	2019	2020
Summary external debt data by debtor type						
Total external debt stocks	**721.6**	**499.4**	**653.8**	**511.3**	**630.3**	**766.1**
Use of IMF credit	74.4	64.9	68.8	67.2	66.8	182.6
Long-term external debt	438.5	374.4	403.0	423.5	536.1	557.1
Public and publicly guaranteed sector	438.5	374.4	403.0	423.5	536.1	557.1
Public sector	438.5	374.4	403.0	423.5	536.1	557.1
of which: General government	431.4	364.4	393.0	413.5	526.1	550.1
Private sector guaranteed by public sector	..	..	..	..	..	..
Private sector not guaranteed	..	..	..	..	..	..
Short-term external debt	208.8	60.1	182.1	20.6	27.5	26.4
Disbursements (long-term)	**17.7**	**99.6**	**47.1**	**63.3**	**142.5**	**55.4**
Public and publicly guaranteed sector	17.7	99.6	47.1	63.3	142.5	55.4
Public sector	17.7	99.6	47.1	63.3	142.5	55.4
of which: General government	17.7	93.6	47.1	63.3	142.5	55.4
Private sector guaranteed by public sector	..	..	..	..	..	..
Private sector not guaranteed	..	..	..	..	..	..
Principal repayments (long-term)	**34.0**	**31.3**	**33.1**	**32.8**	**31.5**	**39.2**
Public and publicly guaranteed sector	34.0	31.3	33.1	32.8	31.5	39.2
Public sector	34.0	31.3	33.1	32.8	31.5	39.2
of which: General government	30.8	31.3	33.1	32.8	31.5	36.2
Private sector guaranteed by public sector	..	..	..	..	..	..
Private sector not guaranteed	..	..	..	..	..	..
Interest payments (long-term)	**17.3**	**8.9**	**11.3**	**13.2**	**23.9**	**23.1**
Public and publicly guaranteed sector	17.3	8.9	11.3	13.2	23.9	23.1
Public sector	17.3	8.9	11.3	13.2	23.9	23.1
of which: General government	16.6	8.9	11.3	13.2	23.9	22.7
Private sector guaranteed by public sector	..	..	..	..	..	..
Private sector not guaranteed	..	..	..	..	..	..
Summary external debt stock by creditor type						
Long-term external debt stocks	**438.5**	**374.4**	**403.0**	**423.5**	**536.1**	**557.1**
Public and publicly guaranteed debt from:	438.5	374.4	403.0	423.5	536.1	557.1
Official creditors	397.6	359.7	387.2	411.2	525.4	546.9
Multilateral	246.0	177.4	208.3	219.4	241.0	261.7
of which: World Bank	4.6	27.6	38.8	39.8	36.4	42.9
Bilateral	151.6	182.3	178.9	191.7	284.4	285.1
Private creditors	40.9	14.7	15.7	12.4	10.7	10.2
Bondholders	..	..	..	..	..	..
Commercial banks and others	40.9	14.7	15.7	12.4	10.7	10.2
Private nonguaranteed debt from:	..	..	..	..	..	..
Bondholders	..	..	..	..	..	..
Commercial banks and others	..	..	..	..	..	..
Use of IMF credit	74.4	64.9	68.8	67.2	66.8	182.6
Net financial inflows						
Net debt inflows						
Use of IMF credit	..	..	..	..	..	109.4
Long-term	-16.3	68.3	14.0	30.5	111.0	16.2
Official creditors	-14.7	69.1	14.6	31.7	112.9	16.2
Multilateral	-20.2	19.4	22.8	18.1	20.6	18.6
of which: World Bank	-5.5	5.8	11.2	1.0	-3.4	6.4
Bilateral	5.5	49.7	-8.2	13.7	92.3	-2.4
Private creditors	-1.6	-0.8	-0.6	-1.2	-1.9	0.0
Bondholders	..	..	..	..	..	..
Banks and others	-1.6	-0.8	-0.6	-1.2	-1.9	0.0
Short-term	181.0	46.7	128.3	-168.5	6.8	7.9
Net equity inflows						
Foreign direct investment	49.3	2.3	45.4	-14.1	112.1	74.5
Portfolio equity	4.7	..	..	..	..	..
Debt ratios						
External debt stocks to exports (%)	31.7	27.3	31.2	25.0	28.7	40.1
External debt stocks to GNI (%)	17.1	13.8	15.9	11.8	15.7	20.4
Debt service to exports (%)	2.4	2.2	2.3	2.3	2.6	3.3
Short-term to external debt stocks (%)	28.9	12.0	27.9	4.0	4.4	3.4
Multilateral to external debt stocks (%)	34.1	35.5	31.9	42.9	38.2	34.2
Reserves to external debt stocks (%)	104.8	113.0	86.1	86.2	69.9	71.2
Gross national income (GNI)	4,212.6	3,610.9	4,107.9	4,345.1	4,018.7	3,751.6

ETHIOPIA

(US$ million, unless otherwise indicated)

	2010	2016	2017	2018	2019	2020
Summary external debt data by debtor type						
Total external debt stocks	**7,286**	**23,396**	**26,170**	**27,842**	**28,375**	**30,364**
Use of IMF credit	485	335	301	242	318	940
Long-term external debt	6,499	22,134	25,235	26,850	27,576	29,016
Public and publicly guaranteed sector	6,499	22,134	25,235	26,850	27,576	29,016
Public sector	6,499	22,134	25,235	26,850	27,576	29,016
of which: General government	4,070	12,236	14,349	15,370	16,658	18,729
Private sector guaranteed by public sector	..	..	..	..	..	..
Private sector not guaranteed	..	..	..	..	..	..
Short-term external debt	302	927	634	750	480	409
Disbursements (long-term)	**1,763**	**3,684**	**3,522**	**3,567**	**2,363**	**2,194**
Public and publicly guaranteed sector	1,763	3,684	3,522	3,567	2,363	2,194
Public sector	1,763	3,684	3,522	3,567	2,363	2,194
of which: General government	747	1,972	1,756	1,969	1,577	1,675
Private sector guaranteed by public sector	..	..	..	..	..	..
Private sector not guaranteed	..	..	..	..	..	..
Principal repayments (long-term)	**129**	**771**	**985**	**1,138**	**1,431**	**1,371**
Public and publicly guaranteed sector	129	771	985	1,138	1,431	1,371
Public sector	129	771	985	1,138	1,431	1,371
of which: General government	32	110	142	167	210	168
Private sector guaranteed by public sector	..	..	..	..	..	..
Private sector not guaranteed	..	..	..	..	..	..
Interest payments (long-term)	**46**	**397**	**430**	**436**	**670**	**599**
Public and publicly guaranteed sector	46	397	430	436	670	599
Public sector	46	397	430	436	670	599
of which: General government	30	168	165	201	207	196
Private sector guaranteed by public sector	..	..	..	..	..	..
Private sector not guaranteed	..	..	..	..	..	..
Summary external debt stock by creditor type						
Long-term external debt stocks	**6,499**	**22,134**	**25,235**	**26,850**	**27,576**	**29,016**
Public and publicly guaranteed debt from:	6,499	22,134	25,235	26,850	27,576	29,016
Official creditors	4,612	15,810	18,497	19,575	20,618	22,505
Multilateral	2,812	8,145	10,086	11,043	12,200	14,024
of which: World Bank	1,804	5,746	7,040	8,338	9,354	10,991
Bilateral	1,799	7,665	8,411	8,532	8,419	8,481
Private creditors	1,887	6,324	6,738	7,276	6,958	6,511
Bondholders	..	1,000	1,000	1,000	1,000	1,000
Commercial banks and others	1,887	5,324	5,738	6,276	5,958	5,511
Private nonguaranteed debt from:	..	..	..	..	..	..
Bondholders	..	..	..	..	..	..
Commercial banks and others	..	..	..	..	..	..
Use of IMF credit	485	335	301	242	318	940
Net financial inflows						
Net debt inflows						
Use of IMF credit	122	-52	-52	-53	78	588
Long-term	1,634	2,913	2,537	2,428	932	824
Official creditors	1,009	2,813	2,161	1,869	1,198	1,307
Multilateral	472	1,610	1,494	1,703	1,220	1,347
of which: World Bank	385	1,177	933	1,494	1,075	1,209
Bilateral	537	1,203	667	166	-21	-40
Private creditors	625	100	376	559	-267	-483
Bondholders	..	..	..	0	0	0
Banks and others	625	100	376	559	-267	-483
Short-term	75	378	-293	115	-270	-71
Net equity inflows						
Foreign direct investment	288	4,143	4,017	3,360	2,549	2,396
Portfolio equity	..	..	..	..	..	..
Debt ratios						
External debt stocks to exports (%)	157	395	393	362	371	393
External debt stocks to GNI (%)	24	32	32	33	30	28
Debt service to exports (%)	4	21	22	21	28	26
Short-term to external debt stocks (%)	4	4	2	3	2	1
Multilateral to external debt stocks (%)	39	35	39	40	43	46
Reserves to external debt stocks (%)	31	13	12	14	11	10
Gross national income (GNI)	29,826	74,054	81,285	83,892	95,323	107,062

FIJI

(US$ million, unless otherwise indicated)

	2010	2016	2017	2018	2019	2020
Summary external debt data by debtor type						
Total external debt stocks	**1,107**	**1,298**	**1,268**	**1,245**	**1,344**	**1,518**
Use of IMF credit	103	90	96	93	93	97
Long-term external debt	926	1,110	1,109	1,108	1,198	1,400
Public and publicly guaranteed sector	426	710	753	738	713	903
Public sector	353	662	717	714	701	903
of which: General government	315	629	683	681	669	871
Private sector guaranteed by public sector	73	49	36	24	12	0
Private sector not guaranteed	500	400	355	370	485	497
Short-term external debt	78	97	64	45	53	22
Disbursements (long-term)	**50**	**146**	**119**	**86**	**153**	**433**
Public and publicly guaranteed sector	38	97	59	37	17	403
Public sector	38	97	59	37	17	403
of which: General government	33	95	58	36	17	403
Private sector guaranteed by public sector	..	..	..	..	..	..
Private sector not guaranteed	13	49	59	49	136	30
Principal repayments (long-term)	**36**	**77**	**137**	**75**	**59**	**250**
Public and publicly guaranteed sector	9	48	33	40	38	231
Public sector	9	36	21	28	26	219
of which: General government	9	32	21	26	26	219
Private sector guaranteed by public sector	..	12	12	12	12	12
Private sector not guaranteed	27	29	104	35	21	19
Interest payments (long-term)	**23**	**27**	**30**	**31**	**150**	**24**
Public and publicly guaranteed sector	15	23	24	26	146	24
Public sector	14	21	23	25	146	24
of which: General government	12	21	23	25	145	24
Private sector guaranteed by public sector	1	2	1	1	1	0
Private sector not guaranteed	7	4	6	5	4	0
Summary external debt stock by creditor type						
Long-term external debt stocks	**926**	**1,110**	**1,109**	**1,108**	**1,198**	**1,400**
Public and publicly guaranteed debt from:	426	710	753	738	713	903
Official creditors	276	510	553	538	513	903
Multilateral	113	173	224	253	263	638
of which: World Bank	0	50	54	73	76	142
Bilateral	162	337	329	284	250	265
Private creditors	150	200	200	200	200	0
Bondholders	150	200	200	200	200	0
Commercial banks and others	..	..	..	..	..	..
Private nonguaranteed debt from:	500	400	355	370	485	497
Bondholders	..	..	..	..	..	..
Commercial banks and others	500	400	355	370	485	497
Use of IMF credit	103	90	96	93	93	97
Net financial inflows						
Net debt inflows						
Use of IMF credit	..	..	..	..	..	..
Long-term	15	68	-18	11	95	183
Official creditors	29	55	27	-4	-21	372
Multilateral	9	42	51	29	10	374
of which: World Bank	0	50	3	20	3	64
Bilateral	19	13	-25	-33	-30	-2
Private creditors	-14	13	-45	15	116	-189
Bondholders	..	-7	0	0	0	-200
Banks and others	-14	20	-45	15	116	11
Short-term	22	16	-34	-19	8	-31
Net equity inflows						
Foreign direct investment	177	379	418	435	397	207
Portfolio equity	..	..	..	..	..	..
Debt ratios						
External debt stocks to exports (%)	59	55	50	45	50	117
External debt stocks to GNI (%)	36	28	26	24	27	37
Debt service to exports (%)	3	4	7	4	8	21
Short-term to external debt stocks (%)	7	7	5	4	4	1
Multilateral to external debt stocks (%)	10	13	18	20	20	42
Reserves to external debt stocks (%)	65	70	88	76	78	..
Gross national income (GNI)	3,043	4,658	4,930	5,222	5,045	4,115

GABON

(US$ million, unless otherwise indicated)

	2010	2016	2017	2018	2019	2020
Summary external debt data by debtor type	4					
Total external debt stocks	**2,929**	**5,336**	**6,499**	**6,811**	**7,199**	**7,616**
Use of IMF credit	226	197	412	601	722	1,063
Long-term external debt	2,532	4,898	5,880	6,022	6,118	6,478
Public and publicly guaranteed sector	2,532	4,898	5,880	6,022	6,118	6,478
Public sector	2,532	4,898	5,880	6,022	6,118	6,478
of which: General government	2,531	4,884	5,830	5,967	6,060	6,399
Private sector guaranteed by public sector	..	..	..	..	..	..
Private sector not guaranteed	..	..	..	..	..	..
Short-term external debt	170	241	207	187	360	76
Disbursements (long-term)	**509**	**433**	**1,173**	**854**	**594**	**1,252**
Public and publicly guaranteed sector	509	433	1,173	854	594	1,252
Public sector	509	433	1,173	854	594	1,252
of which: General government	509	425	1,152	826	589	1,235
Private sector guaranteed by public sector	..	..	..	..	..	..
Private sector not guaranteed	..	..	..	..	..	..
Principal repayments (long-term)	**313**	**172**	**450**	**496**	**424**	**1,128**
Public and publicly guaranteed sector	313	172	450	496	424	1,128
Public sector	313	172	450	496	424	1,128
of which: General government	313	171	449	494	423	1,126
Private sector guaranteed by public sector	..	..	..	..	..	..
Private sector not guaranteed	..	..	..	..	..	..
Interest payments (long-term)	**137**	**195**	**168**	**216**	**252**	**273**
Public and publicly guaranteed sector	137	195	168	216	252	273
Public sector	137	195	168	216	252	273
of which: General government	137	195	167	215	250	272
Private sector guaranteed by public sector	..	..	..	..	..	..
Private sector not guaranteed	..	..	..	..	..	..
Summary external debt stock by creditor type						
Long-term external debt stocks	**2,532**	**4,898**	**5,880**	**6,022**	**6,118**	**6,478**
Public and publicly guaranteed debt from:	2,532	4,898	5,880	6,022	6,118	6,478
Official creditors	1,136	1,672	2,672	3,043	3,397	3,590
Multilateral	466	563	1,450	1,697	1,920	2,081
of which: World Bank	22	67	336	369	581	680
Bilateral	670	1,108	1,222	1,346	1,477	1,508
Private creditors	1,397	3,226	3,207	2,980	2,720	2,888
Bondholders	879	2,218	2,200	2,186	2,186	2,436
Commercial banks and others	518	1,008	1,007	794	534	452
Private nonguaranteed debt from:	..	..	..	..	..	..
Bondholders	..	..	..	..	..	..
Commercial banks and others	..	..	..	..	..	..
Use of IMF credit	226	197	412	601	722	1,063
Net financial inflows						
Net debt inflows						
Use of IMF credit	..	..	198	202	123	301
Long-term	196	262	722	358	169	124
Official creditors	36	66	850	486	400	-26
Multilateral	16	8	786	331	257	-1
of which: World Bank	6	21	249	64	220	46
Bilateral	19	58	64	155	143	-25
Private creditors	160	196	-128	-128	-231	150
Bondholders	-23	..	-18	-14	..	250
Banks and others	183	196	-110	-114	-231	-100
Short-term	67	21	-37	-11	178	-299
Net equity inflows						
Foreign direct investment	651	1,244	1,314	1,379	1,553	1,717
Portfolio equity	0	..	..	..	..	..
Debt ratios						
External debt stocks to exports (%)	31	..	..	..	..	..
External debt stocks to GNI (%)	23	41	46	43	46	53
Debt service to exports (%)	5	..	..	..	..	..
Short-term to external debt stocks (%)	6	5	3	3	5	1
Multilateral to external debt stocks (%)	16	11	22	25	27	27
Reserves to external debt stocks (%)	59	15	15	19	19	..
Gross national income (GNI)	12,484	12,935	13,986	15,755	15,511	14,503

GAMBIA, THE

(US$ million, unless otherwise indicated)

	2010	2016	2017	2018	2019	2020
Summary external debt data by debtor type						
Total external debt stocks	**548.0**	**527.1**	**660.9**	**687.8**	**712.5**	**775.7**
Use of IMF credit	77.0	80.0	93.9	84.1	77.2	103.4
Long-term external debt	426.4	429.4	553.2	585.9	611.3	646.6
Public and publicly guaranteed sector	426.4	429.4	553.2	585.9	611.3	646.6
Public sector	426.4	429.4	553.2	585.9	611.3	646.6
of which: General government	409.1	420.2	546.6	582.7	609.6	645.9
Private sector guaranteed by public sector	..	..	..	..	..	..
Private sector not guaranteed	..	..	..	..	..	..
Short-term external debt	44.7	17.6	13.7	17.8	24.0	25.7
Disbursements (long-term)	**41.1**	**29.7**	**139.9**	**72.1**	**58.0**	**42.7**
Public and publicly guaranteed sector	41.1	29.7	139.9	72.1	58.0	42.7
Public sector	41.1	29.7	139.9	72.1	58.0	42.7
of which: General government	34.7	29.7	139.9	72.1	58.0	42.7
Private sector guaranteed by public sector	..	..	..	..	..	..
Private sector not guaranteed	..	..	..	..	..	..
Principal repayments (long-term)	**16.8**	**30.3**	**30.6**	**32.5**	**31.9**	**19.7**
Public and publicly guaranteed sector	16.8	30.3	30.6	32.5	31.9	19.7
Public sector	16.8	30.3	30.6	32.5	31.9	19.7
of which: General government	12.3	27.2	27.4	29.3	30.4	19.7
Private sector guaranteed by public sector	..	..	..	..	..	..
Private sector not guaranteed	..	..	..	..	..	..
Interest payments (long-term)	**6.6**	**6.0**	**6.5**	**6.7**	**8.6**	**6.1**
Public and publicly guaranteed sector	6.6	6.0	6.5	6.7	8.6	6.1
Public sector	6.6	6.0	6.5	6.7	8.6	6.1
of which: General government	6.3	5.9	6.3	6.6	8.6	6.1
Private sector guaranteed by public sector	..	..	..	..	..	..
Private sector not guaranteed	..	..	..	..	..	..
Summary external debt stock by creditor type						
Long-term external debt stocks	**426.4**	**429.4**	**553.2**	**585.9**	**611.3**	**646.6**
Public and publicly guaranteed debt from:	426.4	429.4	553.2	585.9	611.3	646.6
Official creditors	420.0	425.1	550.3	585.0	611.3	646.6
Multilateral	299.9	303.7	406.5	436.2	451.1	475.4
of which: World Bank	65.0	57.2	105.1	115.8	117.7	128.1
Bilateral	120.1	121.4	143.8	148.8	160.2	171.2
Private creditors	6.4	4.3	2.9	0.9	0.0	..
Bondholders	..	..	..	..	..	..
Commercial banks and others	6.4	4.3	2.9	0.9	0.0	..
Private nonguaranteed debt from:	..	..	..	..	..	..
Bondholders	..	..	..	..	..	..
Commercial banks and others	..	..	..	..	..	..
Use of IMF credit	77.0	80.0	93.9	84.1	77.2	103.4
Net financial inflows						
Net debt inflows						
Use of IMF credit	3.0	-5.9	8.9	-7.8	-6.3	22.2
Long-term	24.3	-0.6	109.3	39.5	26.1	23.0
Official creditors	21.1	1.2	111.1	41.5	27.0	23.0
Multilateral	13.0	-2.5	89.6	36.1	15.7	13.0
of which: World Bank	1.9	4.0	43.9	13.3	2.5	5.4
Bilateral	8.2	3.7	21.6	5.4	11.3	10.0
Private creditors	3.2	-1.8	-1.8	-1.9	-0.9	..
Bondholders	..	..	..	..	..	..
Banks and others	3.2	-1.8	-1.8	-1.9	-0.9	..
Short-term	1.0	7.9	-3.9	3.7	7.5	1.5
Net equity inflows						
Foreign direct investment	37.1	7.9	12.3	33.0	43.9	45.7
Portfolio equity	..	..	..	..	..	..
Debt ratios						
External debt stocks to exports (%)	195.7	214.7	251.7	197.2	200.6	411.2
External debt stocks to GNI (%)	36.2	36.2	44.8	41.9	39.7	41.5
Debt service to exports (%)	8.6	17.3	16.9	13.6	13.4	17.3
Short-term to external debt stocks (%)	8.2	3.3	2.1	2.6	3.4	3.3
Multilateral to external debt stocks (%)	54.7	57.6	61.5	63.4	63.3	61.3
Reserves to external debt stocks (%)	36.8	16.6	25.7	27.9	36.1	49.9
Gross national income (GNI)	1,513.4	1,456.8	1,476.6	1,641.5	1,795.9	1,868.5

GEORGIA

(US$ million, unless otherwise indicated)

	2010	2016	2017	2018	2019	2020
Summary external debt data by debtor type						
Total external debt stocks	**8,790**	**16,320**	**16,424**	**17,326**	**18,757**	**20,089**
Use of IMF credit	1,272	307	397	416	448	792
Long-term external debt	6,418	13,659	13,584	14,593	16,033	16,974
Public and publicly guaranteed sector	3,274	6,224	6,615	6,749	6,993	7,967
Public sector	3,274	6,224	6,615	6,749	6,993	7,967
of which: General government	2,950	4,443	5,032	5,257	5,535	6,978
Private sector guaranteed by public sector	..	..	..	..	..	..
Private sector not guaranteed	3,143	7,435	6,969	7,844	9,040	9,007
Short-term external debt	1,101	2,354	2,443	2,318	2,276	2,322
Disbursements (long-term)	**1,026**	**2,780**	**2,003**	**2,468**	**2,983**	**2,508**
Public and publicly guaranteed sector	651	839	536	567	616	1,452
Public sector	651	839	536	567	616	1,452
of which: General government	401	424	524	555	605	1,421
Private sector guaranteed by public sector	..	..	..	..	..	..
Private sector not guaranteed	375	1,941	1,467	1,900	2,367	1,056
Principal repayments (long-term)	**510**	**1,634**	**1,974**	**1,681**	**1,669**	**1,820**
Public and publicly guaranteed sector	169	256	434	300	324	799
Public sector	169	256	434	300	324	799
of which: General government	71	132	165	227	280	299
Private sector guaranteed by public sector	..	..	..	..	..	..
Private sector not guaranteed	342	1,379	1,540	1,381	1,345	1,022
Interest payments (long-term)	**247**	**905**	**526**	**609**	**676**	**587**
Public and publicly guaranteed sector	87	153	175	167	185	135
Public sector	87	153	175	167	185	135
of which: General government	77	87	99	111	122	115
Private sector guaranteed by public sector	..	..	..	..	..	..
Private sector not guaranteed	160	752	351	442	491	452
Summary external debt stock by creditor type						
Long-term external debt stocks	**6,418**	**13,659**	**13,584**	**14,593**	**16,033**	**16,974**
Public and publicly guaranteed debt from:	3,274	6,224	6,615	6,749	6,993	7,967
Official creditors	2,448	3,882	4,416	4,580	4,880	6,329
Multilateral	1,002	3,154	3,664	3,794	3,934	4,798
of which: World Bank	1,359	1,830	2,026	1,960	1,879	2,054
Bilateral	645	728	752	786	946	1,531
Private creditors	827	2,341	2,199	2,169	2,113	1,638
Bondholders	750	1,500	1,250	1,250	1,250	750
Commercial banks and others	77	841	949	919	863	888
Private nonguaranteed debt from:	3,143	7,435	6,969	7,844	9,040	9,007
Bondholders	..	1,054	1,152	1,660	3,320	3,372
Commercial banks and others	3,143	6,381	5,817	6,184	5,720	5,635
Use of IMF credit	1,272	307	397	416	448	792
Net financial inflows						
Net debt inflows						
Use of IMF credit	275	-14	70	28	35	315
Long-term	516	1,146	29	787	1,314	688
Official creditors	330	253	315	259	344	1,142
Multilateral	294	265	337	212	181	659
of which: World Bank	126	19	125	-31	-58	115
Bilateral	36	-12	-22	48	163	482
Private creditors	186	892	-287	528	970	-454
Bondholders	250	404	-454	236	1,323	-290
Banks and others	-64	488	167	291	-353	-164
Short-term	176	230	181	-262	-19	37
Net equity inflows						
Foreign direct investment	740	2,118	1,724	1,274	1,326	570
Portfolio equity	-22	-4	-2	4	-6	1
Debt ratios						
External debt stocks to exports (%)	191	230	189	170	172	291
External debt stocks to GNI (%)	73	113	106	102	112	133
Debt service to exports (%)	18	37	30	24	23	35
Short-term to external debt stocks (%)	13	14	15	13	12	12
Multilateral to external debt stocks (%)	21	19	22	22	21	24
Reserves to external debt stocks (%)	26	17	19	19	19	19
Gross national income (GNI)	12,026	14,440	15,447	16,915	16,699	15,137

GHANA

(US$ million, unless otherwise indicated)

	2010	2016	2017	2018	2019	2020
Summary external debt data by debtor type						
Total external debt stocks	**8,367**	**21,152**	**22,326**	**23,262**	**26,606**	**31,179**
Use of IMF credit	937	1,366	1,465	1,508	1,576	2,612
Long-term external debt	5,338	16,998	17,539	18,121	20,392	23,537
Public and publicly guaranteed sector	5,338	16,744	17,285	17,867	20,138	23,284
Public sector	5,338	16,744	17,285	17,867	20,138	23,284
of which: General government	4,783	15,725	16,187	16,773	19,071	22,194
Private sector guaranteed by public sector	..	..	..	..	..	..
Private sector not guaranteed	0	253	253	253	253	253
Short-term external debt	2,092	2,789	3,323	3,634	4,638	5,030
Disbursements (long-term)	**1,314**	**2,510**	**1,166**	**2,662**	**3,630**	**4,361**
Public and publicly guaranteed sector	1,314	2,510	1,166	2,662	3,630	4,361
Public sector	1,314	2,510	1,166	2,662	3,630	4,361
of which: General government	1,078	2,473	1,141	2,626	3,630	4,340
Private sector guaranteed by public sector	..	..	..	..	..	..
Private sector not guaranteed	0	..	..	..	..	..
Principal repayments (long-term)	**170**	**875**	**1,100**	**1,879**	**1,300**	**1,615**
Public and publicly guaranteed sector	170	875	1,100	1,879	1,300	1,615
Public sector	170	875	1,100	1,879	1,300	1,615
of which: General government	149	862	1,089	1,866	1,280	1,571
Private sector guaranteed by public sector	..	..	..	..	..	..
Private sector not guaranteed	0	..	..	..	..	..
Interest payments (long-term)	**96**	**554**	**745**	**675**	**688**	**937**
Public and publicly guaranteed sector	96	548	739	669	682	931
Public sector	96	548	739	669	682	931
of which: General government	89	539	731	660	674	921
Private sector guaranteed by public sector	..	..	..	..	..	..
Private sector not guaranteed	0	6	6	6	6	6
Summary external debt stock by creditor type						
Long-term external debt stocks	**5,338**	**16,998**	**17,539**	**18,121**	**20,392**	**23,537**
Public and publicly guaranteed debt from:	5,338	16,744	17,285	17,867	20,138	23,284
Official creditors	4,216	8,681	9,184	8,871	8,706	9,164
Multilateral	2,744	4,728	5,383	5,375	5,482	6,056
of which: World Bank	1,868	3,415	3,945	3,926	3,989	4,477
Bilateral	1,472	3,952	3,800	3,496	3,225	3,108
Private creditors	1,122	8,064	8,102	8,996	11,432	14,120
Bondholders	..	1,000	1,000	3,000	6,000	9,000
Commercial banks and others	1,122	7,064	7,102	5,996	5,432	5,120
Private nonguaranteed debt from:	0	253	253	253	253	253
Bondholders	0	253	253	253	253	253
Commercial banks and others	..	..	..	..	..	..
Use of IMF credit	937	1,366	1,465	1,508	1,576	2,612
Net financial inflows						
Net debt inflows						
Use of IMF credit	124	166	18	78	76	939
Long-term	1,144	1,636	66	783	2,330	2,746
Official creditors	924	162	142	-153	-121	172
Multilateral	436	280	399	107	133	365
of which: World Bank	308	235	323	75	88	309
Bilateral	488	-117	-256	-260	-254	-193
Private creditors	220	1,473	-76	936	2,450	2,574
Bondholders	0	..	..	2,000	3,000	3,000
Banks and others	220	1,473	-76	-1,064	-550	-426
Short-term	571	-503	409	290	1,005	390
Net equity inflows						
Foreign direct investment	2,527	3,485	3,255	2,989	3,880	1,876
Portfolio equity	18	..	..	..	..	..
Debt ratios						
External debt stocks to exports (%)	88	119	108	101	102	137
External debt stocks to GNI (%)	26	39	39	36	41	44
Debt service to exports (%)	3	9	10	12	8	12
Short-term to external debt stocks (%)	25	13	15	16	17	16
Multilateral to external debt stocks (%)	33	22	24	23	21	19
Reserves to external debt stocks (%)	57	26	30	26	27	24
Gross national income (GNI)	31,663	53,962	57,432	64,270	65,527	70,777

GRENADA

(US$ million, unless otherwise indicated)

	2010	2016	2017	2018	2019	2020
Summary external debt data by debtor type						
Total external debt stocks	**560.6**	**622.1**	**561.5**	**568.0**	**567.0**	**700.1**
Use of IMF credit	46.3	43.9	44.5	38.6	35.6	58.8
Long-term external debt	476.7	551.4	495.0	512.7	517.5	539.1
Public and publicly guaranteed sector	476.7	551.4	495.0	512.7	517.5	539.1
Public sector	476.7	551.4	495.0	512.7	517.5	539.1
of which: General government	472.4	550.6	494.6	512.7	517.5	539.1
Private sector guaranteed by public sector	..	..	..	..	..	..
Private sector not guaranteed	..	..	..	..	..	..
Short-term external debt	37.6	26.8	22.0	16.7	13.8	102.2
Disbursements (long-term)	**21.1**	**23.6**	**14.8**	**51.9**	**40.2**	**44.9**
Public and publicly guaranteed sector	21.1	23.6	14.8	51.9	40.2	44.9
Public sector	21.1	23.6	14.8	51.9	40.2	44.9
of which: General government	21.1	23.6	14.8	51.9	40.2	44.9
Private sector guaranteed by public sector	..	..	..	..	..	..
Private sector not guaranteed	..	..	..	..	..	..
Principal repayments (long-term)	**15.1**	**26.2**	**32.1**	**33.3**	**34.4**	**28.7**
Public and publicly guaranteed sector	15.1	26.2	32.1	33.3	34.4	28.7
Public sector	15.1	26.2	32.1	33.3	34.4	28.7
of which: General government	14.8	25.9	31.7	32.9	34.4	28.7
Private sector guaranteed by public sector	..	..	..	..	..	..
Private sector not guaranteed	..	..	..	..	..	..
Interest payments (long-term)	**10.5**	**20.6**	**22.7**	**17.6**	**17.7**	**15.6**
Public and publicly guaranteed sector	10.5	20.6	22.7	17.6	17.7	15.6
Public sector	10.5	20.6	22.7	17.6	17.7	15.6
of which: General government	10.4	20.5	22.7	17.6	17.7	15.6
Private sector guaranteed by public sector	..	..	..	..	..	..
Private sector not guaranteed	..	..	..	..	..	..
Summary external debt stock by creditor type						
Long-term external debt stocks	**476.7**	**551.4**	**495.0**	**512.7**	**517.5**	**539.1**
Public and publicly guaranteed debt from:	476.7	551.4	495.0	512.7	517.5	539.1
Official creditors	278.2	355.9	356.0	383.9	399.9	432.2
Multilateral	107.8	251.0	256.0	278.7	273.6	305.0
of which: World Bank	58.2	89.5	102.0	131.1	131.4	161.4
Bilateral	90.4	104.9	100.0	105.2	126.2	127.1
Private creditors	198.5	195.5	139.0	128.8	117.6	107.0
Bondholders	193.2	195.1	135.6	126.7	115.9	105.4
Commercial banks and others	5.3	0.3	3.3	2.1	1.7	1.6
Private nonguaranteed debt from:	..	..	..	..	..	..
Bondholders	..	..	..	..	..	..
Commercial banks and others	..	..	..	..	..	..
Use of IMF credit	46.3	43.9	44.5	38.6	35.6	58.8
Net financial inflows						
Net debt inflows						
Use of IMF credit	6.4	0.5	-2.0	-4.9	-2.8	21.0
Long-term	6.0	-2.6	-17.3	18.6	5.8	16.2
Official creditors	10.4	8.4	-5.9	30.3	16.9	26.9
Multilateral	13.4	9.2	-0.4	24.8	-4.1	27.4
of which: World Bank	8.6	2.1	7.3	31.3	1.2	26.1
Bilateral	-3.1	-0.8	-5.6	5.5	21.0	-0.5
Private creditors	-4.4	-11.0	-11.4	-11.7	-11.1	-10.7
Bondholders	..	-11.0	-10.6	-10.6	-10.7	-10.6
Banks and others	-4.4	..	-0.8	-1.2	-0.4	-0.1
Short-term	-2.0	5.9	-5.3	-5.8	-3.3	87.9
Net equity inflows						
Foreign direct investment	42.3	91.6	138.7	143.4	206.1	138.0
Portfolio equity	..	0.0	0.0	0.0	0.0	0.0
Debt ratios						
External debt stocks to exports (%)	293.6	116.1	95.2	85.8	88.2	156.9
External debt stocks to GNI (%)	76.7	64.5	55.9	53.8	51.9	71.1
Debt service to exports (%)	13.6	9.7	10.2	8.5	8.6	11.0
Short-term to external debt stocks (%)	6.7	4.3	3.9	2.9	2.4	14.6
Multilateral to external debt stocks (%)	33.5	40.3	45.6	49.1	48.3	43.6
Reserves to external debt stocks (%)	21.3	33.4	35.5	41.2	41.7	41.9
Gross national income (GNI)	731.1	964.6	1,004.1	1,055.1	1,093.0	984.8

GUATEMALA

(US$ million, unless otherwise indicated)

	2010	2016	2017	2018	2019	2020
Summary external debt data by debtor type						
Total external debt stocks	**15,043**	**21,130**	**23,265**	**24,275**	**25,035**	**25,136**
Use of IMF credit	309	270	286	279	278	289
Long-term external debt	13,149	19,939	21,936	22,397	23,419	23,617
Public and publicly guaranteed sector	5,559	8,148	8,366	8,428	9,843	11,192
Public sector	5,559	8,148	8,366	8,428	9,843	11,192
of which: General government	5,061	7,878	8,134	8,234	9,686	11,073
Private sector guaranteed by public sector	..	..	..	..	..	..
Private sector not guaranteed	7,589	11,792	13,570	13,969	13,576	12,425
Short-term external debt	1,585	920	1,042	1,599	1,338	1,229
Disbursements (long-term)	**1,472**	**2,862**	**5,197**	**882**	**1,870**	**1,960**
Public and publicly guaranteed sector	881	953	662	406	1,812	1,748
Public sector	881	953	662	406	1,812	1,748
of which: General government	878	953	662	406	1,812	1,748
Private sector guaranteed by public sector	..	..	..	..	..	..
Private sector not guaranteed	592	1,910	4,536	476	58	212
Principal repayments (long-term)	**949**	**2,116**	**3,226**	**416**	**844**	**1,774**
Public and publicly guaranteed sector	264	352	457	342	394	412
Public sector	264	352	457	342	394	412
of which: General government	242	314	419	305	357	374
Private sector guaranteed by public sector	..	..	..	..	..	..
Private sector not guaranteed	685	1,765	2,768	74	449	1,362
Interest payments (long-term)	**636**	**944**	**922**	**714**	**999**	**1,238**
Public and publicly guaranteed sector	284	354	376	267	408	521
Public sector	284	354	376	267	408	521
of which: General government	253	338	362	255	397	513
Private sector guaranteed by public sector	..	..	..	..	..	..
Private sector not guaranteed	352	591	546	447	591	717
Summary external debt stock by creditor type						
Long-term external debt stocks	**13,149**	**19,939**	**21,936**	**22,397**	**23,419**	**23,617**
Public and publicly guaranteed debt from:	5,559	8,148	8,366	8,428	9,843	11,192
Official creditors	4,600	5,684	5,406	5,470	5,188	5,340
Multilateral	4,241	5,197	4,911	4,977	4,686	4,820
of which: World Bank	1,372	1,679	1,555	1,718	1,641	1,758
Bilateral	359	486	496	493	502	520
Private creditors	959	2,464	2,960	2,958	4,655	5,853
Bondholders	955	2,430	2,930	2,930	4,630	5,830
Commercial banks and others	4	34	30	28	25	23
Private nonguaranteed debt from:	7,589	11,792	13,570	13,969	13,576	12,425
Bondholders	5	1,150	1,650	1,650	1,650	1,850
Commercial banks and others	7,584	10,642	11,920	12,319	11,926	10,575
Use of IMF credit	309	270	286	279	278	289
Net financial inflows						
Net debt inflows						
Use of IMF credit	..	..	..	..	..	..
Long-term	524	746	1,972	466	1,026	186
Official creditors	615	-101	-291	65	-280	140
Multilateral	630	-154	-289	68	-288	133
of which: World Bank	260	-86	-124	163	-78	118
Bilateral	-15	53	-2	-2	8	6
Private creditors	-91	847	2,263	400	1,306	46
Bondholders	..	700	1,000	..	1,700	1,400
Banks and others	-91	147	1,263	400	-394	-1,354
Short-term	359	76	122	556	-261	-109
Net equity inflows						
Foreign direct investment	794	782	880	1,037	929	901
Portfolio equity	0	0	0	0	0	0
Debt ratios						
External debt stocks to exports (%)	151	161	166	170	171	179
External debt stocks to GNI (%)	38	33	33	34	33	33
Debt service to exports (%)	16	24	30	8	13	22
Short-term to external debt stocks (%)	11	4	4	7	5	5
Multilateral to external debt stocks (%)	28	25	21	21	19	19
Reserves to external debt stocks (%)	37	42	49	51	58	72
Gross national income (GNI)	39,643	64,628	70,153	71,702	75,609	76,206

GUINEA

(US$ million, unless otherwise indicated)

	2010	2016	2017	2018	2019	2020
Summary external debt data by debtor type						
Total external debt stocks	**3,245**	**2,218**	**2,388**	**2,589**	**3,000**	**4,175**
Use of IMF credit	205	379	426	464	481	668
Long-term external debt	2,925	1,764	1,860	1,989	2,331	3,363
Public and publicly guaranteed sector	2,925	1,764	1,860	1,989	2,331	3,363
Public sector	2,925	1,764	1,860	1,989	2,331	3,363
of which: General government	2,717	1,729	1,815	1,942	2,273	3,289
Private sector guaranteed by public sector	..	..	..	..	..	..
Private sector not guaranteed	..	..	..	..	..	..
Short-term external debt	115	74	102	136	188	144
Disbursements (long-term)	**36**	**134**	**90**	**239**	**423**	**967**
Public and publicly guaranteed sector	36	134	90	239	423	967
Public sector	36	134	90	239	423	967
of which: General government	24	130	85	235	412	955
Private sector guaranteed by public sector	..	..	..	..	..	..
Private sector not guaranteed	..	..	..	..	..	..
Principal repayments (long-term)	**48**	**36**	**57**	**82**	**73**	**35**
Public and publicly guaranteed sector	48	36	57	82	73	35
Public sector	48	36	57	82	73	35
of which: General government	47	36	57	82	72	35
Private sector guaranteed by public sector	..	..	..	..	..	..
Private sector not guaranteed	..	..	..	..	..	..
Interest payments (long-term)	**21**	**21**	**23**	**29**	**30**	**39**
Public and publicly guaranteed sector	21	21	23	29	30	39
Public sector	21	21	23	29	30	39
of which: General government	14	21	22	28	30	38
Private sector guaranteed by public sector	..	..	..	..	..	..
Private sector not guaranteed	..	..	..	..	..	..
Summary external debt stock by creditor type						
Long-term external debt stocks	**2,925**	**1,764**	**1,860**	**1,989**	**2,331**	**3,363**
Public and publicly guaranteed debt from:	2,925	1,764	1,860	1,989	2,331	3,363
Official creditors	2,900	1,741	1,836	1,966	2,263	3,135
Multilateral	1,875	620	690	823	1,027	1,268
of which: World Bank	1,248	222	252	344	471	572
Bilateral	1,025	1,121	1,146	1,142	1,235	1,867
Private creditors	25	23	24	24	68	228
Bondholders	..	..	..	..	..	..
Commercial banks and others	25	23	24	24	68	228
Private nonguaranteed debt from:	..	..	..	..	..	..
Bondholders	..	..	..	..	..	..
Commercial banks and others	..	..	..	..	..	..
Use of IMF credit	205	379	426	464	481	668
Net financial inflows						
Net debt inflows						
Use of IMF credit	-10	51	24	49	20	162
Long-term	-13	98	33	157	350	931
Official creditors	-13	98	33	157	306	787
Multilateral	-7	39	35	148	208	176
of which: World Bank	0	43	17	98	129	79
Bilateral	-6	59	-2	9	98	610
Private creditors	..	..	..	..	44	145
Bondholders	..	..	..	..	..	..
Banks and others	..	..	..	..	44	145
Short-term	75	-28	28	34	52	-44
Net equity inflows						
Foreign direct investment	..	3	40	-28	13	12
Portfolio equity	..	0	1	0	0	0
Debt ratios						
External debt stocks to exports (%)	210	89	51	62	73	46
External debt stocks to GNI (%)	48	26	23	23	23	29
Debt service to exports (%)	5	2	2	3	3	2
Short-term to external debt stocks (%)	4	3	4	5	6	3
Multilateral to external debt stocks (%)	58	28	29	32	34	30
Reserves to external debt stocks (%)	9	38	41	46	40	30
Gross national income (GNI)	6,776	8,447	10,274	11,448	12,854	14,340

GUINEA-BISSAU

(US$ million, unless otherwise indicated)

	2010	2016	2017	2018	2019	2020
Summary external debt data by debtor type						
Total external debt stocks	**1,096.7**	**323.3**	**425.0**	**520.7**	**611.2**	**805.9**
Use of IMF credit	24.7	42.5	51.6	52.6	50.3	48.9
Long-term external debt	980.3	260.6	352.3	438.2	513.7	708.8
Public and publicly guaranteed sector	980.3	260.6	352.3	438.2	513.7	708.8
Public sector	980.3	260.6	352.3	438.2	513.7	708.8
of which: General government	970.5	260.6	352.3	438.2	513.7	708.8
Private sector guaranteed by public sector	..	..	..	..	..	..
Private sector not guaranteed	..	..	..	..	..	..
Short-term external debt	91.8	20.2	21.2	29.9	47.2	48.3
Disbursements (long-term)	**9.8**	**4.6**	**88.7**	**117.7**	**80.6**	**179.4**
Public and publicly guaranteed sector	9.8	4.6	88.7	117.7	80.6	179.4
Public sector	9.8	4.6	88.7	117.7	80.6	179.4
of which: General government	9.8	4.6	88.7	117.7	80.6	179.4
Private sector guaranteed by public sector	..	..	..	..	..	..
Private sector not guaranteed	..	..	..	..	..	..
Principal repayments (long-term)	**5.9**	**2.6**	**5.5**	**3.3**	**2.9**	**5.7**
Public and publicly guaranteed sector	5.9	2.6	5.5	3.3	2.9	5.7
Public sector	5.9	2.6	5.5	3.3	2.9	5.7
of which: General government	5.5	2.6	5.5	3.3	2.9	5.7
Private sector guaranteed by public sector	..	..	..	..	..	..
Private sector not guaranteed	..	..	..	..	..	..
Interest payments (long-term)	**3.9**	**2.4**	**3.3**	**5.6**	**7.3**	**10.2**
Public and publicly guaranteed sector	3.9	2.4	3.3	5.6	7.3	10.2
Public sector	3.9	2.4	3.3	5.6	7.3	10.2
of which: General government	3.8	2.4	3.3	5.6	7.3	10.2
Private sector guaranteed by public sector	..	..	..	..	..	..
Private sector not guaranteed	..	..	..	..	..	..
Summary external debt stock by creditor type						
Long-term external debt stocks	**980.3**	**260.6**	**352.3**	**438.2**	**513.7**	**708.8**
Public and publicly guaranteed debt from:	980.3	260.6	352.3	438.2	513.7	708.8
Official creditors	980.3	232.7	283.7	341.5	387.5	496.3
Multilateral	495.9	114.8	162.9	221.4	267.9	377.4
of which: World Bank	288.6	54.1	67.0	111.1	126.1	163.7
Bilateral	484.4	117.9	120.9	120.1	119.6	119.0
Private creditors	..	27.9	68.5	96.7	126.2	212.5
Bondholders	..	27.9	68.5	96.7	126.2	212.5
Commercial banks and others	..	..	..	..	..	..
Private nonguaranteed debt from:	..	..	..	..	..	..
Bondholders	..	..	..	..	..	..
Commercial banks and others	..	..	..	..	..	..
Use of IMF credit	24.7	42.5	51.6	52.6	50.3	48.9
Net financial inflows						
Net debt inflows						
Use of IMF credit	7.6	6.1	6.4	2.2	-2.0	-3.4
Long-term	3.9	2.0	83.2	114.4	77.8	173.7
Official creditors	3.9	2.5	42.6	86.2	48.3	87.4
Multilateral	-1.8	2.5	36.7	86.8	48.9	88.0
of which: World Bank	-1.0	2.8	9.4	46.1	15.7	30.5
Bilateral	5.8	0.0	5.9	-0.6	-0.6	-0.6
Private creditors	..	-0.5	40.6	28.2	29.5	86.3
Bondholders	..	-0.5	40.6	28.2	29.5	86.3
Banks and others	..	..	..	..	..	..
Short-term	-6.0	-20.4	1.0	8.7	16.9	0.6
Net equity inflows						
Foreign direct investment	26.2	14.2	15.7	16.7	71.5	20.4
Portfolio equity	2.7	..	..	..	-0.2	..
Debt ratios						
External debt stocks to exports (%)	596.7	148.4	100.8	119.4	164.9	..
External debt stocks to GNI (%)	129.6	26.8	31.4	35.8	41.6	55.3
Debt service to exports (%)	9.8	2.8	2.6	2.6	3.6	..
Short-term to external debt stocks (%)	8.4	6.2	5.0	5.7	7.7	6.0
Multilateral to external debt stocks (%)	45.2	35.5	38.3	42.5	43.8	46.8
Reserves to external debt stocks (%)	14.3	..	..	..	..	..
Gross national income (GNI)	846.2	1,208.7	1,352.9	1,453.5	1,470.0	1,456.3

GUYANA

(US$ million, unless otherwise indicated)

	2010	2016	2017	2018	2019	2020
Summary external debt data by debtor type						
Total external debt stocks	**1,408**	**1,644**	**1,582**	**1,607**	**1,530**	**1,507**
Use of IMF credit	190	117	124	121	120	125
Long-term external debt	885	1,284	1,343	1,362	1,361	1,327
Public and publicly guaranteed sector	885	1,049	1,135	1,205	1,255	1,271
Public sector	885	1,049	1,135	1,205	1,255	1,271
of which: General government	816	1,013	1,099	1,170	1,220	1,237
Private sector guaranteed by public sector	..	..	..	..	..	..
Private sector not guaranteed	0	235	208	157	106	56
Short-term external debt	333	243	116	124	49	54
Disbursements (long-term)	**123**	**141**	**109**	**138**	**92**	**48**
Public and publicly guaranteed sector	123	61	109	138	92	48
Public sector	123	61	109	138	92	48
of which: General government	123	61	109	138	92	48
Private sector guaranteed by public sector	..	..	..	..	..	..
Private sector not guaranteed	0	80	..	..	..	..
Principal repayments (long-term)	**16**	**48**	**66**	**106**	**105**	**103**
Public and publicly guaranteed sector	16	32	39	55	54	52
Public sector	16	32	39	55	54	52
of which: General government	15	32	38	55	54	52
Private sector guaranteed by public sector	..	..	..	..	..	..
Private sector not guaranteed	..	15	27	51	51	51
Interest payments (long-term)	**11**	**28**	**32**	**33**	**33**	**30**
Public and publicly guaranteed sector	11	18	19	22	23	24
Public sector	11	18	19	22	23	24
of which: General government	11	17	19	22	23	24
Private sector guaranteed by public sector	..	..	..	..	..	..
Private sector not guaranteed	..	11	13	11	9	6
Summary external debt stock by creditor type						
Long-term external debt stocks	**885**	**1,284**	**1,343**	**1,362**	**1,361**	**1,327**
Public and publicly guaranteed debt from:	885	1,049	1,135	1,205	1,255	1,271
Official creditors	869	1,033	1,101	1,172	1,223	1,240
Multilateral	533	694	726	788	815	825
of which: World Bank	9	25	36	75	83	90
Bilateral	336	339	376	384	408	415
Private creditors	16	16	33	33	32	31
Bondholders	0	0	0	0	0	0
Commercial banks and others	16	16	33	33	32	31
Private nonguaranteed debt from:	0	235	208	157	106	56
Bondholders	..	..	..	..	..	..
Commercial banks and others	0	235	208	157	106	56
Use of IMF credit	190	117	124	121	120	125
Net financial inflows						
Net debt inflows						
Use of IMF credit	-1	-4	..	..	..	..
Long-term	107	93	44	32	-12	-55
Official creditors	107	29	53	84	39	-4
Multilateral	56	7	26	64	28	6
of which: World Bank	0	5	9	41	8	4
Bilateral	51	22	27	19	11	-9
Private creditors	0	64	-10	-51	-51	-51
Bondholders	..	..	..	..	0	0
Banks and others	0	64	-10	-51	-51	-51
Short-term	-125	-80	-122	6	-7	5
Net equity inflows						
Foreign direct investment	39	137	274	957	1,514	1,834
Portfolio equity	..	0	0	0	0	..
Debt ratios						
External debt stocks to exports (%)	118	95	93	100	82	..
External debt stocks to GNI (%)	41	37	33	34	30	35
Debt service to exports (%)	3	5	6	9	7	..
Short-term to external debt stocks (%)	24	15	7	8	3	4
Multilateral to external debt stocks (%)	38	42	46	49	53	55
Reserves to external debt stocks (%)	56	35	36	32	37	45
Gross national income (GNI)	3,446	4,478	4,737	4,760	5,127	4,267

HAITI

(US$ million, unless otherwise indicated)

	2010	2016	2017	2018	2019	2020
Summary external debt data by debtor type						
Total external debt stocks	**959.1**	**2,167.8**	**2,169.8**	**2,219.7**	**2,213.9**	**2,317.7**
Use of IMF credit	134.9	216.0	212.7	200.6	185.5	291.1
Long-term external debt	824.0	1,950.8	1,955.0	2,019.1	2,012.0	2,026.5
Public and publicly guaranteed sector	824.0	1,946.6	1,954.4	2,018.8	2,012.0	2,026.5
Public sector	824.0	1,946.6	1,954.4	2,018.8	2,012.0	2,026.5
of which: General government	777.5	1,912.8	1,923.4	1,990.4	1,986.5	2,003.9
Private sector guaranteed by public sector	..	..	..	..	..	..
Private sector not guaranteed	..	4.2	0.7	0.2	0.0	0.0
Short-term external debt	0.1	1.0	2.1	0.1	16.3	0.1
Disbursements (long-term)	**287.6**	**106.0**	**16.5**	**40.1**	**3.2**	**..**
Public and publicly guaranteed sector	287.6	102.0	16.5	40.1	3.2	..
Public sector	287.6	102.0	16.5	40.1	3.2	..
of which: General government	287.6	102.0	16.5	39.6	3.2	..
Private sector guaranteed by public sector	..	..	..	..	..	..
Private sector not guaranteed	..	4.0	..	..	..	..
Principal repayments (long-term)	**122.4**	**67.6**	**9.4**	**5.5**	**6.6**	**7.3**
Public and publicly guaranteed sector	122.4	67.2	5.8	5.1	6.4	7.3
Public sector	122.4	67.2	5.8	5.1	6.4	7.3
of which: General government	121.5	64.2	3.0	2.1	3.5	4.4
Private sector guaranteed by public sector	..	..	..	..	..	..
Private sector not guaranteed	..	0.5	3.6	0.4	0.2	..
Interest payments (long-term)	**8.0**	**19.3**	**4.6**	**3.5**	**3.2**	**2.5**
Public and publicly guaranteed sector	8.0	19.2	4.6	3.4	3.2	2.5
Public sector	8.0	19.2	4.6	3.4	3.2	2.5
of which: General government	7.7	18.3	3.8	2.6	2.5	1.8
Private sector guaranteed by public sector	..	..	..	..	..	..
Private sector not guaranteed	..	0.2	0.1	0.1	0.0	..
Summary external debt stock by creditor type						
Long-term external debt stocks	**824.0**	**1,950.8**	**1,955.0**	**2,019.1**	**2,012.0**	**2,026.5**
Public and publicly guaranteed debt from:	824.0	1,946.6	1,954.4	2,018.8	2,012.0	2,026.5
Official creditors	774.0	1,901.3	1,909.0	1,973.5	1,967.9	1,983.5
Multilateral	557.0	89.2	101.3	99.3	96.4	92.1
of which: World Bank	0.0	..	..	..	..	..
Bilateral	217.0	1,812.0	1,807.7	1,874.2	1,871.5	1,891.4
Private creditors	50.0	45.3	45.3	45.3	44.2	43.0
Bondholders	..	..	..	..	..	..
Commercial banks and others	50.0	45.3	45.3	45.3	44.2	43.0
Private nonguaranteed debt from:	..	4.2	0.7	0.2	0.0	0.0
Bondholders	..	..	..	..	..	..
Commercial banks and others	..	4.2	0.7	0.2	0.0	0.0
Use of IMF credit	134.9	216.0	212.7	200.6	185.5	291.1
Net financial inflows						
Net debt inflows						
Use of IMF credit	124.8	39.5	-5.9	-9.6	-10.7	97.6
Long-term	165.1	38.4	7.1	34.6	-3.4	-7.3
Official creditors	165.1	34.9	10.7	35.0	-2.0	-6.1
Multilateral	42.3	10.0	15.0	-1.6	0.7	-3.2
of which: World Bank	-35.9	..	..	..	..	..
Bilateral	122.9	24.8	-4.3	36.6	-2.7	-2.9
Private creditors	..	3.5	-3.6	-0.4	-1.4	-1.2
Bondholders	..	..	..	..	..	..
Banks and others	..	3.5	-3.6	-0.4	-1.4	-1.2
Short-term	-0.1	0.0	0.1	-0.1	0.0	0.0
Net equity inflows						
Foreign direct investment	178.0	104.9	374.9	105.0	75.0	30.0
Portfolio equity	0.0	..	..	..	..	..
Debt ratios						
External debt stocks to exports (%)	91.4	128.6	135.7	120.1	123.0	..
External debt stocks to GNI (%)	8.2	15.7	15.2	13.9	15.4	17.2
Debt service to exports (%)	12.5	5.4	1.2	1.0	1.2	..
Short-term to external debt stocks (%)	0.0	0.0	0.1	0.0	0.7	0.0
Multilateral to external debt stocks (%)	58.1	4.1	4.7	4.5	4.4	4.0
Reserves to external debt stocks (%)	197.2	97.2	107.6	103.4	..	..
Gross national income (GNI)	11,683.9	13,771.2	14,272.3	16,015.9	14,381.8	13,446.6

HONDURAS

(US$ million, unless otherwise indicated)

	2010	2016	2017	2018	2019	2020
Summary external debt data by debtor type						
Total external debt stocks	**4,008**	**7,614**	**8,742**	**9,167**	**9,745**	**11,017**
Use of IMF credit	220	166	176	172	171	664
Long-term external debt	3,413	7,009	8,072	8,293	8,795	9,733
Public and publicly guaranteed sector	2,834	6,084	7,126	7,351	7,751	8,589
Public sector	2,834	6,084	7,126	7,351	7,751	8,589
of which: General government	2,678	5,848	6,793	6,967	7,379	8,305
Private sector guaranteed by public sector	0	..	..	..	..	..
Private sector not guaranteed	579	925	946	942	1,044	1,145
Short-term external debt	374	439	493	702	778	619
Disbursements (long-term)	**906**	**775**	**1,695**	**1,013**	**1,079**	**2,058**
Public and publicly guaranteed sector	454	387	1,160	523	693	1,604
Public sector	454	387	1,160	523	693	1,604
of which: General government	452	311	1,061	466	671	1,604
Private sector guaranteed by public sector	..	..	..	..	..	..
Private sector not guaranteed	452	388	535	490	386	454
Principal repayments (long-term)	**453**	**685**	**713**	**730**	**553**	**1,194**
Public and publicly guaranteed sector	63	179	203	256	276	822
Public sector	63	179	203	256	276	822
of which: General government	54	167	199	251	242	732
Private sector guaranteed by public sector	..	..	..	..	..	..
Private sector not guaranteed	390	506	510	474	277	372
Interest payments (long-term)	**56**	**237**	**238**	**285**	**328**	**321**
Public and publicly guaranteed sector	46	218	220	267	305	302
Public sector	46	218	220	267	305	302
of which: General government	43	213	206	256	286	286
Private sector guaranteed by public sector	..	..	..	..	..	..
Private sector not guaranteed	10	20	19	18	23	19
Summary external debt stock by creditor type						
Long-term external debt stocks	**3,413**	**7,009**	**8,072**	**8,293**	**8,795**	**9,733**
Public and publicly guaranteed debt from:	2,834	6,084	7,126	7,351	7,751	8,589
Official creditors	2,704	4,697	4,965	5,183	5,620	6,392
Multilateral	1,907	3,894	4,135	4,395	4,564	5,404
of which: World Bank	602	940	985	937	908	1,034
Bilateral	796	804	830	788	1,056	988
Private creditors	131	1,387	2,161	2,168	2,131	2,197
Bondholders	..	1,000	1,700	1,700	1,700	1,800
Commercial banks and others	131	387	461	468	431	397
Private nonguaranteed debt from:	579	925	946	942	1,044	1,145
Bondholders	..	..	..	..	..	..
Commercial banks and others	579	925	946	942	1,044	1,145
Use of IMF credit	220	166	176	172	171	664
Net financial inflows						
Net debt inflows						
Use of IMF credit	-2	-1	..	..	..	470
Long-term	454	90	982	283	526	864
Official creditors	393	166	197	255	452	727
Multilateral	389	131	183	284	178	804
of which: World Bank	109	1	-4	-28	-23	95
Bilateral	3	35	14	-29	274	-77
Private creditors	61	-76	785	28	74	137
Bondholders	..	..	700	0	0	100
Banks and others	61	-76	85	28	74	37
Short-term	124	-54	55	210	76	-160
Net equity inflows						
Foreign direct investment	592	1,181	862	766	716	297
Portfolio equity	..	..	..	..	..	..
Debt ratios						
External debt stocks to exports (%)	80	112	117	125	131	171
External debt stocks to GNI (%)	27	38	40	41	42	50
Debt service to exports (%)	10	14	13	14	12	24
Short-term to external debt stocks (%)	9	6	6	8	8	6
Multilateral to external debt stocks (%)	48	51	47	48	47	49
Reserves to external debt stocks (%)	67	50	54	52	59	73
Gross national income (GNI)	15,110	20,197	21,721	22,173	23,175	22,201

INDIA

(US$ million, unless otherwise indicated)

	2010	2016	2017	2018	2019	2020
Summary external debt data by debtor type						
Total external debt stocks	**290,428**	**455,502**	**511,473**	**521,030**	**560,871**	**564,179**
Use of IMF credit	6,127	5,348	5,666	5,533	5,501	5,730
Long-term external debt	227,853	366,221	408,198	411,574	448,590	454,916
Public and publicly guaranteed sector	100,563	152,973	182,914	180,395	191,861	192,785
Public sector	100,507	152,973	182,914	180,395	191,861	192,785
of which: General government	78,545	111,062	141,985	134,209	140,056	139,287
Private sector guaranteed by public sector	56	..	..	..	..	..
Private sector not guaranteed	127,290	213,248	225,284	231,179	256,729	262,131
Short-term external debt	56,448	83,933	97,609	103,924	106,780	103,533
Disbursements (long-term)	**43,406**	**41,942**	**78,141**	**52,132**	**71,708**	**67,570**
Public and publicly guaranteed sector	24,337	11,570	39,420	18,990	24,616	22,372
Public sector	24,337	11,570	39,420	18,990	24,616	22,372
of which: General government	18,716	6,194	33,034	7,864	11,596	13,974
Private sector guaranteed by public sector	0	..	..	..	..	..
Private sector not guaranteed	19,069	30,372	38,721	33,141	47,093	45,197
Principal repayments (long-term)	**19,018**	**65,971**	**38,667**	**46,229**	**34,762**	**63,970**
Public and publicly guaranteed sector	5,164	20,472	11,982	21,016	13,220	24,174
Public sector	5,144	20,472	11,982	21,016	13,220	24,174
of which: General government	2,630	11,409	4,189	15,244	5,822	16,958
Private sector guaranteed by public sector	20	..	..	..	..	..
Private sector not guaranteed	13,854	45,499	26,684	25,213	21,543	39,796
Interest payments (long-term)	**4,675**	**9,540**	**10,346**	**13,975**	**12,888**	**11,192**
Public and publicly guaranteed sector	1,063	2,105	2,151	2,615	3,283	1,650
Public sector	1,061	2,105	2,151	2,615	3,283	1,650
of which: General government	687	770	952	1,217	1,496	1,281
Private sector guaranteed by public sector	2	..	..	..	..	..
Private sector not guaranteed	3,612	7,435	8,195	11,361	9,605	9,543
Summary external debt stock by creditor type						
Long-term external debt stocks	**227,853**	**366,221**	**408,198**	**411,574**	**448,590**	**454,916**
Public and publicly guaranteed debt from:	100,563	152,973	182,914	180,395	191,861	192,785
Official creditors	72,499	73,229	78,044	81,001	84,366	95,969
Multilateral	46,513	50,789	52,976	54,165	56,404	64,268
of which: World Bank	37,068	36,348	37,234	36,464	36,809	39,577
Bilateral	25,986	22,440	25,068	26,836	27,961	31,700
Private creditors	28,065	79,744	104,870	99,394	107,495	96,817
Bondholders	14,700	53,246	81,997	73,809	81,351	71,333
Commercial banks and others	13,364	26,499	22,873	25,585	26,144	25,484
Private nonguaranteed debt from:	127,290	213,248	225,284	231,179	256,729	262,131
Bondholders	13,217	10,040	14,645	13,962	19,197	25,820
Commercial banks and others	114,073	203,208	210,639	217,216	237,532	236,310
Use of IMF credit	6,127	5,348	5,666	5,533	5,501	5,730
Net financial inflows						
Net debt inflows						
Use of IMF credit	..	..	..	..	..	..
Long-term	24,388	-24,029	39,474	5,903	36,946	3,600
Official creditors	5,221	1,978	2,450	3,420	3,301	9,103
Multilateral	4,581	1,014	885	1,747	2,381	6,997
of which: World Bank	3,027	506	-369	-243	465	1,985
Bilateral	640	965	1,564	1,673	920	2,107
Private creditors	19,168	-26,008	37,025	2,482	33,645	-5,503
Bondholders	10,339	-3,796	33,310	-8,417	12,784	-3,460
Banks and others	8,829	-22,211	3,715	10,899	20,861	-2,044
Short-term	9,845	2,370	13,676	6,315	2,856	-3,246
Net equity inflows						
Foreign direct investment	27,357	41,987	37,098	39,234	43,136	59,496
Portfolio equity	30,442	2,337	5,928	-4,361	13,769	24,854
Debt ratios						
External debt stocks to exports (%)	81	102	101	93	99	111
External debt stocks to GNI (%)	18	20	20	19	20	22
Debt service to exports (%)	7	17	10	11	9	15
Short-term to external debt stocks (%)	19	18	19	20	19	18
Multilateral to external debt stocks (%)	16	11	10	10	10	11
Reserves to external debt stocks (%)	95	75	76	72	77	97
Gross national income (GNI)	1,657,660	2,247,940	2,622,800	2,672,176	2,843,265	2,598,299

INDONESIA

(US$ million, unless otherwise indicated)

	2010	2016	2017	2018	2019	2020
Summary external debt data by debtor type						
Total external debt stocks	**198,278**	**318,942**	**353,564**	**379,589**	**402,106**	**417,532**
Use of IMF credit	3,050	2,662	2,820	2,754	2,739	2,852
Long-term external debt	162,181	275,595	304,012	328,875	354,569	370,192
Public and publicly guaranteed sector	102,748	177,073	194,953	215,072	233,528	248,419
Public sector	102,748	177,073	194,953	215,072	233,528	248,419
of which: General government	94,026	154,762	175,600	183,262	199,076	206,991
Private sector guaranteed by public sector	..	..	..	..	..	..
Private sector not guaranteed	59,433	98,522	109,059	113,802	121,041	121,773
Short-term external debt	33,047	40,685	46,731	47,960	44,799	44,488
Disbursements (long-term)	**34,335**	**68,083**	**78,616**	**72,086**	**94,778**	**65,672**
Public and publicly guaranteed sector	13,695	26,669	27,535	31,060	31,656	30,834
Public sector	13,695	26,669	27,535	31,060	31,656	30,834
of which: General government	8,139	23,903	24,690	15,822	25,950	21,355
Private sector guaranteed by public sector	..	..	..	..	..	..
Private sector not guaranteed	20,640	41,414	51,081	41,026	63,122	34,838
Principal repayments (long-term)	**26,202**	**53,835**	**46,884**	**42,905**	**68,392**	**52,577**
Public and publicly guaranteed sector	8,072	10,029	11,765	10,614	13,235	18,469
Public sector	8,072	10,029	11,765	10,614	13,235	18,469
of which: General government	7,823	5,951	5,961	7,858	10,178	15,905
Private sector guaranteed by public sector	..	..	..	..	..	..
Private sector not guaranteed	18,129	43,806	35,119	32,291	55,157	34,108
Interest payments (long-term)	**4,944**	**9,730**	**10,595**	**10,703**	**12,046**	**13,531**
Public and publicly guaranteed sector	3,034	5,959	6,579	6,767	7,867	9,360
Public sector	3,034	5,959	6,579	6,767	7,867	9,360
of which: General government	2,834	4,906	5,520	5,873	6,281	6,742
Private sector guaranteed by public sector	..	..	..	..	..	..
Private sector not guaranteed	1,910	3,771	4,015	3,936	4,179	4,170
Summary external debt stock by creditor type						
Long-term external debt stocks	**162,181**	**275,595**	**304,012**	**328,875**	**354,569**	**370,192**
Public and publicly guaranteed debt from:	102,748	177,073	194,953	215,072	233,528	248,419
Official creditors	66,176	51,549	51,666	53,072	52,276	57,928
Multilateral	22,567	27,496	28,363	30,099	31,447	34,077
of which: World Bank	11,367	17,224	17,941	18,507	19,109	19,669
Bilateral	43,609	24,052	23,302	22,973	20,829	23,851
Private creditors	36,572	125,524	143,287	162,000	181,251	190,491
Bondholders	28,698	114,376	135,396	151,001	173,224	182,704
Commercial banks and others	7,874	11,149	7,891	10,999	8,027	7,786
Private nonguaranteed debt from:	59,433	98,522	109,059	113,802	121,041	121,773
Bondholders	8,437	13,306	14,383	15,038	16,515	18,208
Commercial banks and others	50,996	85,216	94,677	98,764	104,526	103,565
Use of IMF credit	3,050	2,662	2,820	2,754	2,739	2,852
Net financial inflows						
Net debt inflows						
Use of IMF credit	..	..	..	..	..	..
Long-term	8,134	14,248	31,732	29,182	26,386	13,095
Official creditors	1,406	-472	-905	1,401	-927	3,978
Multilateral	1,367	1,595	736	1,785	1,354	2,149
of which: World Bank	1,287	1,221	645	594	617	472
Bilateral	39	-2,067	-1,641	-384	-2,282	1,829
Private creditors	6,727	14,720	32,637	27,780	27,313	9,116
Bondholders	3,198	17,144	21,257	16,496	23,767	10,493
Banks and others	3,529	-2,424	11,380	11,284	3,546	-1,377
Short-term	8,998	2,254	6,046	1,229	-3,161	-311
Net equity inflows						
Foreign direct investment	12,447	4,684	18,839	19,993	25,069	19,348
Portfolio equity	2,132	1,319	-2,538	-3,668	-397	-4,362
Debt ratios						
External debt stocks to exports (%)	118	186	177	172	194	228
External debt stocks to GNI (%)	27	35	36	38	37	41
Debt service to exports (%)	19	37	29	25	39	37
Short-term to external debt stocks (%)	17	13	13	13	11	11
Multilateral to external debt stocks (%)	11	9	8	8	8	8
Reserves to external debt stocks (%)	47	36	36	31	31	31
Gross national income (GNI)	734,988	902,045	983,438	1,011,213	1,085,070	1,029,919

IRAN, ISLAMIC REPUBLIC OF

(US$ million, unless otherwise indicated)

	2010	2016	2017	2018	2019	2020
Summary external debt data by debtor type						
Total external debt stocks	**19,769**	**6,058**	**6,819**	**5,774**	**4,855**	**5,451**
Use of IMF credit	2,196	1,917	2,031	1,983	1,972	2,054
Long-term external debt	5,960	827	589	1,637	1,285	1,313
Public and publicly guaranteed sector	5,960	827	589	437	370	419
Public sector	5,947	827	589	437	370	419
of which: General government	929	378	280	206	141	132
Private sector guaranteed by public sector	12	..	..	..	..	..
Private sector not guaranteed	0	0	0	1,200	915	894
Short-term external debt	11,613	3,314	4,199	2,154	1,599	2,085
Disbursements (long-term)	**249**	**37**	**123**	**0**	**29**	**116**
Public and publicly guaranteed sector	249	37	123	0	29	116
Public sector	244	37	123	0	29	116
of which: General government	72	0	0	0	..	52
Private sector guaranteed by public sector	5	..	..	..	..	..
Private sector not guaranteed	..	..	..	..	..	..
Principal repayments (long-term)	**1,532**	**1,934**	**387**	**138**	**256**	**263**
Public and publicly guaranteed sector	1,532	1,934	387	138	93	84
Public sector	1,530	1,934	387	138	93	84
of which: General government	33	99	99	74	65	65
Private sector guaranteed by public sector	2	..	..	..	..	..
Private sector not guaranteed	..	..	..	..	163	178
Interest payments (long-term)	**136**	**88**	**22**	**18**	**33**	**26**
Public and publicly guaranteed sector	136	88	22	18	15	15
Public sector	135	88	22	18	15	15
of which: General government	13	6	7	6	7	4
Private sector guaranteed by public sector	0	..	..	..	..	..
Private sector not guaranteed	..	..	..	..	18	11
Summary external debt stock by creditor type						
Long-term external debt stocks	**5,960**	**827**	**589**	**1,637**	**1,285**	**1,313**
Public and publicly guaranteed debt from:	5,960	827	589	437	370	419
Official creditors	2,068	593	520	413	325	300
Multilateral	833	407	342	272	199	190
of which: World Bank	801	355	271	206	141	132
Bilateral	1,234	186	177	141	126	110
Private creditors	3,892	234	70	24	45	118
Bondholders	..	..	..	..	..	..
Commercial banks and others	3,892	234	70	24	45	118
Private nonguaranteed debt from:	0	0	0	1,200	915	894
Bondholders	..	..	..	..	..	..
Commercial banks and others	0	0	0	1,200	915	894
Use of IMF credit	2,196	1,917	2,031	1,983	1,972	2,054
Net financial inflows						
Net debt inflows						
Use of IMF credit	..	..	..	..	..	..
Long-term	-1,283	-1,897	-264	-138	-227	-146
Official creditors	-202	-162	-88	-93	-86	-33
Multilateral	78	-72	-72	-67	-72	-18
of which: World Bank	64	-83	-84	-65	-65	-13
Bilateral	-281	-90	-16	-26	-14	-15
Private creditors	-1,081	-1,735	-176	-45	-141	-113
Bondholders	..	..	..	..	..	..
Banks and others	-1,081	-1,735	-176	-45	-141	-113
Short-term	2,826	1,292	886	-2,047	-612	445
Net equity inflows						
Foreign direct investment	3,649	3,372	5,019	2,373	1,508	1,342
Portfolio equity	..	..	..	..	..	..
Debt ratios						
External debt stocks to exports (%)	20	6	6	5	7	14
External debt stocks to GNI (%)	4	1	2	2	2	3
Debt service to exports (%)	2	2	0	0	0	1
Short-term to external debt stocks (%)	59	55	62	37	33	38
Multilateral to external debt stocks (%)	4	7	5	5	4	3
Reserves to external debt stocks (%)	..	..	..	..	..	..
Gross national income (GNI)	486,887	419,265	446,174	295,974	258,444	192,237

JAMAICA

(US$ million, unless otherwise indicated)

	2010	2016	2017	2018	2019	2020
Summary external debt data by debtor type						
Total external debt stocks	**14,193**	**14,127**	**14,808**	**18,381**	**18,577**	**18,035**
Use of IMF credit	1,188	1,103	1,152	1,074	978	1,449
Long-term external debt	11,916	11,363	11,862	15,102	15,330	14,801
Public and publicly guaranteed sector	7,609	9,507	9,929	9,759	9,407	9,151
Public sector	7,608	9,507	9,929	9,759	9,407	9,151
of which: General government	6,391	8,398	9,190	9,115	8,798	8,575
Private sector guaranteed by public sector	1	..	..	..	..	..
Private sector not guaranteed	4,307	1,856	1,932	5,344	5,923	5,650
Short-term external debt	1,089	1,662	1,794	2,205	2,269	1,785
Disbursements (long-term)	**2,360**	**1,097**	**1,184**	**1,389**	**1,613**	**487**
Public and publicly guaranteed sector	1,285	1,054	1,079	294	1,009	260
Public sector	1,285	1,054	1,079	294	1,009	260
of which: General government	1,054	1,018	1,073	285	993	257
Private sector guaranteed by public sector	..	..	..	..	..	..
Private sector not guaranteed	1,075	44	105	1,096	604	227
Principal repayments (long-term)	**345**	**1,206**	**712**	**460**	**1,405**	**1,008**
Public and publicly guaranteed sector	337	1,170	683	456	1,355	521
Public sector	337	1,170	683	456	1,355	521
of which: General government	226	1,093	595	352	1,305	483
Private sector guaranteed by public sector	..	..	..	..	..	..
Private sector not guaranteed	9	37	28	4	50	487
Interest payments (long-term)	**829**	**667**	**652**	**688**	**775**	**713**
Public and publicly guaranteed sector	489	575	558	591	607	552
Public sector	489	575	558	591	607	552
of which: General government	401	514	503	541	559	513
Private sector guaranteed by public sector	..	..	..	..	..	..
Private sector not guaranteed	341	92	94	96	168	161
Summary external debt stock by creditor type						
Long-term external debt stocks	**11,916**	**11,363**	**11,862**	**15,102**	**15,330**	**14,801**
Public and publicly guaranteed debt from:	7,609	9,507	9,929	9,759	9,407	9,151
Official creditors	3,271	3,643	3,609	3,645	3,585	3,566
Multilateral	2,352	2,967	2,922	2,940	2,915	2,947
of which: World Bank	579	809	862	865	886	945
Bilateral	919	677	687	705	670	619
Private creditors	4,338	5,863	6,320	6,114	5,822	5,585
Bondholders	3,786	5,632	6,163	6,064	5,810	5,585
Commercial banks and others	552	232	157	50	12	0
Private nonguaranteed debt from:	4,307	1,856	1,932	5,344	5,923	5,650
Bondholders	4,290	1,175	1,175	1,175	1,775	2,000
Commercial banks and others	17	681	757	4,169	4,148	3,650
Use of IMF credit	1,188	1,103	1,152	1,074	978	1,449
Net financial inflows						
Net debt inflows						
Use of IMF credit	778	113	-16	-53	-90	417
Long-term	2,015	-109	472	929	208	-521
Official creditors	863	51	-50	42	-54	-23
Multilateral	835	90	-49	18	-22	34
of which: World Bank	181	-16	53	3	21	60
Bilateral	29	-39	-1	24	-32	-57
Private creditors	1,151	-160	522	887	263	-497
Bondholders	1,007	-90	532	-100	347	-250
Banks and others	145	-70	-9	987	-84	-247
Short-term	350	119	130	409	64	-441
Net equity inflows						
Foreign direct investment	183	928	889	775	665	265
Portfolio equity	0	33	251	181	257	261
Debt ratios						
External debt stocks to exports (%)	334	300	285	299	292	486
External debt stocks to GNI (%)	112	105	103	121	120	136
Debt service to exports (%)	28	41	27	20	36	50
Short-term to external debt stocks (%)	8	12	12	12	12	10
Multilateral to external debt stocks (%)	17	21	20	16	16	16
Reserves to external debt stocks (%)	18	23	26	19	20	22
Gross national income (GNI)	12,726	13,480	14,386	15,131	15,422	13,253

JORDAN

(US$ million, unless otherwise indicated)

	2010	2016	2017	2018	2019	2020
Summary external debt data by debtor type						
Total external debt stocks	**16,894**	**27,110**	**30,051**	**31,925**	**33,482**	**38,016**
Use of IMF credit	257	1,820	1,500	981	729	1,271
Long-term external debt	7,588	14,821	17,619	19,434	20,455	22,662
Public and publicly guaranteed sector	6,323	12,507	15,158	16,363	16,841	18,756
Public sector	6,190	12,430	15,089	16,329	16,811	18,729
of which: General government	5,755	11,839	14,479	15,734	16,142	18,079
Private sector guaranteed by public sector	133	76	69	34	30	28
Private sector not guaranteed	1,265	2,314	2,460	3,071	3,614	3,905
Short-term external debt	9,049	10,470	10,933	11,511	12,297	14,084
Disbursements (long-term)	**1,508**	**3,501**	**3,230**	**2,782**	**2,812**	**4,043**
Public and publicly guaranteed sector	1,358	3,241	2,983	2,013	2,037	3,439
Public sector	1,358	3,241	2,983	2,013	2,037	3,439
of which: General government	1,087	3,232	2,938	1,884	1,928	3,439
Private sector guaranteed by public sector	0	0	0	0	0	0
Private sector not guaranteed	150	259	247	769	775	604
Principal repayments (long-term)	**506**	**1,641**	**651**	**749**	**1,777**	**2,089**
Public and publicly guaranteed sector	480	1,566	553	591	1,545	1,775
Public sector	472	1,558	545	583	1,541	1,773
of which: General government	464	1,531	507	542	1,506	1,752
Private sector guaranteed by public sector	8	8	8	8	4	2
Private sector not guaranteed	26	75	98	158	231	313
Interest payments (long-term)	**161**	**324**	**441**	**603**	**734**	**580**
Public and publicly guaranteed sector	145	282	387	504	581	523
Public sector	139	279	383	501	579	523
of which: General government	130	258	363	481	557	508
Private sector guaranteed by public sector	6	4	3	3	1	1
Private sector not guaranteed	16	42	55	99	153	56
Summary external debt stock by creditor type						
Long-term external debt stocks	**7,588**	**14,821**	**17,619**	**19,434**	**20,455**	**22,662**
Public and publicly guaranteed debt from:	6,323	12,507	15,158	16,363	16,841	18,756
Official creditors	5,284	5,914	6,563	7,097	8,203	9,427
Multilateral	2,526	3,290	3,449	3,795	4,731	5,491
of which: World Bank	1,040	1,857	1,876	2,252	2,985	3,329
Bilateral	2,757	2,624	3,115	3,301	3,472	3,936
Private creditors	1,040	6,593	8,595	9,266	8,638	9,330
Bondholders	881	6,444	8,429	9,115	8,500	9,198
Commercial banks and others	159	149	166	152	138	132
Private nonguaranteed debt from:	1,265	2,314	2,460	3,071	3,614	3,905
Bondholders	..	..	..	..	..	..
Commercial banks and others	1,265	2,314	2,460	3,071	3,614	3,905
Use of IMF credit	257	1,820	1,500	981	729	1,271
Net financial inflows						
Net debt inflows						
Use of IMF credit	-4	-195	-416	-493	-246	495
Long-term	1,002	1,860	2,579	2,033	1,035	1,955
Official creditors	151	647	438	747	1,118	979
Multilateral	152	428	101	371	941	691
of which: World Bank	-71	308	19	376	733	344
Bilateral	-1	220	338	376	177	288
Private creditors	851	1,212	2,140	1,286	-83	976
Bondholders	736	986	1,986	686	-615	700
Banks and others	116	227	155	600	531	276
Short-term	530	163	463	578	787	1,786
Net equity inflows						
Foreign direct investment	1,688	1,553	2,030	955	825	718
Portfolio equity	-21	334	-476	41	-62	..
Debt ratios						
External debt stocks to exports (%)	124	190	198	198	191	337
External debt stocks to GNI (%)	63	68	73	75	75	87
Debt service to exports (%)	6	17	12	14	19	28
Short-term to external debt stocks (%)	54	39	36	36	37	37
Multilateral to external debt stocks (%)	15	12	11	12	14	14
Reserves to external debt stocks (%)	77	52	..	..	..	..
Gross national income (GNI)	26,919	39,587	41,203	42,733	44,510	43,567

KAZAKHSTAN

(US$ million, unless otherwise indicated)

	2010	2016	2017	2018	2019	2020
Summary external debt data by debtor type						
Total external debt stocks	**119,151**	**163,488**	**158,949**	**156,979**	**158,958**	**162,974**
Use of IMF credit	529	462	489	478	475	495
Long-term external debt	109,757	156,294	150,781	148,135	149,494	152,445
Public and publicly guaranteed sector	3,845	21,425	21,295	24,181	24,716	25,430
Public sector	3,845	21,425	21,295	24,181	24,716	25,430
of which: General government	3,712	14,071	13,806	14,652	15,220	15,666
Private sector guaranteed by public sector	..	..	..	..	..	..
Private sector not guaranteed	105,912	134,869	129,486	123,954	124,779	127,015
Short-term external debt	8,864	6,732	7,678	8,366	8,989	10,034
Disbursements (long-term)	**45,054**	**30,505**	**31,525**	**33,912**	**31,801**	**34,189**
Public and publicly guaranteed sector	1,522	1,712	892	3,504	1,975	1,570
Public sector	1,522	1,712	892	3,504	1,975	1,570
of which: General government	1,508	1,454	243	1,447	1,581	1,300
Private sector guaranteed by public sector	..	..	..	..	..	..
Private sector not guaranteed	43,532	28,793	30,632	30,408	29,826	32,618
Principal repayments (long-term)	**34,639**	**17,415**	**24,529**	**29,807**	**29,334**	**27,125**
Public and publicly guaranteed sector	278	418	1,042	581	1,433	1,082
Public sector	278	418	1,042	581	1,433	1,082
of which: General government	99	401	528	565	1,003	1,066
Private sector guaranteed by public sector	..	..	..	..	..	..
Private sector not guaranteed	34,361	16,997	23,487	29,226	27,901	26,042
Interest payments (long-term)	**4,517**	**2,668**	**3,185**	**3,518**	**3,177**	**3,353**
Public and publicly guaranteed sector	54	801	859	902	1,079	1,022
Public sector	54	801	859	902	1,079	1,022
of which: General government	48	434	489	525	586	516
Private sector guaranteed by public sector	..	..	..	..	..	..
Private sector not guaranteed	4,463	1,866	2,325	2,617	2,098	2,331
Summary external debt stock by creditor type						
Long-term external debt stocks	**109,757**	**156,294**	**150,781**	**148,135**	**149,494**	**152,445**
Public and publicly guaranteed debt from:	3,845	21,425	21,295	24,181	24,716	25,430
Official creditors	3,845	7,990	8,361	8,372	7,634	8,097
Multilateral	2,785	7,175	6,925	6,638	6,010	6,265
of which: World Bank	1,830	4,313	4,185	3,977	3,802	3,615
Bilateral	1,060	815	1,435	1,734	1,624	1,833
Private creditors	0	13,435	12,935	15,810	17,082	17,333
Bondholders	..	13,435	12,935	15,810	17,082	17,333
Commercial banks and others	0	..	..	..	..	..
Private nonguaranteed debt from:	105,912	134,869	129,486	123,954	124,779	127,015
Bondholders	21,044	6,273	9,272	7,908	6,684	7,717
Commercial banks and others	84,868	128,596	120,213	116,046	118,094	119,299
Use of IMF credit	529	462	489	478	475	495
Net financial inflows						
Net debt inflows						
Use of IMF credit	..	..	..	..	..	..
Long-term	10,415	13,090	6,995	4,105	2,467	7,064
Official creditors	1,244	1,294	350	9	-746	480
Multilateral	1,436	1,082	-250	-281	-629	295
of which: World Bank	1,283	1,053	-128	-208	-175	-187
Bilateral	-192	212	600	290	-117	185
Private creditors	9,170	11,796	6,645	4,096	3,213	6,584
Bondholders	-1,053	-482	1,499	2,797	-101	1,098
Banks and others	10,224	12,278	5,146	1,299	3,314	5,486
Short-term	1,879	300	929	661	617	1,231
Net equity inflows						
Foreign direct investment	4,162	9,042	5,748	2,649	6,684	5,695
Portfolio equity	134	-27	22	-1,520	481	346
Debt ratios						
External debt stocks to exports (%)	175	373	283	225	232	303
External debt stocks to GNI (%)	93	132	107	100	100	105
Debt service to exports (%)	58	46	50	48	48	57
Short-term to external debt stocks (%)	7	4	5	5	6	6
Multilateral to external debt stocks (%)	2	4	4	4	4	4
Reserves to external debt stocks (%)	21	12	11	11	6	7
Gross national income (GNI)	128,672	123,828	148,657	157,279	158,975	154,905

KENYA

(US$ million, unless otherwise indicated)

	2010	2016	2017	2018	2019	2020
Summary external debt data by debtor type						
Total external debt stocks	**8,862**	**21,037**	**26,930**	**31,414**	**34,941**	**38,194**
Use of IMF credit	817	1,103	1,047	879	720	1,391
Long-term external debt	7,004	17,800	23,226	27,989	31,611	34,509
Public and publicly guaranteed sector	7,004	17,126	22,378	26,968	30,793	33,688
Public sector	7,004	17,126	22,378	26,968	30,793	33,688
of which: General government	6,566	16,629	21,067	25,459	29,238	32,133
Private sector guaranteed by public sector	..	..	..	..	..	..
Private sector not guaranteed	..	673	849	1,021	817	821
Short-term external debt	1,041	2,134	2,657	2,546	2,611	2,294
Disbursements (long-term)	**532**	**2,784**	**5,217**	**6,621**	**6,722**	**3,557**
Public and publicly guaranteed sector	532	2,649	5,183	6,247	6,712	3,413
Public sector	532	2,649	5,183	6,247	6,712	3,413
of which: General government	522	2,538	4,343	6,016	6,638	3,406
Private sector guaranteed by public sector	..	..	..	..	..	..
Private sector not guaranteed	..	135	34	374	10	144
Principal repayments (long-term)	**260**	**529**	**710**	**1,566**	**3,012**	**1,428**
Public and publicly guaranteed sector	260	332	569	1,370	2,802	1,273
Public sector	260	332	569	1,370	2,802	1,273
of which: General government	233	315	519	1,331	2,764	1,223
Private sector guaranteed by public sector	..	..	..	..	..	..
Private sector not guaranteed	..	196	141	196	210	154
Interest payments (long-term)	**90**	**479**	**657**	**996**	**1,242**	**1,195**
Public and publicly guaranteed sector	90	437	606	941	1,181	1,150
Public sector	90	437	606	941	1,181	1,150
of which: General government	81	435	602	917	1,156	1,125
Private sector guaranteed by public sector	..	..	..	..	..	..
Private sector not guaranteed	..	42	51	55	61	45
Summary external debt stock by creditor type						
Long-term external debt stocks	**7,004**	**17,800**	**23,226**	**27,989**	**31,611**	**34,509**
Public and publicly guaranteed debt from:	7,004	17,126	22,378	26,968	30,793	33,688
Official creditors	6,716	13,265	17,511	20,334	23,692	26,283
Multilateral	4,110	6,975	8,779	10,116	12,716	15,157
of which: World Bank	3,238	4,568	5,303	5,802	7,125	9,334
Bilateral	2,606	6,290	8,732	10,218	10,976	11,126
Private creditors	289	3,861	4,867	6,634	7,101	7,406
Bondholders	..	2,750	2,750	4,750	6,100	6,100
Commercial banks and others	289	1,111	2,117	1,884	1,001	1,306
Private nonguaranteed debt from:	..	673	849	1,021	817	821
Bondholders	..	..	..	..	..	..
Commercial banks and others	..	673	849	1,021	817	821
Use of IMF credit	817	1,103	1,047	879	720	1,391
Net financial inflows						
Net debt inflows						
Use of IMF credit	-26	-68	-119	-146	-154	620
Long-term	272	2,255	4,507	5,056	3,711	2,129
Official creditors	270	2,166	3,652	3,082	3,430	1,921
Multilateral	223	813	1,428	1,510	2,641	2,015
of which: World Bank	132	334	455	631	1,359	1,866
Bilateral	47	1,353	2,224	1,572	790	-94
Private creditors	2	90	855	1,973	280	208
Bondholders	..	..	..	2,000	1,350	0
Banks and others	2	90	855	-27	-1,070	208
Short-term	73	-593	457	-132	139	-338
Net equity inflows						
Foreign direct investment	89	432	793	627	901	717
Portfolio equity	22	57	-126	-293	14	..
Debt ratios						
External debt stocks to exports (%)	97	210	254	267	298	380
External debt stocks to GNI (%)	22	31	35	36	37	39
Debt service to exports (%)	4	11	15	24	38	28
Short-term to external debt stocks (%)	12	10	10	8	7	6
Multilateral to external debt stocks (%)	46	33	33	32	36	40
Reserves to external debt stocks (%)	49	36	27	26	26	22
Gross national income (GNI)	39,852	68,178	77,456	86,329	93,578	97,005

KOSOVO

(US$ million, unless otherwise indicated)

	2010	2016	2017	2018	2019	2020
Summary external debt data by debtor type						
Total external debt stocks	**1,456**	**2,125**	**2,504**	**2,326**	**2,428**	**3,108**
Use of IMF credit	114	195	272	260	225	216
Long-term external debt	886	1,309	1,397	1,265	1,357	1,931
Public and publicly guaranteed sector	319	274	313	305	320	517
Public sector	319	274	313	305	320	517
of which: General government	319	240	263	250	267	467
Private sector guaranteed by public sector	..	0	0	0	0	0
Private sector not guaranteed	567	1,035	1,083	961	1,037	1,414
Short-term external debt	455	621	836	800	846	962
Disbursements (long-term)	**169**	**193**	**196**	**225**	**283**	**567**
Public and publicly guaranteed sector	0	36	25	25	44	193
Public sector	0	36	25	25	44	193
of which: General government	0	14	10	13	39	192
Private sector guaranteed by public sector	..	..	..	..	..	0
Private sector not guaranteed	169	157	171	200	239	375
Principal repayments (long-term)	**76**	**107**	**97**	**208**	**171**	**251**
Public and publicly guaranteed sector	14	19	20	21	24	27
Public sector	14	19	20	21	24	27
of which: General government	14	15	15	16	17	21
Private sector guaranteed by public sector	..	..	..	..	..	0
Private sector not guaranteed	61	89	78	187	148	224
Interest payments (long-term)	**34**	**56**	**50**	**55**	**47**	**47**
Public and publicly guaranteed sector	11	11	11	11	10	11
Public sector	11	11	11	11	10	11
of which: General government	11	10	9	9	9	9
Private sector guaranteed by public sector	..	..	..	..	..	0
Private sector not guaranteed	23	45	39	45	37	36
Summary external debt stock by creditor type						
Long-term external debt stocks	**886**	**1,309**	**1,397**	**1,265**	**1,357**	**1,931**
Public and publicly guaranteed debt from:	319	274	313	305	320	517
Official creditors	319	267	305	297	304	488
Multilateral	319	217	239	240	254	441
of which: World Bank	319	217	239	225	220	314
Bilateral	0	50	66	56	50	46
Private creditors	..	7	8	8	16	30
Bondholders	..	..	..	..	..	..
Commercial banks and others	..	7	8	8	16	30
Private nonguaranteed debt from:	567	1,035	1,083	961	1,037	1,414
Bondholders	..	..	..	..	..	..
Commercial banks and others	567	1,035	1,083	961	1,037	1,414
Use of IMF credit	114	195	272	260	225	216
Net financial inflows						
Net debt inflows						
Use of IMF credit	29	-15	64	-5	-34	-18
Long-term	94	86	99	17	112	316
Official creditors	-14	14	4	4	12	154
Multilateral	-14	-5	-4	11	17	162
of which: World Bank	-14	-5	-4	-5	-1	77
Bilateral	..	19	8	-7	-5	-8
Private creditors	108	72	94	13	100	162
Bondholders	..	..	..	..	..	..
Banks and others	108	72	94	13	100	162
Short-term	-366	-58	215	-36	46	116
Net equity inflows						
Foreign direct investment	439	202	262	309	266	368
Portfolio equity	0	0	0	0	0	0
Debt ratios						
External debt stocks to exports (%)	104	116	111	90	93	154
External debt stocks to GNI (%)	25	31	34	29	30	40
Debt service to exports (%)	8	12	9	11	10	19
Short-term to external debt stocks (%)	31	29	33	34	35	31
Multilateral to external debt stocks (%)	22	10	10	10	10	14
Reserves to external debt stocks (%)	56	30	33	38	40	35
Gross national income (GNI)	5,925	6,802	7,390	8,076	8,133	7,799

KYRGYZ REPUBLIC

(US$ million, unless otherwise indicated)

	2010	2016	2017	2018	2019	2020
Summary external debt data by debtor type						
Total external debt stocks	**4,118**	**7,972**	**8,125**	**8,158**	**8,448**	**8,697**
Use of IMF credit	307	302	321	285	258	498
Long-term external debt	3,616	7,308	7,448	7,416	7,674	7,647
Public and publicly guaranteed sector	2,446	3,606	3,886	3,647	3,706	3,837
Public sector	2,446	3,606	3,886	3,647	3,706	3,837
of which: General government	2,446	3,606	3,886	3,647	3,706	3,837
Private sector guaranteed by public sector	..	..	..	..	..	..
Private sector not guaranteed	1,171	3,702	3,562	3,769	3,968	3,809
Short-term external debt	195	362	356	457	517	552
Disbursements (long-term)	**672**	**900**	**526**	**680**	**898**	**390**
Public and publicly guaranteed sector	151	341	283	143	189	166
Public sector	151	341	283	143	189	166
of which: General government	151	341	283	143	189	166
Private sector guaranteed by public sector	..	..	..	..	..	..
Private sector not guaranteed	521	558	243	537	708	224
Principal repayments (long-term)	**462**	**574**	**465**	**432**	**631**	**508**
Public and publicly guaranteed sector	38	86	82	102	122	125
Public sector	38	86	82	102	122	125
of which: General government	38	86	82	102	122	125
Private sector guaranteed by public sector	..	..	..	..	..	..
Private sector not guaranteed	424	488	383	331	509	384
Interest payments (long-term)	**69**	**75**	**83**	**84**	**88**	**87**
Public and publicly guaranteed sector	23	47	51	54	56	55
Public sector	23	47	51	54	56	55
of which: General government	23	47	51	54	56	55
Private sector guaranteed by public sector	..	..	..	..	..	..
Private sector not guaranteed	46	28	32	30	32	32
Summary external debt stock by creditor type						
Long-term external debt stocks	**3,616**	**7,308**	**7,448**	**7,416**	**7,674**	**7,647**
Public and publicly guaranteed debt from:	2,446	3,606	3,886	3,647	3,706	3,837
Official creditors	2,446	3,606	3,886	3,647	3,706	3,837
Multilateral	1,296	1,349	1,446	1,442	1,455	1,582
of which: World Bank	649	631	667	660	657	677
Bilateral	1,150	2,257	2,440	2,205	2,250	2,255
Private creditors	..	..	..	..	..	..
Bondholders	..	..	..	..	..	..
Commercial banks and others	..	..	..	..	..	..
Private nonguaranteed debt from:	1,171	3,702	3,562	3,769	3,968	3,809
Bondholders	..	..	..	0	0	0
Commercial banks and others	1,171	3,702	3,562	3,768	3,968	3,809
Use of IMF credit	307	302	321	285	258	498
Net financial inflows						
Net debt inflows						
Use of IMF credit	12	6	1	-29	-26	223
Long-term	210	326	61	248	267	-118
Official creditors	113	255	201	41	67	41
Multilateral	8	29	16	30	22	65
of which: World Bank	5	-2	-1	8	1	-7
Bilateral	105	226	185	11	46	-23
Private creditors	97	71	-141	206	200	-159
Bondholders	..	..	..	..	0	0
Banks and others	97	71	-141	206	200	-159
Short-term	-238	10	-6	101	59	35
Net equity inflows						
Foreign direct investment	231	446	-17	86	490	262
Portfolio equity	-18	-1	0	0	0	..
Debt ratios						
External debt stocks to exports (%)	181	328	312	294	269	354
External debt stocks to GNI (%)	92	123	111	102	104	117
Debt service to exports (%)	25	28	22	20	24	26
Short-term to external debt stocks (%)	5	5	4	6	6	6
Multilateral to external debt stocks (%)	31	17	18	18	17	18
Reserves to external debt stocks (%)	39	23	23	21	20	21
Gross national income (GNI)	4,489	6,455	7,331	8,020	8,092	7,406

LAO PEOPLE'S DEMOCRATIC REPUBLIC

(US$ million, unless otherwise indicated)

	2010	2016	2017	2018	2019	2020
Summary external debt data by debtor type						
Total external debt stocks	**6,554**	**13,535**	**14,696**	**15,377**	**16,701**	**17,164**
Use of IMF credit	88	68	72	70	70	73
Long-term external debt	6,410	12,745	13,879	14,903	16,046	16,106
Public and publicly guaranteed sector	3,751	7,313	8,419	9,315	10,329	10,393
Public sector	3,751	7,313	8,419	9,315	10,329	10,393
of which: General government	3,528	7,117	8,252	9,151	10,170	10,239
Private sector guaranteed by public sector	..	0	0	0	0	0
Private sector not guaranteed	2,659	5,433	5,461	5,588	5,717	5,714
Short-term external debt	56	722	745	404	585	985
Disbursements (long-term)	**460**	**2,308**	**1,332**	**1,650**	**1,331**	**633**
Public and publicly guaranteed sector	267	968	1,156	1,402	1,208	633
Public sector	267	968	1,156	1,402	1,208	633
of which: General government	267	968	1,156	1,377	1,208	633
Private sector guaranteed by public sector	..	..	..	..	..	0
Private sector not guaranteed	193	1,340	176	248	124	..
Principal repayments (long-term)	**217**	**326**	**446**	**536**	**261**	**730**
Public and publicly guaranteed sector	59	236	298	416	259	726
Public sector	59	236	298	416	259	726
of which: General government	59	231	269	389	254	721
Private sector guaranteed by public sector	..	..	..	..	..	..
Private sector not guaranteed	159	91	148	120	2	4
Interest payments (long-term)	**78**	**223**	**281**	**328**	**244**	**294**
Public and publicly guaranteed sector	28	138	176	222	211	259
Public sector	28	138	176	222	211	259
of which: General government	28	138	176	222	211	259
Private sector guaranteed by public sector	..	..	..	..	..	..
Private sector not guaranteed	50	85	105	106	33	34
Summary external debt stock by creditor type						
Long-term external debt stocks	**6,410**	**12,745**	**13,879**	**14,903**	**16,046**	**16,106**
Public and publicly guaranteed debt from:	3,751	7,313	8,419	9,315	10,329	10,393
Official creditors	3,652	6,050	6,696	7,428	8,395	8,719
Multilateral	2,084	1,478	1,600	1,577	1,701	1,801
of which: World Bank	655	493	582	588	659	717
Bilateral	1,569	4,572	5,097	5,851	6,694	6,918
Private creditors	98	1,263	1,722	1,887	1,934	1,673
Bondholders	..	1,082	1,484	1,596	1,671	1,434
Commercial banks and others	98	181	238	291	263	239
Private nonguaranteed debt from:	2,659	5,433	5,461	5,588	5,717	5,714
Bondholders	..	558	510	560	691	692
Commercial banks and others	2,659	4,874	4,951	5,028	5,026	5,022
Use of IMF credit	88	68	72	70	70	73
Net financial inflows						
Net debt inflows						
Use of IMF credit	-6	..	..	..	..	..
Long-term	243	1,982	886	1,113	1,070	-98
Official creditors	202	451	461	819	974	181
Multilateral	13	-25	36	13	133	33
of which: World Bank	-13	-4	60	19	74	30
Bilateral	189	475	425	806	842	148
Private creditors	41	1,531	425	294	96	-278
Bondholders	..	560	309	158	124	-238
Banks and others	41	971	116	137	-28	-41
Short-term	-148	23	23	-341	181	400
Net equity inflows						
Foreign direct investment	279	935	1,693	1,358	756	968
Portfolio equity	54	-5	-34	1	0	-1
Debt ratios						
External debt stocks to exports (%)	284	260	254	238	236	262
External debt stocks to GNI (%)	98	89	92	90	97	95
Debt service to exports (%)	13	11	13	13	7	16
Short-term to external debt stocks (%)	1	5	5	3	4	6
Multilateral to external debt stocks (%)	32	11	11	10	10	10
Reserves to external debt stocks (%)	11	7	7	6	6	8
Gross national income (GNI)	6,676	15,126	15,964	17,116	17,161	18,094

LEBANON

(US$ million, unless otherwise indicated)

	2010	2016	2017	2018	2019	2020
Summary external debt data by debtor type						
Total external debt stocks	**47,819**	**69,509**	**74,165**	**79,650**	**73,893**	**68,865**
Use of IMF credit	395	260	275	269	267	278
Long-term external debt	43,857	61,395	65,127	73,834	68,663	58,433
Public and publicly guaranteed sector	20,386	27,702	29,987	33,072	33,319	33,359
Public sector	20,386	27,702	29,987	33,072	33,319	33,359
of which: General government	20,386	27,702	29,987	33,072	33,319	33,359
Private sector guaranteed by public sector	..	..	..	..	..	..
Private sector not guaranteed	23,471	33,693	35,140	40,763	35,343	25,074
Short-term external debt	3,567	7,854	8,764	5,547	4,963	10,154
Disbursements (long-term)	**9,615**	**13,374**	**16,061**	**20,746**	**8,597**	**202**
Public and publicly guaranteed sector	2,186	3,651	5,152	5,716	3,173	202
Public sector	2,186	3,651	5,152	5,716	3,173	202
of which: General government	2,186	3,651	5,152	5,716	3,173	202
Private sector guaranteed by public sector	..	..	..	..	..	..
Private sector not guaranteed	7,430	9,724	10,909	15,030	5,424	..
Principal repayments (long-term)	**8,395**	**11,307**	**12,492**	**11,996**	**13,761**	**10,467**
Public and publicly guaranteed sector	2,477	2,626	3,030	2,589	2,917	198
Public sector	2,477	2,626	3,030	2,589	2,917	198
of which: General government	2,477	2,626	3,030	2,589	2,917	198
Private sector guaranteed by public sector	..	..	..	..	..	..
Private sector not guaranteed	5,918	8,680	9,462	9,407	10,844	10,269
Interest payments (long-term)	**2,735**	**3,690**	**3,779**	**4,275**	**4,597**	**2,287**
Public and publicly guaranteed sector	1,406	1,719	1,761	2,150	2,142	157
Public sector	1,406	1,719	1,761	2,150	2,142	157
of which: General government	1,406	1,719	1,761	2,150	2,142	157
Private sector guaranteed by public sector	..	..	..	..	..	..
Private sector not guaranteed	1,328	1,971	2,018	2,125	2,455	2,130
Summary external debt stock by creditor type						
Long-term external debt stocks	**43,857**	**61,395**	**65,127**	**73,834**	**68,663**	**58,433**
Public and publicly guaranteed debt from:	20,386	27,702	29,987	33,072	33,319	33,359
Official creditors	2,358	1,758	2,026	1,943	1,875	1,936
Multilateral	1,368	1,033	1,333	1,369	1,373	1,460
of which: World Bank	321	254	441	510	536	615
Bilateral	990	726	692	574	502	476
Private creditors	18,028	25,944	27,961	31,128	31,444	31,423
Bondholders	17,422	25,727	27,768	30,964	31,314	31,314
Commercial banks and others	606	217	194	164	130	109
Private nonguaranteed debt from:	23,471	33,693	35,140	40,763	35,343	25,074
Bondholders	500	500	300	600	600	600
Commercial banks and others	22,971	33,193	34,840	40,163	34,743	24,474
Use of IMF credit	395	260	275	269	267	278
Net financial inflows						
Net debt inflows						
Use of IMF credit	-19	..	..	..	..	..
Long-term	1,221	2,068	3,569	8,750	-5,164	-10,265
Official creditors	-59	-42	178	-51	-61	32
Multilateral	-13	64	265	53	7	70
of which: World Bank	3	67	186	70	26	75
Bilateral	-45	-106	-86	-105	-68	-38
Private creditors	1,279	2,110	3,390	8,802	-5,102	-10,297
Bondholders	-396	1,114	1,776	3,504	350	0
Banks and others	1,675	996	1,614	5,297	-5,452	-10,297
Short-term	568	-525	909	-3,217	-584	3,106
Net equity inflows						
Foreign direct investment	4,280	2,568	2,519	2,650	2,220	3,028
Portfolio equity	154	-135	-294	-266	344	..
Debt ratios						
External debt stocks to exports (%)	216	326	336	362	352	..
External debt stocks to GNI (%)	126	138	140	146	144	212
Debt service to exports (%)	50	71	75	75	88	..
Short-term to external debt stocks (%)	7	11	12	7	7	15
Multilateral to external debt stocks (%)	3	1	2	2	2	2
Reserves to external debt stocks (%)	66	62	59	51	52	36
Gross national income (GNI)	37,935	50,390	52,931	54,647	51,373	32,478

LESOTHO

(US$ million, unless otherwise indicated)

	2010	2016	2017	2018	2019	2020
Summary external debt data by debtor type						
Total external debt stocks	**788.1**	**921.5**	**936.0**	**903.6**	**935.9**	**1,052.2**
Use of IMF credit	78.8	108.3	108.1	93.8	79.3	119.4
Long-term external debt	709.2	774.8	827.5	809.3	856.2	930.8
Public and publicly guaranteed sector	709.2	774.8	827.5	809.3	856.2	930.8
Public sector	709.2	774.8	827.5	809.3	856.2	930.8
of which: General government	697.9	774.1	826.4	807.1	851.6	925.9
Private sector guaranteed by public sector	..	..	..	..	..	..
Private sector not guaranteed	..	..	..	..	..	..
Short-term external debt	0.0	38.4	0.4	0.5	0.4	2.1
Disbursements (long-term)	**45.4**	**59.6**	**38.9**	**42.7**	**91.2**	**79.2**
Public and publicly guaranteed sector	45.4	59.6	38.9	42.7	91.2	79.2
Public sector	45.4	59.6	38.9	42.7	91.2	79.2
of which: General government	45.4	59.3	38.5	41.6	88.7	79.1
Private sector guaranteed by public sector	..	..	..	..	..	..
Private sector not guaranteed	..	..	..	..	..	..
Principal repayments (long-term)	**19.4**	**40.2**	**33.2**	**42.0**	**37.2**	**43.8**
Public and publicly guaranteed sector	19.4	40.2	33.2	42.0	37.2	43.8
Public sector	19.4	40.2	33.2	42.0	37.2	43.8
of which: General government	18.6	40.1	33.2	42.0	37.2	43.8
Private sector guaranteed by public sector	..	..	..	..	..	..
Private sector not guaranteed	..	..	..	..	..	..
Interest payments (long-term)	**7.8**	**14.2**	**16.1**	**16.9**	**23.8**	**16.0**
Public and publicly guaranteed sector	7.8	14.2	16.1	16.9	23.8	16.0
Public sector	7.8	14.2	16.1	16.9	23.8	16.0
of which: General government	6.4	14.2	16.1	16.9	23.8	16.0
Private sector guaranteed by public sector	..	..	..	..	..	..
Private sector not guaranteed	..	..	..	..	..	..
Summary external debt stock by creditor type						
Long-term external debt stocks	**709.2**	**774.8**	**827.5**	**809.3**	**856.2**	**930.8**
Public and publicly guaranteed debt from:	709.2	774.8	827.5	809.3	856.2	930.8
Official creditors	687.8	769.2	821.9	804.7	852.4	926.7
Multilateral	632.7	648.5	703.5	697.0	721.7	755.5
of which: World Bank	330.2	284.1	321.4	338.3	362.8	399.5
Bilateral	55.0	120.7	118.4	107.7	130.8	171.2
Private creditors	21.5	5.6	5.6	4.6	3.8	4.1
Bondholders	..	..	..	..	..	..
Commercial banks and others	21.5	5.6	5.6	4.6	3.8	4.1
Private nonguaranteed debt from:	..	..	..	..	..	..
Bondholders	..	..	..	..	..	..
Commercial banks and others	..	..	..	..	..	..
Use of IMF credit	78.8	108.3	108.1	93.8	79.3	119.4
Net financial inflows						
Net debt inflows						
Use of IMF credit	4.4	-3.0	-6.5	-11.9	-14.0	35.6
Long-term	26.0	19.4	5.7	0.7	54.0	35.4
Official creditors	27.1	20.3	6.4	1.4	54.7	35.5
Multilateral	24.2	7.5	12.3	9.6	30.5	2.5
of which: World Bank	21.5	8.7	20.9	24.6	27.7	21.5
Bilateral	2.9	12.8	-5.9	-8.3	24.2	32.9
Private creditors	-1.1	-0.8	-0.7	-0.7	-0.8	-0.1
Bondholders	..	..	..	..	..	..
Banks and others	-1.1	-0.8	-0.7	-0.7	-0.8	-0.1
Short-term	-3.0	5.2	-37.9	-0.3	0.3	1.0
Net equity inflows						
Foreign direct investment	46.6	45.7	45.9	50.6	46.5	40.9
Portfolio equity	..	0.2	0.2	0.3	0.2	0.2
Debt ratios						
External debt stocks to exports (%)	47.3	62.5	55.9	48.6	56.8	76.6
External debt stocks to GNI (%)	27.4	38.4	35.7	31.5	34.8	50.1
Debt service to exports (%)	2.1	3.9	3.3	3.8	4.6	5.3
Short-term to external debt stocks (%)	0.0	4.2	0.0	0.1	0.0	0.2
Multilateral to external debt stocks (%)	80.3	70.4	75.2	77.1	77.1	71.8
Reserves to external debt stocks (%)	135.9	100.4	70.3	80.6	82.7	..
Gross national income (GNI)	2,872.1	2,400.9	2,620.8	2,864.8	2,690.4	2,098.2

LIBERIA

(US$ million, unless otherwise indicated)

	2010	2016	2017	2018	2019	2020
Summary external debt data by debtor type						
Total external debt stocks	**418.9**	**952.6**	**1,122.2**	**1,163.4**	**1,296.4**	**1,480.6**
Use of IMF credit	235.3	359.4	401.8	389.5	396.3	472.9
Long-term external debt	183.1	593.2	720.4	773.9	900.0	1,007.7
Public and publicly guaranteed sector	183.1	528.3	659.7	718.7	851.5	966.3
Public sector	183.1	528.3	659.7	718.7	851.5	966.3
of which: General government	183.1	528.3	659.7	718.7	851.5	966.3
Private sector guaranteed by public sector	..	..	..	..	..	..
Private sector not guaranteed	..	64.9	60.8	55.2	48.5	41.4
Short-term external debt	0.4	0.0	0.0	0.0	0.1	0.0
Disbursements (long-term)	**0.0**	**103.7**	**112.4**	**155.8**	**147.1**	**98.9**
Public and publicly guaranteed sector	0.0	103.7	110.3	153.4	145.8	97.5
Public sector	0.0	103.7	110.3	153.4	145.8	97.5
of which: General government	0.0	103.7	110.3	153.4	145.8	97.5
Private sector guaranteed by public sector	..	..	..	..	..	..
Private sector not guaranteed	..	..	2.1	2.5	1.3	1.3
Principal repayments (long-term)	**3.7**	**7.7**	**9.3**	**13.1**	**16.7**	**19.6**
Public and publicly guaranteed sector	3.7	1.6	3.0	5.2	8.9	11.8
Public sector	3.7	1.6	3.0	5.2	8.9	11.8
of which: General government	3.7	1.6	3.0	5.2	8.9	11.8
Private sector guaranteed by public sector	..	..	..	..	..	..
Private sector not guaranteed	..	6.1	6.3	7.9	7.9	7.9
Interest payments (long-term)	**0.6**	**4.2**	**5.6**	**8.4**	**8.8**	**11.2**
Public and publicly guaranteed sector	0.6	3.0	4.7	7.3	7.3	10.3
Public sector	0.6	3.0	4.7	7.3	7.3	10.3
of which: General government	0.6	3.0	4.7	7.3	7.3	10.3
Private sector guaranteed by public sector	..	..	..	..	..	..
Private sector not guaranteed	..	1.2	0.9	1.1	1.5	0.9
Summary external debt stock by creditor type						
Long-term external debt stocks	**183.1**	**593.2**	**720.4**	**773.9**	**900.0**	**1,007.7**
Public and publicly guaranteed debt from:	183.1	528.3	659.7	718.7	851.5	966.3
Official creditors	183.1	528.3	659.7	718.7	851.5	966.3
Multilateral	63.3	395.6	506.0	601.0	721.2	833.4
of which: World Bank	0.0	231.3	306.4	367.6	454.9	550.1
Bilateral	119.8	132.7	153.6	117.7	130.3	132.9
Private creditors	0.0	..	..	0.0	..	..
Bondholders	..	..	..	..	..	..
Commercial banks and others	0.0	..	..	0.0	..	..
Private nonguaranteed debt from:	..	64.9	60.8	55.2	48.5	41.4
Bondholders	..	..	..	..	..	..
Commercial banks and others	..	64.9	60.8	55.2	48.5	41.4
Use of IMF credit	235.3	359.4	401.8	389.5	396.3	472.9
Net financial inflows						
Net debt inflows						
Use of IMF credit	13.6	38.5	20.5	-3.0	9.0	58.2
Long-term	-3.7	95.9	103.1	142.8	130.3	79.2
Official creditors	-3.7	102.0	107.3	148.2	136.9	85.8
Multilateral	-3.7	83.6	87.1	106.1	123.4	86.6
of which: World Bank	-1.7	74.3	59.6	69.3	89.4	75.3
Bilateral	..	18.4	20.3	42.1	13.5	-0.8
Private creditors	..	-6.1	-4.3	-5.4	-6.6	-6.6
Bondholders	..	..	..	..	..	..
Banks and others	..	-6.1	-4.3	-5.4	-6.6	-6.6
Short-term	0.0	0.0	0.0	0.0	0.0	0.0
Net equity inflows						
Foreign direct investment	1,768.7	141.7	188.4	59.1	19.5	87.0
Portfolio equity	-1.1	0.0	0.0	..	..	..
Debt ratios						
External debt stocks to exports (%)	116.6	240.0	249.5	208.2	221.2	229.7
External debt stocks to GNI (%)	23.0	31.8	37.6	41.2	47.7	57.2
Debt service to exports (%)	1.7	3.0	3.4	4.4	7.1	11.0
Short-term to external debt stocks (%)	0.1	0.0	0.0	0.0	0.0	0.0
Multilateral to external debt stocks (%)	15.1	41.5	45.1	51.7	55.6	56.3
Reserves to external debt stocks (%)	105.5	61.5	52.2	48.4	42.3	36.4
Gross national income (GNI)	1,818.6	2,996.8	2,982.6	2,827.0	2,717.6	2,589.5

MADAGASCAR

(US$ million, unless otherwise indicated)

	2010	2016	2017	2018	2019	2020
Summary external debt data by debtor type						
Total external debt stocks	**2,756**	**2,976**	**3,382**	**3,730**	**4,065**	**4,873**
Use of IMF credit	278	301	440	465	545	956
Long-term external debt	2,054	2,470	2,765	2,994	3,239	3,644
Public and publicly guaranteed sector	2,039	2,465	2,735	2,902	3,120	3,514
Public sector	2,038	2,465	2,735	2,902	3,120	3,514
of which: General government	2,006	2,387	2,670	2,826	2,990	3,336
Private sector guaranteed by public sector	1	..	..	..	..	..
Private sector not guaranteed	15	5	30	92	119	130
Short-term external debt	425	204	177	271	281	273
Disbursements (long-term)	**198**	**133**	**272**	**363**	**328**	**348**
Public and publicly guaranteed sector	198	133	246	297	302	337
Public sector	198	133	246	297	302	337
of which: General government	180	133	246	285	247	299
Private sector guaranteed by public sector	0	..	..	..	..	..
Private sector not guaranteed	..	..	26	66	26	11
Principal repayments (long-term)	**39**	**84**	**93**	**72**	**67**	**73**
Public and publicly guaranteed sector	37	76	92	72	67	73
Public sector	37	76	92	72	67	73
of which: General government	29	68	77	71	67	72
Private sector guaranteed by public sector	0	..	..	..	..	..
Private sector not guaranteed	1	8	1	..	..	..
Interest payments (long-term)	**16**	**20**	**23**	**30**	**36**	**38**
Public and publicly guaranteed sector	16	20	23	29	30	31
Public sector	16	20	23	29	30	31
of which: General government	16	20	22	29	29	29
Private sector guaranteed by public sector	0	..	..	..	..	..
Private sector not guaranteed	0	0	0	1	7	8
Summary external debt stock by creditor type						
Long-term external debt stocks	**2,054**	**2,470**	**2,765**	**2,994**	**3,239**	**3,644**
Public and publicly guaranteed debt from:	2,039	2,465	2,735	2,902	3,120	3,514
Official creditors	2,031	2,387	2,609	2,738	2,966	3,368
Multilateral	1,575	2,015	2,254	2,349	2,491	2,814
of which: World Bank	1,161	1,433	1,595	1,648	1,686	1,874
Bilateral	456	372	355	390	475	553
Private creditors	8	78	127	164	154	146
Bondholders	..	..	..	..	..	..
Commercial banks and others	8	78	127	164	154	146
Private nonguaranteed debt from:	15	5	30	92	119	130
Bondholders	..	..	..	..	..	..
Commercial banks and others	15	5	30	92	119	130
Use of IMF credit	278	301	440	465	545	956
Net financial inflows						
Net debt inflows						
Use of IMF credit	-2	29	118	36	83	376
Long-term	159	49	178	291	261	276
Official creditors	160	65	110	185	244	277
Multilateral	106	94	133	145	156	217
of which: World Bank	75	65	77	93	48	117
Bilateral	54	-30	-23	40	88	60
Private creditors	-1	-15	68	106	17	-1
Bondholders	..	..	..	..	..	..
Banks and others	-1	-15	68	106	17	-1
Short-term	-224	26	-26	94	11	-8
Net equity inflows						
Foreign direct investment	380	54	61	74	65	359
Portfolio equity	2	0	0	0	0	..
Debt ratios						
External debt stocks to exports (%)	124	87	81	84	98	186
External debt stocks to GNI (%)	28	26	26	28	30	37
Debt service to exports (%)	3	4	3	3	3	5
Short-term to external debt stocks (%)	15	7	5	7	7	6
Multilateral to external debt stocks (%)	57	68	67	63	61	58
Reserves to external debt stocks (%)	37	40	47	47	42	41
Gross national income (GNI)	9,834	11,432	12,817	13,390	13,596	13,303

MALAWI

(US$ million, unless otherwise indicated)

	2010	2016	2017	2018	2019	2020
Summary external debt data by debtor type						
Total external debt stocks	**1,021**	**1,847**	**2,162**	**2,266**	**2,429**	**2,943**
Use of IMF credit	248	296	319	314	339	528
Long-term external debt	730	1,507	1,790	1,926	2,021	2,237
Public and publicly guaranteed sector	730	1,507	1,790	1,926	2,021	2,237
Public sector	730	1,507	1,790	1,926	2,021	2,237
of which: General government	721	1,493	1,775	1,913	2,009	2,225
Private sector guaranteed by public sector	..	..	..	..	..	..
Private sector not guaranteed	..	..	..	..	..	..
Short-term external debt	43	44	54	25	68	178
Disbursements (long-term)	**81**	**135**	**240**	**223**	**168**	**193**
Public and publicly guaranteed sector	81	135	240	223	168	193
Public sector	81	135	240	223	168	193
of which: General government	78	135	240	223	168	193
Private sector guaranteed by public sector	..	..	..	..	..	..
Private sector not guaranteed	..	..	..	..	..	..
Principal repayments (long-term)	**13**	**33**	**33**	**42**	**62**	**52**
Public and publicly guaranteed sector	13	33	33	42	62	52
Public sector	13	33	33	42	62	52
of which: General government	12	32	32	41	61	51
Private sector guaranteed by public sector	..	..	..	..	..	..
Private sector not guaranteed	..	..	..	..	..	..
Interest payments (long-term)	**7**	**17**	**16**	**12**	**17**	**21**
Public and publicly guaranteed sector	7	17	16	12	17	21
Public sector	7	17	16	12	17	21
of which: General government	7	17	16	12	17	21
Private sector guaranteed by public sector	..	..	..	..	..	..
Private sector not guaranteed	..	..	..	..	..	..
Summary external debt stock by creditor type						
Long-term external debt stocks	**730**	**1,507**	**1,790**	**1,926**	**2,021**	**2,237**
Public and publicly guaranteed debt from:	730	1,507	1,790	1,926	2,021	2,237
Official creditors	724	1,507	1,790	1,926	2,021	2,237
Multilateral	586	1,088	1,369	1,487	1,600	1,799
of which: World Bank	243	642	862	917	969	1,104
Bilateral	138	419	420	439	421	438
Private creditors	5	..	..	..	..	..
Bondholders	..	..	..	..	..	..
Commercial banks and others	5	..	..	..	..	..
Private nonguaranteed debt from:	..	..	..	..	..	..
Bondholders	..	..	..	..	..	..
Commercial banks and others	..	..	..	..	..	..
Use of IMF credit	248	296	319	314	339	528
Net financial inflows						
Net debt inflows						
Use of IMF credit	21	51	5	3	27	169
Long-term	68	102	207	181	106	141
Official creditors	68	102	207	181	106	141
Multilateral	46	108	221	150	120	139
of which: World Bank	34	76	180	78	58	92
Bilateral	22	-6	-14	31	-14	2
Private creditors	..	..	..	..	..	..
Bondholders	..	..	..	..	..	..
Banks and others	..	..	..	..	..	..
Short-term	-24	31	5	-26	43	110
Net equity inflows						
Foreign direct investment	133	25	81	91	89	98
Portfolio equity	1	..	..	..	..	..
Debt ratios						
External debt stocks to exports (%)	83	156	204	201	207	262
External debt stocks to GNI (%)	15	34	25	24	23	25
Debt service to exports (%)	2	6	7	7	8	9
Short-term to external debt stocks (%)	4	2	2	1	3	6
Multilateral to external debt stocks (%)	57	59	63	66	66	61
Reserves to external debt stocks (%)	30	33	36	34	34	20
Gross national income (GNI)	6,851	5,410	8,634	9,548	10,681	11,771

MALDIVES

(US$ million, unless otherwise indicated)

	2010	2016	2017	2018	2019	2020
Summary external debt data by debtor type						
Total external debt stocks	**916.6**	**1,222.0**	**1,515.7**	**2,339.7**	**2,679.2**	**3,403.6**
Use of IMF credit	27.6	12.1	12.3	11.4	10.8	41.6
Long-term external debt	743.1	1,080.0	1,392.1	2,089.9	2,331.9	3,013.0
Public and publicly guaranteed sector	627.8	911.8	1,234.1	2,003.9	2,228.2	2,895.1
Public sector	615.8	911.8	1,234.1	1,949.6	2,121.4	2,774.0
of which: General government	606.9	760.5	1,078.3	1,321.0	1,432.6	1,655.5
Private sector guaranteed by public sector	12.0	0.0	0.0	54.3	106.8	121.1
Private sector not guaranteed	115.2	168.2	158.1	86.0	103.7	117.9
Short-term external debt	145.9	129.8	111.3	238.4	336.5	349.0
Disbursements (long-term)	**168.5**	**387.7**	**420.1**	**1,124.0**	**612.7**	**787.0**
Public and publicly guaranteed sector	142.4	330.4	388.1	1,124.0	562.1	772.8
Public sector	142.4	330.4	388.1	1,069.7	509.6	752.1
of which: General government	142.4	198.9	349.8	330.2	179.1	184.7
Private sector guaranteed by public sector	..	..	..	54.3	52.5	20.7
Private sector not guaranteed	26.1	57.3	32.0	..	50.7	14.2
Principal repayments (long-term)	**59.8**	**122.9**	**144.6**	**373.9**	**364.1**	**197.8**
Public and publicly guaranteed sector	50.9	83.1	102.4	333.9	331.1	197.8
Public sector	47.9	83.1	102.4	333.9	331.1	191.4
of which: General government	44.5	71.6	68.5	67.3	60.7	53.6
Private sector guaranteed by public sector	3.0	..	..	0.0	0.0	6.4
Private sector not guaranteed	8.9	39.7	42.2	40.1	33.0	..
Interest payments (long-term)	**10.6**	**17.4**	**19.1**	**58.0**	**83.6**	**78.4**
Public and publicly guaranteed sector	9.2	14.5	15.0	54.6	80.4	75.0
Public sector	8.6	14.5	15.0	53.8	75.4	69.2
of which: General government	8.3	12.3	11.6	31.5	40.0	35.5
Private sector guaranteed by public sector	0.5	..	..	0.8	5.0	5.7
Private sector not guaranteed	1.5	2.9	4.1	3.5	3.3	3.4
Summary external debt stock by creditor type						
Long-term external debt stocks	**743.1**	**1,080.0**	**1,392.1**	**2,089.9**	**2,331.9**	**3,013.0**
Public and publicly guaranteed debt from:	627.8	911.8	1,234.1	2,003.9	2,228.2	2,895.1
Official creditors	536.2	866.2	934.4	1,294.1	1,446.1	2,031.3
Multilateral	300.5	252.6	275.9	339.7	383.8	411.2
of which: World Bank	98.6	87.5	90.1	85.4	92.2	105.6
Bilateral	235.7	613.5	658.6	954.4	1,062.4	1,620.1
Private creditors	91.6	45.7	299.6	709.8	782.0	863.8
Bondholders	..	..	250.0	350.0	350.0	350.0
Commercial banks and others	91.6	45.7	49.6	359.8	432.0	513.8
Private nonguaranteed debt from:	115.2	168.2	158.1	86.0	103.7	117.9
Bondholders	..	..	..	..	..	..
Commercial banks and others	115.2	168.2	158.1	86.0	103.7	117.9
Use of IMF credit	27.6	12.1	12.3	11.4	10.8	41.6
Net financial inflows						
Net debt inflows						
Use of IMF credit	7.0	-0.6	-0.6	-0.6	-0.6	29.4
Long-term	108.6	264.8	275.5	750.0	248.6	589.2
Official creditors	79.1	261.0	34.9	379.2	158.4	493.6
Multilateral	28.1	-8.8	7.5	69.9	45.5	15.0
of which: World Bank	15.7	-2.5	-2.5	-2.7	7.2	9.4
Bilateral	50.9	269.9	27.4	309.2	112.9	478.6
Private creditors	29.6	3.8	240.6	370.9	90.2	95.6
Bondholders	..	..	250.0	100.0	..	..
Banks and others	29.6	3.8	-9.4	270.9	90.2	95.6
Short-term	-460.0	-26.3	-17.6	126.0	96.7	-24.8
Net equity inflows						
Foreign direct investment	216.5	456.6	457.8	575.7	956.2	348.3
Portfolio equity	-10.4	-0.7	-0.8	31.8	-30.4	124.2
Debt ratios						
External debt stocks to exports (%)	45.6	38.7	45.5	64.9	71.2	187.5
External debt stocks to GNI (%)	40.3	30.4	34.6	48.7	52.7	90.5
Debt service to exports (%)	4.0	4.6	5.0	12.3	12.2	15.9
Short-term to external debt stocks (%)	15.9	10.6	7.3	10.2	12.6	10.3
Multilateral to external debt stocks (%)	32.8	20.7	18.2	14.5	14.3	12.1
Reserves to external debt stocks (%)	39.7	39.1	39.5	30.9	28.5	29.2
Gross national income (GNI)	2,276.9	4,025.5	4,378.5	4,807.1	5,082.0	3,759.3

MALI

(US$ million, unless otherwise indicated)

	2010	2016	2017	2018	2019	2020
Summary external debt data by debtor type						
Total external debt stocks	**2,446**	**3,782**	**4,279**	**4,631**	**5,104**	**6,081**
Use of IMF credit	187	288	334	441	447	681
Long-term external debt	2,253	3,413	3,851	4,080	4,549	5,317
Public and publicly guaranteed sector	2,253	3,413	3,851	4,080	4,549	5,317
Public sector	2,253	3,413	3,851	4,080	4,549	5,317
of which: General government	2,250	3,411	3,850	4,079	4,547	5,316
Private sector guaranteed by public sector	..	..	..	..	..	..
Private sector not guaranteed	..	..	..	..	..	..
Short-term external debt	6	80	93	110	109	83
Disbursements (long-term)	**310**	**244**	**290**	**474**	**656**	**674**
Public and publicly guaranteed sector	310	244	290	474	656	674
Public sector	310	244	290	474	656	674
of which: General government	310	244	290	474	656	674
Private sector guaranteed by public sector	..	..	..	..	..	..
Private sector not guaranteed	..	..	..	..	..	..
Principal repayments (long-term)	**39**	**71**	**89**	**129**	**140**	**180**
Public and publicly guaranteed sector	39	71	89	129	140	180
Public sector	39	71	89	129	140	180
of which: General government	38	71	89	129	140	179
Private sector guaranteed by public sector	..	..	..	..	..	..
Private sector not guaranteed	..	..	..	..	..	..
Interest payments (long-term)	**21**	**35**	**35**	**42**	**51**	**40**
Public and publicly guaranteed sector	21	35	35	42	51	40
Public sector	21	35	35	42	51	40
of which: General government	21	35	35	42	51	40
Private sector guaranteed by public sector	..	..	..	..	..	..
Private sector not guaranteed	..	..	..	..	..	..
Summary external debt stock by creditor type						
Long-term external debt stocks	**2,253**	**3,413**	**3,851**	**4,080**	**4,549**	**5,317**
Public and publicly guaranteed debt from:	2,253	3,413	3,851	4,080	4,549	5,317
Official creditors	2,248	3,413	3,851	4,080	4,549	5,317
Multilateral	1,788	2,505	2,904	3,090	3,476	4,024
of which: World Bank	840	1,364	1,574	1,682	1,970	2,146
Bilateral	460	908	947	990	1,072	1,293
Private creditors	5	0	0	0	0	0
Bondholders	..	..	..	..	..	..
Commercial banks and others	5	0	0	0	0	0
Private nonguaranteed debt from:	..	..	..	..	..	..
Bondholders	..	..	..	..	..	..
Commercial banks and others	..	..	..	..	..	..
Use of IMF credit	187	288	334	441	447	681
Net financial inflows						
Net debt inflows						
Use of IMF credit	6	41	28	116	9	208
Long-term	271	174	201	345	516	495
Official creditors	272	174	201	345	516	495
Multilateral	229	87	204	274	417	332
of which: World Bank	151	57	123	149	298	70
Bilateral	43	87	-3	71	99	163
Private creditors	-1	0	0	0	0	0
Bondholders	..	..	..	..	..	..
Banks and others	-1	0	0	0	0	0
Short-term	-18	-3	12	19	10	-22
Net equity inflows						
Foreign direct investment	373	237	365	358	721	308
Portfolio equity	1	5	2	-1	..	..
Debt ratios						
External debt stocks to exports (%)	98	112	121	106	..	..
External debt stocks to GNI (%)	24	28	29	28	31	36
Debt service to exports (%)	2	4	4	4	..	..
Short-term to external debt stocks (%)	0	2	2	2	2	1
Multilateral to external debt stocks (%)	73	66	68	67	68	66
Reserves to external debt stocks (%)	55	..	..	..	..	..
Gross national income (GNI)	10,269	13,651	14,865	16,561	16,671	16,749

MAURITANIA

(US$ million, unless otherwise indicated)

	2010	2016	2017	2018	2019	2020
Summary external debt data by debtor type						
Total external debt stocks	**3,556**	**5,080**	**5,241**	**5,226**	**5,370**	**5,710**
Use of IMF credit	145	180	200	221	244	424
Long-term external debt	2,326	3,865	4,002	3,952	4,043	4,211
Public and publicly guaranteed sector	2,326	3,865	4,002	3,952	4,043	4,211
Public sector	2,326	3,865	4,002	3,952	4,043	4,211
of which: General government	1,993	3,011	3,214	3,238	3,383	3,606
Private sector guaranteed by public sector	..	..	..	..	..	..
Private sector not guaranteed	..	..	..	..	..	..
Short-term external debt	1,086	1,035	1,040	1,052	1,083	1,075
Disbursements (long-term)	**412**	**390**	**250**	**270**	**367**	**228**
Public and publicly guaranteed sector	412	390	250	270	367	228
Public sector	412	390	250	270	367	228
of which: General government	262	390	248	270	345	228
Private sector guaranteed by public sector	..	..	..	..	..	..
Private sector not guaranteed	..	..	..	..	..	..
Principal repayments (long-term)	**77**	**173**	**224**	**270**	**266**	**211**
Public and publicly guaranteed sector	77	173	224	270	266	211
Public sector	77	173	224	270	266	211
of which: General government	23	96	149	198	190	155
Private sector guaranteed by public sector	..	..	..	..	..	..
Private sector not guaranteed	..	..	..	..	..	..
Interest payments (long-term)	**35**	**75**	**80**	**92**	**88**	**59**
Public and publicly guaranteed sector	35	75	80	92	88	59
Public sector	35	75	80	92	88	59
of which: General government	25	42	50	62	60	43
Private sector guaranteed by public sector	..	..	..	..	..	..
Private sector not guaranteed	..	..	..	..	..	..
Summary external debt stock by creditor type						
Long-term external debt stocks	**2,326**	**3,865**	**4,002**	**3,952**	**4,043**	**4,211**
Public and publicly guaranteed debt from:	2,326	3,865	4,002	3,952	4,043	4,211
Official creditors	2,325	3,865	4,002	3,952	4,043	4,211
Multilateral	1,501	2,239	2,358	2,284	2,379	2,481
of which: World Bank	316	366	390	382	388	418
Bilateral	824	1,627	1,644	1,668	1,664	1,729
Private creditors	1	..	..	..	..	..
Bondholders	..	..	..	..	..	..
Commercial banks and others	1	..	..	..	..	..
Private nonguaranteed debt from:	..	..	..	..	..	..
Bondholders	..	..	..	..	..	..
Commercial banks and others	..	..	..	..	..	..
Use of IMF credit	145	180	200	221	244	424
Net financial inflows						
Net debt inflows						
Use of IMF credit	34	-10	9	26	24	165
Long-term	335	217	27	0	101	17
Official creditors	346	217	27	0	101	17
Multilateral	269	181	48	-45	99	-6
of which: World Bank	39	9	2	2	8	14
Bilateral	77	36	-21	45	2	23
Private creditors	-11	..	..	..	..	..
Bondholders	..	..	..	..	..	..
Banks and others	-11	..	..	..	..	..
Short-term	103	-50	4	13	30	-8
Net equity inflows						
Foreign direct investment	131	271	588	773	-884	978
Portfolio equity	..	..	..	..	..	..
Debt ratios						
External debt stocks to exports (%)	154	294	257	235	198	193
External debt stocks to GNI (%)	64	81	79	75	72	74
Debt service to exports (%)	5	15	16	17	14	10
Short-term to external debt stocks (%)	31	20	20	20	20	19
Multilateral to external debt stocks (%)	42	44	45	44	44	43
Reserves to external debt stocks (%)	8	16	16	18	19	26
Gross national income (GNI)	5,560	6,282	6,661	7,013	7,504	7,746

MAURITIUS

(US$ million, unless otherwise indicated)

	2010	2016	2017	2018	2019	2020
Summary external debt data by debtor type						
Total external debt stocks	**7,929**	**10,464**	**15,847**	**16,112**	**18,162**	**18,527**
Use of IMF credit	149	130	138	135	134	139
Long-term external debt	6,294	5,707	10,469	11,123	12,267	12,143
Public and publicly guaranteed sector	1,007	1,628	1,547	1,430	1,378	1,909
Public sector	1,007	1,628	1,547	1,430	1,378	1,909
of which: General government	735	1,320	1,273	1,151	1,121	1,531
Private sector guaranteed by public sector	..	..	..	..	..	..
Private sector not guaranteed	5,287	4,079	8,921	9,693	10,889	10,234
Short-term external debt	1,485	4,627	5,241	4,855	5,761	6,245
Disbursements (long-term)	**2,568**	**1,830**	**2,196**	**3,535**	**3,668**	**1,980**
Public and publicly guaranteed sector	356	74	71	63	131	783
Public sector	356	74	71	63	131	783
of which: General government	211	73	70	18	112	625
Private sector guaranteed by public sector	..	..	..	..	..	..
Private sector not guaranteed	2,212	1,756	2,125	3,471	3,536	1,197
Principal repayments (long-term)	**2,118**	**1,510**	**2,637**	**2,845**	**2,499**	**2,193**
Public and publicly guaranteed sector	69	111	243	146	159	341
Public sector	69	111	243	146	159	341
of which: General government	28	73	204	106	119	303
Private sector guaranteed by public sector	..	..	..	..	..	..
Private sector not guaranteed	2,049	1,398	2,394	2,699	2,341	1,852
Interest payments (long-term)	**73**	**205**	**197**	**297**	**622**	**314**
Public and publicly guaranteed sector	17	27	30	28	29	27
Public sector	17	27	30	28	29	27
of which: General government	13	20	21	22	23	21
Private sector guaranteed by public sector	..	..	..	..	..	..
Private sector not guaranteed	56	178	167	269	593	287
Summary external debt stock by creditor type						
Long-term external debt stocks	**6,294**	**5,707**	**10,469**	**11,123**	**12,267**	**12,143**
Public and publicly guaranteed debt from:	1,007	1,628	1,547	1,430	1,378	1,909
Official creditors	888	1,601	1,522	1,411	1,366	1,883
Multilateral	501	877	815	757	789	790
of which: World Bank	204	271	263	231	207	189
Bilateral	387	724	706	654	577	1,093
Private creditors	119	28	26	19	13	26
Bondholders	..	..	..	..	..	..
Commercial banks and others	119	28	26	19	13	26
Private nonguaranteed debt from:	5,287	4,079	8,921	9,693	10,889	10,234
Bondholders	..	..	44	50	59	39
Commercial banks and others	5,287	4,079	8,878	9,643	10,830	10,195
Use of IMF credit	149	130	138	135	134	139
Net financial inflows						
Net debt inflows						
Use of IMF credit	..	..	..	..	..	..
Long-term	450	320	-441	689	1,168	-213
Official creditors	249	-33	-167	-77	-22	430
Multilateral	137	8	-108	-42	38	-36
of which: World Bank	-4	-8	-26	-25	-24	-24
Bilateral	112	-41	-59	-34	-60	466
Private creditors	201	353	-274	766	1,190	-643
Bondholders	..	..	44	6	9	-20
Banks and others	201	353	-318	760	1,181	-623
Short-term	183	-126	613	-383	906	484
Net equity inflows						
Foreign direct investment	430	379	480	461	471	246
Portfolio equity	7,821	-3,781	3,306	-691	419	-372
Debt ratios						
External debt stocks to exports (%)	78	75	92	113	118	186
External debt stocks to GNI (%)	80	79	109	101	115	156
Debt service to exports (%)	22	13	17	23	21	26
Short-term to external debt stocks (%)	19	44	33	30	32	34
Multilateral to external debt stocks (%)	6	8	5	5	4	4
Reserves to external debt stocks (%)	31	43	34	36	37	35
Gross national income (GNI)	9,913	13,230	14,573	15,880	15,788	11,896

MEXICO

(US$ million, unless otherwise indicated)

	2010	2016	2017	2018	2019	2020
Summary external debt data by debtor type						
Total external debt stocks	**245,906**	**424,268**	**444,153**	**455,828**	**472,378**	**467,512**
Use of IMF credit	4,391	3,833	4,060	3,965	3,943	4,106
Long-term external debt	198,455	367,339	387,659	390,715	405,742	413,696
Public and publicly guaranteed sector	145,925	269,136	289,216	297,827	306,466	308,532
Public sector	145,925	269,136	289,016	297,627	306,266	308,332
of which: General government	91,010	176,253	185,818	191,327	201,787	199,963
Private sector guaranteed by public sector	..	0	200	200	200	200
Private sector not guaranteed	52,529	98,203	98,443	92,888	99,276	105,164
Short-term external debt	43,061	53,096	52,433	61,147	62,693	49,709
Disbursements (long-term)	**54,656**	**63,246**	**59,556**	**37,785**	**55,190**	**56,658**
Public and publicly guaranteed sector	41,812	43,371	35,191	25,731	37,532	33,031
Public sector	41,812	43,371	34,991	25,731	37,532	33,031
of which: General government	26,246	12,806	13,424	8,417	18,303	21,260
Private sector guaranteed by public sector	..	..	200	0	0	..
Private sector not guaranteed	12,844	19,875	24,365	12,054	17,658	23,627
Principal repayments (long-term)	**21,683**	**59,177**	**38,185**	**32,563**	**36,425**	**45,124**
Public and publicly guaranteed sector	13,941	28,430	17,635	15,051	25,172	25,548
Public sector	13,941	28,430	17,635	15,051	25,172	25,548
of which: General government	2,527	12,933	4,769	1,498	4,386	16,276
Private sector guaranteed by public sector	..	0	0	0	0	0
Private sector not guaranteed	7,742	30,747	20,550	17,512	11,253	19,576
Interest payments (long-term)	**8,345**	**17,367**	**25,059**	**23,046**	**22,791**	**21,648**
Public and publicly guaranteed sector	5,859	12,362	18,712	15,899	17,120	16,415
Public sector	5,859	12,362	18,710	15,892	17,113	16,411
of which: General government	3,974	8,886	14,347	10,923	11,964	11,105
Private sector guaranteed by public sector	..	0	2	6	7	4
Private sector not guaranteed	2,486	5,005	6,347	7,148	5,671	5,233
Summary external debt stock by creditor type						
Long-term external debt stocks	**198,455**	**367,339**	**387,659**	**390,715**	**405,742**	**413,696**
Public and publicly guaranteed debt from:	145,925	269,136	289,216	297,827	306,466	308,532
Official creditors	25,389	31,139	32,723	32,605	33,509	34,347
Multilateral	21,433	27,927	29,304	29,794	31,022	31,685
of which: World Bank	12,462	14,656	14,887	14,611	14,942	15,714
Bilateral	3,956	3,212	3,419	2,810	2,487	2,662
Private creditors	120,536	237,996	256,494	265,222	272,957	274,185
Bondholders	97,656	208,310	225,580	237,164	247,179	250,632
Commercial banks and others	22,880	29,686	30,914	28,059	25,778	23,552
Private nonguaranteed debt from:	52,529	98,203	98,443	92,888	99,276	105,164
Bondholders	32,898	78,753	80,120	74,589	77,355	82,796
Commercial banks and others	19,631	19,450	18,323	18,299	21,921	22,368
Use of IMF credit	4,391	3,833	4,060	3,965	3,943	4,106
Net financial inflows						
Net debt inflows						
Use of IMF credit	..	..	..	..	..	..
Long-term	32,973	4,069	21,372	5,222	18,765	11,534
Official creditors	4,875	-1	1,344	-276	820	847
Multilateral	4,022	231	1,297	269	1,118	803
of which: World Bank	2,256	27	178	-278	298	816
Bilateral	853	-233	46	-544	-298	44
Private creditors	28,098	4,071	20,028	5,498	17,945	10,687
Bondholders	27,843	15,654	20,062	7,974	16,370	13,985
Banks and others	255	-11,584	-34	-2,476	1,575	-3,298
Short-term	17,506	-17,159	-663	8,714	1,546	-12,984
Net equity inflows						
Foreign direct investment	20,945	21,633	23,896	24,555	31,228	22,687
Portfolio equity	373	9,477	10,320	2,421	-10	186
Debt ratios						
External debt stocks to exports (%)	76	104	99	92	93	105
External debt stocks to GNI (%)	24	40	39	38	38	45
Debt service to exports (%)	10	19	15	12	12	16
Short-term to external debt stocks (%)	18	13	12	13	13	11
Multilateral to external debt stocks (%)	9	7	7	7	7	7
Reserves to external debt stocks (%)	49	41	38	38	38	41
Gross national income (GNI)	1,045,221	1,049,583	1,128,823	1,189,368	1,232,371	1,038,394

MOLDOVA

(US$ million, unless otherwise indicated)

	2010	2016	2017	2018	2019	2020
Summary external debt data by debtor type						
Total external debt stocks	**4,725**	**6,222**	**6,969**	**7,440**	**7,524**	**8,476**
Use of IMF credit	509	574	562	496	458	669
Long-term external debt	2,745	4,313	4,756	4,925	5,074	5,561
Public and publicly guaranteed sector	839	1,212	1,442	1,450	1,464	1,761
Public sector	839	1,212	1,442	1,450	1,464	1,761
of which: General government	814	1,209	1,437	1,442	1,450	1,746
Private sector guaranteed by public sector	..	..	..	..	..	..
Private sector not guaranteed	1,906	3,101	3,315	3,476	3,610	3,800
Short-term external debt	1,471	1,335	1,650	2,020	1,992	2,246
Disbursements (long-term)	**464**	**381**	**596**	**551**	**549**	**815**
Public and publicly guaranteed sector	94	207	183	138	130	312
Public sector	94	207	183	138	130	312
of which: General government	89	207	180	134	122	309
Private sector guaranteed by public sector	..	..	..	..	..	..
Private sector not guaranteed	370	174	413	413	419	503
Principal repayments (long-term)	**306**	**265**	**249**	**375**	**427**	**544**
Public and publicly guaranteed sector	55	37	50	89	101	122
Public sector	55	37	50	89	101	122
of which: General government	47	34	48	88	100	119
Private sector guaranteed by public sector	..	..	..	..	..	..
Private sector not guaranteed	251	229	200	286	325	422
Interest payments (long-term)	**49**	**61**	**55**	**67**	**63**	**65**
Public and publicly guaranteed sector	16	15	20	22	23	20
Public sector	16	15	20	22	23	20
of which: General government	14	15	20	22	22	19
Private sector guaranteed by public sector	..	..	..	..	..	..
Private sector not guaranteed	33	45	35	44	40	45
Summary external debt stock by creditor type						
Long-term external debt stocks	**2,745**	**4,313**	**4,756**	**4,925**	**5,074**	**5,561**
Public and publicly guaranteed debt from:	839	1,212	1,442	1,450	1,464	1,761
Official creditors	816	1,189	1,417	1,425	1,440	1,736
Multilateral	565	960	1,086	1,152	1,226	1,574
of which: World Bank	479	634	696	712	716	792
Bilateral	251	229	331	273	214	163
Private creditors	23	23	25	25	24	24
Bondholders	..	..	..	..	..	..
Commercial banks and others	23	23	25	25	24	24
Private nonguaranteed debt from:	1,906	3,101	3,315	3,476	3,610	3,800
Bondholders	..	..	..	..	..	..
Commercial banks and others	1,906	3,101	3,315	3,476	3,610	3,800
Use of IMF credit	509	574	562	496	458	669
Net financial inflows						
Net debt inflows						
Use of IMF credit	175	-37	-44	-54	-35	186
Long-term	159	116	347	175	122	271
Official creditors	44	169	134	48	29	192
Multilateral	49	111	51	100	85	252
of which: World Bank	42	81	28	31	8	38
Bilateral	-5	58	83	-52	-57	-60
Private creditors	115	-53	213	127	94	79
Bondholders	..	..	..	..	..	..
Banks and others	115	-53	213	127	94	79
Short-term	106	129	336	366	-20	219
Net equity inflows						
Foreign direct investment	172	135	66	166	435	92
Portfolio equity	6	0	0	-1	0	0
Debt ratios						
External debt stocks to exports (%)	174	184	174	167	161	207
External debt stocks to GNI (%)	63	73	68	62	60	68
Debt service to exports (%)	15	13	11	14	14	17
Short-term to external debt stocks (%)	31	21	24	27	26	26
Multilateral to external debt stocks (%)	12	15	16	15	16	19
Reserves to external debt stocks (%)	36	35	40	40	41	45
Gross national income (GNI)	7,481	8,517	10,221	12,007	12,594	12,387

MONGOLIA

(US$ million, unless otherwise indicated)

	2010	2016	2017	2018	2019	2020
Summary external debt data by debtor type						
Total external debt stocks	**5,928**	**24,612**	**27,963**	**29,789**	**31,650**	**33,236**
Use of IMF credit	273	66	189	287	285	401
Long-term external debt	5,290	21,958	24,612	26,404	28,405	29,717
Public and publicly guaranteed sector	1,782	5,137	7,511	8,006	8,355	9,728
Public sector	1,782	5,137	7,511	8,006	8,355	9,728
of which: General government	1,763	5,130	7,504	8,000	8,349	9,723
Private sector guaranteed by public sector	..	..	..	..	..	..
Private sector not guaranteed	3,508	16,821	17,101	18,398	20,050	19,989
Short-term external debt	365	2,589	3,163	3,098	2,960	3,118
Disbursements (long-term)	**2,929**	**5,106**	**4,325**	**8,363**	**12,750**	**3,604**
Public and publicly guaranteed sector	67	1,189	2,327	1,098	520	1,669
Public sector	67	1,189	2,327	1,098	520	1,669
of which: General government	67	1,189	2,327	1,098	520	1,669
Private sector guaranteed by public sector	..	..	..	..	..	..
Private sector not guaranteed	2,863	3,916	1,997	7,265	12,229	1,935
Principal repayments (long-term)	**139**	**938**	**2,788**	**6,614**	**11,131**	**1,322**
Public and publicly guaranteed sector	121	84	68	630	165	445
Public sector	121	84	68	630	165	445
of which: General government	46	83	68	630	164	445
Private sector guaranteed by public sector	..	..	..	..	..	..
Private sector not guaranteed	18	855	2,720	5,984	10,966	876
Interest payments (long-term)	**89**	**471**	**826**	**1,037**	**504**	**484**
Public and publicly guaranteed sector	20	112	217	244	309	319
Public sector	20	112	217	244	309	319
of which: General government	19	112	217	244	308	319
Private sector guaranteed by public sector	..	..	..	..	..	..
Private sector not guaranteed	70	358	609	793	196	165
Summary external debt stock by creditor type						
Long-term external debt stocks	**5,290**	**21,958**	**24,612**	**26,404**	**28,405**	**29,717**
Public and publicly guaranteed debt from:	1,782	5,137	7,511	8,006	8,355	9,728
Official creditors	1,776	2,857	3,814	4,334	4,744	5,809
Multilateral	1,073	1,205	1,644	1,878	2,099	2,691
of which: World Bank	403	423	579	570	579	760
Bilateral	703	1,652	2,170	2,457	2,645	3,118
Private creditors	7	2,280	3,697	3,672	3,611	3,919
Bondholders	0	2,000	3,400	3,400	3,400	3,799
Commercial banks and others	7	280	297	272	211	120
Private nonguaranteed debt from:	3,508	16,821	17,101	18,398	20,050	19,989
Bondholders	..	1,495	1,317	1,865	2,228	1,818
Commercial banks and others	3,508	15,326	15,783	16,533	17,822	18,171
Use of IMF credit	273	66	189	287	285	401
Net financial inflows						
Net debt inflows						
Use of IMF credit	19	..	116	104	0	101
Long-term	2,790	4,167	1,536	1,748	1,619	2,282
Official creditors	23	343	848	490	416	920
Multilateral	20	85	377	263	229	536
of which: World Bank	17	2	130	5	13	153
Bilateral	2	257	471	227	187	384
Private creditors	2,768	3,825	688	1,258	1,203	1,362
Bondholders	-75	500	1,232	525	440	526
Banks and others	2,843	3,325	-544	733	763	835
Short-term	117	154	574	-64	-138	154
Net equity inflows						
Foreign direct investment	1,331	-399	828	799	1,231	681
Portfolio equity	680	4	-10	-7	7	6
Debt ratios						
External debt stocks to exports (%)	173	434	407	375	359	416
External debt stocks to GNI (%)	90	240	285	253	255	280
Debt service to exports (%)	7	26	54	98	133	24
Short-term to external debt stocks (%)	6	11	11	10	9	9
Multilateral to external debt stocks (%)	18	5	6	6	7	8
Reserves to external debt stocks (%)	37	5	10	9	10	12
Gross national income (GNI)	6,610	10,265	9,817	11,765	12,425	11,871

MONTENEGRO

(US$ million, unless otherwise indicated)

	2010	2016	2017	2018	2019	2020
Summary external debt data by debtor type						
Total external debt stocks	**4,522**	**6,220**	**7,219**	**8,027**	**8,339**	**9,723**
Use of IMF credit	40	35	37	36	36	124
Long-term external debt	4,296	6,011	7,008	7,776	8,026	9,282
Public and publicly guaranteed sector	1,349	2,428	2,978	3,443	3,726	4,858
Public sector	1,340	2,380	2,935	3,417	3,717	4,852
of which: General government	1,036	2,088	2,644	3,163	3,479	4,621
Private sector guaranteed by public sector	9	49	44	26	9	6
Private sector not guaranteed	2,947	3,583	4,029	4,333	4,301	4,424
Short-term external debt	186	174	174	215	277	316
Disbursements (long-term)	**688**	**1,278**	**1,640**	**2,315**	**1,607**	**1,327**
Public and publicly guaranteed sector	383	414	456	1,175	788	1,314
Public sector	374	414	456	1,175	788	1,314
of which: General government	297	384	438	1,156	765	1,298
Private sector guaranteed by public sector	9	..	..	..	..	..
Private sector not guaranteed	305	864	1,184	1,140	819	12
Principal repayments (long-term)	**61**	**1,090**	**953**	**1,421**	**1,293**	**1,353**
Public and publicly guaranteed sector	59	375	197	591	444	518
Public sector	59	362	186	575	428	514
of which: General government	47	327	142	527	392	476
Private sector guaranteed by public sector	..	13	11	17	16	4
Private sector not guaranteed	2	715	755	830	849	836
Interest payments (long-term)	**34**	**171**	**208**	**267**	**229**	**247**
Public and publicly guaranteed sector	33	88	96	102	105	109
Public sector	33	86	94	101	105	108
of which: General government	25	79	87	95	100	104
Private sector guaranteed by public sector	..	2	2	1	0	0
Private sector not guaranteed	1	82	113	165	123	138
Summary external debt stock by creditor type						
Long-term external debt stocks	**4,296**	**6,011**	**7,008**	**7,776**	**8,026**	**9,282**
Public and publicly guaranteed debt from:	1,349	2,428	2,978	3,443	3,726	4,858
Official creditors	818	1,091	1,323	1,459	1,551	1,690
Multilateral	546	600	634	589	556	670
of which: World Bank	306	287	297	271	243	252
Bilateral	271	490	689	871	995	1,020
Private creditors	531	1,337	1,655	1,984	2,175	3,168
Bondholders	267	1,138	1,295	1,394	1,740	2,427
Commercial banks and others	264	199	360	589	435	741
Private nonguaranteed debt from:	2,947	3,583	4,029	4,333	4,301	4,424
Bondholders	..	..	..	..	..	..
Commercial banks and others	2,947	3,583	4,029	4,333	4,301	4,424
Use of IMF credit	40	35	37	36	36	124
Net financial inflows						
Net debt inflows						
Use of IMF credit	..	..	..	..	..	84
Long-term	627	187	687	894	314	-27
Official creditors	2	-10	133	167	116	59
Multilateral	-5	-14	-44	-22	-12	48
of which: World Bank	-3	-17	-26	-18	-12	-12
Bilateral	8	3	177	190	128	11
Private creditors	625	198	554	726	197	-86
Bondholders	265	135	0	163	370	490
Banks and others	359	63	554	564	-173	-575
Short-term	-1,021	-69	0	41	62	39
Net equity inflows						
Foreign direct investment	566	91	386	342	232	220
Portfolio equity	-8	17	14	0	3	-1
Debt ratios						
External debt stocks to exports (%)	263	301	309	297	302	621
External debt stocks to GNI (%)	110	141	146	144	150	201
Debt service to exports (%)	6	61	50	63	55	103
Short-term to external debt stocks (%)	4	3	2	3	3	3
Multilateral to external debt stocks (%)	12	10	9	7	7	7
Reserves to external debt stocks (%)	12	13	14	15	18	22
Gross national income (GNI)	4,114	4,415	4,956	5,572	5,562	4,849

MOROCCO

(US$ million, unless otherwise indicated)

	2010	2016	2017	2018	2019	2020
Summary external debt data by debtor type						
Total external debt stocks	**27,296**	**47,614**	**51,023**	**50,431**	**55,058**	**65,683**
Use of IMF credit	865	755	800	781	776	3,906
Long-term external debt	23,684	37,937	42,816	42,204	45,586	53,630
Public and publicly guaranteed sector	21,095	31,448	34,705	33,504	36,562	43,657
Public sector	21,092	31,448	34,705	33,504	36,551	43,622
of which: General government	13,056	19,582	21,636	20,794	23,664	29,972
Private sector guaranteed by public sector	3	..	..	0	11	35
Private sector not guaranteed	2,589	6,489	8,111	8,700	9,025	9,973
Short-term external debt	2,747	8,923	7,408	7,446	8,695	8,146
Disbursements (long-term)	**4,999**	**4,635**	**4,478**	**3,261**	**6,691**	**9,120**
Public and publicly guaranteed sector	3,882	3,042	2,965	1,799	5,448	8,025
Public sector	3,882	3,042	2,965	1,799	5,438	8,003
of which: General government	2,879	2,119	1,826	1,009	4,338	7,054
Private sector guaranteed by public sector	0	..	..	..	11	22
Private sector not guaranteed	1,116	1,593	1,513	1,462	1,243	1,095
Principal repayments (long-term)	**2,428**	**2,657**	**2,797**	**2,728**	**2,904**	**3,930**
Public and publicly guaranteed sector	1,274	2,100	2,389	2,046	2,024	3,253
Public sector	1,271	2,100	2,389	2,046	2,024	3,253
of which: General government	730	1,075	1,611	1,197	1,208	2,414
Private sector guaranteed by public sector	3	..	..	..	..	0
Private sector not guaranteed	1,154	557	408	682	880	677
Interest payments (long-term)	**850**	**1,023**	**1,016**	**1,088**	**1,053**	**1,042**
Public and publicly guaranteed sector	820	929	927	932	947	936
Public sector	819	929	927	932	947	935
of which: General government	559	512	522	519	558	561
Private sector guaranteed by public sector	0	..	..	..	0	1
Private sector not guaranteed	31	94	88	155	106	106
Summary external debt stock by creditor type						
Long-term external debt stocks	**23,684**	**37,937**	**42,816**	**42,204**	**45,586**	**53,630**
Public and publicly guaranteed debt from:	21,095	31,448	34,705	33,504	36,562	43,657
Official creditors	17,249	21,001	24,222	23,218	23,746	27,178
Multilateral	10,186	13,589	16,110	15,738	16,732	19,720
of which: World Bank	2,518	4,565	5,560	5,529	6,414	7,886
Bilateral	7,063	7,413	8,112	7,480	7,013	7,458
Private creditors	3,846	10,447	10,483	10,286	12,816	16,479
Bondholders	1,336	6,208	6,499	6,390	7,590	10,912
Commercial banks and others	2,510	4,238	3,984	3,896	5,226	5,567
Private nonguaranteed debt from:	2,589	6,489	8,111	8,700	9,025	9,973
Bondholders	..	..	..	..	..	..
Commercial banks and others	2,589	6,489	8,111	8,700	9,025	9,973
Use of IMF credit	865	755	800	781	776	3,906
Net financial inflows						
Net debt inflows						
Use of IMF credit	..	..	..	..	..	2,996
Long-term	2,571	1,978	1,681	533	3,787	5,191
Official creditors	1,123	1,093	1,230	-293	805	1,795
Multilateral	622	719	1,166	139	1,205	1,812
of which: World Bank	64	521	532	146	957	985
Bilateral	501	374	63	-432	-400	-17
Private creditors	1,448	885	451	826	2,982	3,396
Bondholders	1,327	0	0	0	1,239	3,000
Banks and others	121	885	451	826	1,743	396
Short-term	537	2,055	-1,515	38	1,250	-549
Net equity inflows						
Foreign direct investment	1,369	1,626	1,952	2,926	1,359	1,482
Portfolio equity	132	-26	-33	-184	280	-42
Debt ratios						
External debt stocks to exports (%)	98	136	129	115	123	171
External debt stocks to GNI (%)	30	47	47	44	47	59
Debt service to exports (%)	12	11	10	9	9	13
Short-term to external debt stocks (%)	10	19	15	15	16	12
Multilateral to external debt stocks (%)	37	29	32	31	30	30
Reserves to external debt stocks (%)	83	51	50	47	46	53
Gross national income (GNI)	91,933	101,326	107,533	115,795	117,366	111,167

MOZAMBIQUE

(US$ million, unless otherwise indicated)

	2010	2016	2017	2018	2019	2020
Summary external debt data by debtor type						
Total external debt stocks	**5,936**	**14,205**	**15,822**	**18,679**	**20,110**	**20,932**
Use of IMF credit	357	355	343	303	375	689
Long-term external debt	4,975	13,275	14,390	17,145	18,088	18,415
Public and publicly guaranteed sector	3,399	9,709	10,512	10,676	10,755	10,192
Public sector	3,399	9,709	10,512	10,676	10,755	10,192
of which: General government	3,300	7,989	8,897	9,180	9,464	9,775
Private sector guaranteed by public sector	..	..	..	..	..	..
Private sector not guaranteed	1,576	3,566	3,877	6,470	7,333	8,223
Short-term external debt	604	576	1,089	1,230	1,648	1,829
Disbursements (long-term)	**631**	**955**	**1,058**	**3,242**	**1,568**	**1,272**
Public and publicly guaranteed sector	403	761	720	603	705	382
Public sector	403	761	720	603	705	382
of which: General government	397	761	720	603	705	382
Private sector guaranteed by public sector	..	..	..	..	..	..
Private sector not guaranteed	228	194	338	2,639	863	890
Principal repayments (long-term)	**409**	**300**	**266**	**334**	**583**	**1,235**
Public and publicly guaranteed sector	43	243	240	287	583	1,235
Public sector	43	243	240	287	583	1,235
of which: General government	40	135	130	170	379	359
Private sector guaranteed by public sector	..	..	..	..	..	..
Private sector not guaranteed	366	57	27	47	..	..
Interest payments (long-term)	**259**	**143**	**129**	**147**	**198**	**276**
Public and publicly guaranteed sector	49	100	110	134	147	172
Public sector	49	100	110	134	147	172
of which: General government	47	96	107	130	128	118
Private sector guaranteed by public sector	..	..	..	..	..	..
Private sector not guaranteed	210	43	20	13	51	103
Summary external debt stock by creditor type						
Long-term external debt stocks	**4,975**	**13,275**	**14,390**	**17,145**	**18,088**	**18,415**
Public and publicly guaranteed debt from:	3,399	9,709	10,512	10,676	10,755	10,192
Official creditors	3,303	7,888	8,770	9,072	9,340	9,601
Multilateral	2,195	3,716	4,073	4,213	4,433	4,693
of which: World Bank	1,491	2,555	2,822	2,904	3,039	3,224
Bilateral	1,108	4,172	4,697	4,859	4,907	4,908
Private creditors	96	1,820	1,742	1,603	1,414	591
Bondholders	..	727	727	727	727	0
Commercial banks and others	96	1,094	1,015	877	688	591
Private nonguaranteed debt from:	1,576	3,566	3,877	6,470	7,333	8,223
Bondholders	..	..	..	..	..	..
Commercial banks and others	1,576	3,566	3,877	6,470	7,333	8,223
Use of IMF credit	357	355	343	303	375	689
Net financial inflows						
Net debt inflows						
Use of IMF credit	21	-33	-32	-32	73	288
Long-term	221	656	792	2,908	984	36
Official creditors	289	630	585	445	306	-9
Multilateral	255	227	162	231	242	101
of which: World Bank	158	174	113	153	154	56
Bilateral	33	403	423	214	64	-110
Private creditors	-67	26	207	2,463	678	45
Bondholders	..	..	..	..	..	-727
Banks and others	-67	26	207	2,463	678	772
Short-term	-68	-223	445	77	418	186
Net equity inflows						
Foreign direct investment	410	805	668	491	382	254
Portfolio equity	..	0	-5	0	0	3
Debt ratios						
External debt stocks to exports (%)	219	367	285	300	343	458
External debt stocks to GNI (%)	55	122	123	128	134	154
Debt service to exports (%)	25	13	8	9	15	34
Short-term to external debt stocks (%)	10	4	7	7	8	9
Multilateral to external debt stocks (%)	37	26	26	23	22	22
Reserves to external debt stocks (%)	36	14	20	16	18	18
Gross national income (GNI)	10,745	11,676	12,826	14,550	14,995	13,559

MYANMAR

(US$ million, unless otherwise indicated)

	2010	2016	2017	2018	2019	2020
Summary external debt data by debtor type						
Total external debt stocks	**10,164**	**10,107**	**10,759**	**10,685**	**11,120**	**13,348**
Use of IMF credit	378	330	350	342	340	726
Long-term external debt	8,607	9,685	10,312	10,238	10,714	12,554
Public and publicly guaranteed sector	8,607	9,638	10,284	10,224	10,686	12,519
Public sector	8,462	9,638	10,284	10,224	10,686	12,519
of which: General government	1,899	4,815	5,490	5,938	6,755	8,697
Private sector guaranteed by public sector	146	..	..	..	..	..
Private sector not guaranteed	..	47	28	14	28	35
Short-term external debt	1,179	91	97	105	66	68
Disbursements (long-term)	**887**	**446**	**400**	**757**	**1,014**	**1,655**
Public and publicly guaranteed sector	887	446	400	757	949	1,574
Public sector	887	446	400	757	949	1,574
of which: General government	14	368	381	696	864	1,538
Private sector guaranteed by public sector	0	..	..	..	..	..
Private sector not guaranteed	..	..	..	..	65	81
Principal repayments (long-term)	**201**	**493**	**430**	**530**	**493**	**454**
Public and publicly guaranteed sector	201	475	411	516	441	380
Public sector	201	475	411	516	441	380
of which: General government	25	94	41	84	52	132
Private sector guaranteed by public sector	..	..	..	..	..	..
Private sector not guaranteed	..	19	19	14	51	74
Interest payments (long-term)	**42**	**280**	**226**	**309**	**207**	**132**
Public and publicly guaranteed sector	42	279	225	309	197	117
Public sector	42	279	225	309	197	117
of which: General government	3	112	53	150	46	32
Private sector guaranteed by public sector	..	..	..	..	..	..
Private sector not guaranteed	..	1	1	..	10	15
Summary external debt stock by creditor type						
Long-term external debt stocks	**8,607**	**9,685**	**10,312**	**10,238**	**10,714**	**12,554**
Public and publicly guaranteed debt from:	8,607	9,638	10,284	10,224	10,686	12,519
Official creditors	8,005	9,278	9,931	9,911	10,401	12,257
Multilateral	1,447	1,462	1,788	1,859	2,081	2,629
of which: World Bank	799	914	1,192	1,266	1,468	1,804
Bilateral	6,558	7,816	8,144	8,053	8,320	9,628
Private creditors	602	360	353	312	285	262
Bondholders	..	..	..	..	..	..
Commercial banks and others	602	360	353	312	285	262
Private nonguaranteed debt from:	..	47	28	14	28	35
Bondholders	..	..	..	..	..	..
Commercial banks and others	..	47	28	14	28	35
Use of IMF credit	378	330	350	342	340	726
Net financial inflows						
Net debt inflows						
Use of IMF credit	..	..	..	..	..	360
Long-term	686	-47	-30	227	522	1,201
Official creditors	690	-14	1	281	535	1,220
Multilateral	0	120	226	207	232	458
of which: World Bank	..	108	214	181	208	271
Bilateral	690	-134	-224	74	304	762
Private creditors	-4	-33	-31	-53	-14	-18
Bondholders	..	..	..	..	..	..
Banks and others	-4	-33	-31	-53	-14	-18
Short-term	0	0	0	0	0	0
Net equity inflows						
Foreign direct investment	901	3,319	2,937	2,201	1,978	1,770
Portfolio equity	..	0	0	0	0	..
Debt ratios						
External debt stocks to exports (%)	129	72	73	63	59	..
External debt stocks to GNI (%)	20	17	16	16	14	18
Debt service to exports (%)	3	6	4	5	4	..
Short-term to external debt stocks (%)	12	1	1	1	1	1
Multilateral to external debt stocks (%)	14	14	17	17	19	20
Reserves to external debt stocks (%)	56	46	46	50	49	54
Gross national income (GNI)	51,506	59,831	65,232	66,675	77,688	73,922

NEPAL

(US$ million, unless otherwise indicated)

	2010	2016	2017	2018	2019	2020
Summary external debt data by debtor type						
Total external debt stocks	**3,787**	**4,297**	**4,963**	**5,511**	**6,513**	**7,905**
Use of IMF credit	219	171	168	156	147	370
Long-term external debt	3,507	3,748	4,374	5,103	5,963	7,174
Public and publicly guaranteed sector	3,507	3,665	4,299	4,974	5,845	7,056
Public sector	3,507	3,665	4,299	4,974	5,845	7,056
of which: General government	3,493	3,659	4,294	4,969	5,841	7,052
Private sector guaranteed by public sector	..	..	..	..	..	..
Private sector not guaranteed	..	83	75	129	118	118
Short-term external debt	61	379	421	252	403	361
Disbursements (long-term)	**126**	**431**	**606**	**1,017**	**1,096**	**1,157**
Public and publicly guaranteed sector	126	397	591	955	1,096	1,157
Public sector	126	397	591	955	1,096	1,157
of which: General government	126	397	591	955	1,096	1,157
Private sector guaranteed by public sector	..	..	..	..	..	..
Private sector not guaranteed	..	34	15	63	..	..
Principal repayments (long-term)	**148**	**177**	**195**	**181**	**205**	**202**
Public and publicly guaranteed sector	148	170	172	174	194	202
Public sector	148	170	172	174	194	202
of which: General government	147	169	172	173	193	201
Private sector guaranteed by public sector	..	..	..	..	..	..
Private sector not guaranteed	..	8	23	8	11	..
Interest payments (long-term)	**32**	**37**	**38**	**45**	**57**	**60**
Public and publicly guaranteed sector	32	35	36	41	52	54
Public sector	32	35	36	41	52	54
of which: General government	32	35	36	41	52	54
Private sector guaranteed by public sector	..	..	..	..	..	..
Private sector not guaranteed	..	1	2	4	6	6
Summary external debt stock by creditor type						
Long-term external debt stocks	**3,507**	**3,748**	**4,374**	**5,103**	**5,963**	**7,174**
Public and publicly guaranteed debt from:	3,507	3,665	4,299	4,974	5,845	7,056
Official creditors	3,504	3,665	4,299	4,974	5,845	7,056
Multilateral	3,130	3,318	3,901	4,458	5,080	6,152
of which: World Bank	1,426	1,708	2,022	2,477	2,877	3,469
Bilateral	374	347	399	516	765	904
Private creditors	3	0	0	0	0	0
Bondholders	..	..	..	..	..	..
Commercial banks and others	3	0	0	0	0	0
Private nonguaranteed debt from:	..	83	75	129	118	118
Bondholders	..	..	..	..	..	..
Commercial banks and others	..	83	75	129	118	118
Use of IMF credit	219	171	168	156	147	370
Net financial inflows						
Net debt inflows						
Use of IMF credit	39	-18	-12	-8	-8	210
Long-term	-22	254	411	836	891	955
Official creditors	-22	228	419	781	902	955
Multilateral	-19	203	386	658	651	853
of which: World Bank	-32	120	211	512	415	459
Bilateral	-3	25	34	123	251	103
Private creditors	0	26	-8	55	-11	0
Bondholders	..	..	..	..	..	..
Banks and others	0	26	-8	55	-11	0
Short-term	17	29	43	-170	151	-42
Net equity inflows						
Foreign direct investment	87	106	196	68	186	127
Portfolio equity	..	..	..	..	..	..
Debt ratios						
External debt stocks to exports (%)	213	167	166	163	188	344
External debt stocks to GNI (%)	23	17	17	17	19	23
Debt service to exports (%)	11	9	8	7	8	12
Short-term to external debt stocks (%)	2	9	8	5	6	5
Multilateral to external debt stocks (%)	83	77	79	81	78	78
Reserves to external debt stocks (%)	78	198	185	146	129	140
Gross national income (GNI)	16,125	24,844	29,263	33,328	34,540	34,054

NICARAGUA

(US$ million, unless otherwise indicated)

	2010	2016	2017	2018	2019	2020
Summary external debt data by debtor type						
Total external debt stocks	**7,017**	**11,035**	**11,521**	**11,679**	**11,681**	**12,050**
Use of IMF credit	359	228	219	195	181	369
Long-term external debt	5,256	9,389	9,858	10,108	10,294	10,513
Public and publicly guaranteed sector	2,704	4,218	4,709	5,108	5,428	5,899
Public sector	2,704	4,218	4,709	5,108	5,428	5,899
of which: General government	2,006	3,410	3,925	4,150	4,516	5,060
Private sector guaranteed by public sector	0	..	..	..	..	..
Private sector not guaranteed	2,552	5,171	5,149	5,000	4,867	4,614
Short-term external debt	1,402	1,419	1,444	1,375	1,205	1,168
Disbursements (long-term)	**1,181**	**988**	**1,235**	**1,057**	**981**	**944**
Public and publicly guaranteed sector	267	373	539	572	509	652
Public sector	267	373	539	572	509	652
of which: General government	267	373	539	372	509	652
Private sector guaranteed by public sector	..	..	..	..	..	..
Private sector not guaranteed	914	615	695	485	472	292
Principal repayments (long-term)	**459**	**575**	**849**	**775**	**820**	**915**
Public and publicly guaranteed sector	56	89	122	135	177	229
Public sector	56	89	122	135	177	229
of which: General government	33	74	96	110	131	156
Private sector guaranteed by public sector	..	..	..	..	..	..
Private sector not guaranteed	403	486	727	640	643	686
Interest payments (long-term)	**103**	**213**	**262**	**265**	**301**	**283**
Public and publicly guaranteed sector	34	74	83	94	119	117
Public sector	34	74	83	94	119	117
of which: General government	29	70	79	89	102	107
Private sector guaranteed by public sector	..	..	..	..	..	..
Private sector not guaranteed	70	138	179	172	182	165
Summary external debt stock by creditor type						
Long-term external debt stocks	**5,256**	**9,389**	**9,858**	**10,108**	**10,294**	**10,513**
Public and publicly guaranteed debt from:	2,704	4,218	4,709	5,108	5,428	5,899
Official creditors	2,694	4,207	4,695	5,083	5,402	5,874
Multilateral	1,661	3,081	3,529	3,914	4,215	4,652
of which: World Bank	447	531	595	624	692	771
Bilateral	1,033	1,126	1,166	1,170	1,187	1,222
Private creditors	11	11	14	24	26	25
Bondholders	..	..	..	..	..	..
Commercial banks and others	11	11	14	24	26	25
Private nonguaranteed debt from:	2,552	5,171	5,149	5,000	4,867	4,614
Bondholders	..	..	..	..	..	..
Commercial banks and others	2,552	5,171	5,149	5,000	4,867	4,614
Use of IMF credit	359	228	219	195	181	369
Net financial inflows						
Net debt inflows						
Use of IMF credit	20	-29	-22	-19	-13	174
Long-term	721	413	386	281	161	28
Official creditors	212	278	417	426	330	425
Multilateral	214	261	404	411	306	412
of which: World Bank	36	15	33	44	71	58
Bilateral	-2	17	13	15	25	14
Private creditors	509	135	-31	-144	-169	-397
Bondholders	..	..	..	..	..	..
Banks and others	509	135	-31	-144	-169	-397
Short-term	389	129	15	-105	-193	-52
Net equity inflows						
Foreign direct investment	490	781	980	798	394	152
Portfolio equity	0	0	0	0	0	0
Debt ratios						
External debt stocks to exports (%)	197	211	199	207	201	224
External debt stocks to GNI (%)	82	87	88	94	96	98
Debt service to exports (%)	16	16	20	19	20	22
Short-term to external debt stocks (%)	20	13	13	12	10	10
Multilateral to external debt stocks (%)	24	28	31	34	36	39
Reserves to external debt stocks (%)	26	22	24	19	21	27
Gross national income (GNI)	8,514	12,652	13,074	12,373	12,145	12,258

NIGER

(US$ million, unless otherwise indicated)

	2010	2016	2017	2018	2019	2020
Summary external debt data by debtor type						
Total external debt stocks	**1,534**	**2,529**	**3,055**	**3,197**	**3,609**	**4,591**
Use of IMF credit	158	239	287	311	346	498
Long-term external debt	1,206	2,250	2,698	2,819	3,170	4,031
Public and publicly guaranteed sector	1,206	2,250	2,698	2,819	3,170	4,031
Public sector	1,206	2,250	2,698	2,819	3,170	4,031
of which: General government	1,205	2,249	2,697	2,818	3,169	4,030
Private sector guaranteed by public sector	..	..	..	..	..	..
Private sector not guaranteed	0	..	..	..	..	..
Short-term external debt	170	40	70	67	93	62
Disbursements (long-term)	**279**	**403**	**361**	**278**	**422**	**745**
Public and publicly guaranteed sector	279	403	361	278	422	745
Public sector	279	403	361	278	422	745
of which: General government	279	403	361	278	422	745
Private sector guaranteed by public sector	..	..	..	..	..	..
Private sector not guaranteed	..	..	..	..	..	..
Principal repayments (long-term)	**16**	**72**	**88**	**72**	**93**	**112**
Public and publicly guaranteed sector	9	72	88	72	93	112
Public sector	9	72	88	72	93	112
of which: General government	9	72	88	72	93	112
Private sector guaranteed by public sector	..	..	..	..	..	..
Private sector not guaranteed	7	..	..	..	..	..
Interest payments (long-term)	**8**	**32**	**38**	**44**	**35**	**50**
Public and publicly guaranteed sector	8	32	38	44	35	50
Public sector	8	32	38	44	35	50
of which: General government	8	32	38	44	35	50
Private sector guaranteed by public sector	..	..	..	..	..	..
Private sector not guaranteed	0	..	..	..	..	..
Summary external debt stock by creditor type						
Long-term external debt stocks	**1,206**	**2,250**	**2,698**	**2,819**	**3,170**	**4,031**
Public and publicly guaranteed debt from:	1,206	2,250	2,698	2,819	3,170	4,031
Official creditors	1,205	2,250	2,698	2,819	3,170	3,812
Multilateral	664	1,646	2,037	2,095	2,466	3,084
of which: World Bank	275	773	988	1,044	1,347	1,694
Bilateral	541	603	661	724	703	728
Private creditors	1	..	..	..	..	219
Bondholders	..	..	..	..	..	..
Commercial banks and others	1	..	..	..	..	219
Private nonguaranteed debt from:	0	..	..	..	..	..
Bondholders	..	..	..	..	..	..
Commercial banks and others	0	..	..	..	..	..
Use of IMF credit	158	239	287	311	346	498
Net financial inflows						
Net debt inflows						
Use of IMF credit	5	10	32	32	36	133
Long-term	263	331	273	206	329	633
Official creditors	270	331	273	206	329	429
Multilateral	62	262	240	127	342	439
of which: World Bank	14	170	159	87	257	259
Bilateral	208	69	33	79	-14	-9
Private creditors	-7	..	..	..	..	204
Bondholders	..	..	..	..	..	..
Banks and others	-7	..	..	..	..	204
Short-term	35	9	21	-11	16	-5
Net equity inflows						
Foreign direct investment	0	146	128	211	306	367
Portfolio equity	6	18	16	21	27	..
Debt ratios						
External debt stocks to exports (%)	115	189	197	202	237	..
External debt stocks to GNI (%)	19	24	26	24	27	35
Debt service to exports (%)	2	8	9	8	9	..
Short-term to external debt stocks (%)	11	2	2	2	3	1
Multilateral to external debt stocks (%)	43	65	67	66	68	67
Reserves to external debt stocks (%)	50	..	..	..	..	..
Gross national income (GNI)	8,284	10,735	11,600	13,406	13,479	13,156

NIGERIA

(US$ million, unless otherwise indicated)

	2010	2016	2017	2018	2019	2020
Summary external debt data by debtor type						
Total external debt stocks	**18,822**	**35,715**	**45,772**	**54,184**	**60,006**	**70,318**
Use of IMF credit	2,580	2,252	2,386	2,330	2,317	5,948
Long-term external debt	16,241	33,462	43,386	51,854	57,689	64,370
Public and publicly guaranteed sector	4,686	11,317	18,822	25,232	27,531	29,498
Public sector	4,686	11,317	18,822	25,232	27,531	29,498
of which: General government	4,686	11,059	18,496	24,840	27,131	29,056
Private sector guaranteed by public sector	0	..	..	..	..	..
Private sector not guaranteed	11,556	22,146	24,564	26,622	30,158	34,873
Short-term external debt	0	0	0	0	0	0
Disbursements (long-term)	**1,111**	**5,535**	**12,114**	**12,640**	**9,190**	**9,811**
Public and publicly guaranteed sector	1,051	1,134	7,126	7,363	2,673	1,962
Public sector	1,051	1,134	7,126	7,363	2,673	1,962
of which: General government	1,051	1,082	7,075	7,289	2,662	1,931
Private sector guaranteed by public sector	0	..	..	..	..	..
Private sector not guaranteed	60	4,401	4,988	5,277	6,517	7,849
Principal repayments (long-term)	**1,189**	**1,849**	**2,707**	**3,954**	**3,275**	**3,667**
Public and publicly guaranteed sector	248	180	137	735	295	437
Public sector	241	180	137	735	295	437
of which: General government	227	180	137	735	295	437
Private sector guaranteed by public sector	7	..	..	..	..	..
Private sector not guaranteed	942	1,670	2,570	3,219	2,980	3,230
Interest payments (long-term)	**59**	**640**	**822**	**1,411**	**1,832**	**1,845**
Public and publicly guaranteed sector	59	175	207	698	1,095	1,114
Public sector	59	175	207	698	1,095	1,114
of which: General government	58	173	205	696	1,092	1,111
Private sector guaranteed by public sector	1	..	..	..	..	..
Private sector not guaranteed	..	465	615	713	737	731
Summary external debt stock by creditor type						
Long-term external debt stocks	**16,241**	**33,462**	**43,386**	**51,854**	**57,689**	**64,370**
Public and publicly guaranteed debt from:	4,686	11,317	18,822	25,232	27,531	29,498
Official creditors	4,686	9,817	12,522	14,063	16,363	18,329
Multilateral	4,304	7,885	10,110	10,932	12,516	14,303
of which: World Bank	3,705	6,640	7,913	8,557	9,959	11,415
Bilateral	381	1,932	2,412	3,131	3,846	4,026
Private creditors	0	1,500	6,300	11,168	11,168	11,168
Bondholders	..	1,500	6,300	11,168	11,168	11,168
Commercial banks and others	0	..	..	..	..	..
Private nonguaranteed debt from:	11,556	22,146	24,564	26,622	30,158	34,873
Bondholders	..	5,942	6,942	6,017	6,367	5,817
Commercial banks and others	11,556	16,203	17,622	20,605	23,791	29,055
Use of IMF credit	2,580	2,252	2,386	2,330	2,317	5,948
Net financial inflows						
Net debt inflows						
Use of IMF credit	..	..	..	..	..	3,419
Long-term	-79	3,686	9,407	8,685	5,914	6,144
Official creditors	807	955	2,189	1,759	2,378	1,525
Multilateral	865	707	1,713	1,041	1,663	1,351
of which: World Bank	905	650	858	851	1,475	1,058
Bilateral	-58	248	476	719	715	174
Private creditors	-886	2,731	7,218	6,926	3,536	4,619
Bondholders	..	667	5,800	3,943	350	-550
Banks and others	-886	2,064	1,418	2,983	3,186	5,169
Short-term	0	0	0	0	0	0
Net equity inflows						
Foreign direct investment	5,966	2,134	1,150	-563	851	930
Portfolio equity	2,153	325	1,360	1,259	-1,548	-255
Debt ratios						
External debt stocks to exports (%)	22	90	87	80	83	169
External debt stocks to GNI (%)	6	9	13	14	14	17
Debt service to exports (%)	2	6	7	8	7	13
Short-term to external debt stocks (%)	0	0	0	0	0	0
Multilateral to external debt stocks (%)	23	22	22	20	21	20
Reserves to external debt stocks (%)	186	76	87	79	64	52
Gross national income (GNI)	342,044	395,951	364,254	378,867	433,449	416,521

NORTH MACEDONIA

(US$ million, unless otherwise indicated)

	2010	2016	2017	2018	2019	2020
Summary external debt data by debtor type						
Total external debt stocks	**5,159**	**7,513**	**8,544**	**8,666**	**8,986**	**10,607**
Use of IMF credit	101	88	93	91	91	297
Long-term external debt	3,840	6,320	7,133	7,237	7,499	8,806
Public and publicly guaranteed sector	1,880	3,473	3,829	4,061	4,163	5,102
Public sector	1,880	3,473	3,829	4,061	4,163	5,102
of which: General government	1,660	2,655	2,920	3,142	3,152	3,993
Private sector guaranteed by public sector	0	..	..	..	..	..
Private sector not guaranteed	1,959	2,847	3,304	3,176	3,336	3,704
Short-term external debt	1,218	1,105	1,318	1,339	1,396	1,504
Disbursements (long-term)	**596**	**1,465**	**1,020**	**1,400**	**821**	**1,802**
Public and publicly guaranteed sector	197	777	221	794	383	1,202
Public sector	197	777	221	794	383	1,202
of which: General government	123	604	110	672	181	1,032
Private sector guaranteed by public sector	..	..	..	..	..	..
Private sector not guaranteed	399	688	798	606	438	600
Principal repayments (long-term)	**443**	**702**	**645**	**1,077**	**513**	**948**
Public and publicly guaranteed sector	98	309	262	406	219	625
Public sector	98	309	262	406	219	625
of which: General government	87	235	177	317	118	505
Private sector guaranteed by public sector	0	..	..	..	..	..
Private sector not guaranteed	344	394	383	671	293	323
Interest payments (long-term)	**128**	**124**	**177**	**159**	**151**	**149**
Public and publicly guaranteed sector	56	86	112	105	115	112
Public sector	56	86	112	105	115	112
of which: General government	51	75	100	92	101	97
Private sector guaranteed by public sector	0	..	..	..	..	..
Private sector not guaranteed	71	38	65	54	36	36
Summary external debt stock by creditor type						
Long-term external debt stocks	**3,840**	**6,320**	**7,133**	**7,237**	**7,499**	**8,806**
Public and publicly guaranteed debt from:	1,880	3,473	3,829	4,061	4,163	5,102
Official creditors	1,369	1,737	1,921	1,865	2,051	2,390
Multilateral	1,127	1,232	1,336	1,245	1,387	1,735
of which: World Bank	681	620	658	614	732	856
Bilateral	242	505	585	620	665	655
Private creditors	512	1,736	1,907	2,196	2,112	2,712
Bondholders	434	1,286	1,463	1,864	1,829	2,638
Commercial banks and others	77	450	444	332	283	74
Private nonguaranteed debt from:	1,959	2,847	3,304	3,176	3,336	3,704
Bondholders	..	..	..	..	..	..
Commercial banks and others	1,959	2,847	3,304	3,176	3,336	3,704
Use of IMF credit	101	88	93	91	91	297
Net financial inflows						
Net debt inflows						
Use of IMF credit	..	..	..	..	..	195
Long-term	153	763	375	323	309	854
Official creditors	101	99	22	1	206	199
Multilateral	101	-10	-40	-39	161	219
of which: World Bank	53	-16	-24	-21	125	66
Bilateral	0	109	62	39	46	-20
Private creditors	53	664	352	323	102	654
Bondholders	..	498	0	482	0	595
Banks and others	53	166	352	-160	102	59
Short-term	-229	68	230	8	50	70
Net equity inflows						
Foreign direct investment	202	325	246	471	444	111
Portfolio equity	-4	-8	-12	-34	-16	-8
Debt ratios						
External debt stocks to exports (%)	136	134	133	111	113	144
External debt stocks to GNI (%)	56	73	79	71	75	90
Debt service to exports (%)	16	16	14	17	9	16
Short-term to external debt stocks (%)	24	15	15	15	16	14
Multilateral to external debt stocks (%)	22	16	16	14	15	16
Reserves to external debt stocks (%)	38	33	29	35	37	35
Gross national income (GNI)	9,281	10,256	10,862	12,148	11,965	11,797

PAKISTAN

(US$ million, unless otherwise indicated)

	2010	2016	2017	2018	2019	2020
Summary external debt data by debtor type						
Total external debt stocks	**63,098**	**73,057**	**86,047**	**93,546**	**100,831**	**108,530**
Use of IMF credit	10,258	7,235	7,664	7,276	8,097	8,902
Long-term external debt	48,173	58,702	69,673	78,182	83,208	92,398
Public and publicly guaranteed sector	43,700	52,577	61,083	67,275	71,125	78,751
Public sector	43,654	52,548	61,053	67,249	71,101	78,728
of which: General government	43,541	51,788	60,241	64,943	68,270	76,008
Private sector guaranteed by public sector	46	29	29	26	24	23
Private sector not guaranteed	4,473	6,125	8,591	10,906	12,083	13,647
Short-term external debt	4,667	7,121	8,709	8,088	9,526	7,230
Disbursements (long-term)	**3,958**	**8,148**	**14,017**	**12,752**	**13,183**	**12,900**
Public and publicly guaranteed sector	1,867	6,388	11,189	9,997	11,400	10,428
Public sector	1,867	6,388	11,189	9,997	11,400	10,428
of which: General government	1,867	6,258	10,883	8,238	10,652	10,337
Private sector guaranteed by public sector	0	0	0	0	0	0
Private sector not guaranteed	2,091	1,760	2,828	2,755	1,782	2,472
Principal repayments (long-term)	**3,022**	**2,985**	**4,958**	**3,311**	**7,478**	**5,734**
Public and publicly guaranteed sector	2,139	2,610	4,597	2,871	6,871	4,827
Public sector	2,137	2,608	4,595	2,869	6,869	4,825
of which: General government	2,106	2,422	4,341	2,605	6,646	4,623
Private sector guaranteed by public sector	2	1	1	2	2	2
Private sector not guaranteed	883	375	362	439	606	907
Interest payments (long-term)	**883**	**1,223**	**1,563**	**2,196**	**2,627**	**2,159**
Public and publicly guaranteed sector	783	1,112	1,322	1,762	2,084	1,595
Public sector	783	1,112	1,322	1,762	2,084	1,595
of which: General government	780	1,093	1,304	1,711	1,984	1,461
Private sector guaranteed by public sector	0	0	0	0	0	0
Private sector not guaranteed	100	111	240	434	543	564
Summary external debt stock by creditor type						
Long-term external debt stocks	**48,173**	**58,702**	**69,673**	**78,182**	**83,208**	**92,398**
Public and publicly guaranteed debt from:	43,700	52,577	61,083	67,275	71,125	78,751
Official creditors	42,049	45,257	50,390	56,423	62,205	68,148
Multilateral	24,670	25,533	27,845	27,880	30,141	33,817
of which: World Bank	11,806	14,049	15,300	15,162	15,305	17,176
Bilateral	17,379	19,724	22,545	28,543	32,065	34,331
Private creditors	1,651	7,320	10,693	10,852	8,920	10,603
Bondholders	1,550	5,550	7,300	7,300	5,300	5,300
Commercial banks and others	101	1,770	3,393	3,552	3,620	5,303
Private nonguaranteed debt from:	4,473	6,125	8,591	10,906	12,083	13,647
Bondholders	250	12	12	12	12	12
Commercial banks and others	4,223	6,113	8,579	10,894	12,071	13,635
Use of IMF credit	10,258	7,235	7,664	7,276	8,097	8,902
Net financial inflows						
Net debt inflows						
Use of IMF credit	1,360	1,102	0	-212	862	453
Long-term	936	5,164	9,058	9,442	5,705	7,165
Official creditors	402	2,736	3,219	6,967	6,461	3,920
Multilateral	452	1,073	1,173	482	2,418	2,844
of which: World Bank	78	654	491	183	223	1,269
Bilateral	-50	1,662	2,046	6,485	4,043	1,075
Private creditors	534	2,428	5,839	2,475	-756	3,246
Bondholders	-1,200	500	1,750	0	-2,000	..
Banks and others	1,734	1,928	4,089	2,475	1,244	3,246
Short-term	3,201	647	1,588	-621	1,438	-2,296
Net equity inflows						
Foreign direct investment	2,022	2,484	2,583	1,479	1,981	1,885
Portfolio equity	511	-339	-391	-528	22	-542
Debt ratios						
External debt stocks to exports (%)	220	265	285	297	324	390
External debt stocks to GNI (%)	36	27	29	30	37	42
Debt service to exports (%)	15	16	22	19	35	33
Short-term to external debt stocks (%)	7	10	10	9	9	7
Multilateral to external debt stocks (%)	39	35	32	30	30	31
Reserves to external debt stocks (%)	23	27	18	10	13	13
Gross national income (GNI)	173,884	273,310	299,553	309,131	272,612	258,005

PANAMA

(US$ million, unless otherwise indicated)

	2010	2016	2017	2018	2019	2020
Summary external debt data by debtor type						
Total external debt stocks	**48,882**	**89,440**	**93,149**	**100,311**	**107,416**	**108,866**
Use of IMF credit	303	265	281	274	272	826
Long-term external debt	23,692	45,878	54,418	61,131	70,316	72,369
Public and publicly guaranteed sector	10,420	17,256	18,750	20,937	24,619	29,699
Public sector	10,420	17,256	18,750	20,937	24,619	29,699
of which: General government	10,367	16,643	18,150	20,342	24,025	29,108
Private sector guaranteed by public sector	..	0	0	0	..	..
Private sector not guaranteed	13,272	28,622	35,668	40,194	45,697	42,670
Short-term external debt	24,887	43,297	38,450	38,906	36,828	35,671
Disbursements (long-term)	**2,220**	**5,887**	**10,098**	**7,758**	**10,893**	**6,721**
Public and publicly guaranteed sector	440	2,270	2,358	2,608	4,113	6,721
Public sector	440	2,270	2,358	2,608	4,113	6,721
of which: General government	430	1,695	2,358	2,608	4,113	6,721
Private sector guaranteed by public sector	..	..	0	0	..	..
Private sector not guaranteed	1,780	3,618	7,740	5,151	6,779	..
Principal repayments (long-term)	**556**	**4,436**	**1,577**	**1,256**	**1,516**	**4,703**
Public and publicly guaranteed sector	170	441	881	430	440	1,666
Public sector	170	440	881	430	440	1,666
of which: General government	165	437	869	426	438	1,663
Private sector guaranteed by public sector	..	0	0	0	..	..
Private sector not guaranteed	386	3,995	696	826	1,076	3,038
Interest payments (long-term)	**797**	**1,309**	**1,738**	**2,283**	**2,216**	**1,617**
Public and publicly guaranteed sector	670	818	930	962	1,098	1,176
Public sector	670	818	930	962	1,098	1,176
of which: General government	668	801	896	929	1,064	1,143
Private sector guaranteed by public sector	..	0	0	0	..	..
Private sector not guaranteed	126	491	808	1,321	1,118	441
Summary external debt stock by creditor type						
Long-term external debt stocks	**23,692**	**45,878**	**54,418**	**61,131**	**70,316**	**72,369**
Public and publicly guaranteed debt from:	10,420	17,256	18,750	20,937	24,619	29,699
Official creditors	2,126	4,752	5,261	5,759	6,173	7,493
Multilateral	1,814	4,547	5,068	5,580	6,006	7,334
of which: World Bank	420	1,001	1,239	1,264	1,183	1,456
Bilateral	313	205	192	179	167	159
Private creditors	8,293	12,504	13,490	15,178	18,445	22,206
Bondholders	8,071	11,963	13,052	14,809	18,115	21,700
Commercial banks and others	223	541	438	369	330	507
Private nonguaranteed debt from:	13,272	28,622	35,668	40,194	45,697	42,670
Bondholders	911	3,579	5,500	5,332	5,582	5,593
Commercial banks and others	12,361	25,043	30,168	34,861	40,115	37,077
Use of IMF credit	303	265	281	274	272	826
Net financial inflows						
Net debt inflows						
Use of IMF credit	..	..	..	..	..	525
Long-term	1,664	1,452	8,521	6,503	9,377	2,017
Official creditors	275	373	503	496	412	1,314
Multilateral	188	394	520	512	426	1,328
of which: World Bank	-15	-28	237	25	-81	273
Bilateral	87	-21	-17	-16	-14	-14
Private creditors	1,389	1,079	8,018	6,007	8,964	703
Bondholders	-150	-1,454	2,997	1,381	3,750	3,565
Banks and others	1,539	2,533	5,020	4,625	5,214	-2,861
Short-term	1,604	-521	-4,847	456	-2,078	-1,157
Net equity inflows						
Foreign direct investment	1,967	3,042	1,766	1,931	2,404	-890
Portfolio equity	0	0	0	0	0	0
Debt ratios						
External debt stocks to exports (%)	222	330	317	326	350	504
External debt stocks to GNI (%)	180	166	159	166	172	220
Debt service to exports (%)	6	24	15	16	16	31
Short-term to external debt stocks (%)	51	48	41	39	34	33
Multilateral to external debt stocks (%)	4	5	5	6	6	7
Reserves to external debt stocks (%)	6	4	3	2	3	9
Gross national income (GNI)	27,129	53,771	58,443	60,383	62,286	49,446

PAPUA NEW GUINEA

(US$ million, unless otherwise indicated)

	2010	2016	2017	2018	2019	2020
Summary external debt data by debtor type						
Total external debt stocks	**5,987**	**19,247**	**17,224**	**17,724**	**18,745**	**17,971**
Use of IMF credit	193	169	179	175	174	560
Long-term external debt	5,380	18,416	16,968	17,085	17,914	17,012
Public and publicly guaranteed sector	1,042	1,922	2,306	3,411	4,313	5,112
Public sector	1,042	1,922	2,306	3,411	4,313	5,112
of which: General government	1,038	1,919	2,303	3,408	4,311	5,109
Private sector guaranteed by public sector	..	..	..	..	..	..
Private sector not guaranteed	4,337	16,494	14,663	13,674	13,601	11,900
Short-term external debt	414	663	77	464	657	400
Disbursements (long-term)	**3,153**	**1,538**	**1,320**	**3,046**	**1,501**	**1,554**
Public and publicly guaranteed sector	37	534	394	1,234	1,201	1,554
Public sector	37	534	394	1,234	1,201	1,554
of which: General government	37	534	394	1,234	1,201	1,554
Private sector guaranteed by public sector	..	..	..	..	..	..
Private sector not guaranteed	3,116	1,004	926	1,812	300	..
Principal repayments (long-term)	**758**	**2,659**	**2,111**	**2,029**	**1,568**	**1,095**
Public and publicly guaranteed sector	67	73	84	93	281	845
Public sector	67	73	84	93	281	845
of which: General government	67	73	84	93	281	845
Private sector guaranteed by public sector	..	..	..	..	..	..
Private sector not guaranteed	691	2,586	2,027	1,937	1,286	250
Interest payments (long-term)	**50**	**651**	**673**	**741**	**772**	**221**
Public and publicly guaranteed sector	16	25	51	88	149	163
Public sector	16	25	51	88	149	163
of which: General government	16	25	51	88	149	163
Private sector guaranteed by public sector	..	..	..	..	..	..
Private sector not guaranteed	33	626	622	653	623	58
Summary external debt stock by creditor type						
Long-term external debt stocks	**5,380**	**18,416**	**16,968**	**17,085**	**17,914**	**17,012**
Public and publicly guaranteed debt from:	1,042	1,922	2,306	3,411	4,313	5,112
Official creditors	1,009	1,705	1,957	2,374	3,161	4,180
Multilateral	712	1,168	1,278	1,633	1,853	2,565
of which: World Bank	225	262	277	446	448	480
Bilateral	297	537	679	741	1,307	1,616
Private creditors	33	216	349	1,037	1,152	931
Bondholders	..	..	..	500	500	500
Commercial banks and others	33	216	349	537	652	431
Private nonguaranteed debt from:	4,337	16,494	14,663	13,674	13,601	11,900
Bondholders	..	..	..	..	..	..
Commercial banks and others	4,337	16,494	14,663	13,674	13,601	11,900
Use of IMF credit	193	169	179	175	174	560
Net financial inflows						
Net debt inflows						
Use of IMF credit	..	..	..	..	..	367
Long-term	2,395	-1,121	-791	1,017	-66	458
Official creditors	-23	245	181	452	804	938
Multilateral	-2	101	68	373	232	670
of which: World Bank	-6	17	4	174	8	16
Bilateral	-21	143	114	79	572	268
Private creditors	2,418	-1,366	-972	565	-870	-479
Bondholders	..	..	..	500	..	..
Banks and others	2,418	-1,366	-972	65	-870	-479
Short-term	302	144	-383	235	334	-243
Net equity inflows						
Foreign direct investment	35	19	99	168	-901	-935
Portfolio equity	0	-1	0	0	..	..
Debt ratios						
External debt stocks to exports (%)	98	231	168	167	159	192
External debt stocks to GNI (%)	45	94	77	75	79	78
Debt service to exports (%)	13	40	27	26	20	14
Short-term to external debt stocks (%)	7	3	0	3	4	2
Multilateral to external debt stocks (%)	12	6	7	9	10	14
Reserves to external debt stocks (%)	51	8	10	12	12	..
Gross national income (GNI)	13,182	20,529	22,294	23,492	23,780	23,142

PARAGUAY

(US$ million, unless otherwise indicated)

	2010	2016	2017	2018	2019	2020
Summary external debt data by debtor type						
Total external debt stocks	**15,903**	**16,228**	**15,929**	**15,799**	**16,388**	**19,763**
Use of IMF credit	147	128	136	132	132	137
Long-term external debt	11,383	11,503	11,173	11,026	11,543	15,013
Public and publicly guaranteed sector	2,390	4,828	5,609	6,402	7,183	10,258
Public sector	2,390	4,825	5,605	6,383	7,148	10,212
of which: General government	2,148	4,662	5,421	6,196	6,978	10,058
Private sector guaranteed by public sector	..	4	4	19	35	46
Private sector not guaranteed	8,992	6,675	5,564	4,625	4,360	4,755
Short-term external debt	4,373	4,596	4,620	4,640	4,713	4,614
Disbursements (long-term)	**1,912**	**1,216**	**996**	**1,535**	**1,453**	**4,751**
Public and publicly guaranteed sector	308	1,040	978	1,003	994	3,281
Public sector	308	1,036	978	988	978	3,270
of which: General government	298	1,001	945	969	973	3,268
Private sector guaranteed by public sector	..	4	0	15	16	12
Private sector not guaranteed	1,605	176	18	533	459	1,470
Principal repayments (long-term)	**314**	**913**	**1,338**	**1,680**	**924**	**237**
Public and publicly guaranteed sector	240	233	209	208	207	218
Public sector	240	233	209	208	207	218
of which: General government	210	217	194	193	187	198
Private sector guaranteed by public sector	..	0	0	0	0	0
Private sector not guaranteed	75	681	1,129	1,472	717	19
Interest payments (long-term)	**131**	**371**	**356**	**553**	**390**	**414**
Public and publicly guaranteed sector	65	178	211	254	330	359
Public sector	65	178	211	254	329	358
of which: General government	58	174	206	249	323	353
Private sector guaranteed by public sector	..	0	0	0	1	1
Private sector not guaranteed	66	194	145	299	60	55
Summary external debt stock by creditor type						
Long-term external debt stocks	**11,383**	**11,503**	**11,173**	**11,026**	**11,543**	**15,013**
Public and publicly guaranteed debt from:	2,390	4,828	5,609	6,402	7,183	10,258
Official creditors	2,123	2,384	2,690	2,979	3,273	4,898
Multilateral	1,510	2,167	2,501	2,790	3,062	4,653
of which: World Bank	270	544	605	636	619	852
Bilateral	613	217	189	189	211	245
Private creditors	267	2,445	2,919	3,423	3,910	5,360
Bondholders	..	2,380	2,880	3,410	3,910	5,360
Commercial banks and others	267	65	39	13	0	0
Private nonguaranteed debt from:	8,992	6,675	5,564	4,625	4,360	4,755
Bondholders	..	800	600	600	600	1,150
Commercial banks and others	8,992	5,875	4,964	4,025	3,760	3,605
Use of IMF credit	147	128	136	132	132	137
Net financial inflows						
Net debt inflows						
Use of IMF credit	..	..	..	..	..	..
Long-term	1,598	303	-342	-145	529	4,515
Official creditors	83	246	295	290	300	1,614
Multilateral	146	306	330	293	280	1,588
of which: World Bank	-26	113	62	31	-11	233
Bilateral	-63	-60	-35	-2	20	25
Private creditors	1,515	57	-637	-435	229	2,901
Bondholders	..	600	300	530	500	2,000
Banks and others	1,515	-543	-937	-965	-271	901
Short-term	312	-178	24	20	72	-99
Net equity inflows						
Foreign direct investment	313	355	350	361	288	314
Portfolio equity	..	..	..	..	..	..
Debt ratios						
External debt stocks to exports (%)	143	127	112	109	122	165
External debt stocks to GNI (%)	61	47	42	41	45	58
Debt service to exports (%)	5	11	12	16	10	6
Short-term to external debt stocks (%)	28	28	29	29	29	23
Multilateral to external debt stocks (%)	9	13	16	18	19	24
Reserves to external debt stocks (%)	26	41	47	47	45	44
Gross national income (GNI)	25,927	34,643	37,707	38,877	36,774	34,156

PERU

(US$ million, unless otherwise indicated)

	2010	2016	2017	2018	2019	2020
Summary external debt data by debtor type						
Total external debt stocks	**42,154**	**69,613**	**67,604**	**66,769**	**64,247**	**73,549**
Use of IMF credit	939	820	869	848	843	878
Long-term external debt	34,822	61,028	58,040	55,923	54,837	62,387
Public and publicly guaranteed sector	20,009	19,733	18,978	18,145	18,606	28,027
Public sector	19,563	19,733	18,978	18,145	18,606	28,027
of which: General government	19,554	19,728	16,823	15,990	16,451	25,872
Private sector guaranteed by public sector	445	..	..	..	..	..
Private sector not guaranteed	14,813	41,295	39,062	37,778	36,231	34,360
Short-term external debt	6,393	7,765	8,695	9,998	8,567	10,284
Disbursements (long-term)	**5,425**	**7,982**	**5,371**	**3,513**	**3,291**	**11,457**
Public and publicly guaranteed sector	3,862	1,978	2,631	569	1,866	9,427
Public sector	3,862	1,978	2,631	569	1,866	9,427
of which: General government	3,862	1,978	481	569	1,866	9,427
Private sector guaranteed by public sector	0	..	..	..	..	..
Private sector not guaranteed	1,563	6,004	2,740	2,945	1,425	2,030
Principal repayments (long-term)	**4,060**	**5,545**	**8,718**	**4,583**	**4,327**	**4,191**
Public and publicly guaranteed sector	3,490	980	3,746	1,263	1,356	290
Public sector	3,372	980	3,746	1,263	1,356	290
of which: General government	3,370	979	3,745	1,263	1,356	290
Private sector guaranteed by public sector	118	..	..	..	..	..
Private sector not guaranteed	570	4,565	4,973	3,320	2,972	3,901
Interest payments (long-term)	**2,550**	**2,090**	**2,151**	**2,328**	**2,103**	**2,049**
Public and publicly guaranteed sector	1,096	876	969	982	979	919
Public sector	1,084	876	969	982	979	919
of which: General government	1,083	876	914	872	870	810
Private sector guaranteed by public sector	12	..	..	..	..	..
Private sector not guaranteed	1,454	1,214	1,182	1,346	1,124	1,130
Summary external debt stock by creditor type						
Long-term external debt stocks	**34,822**	**61,028**	**58,040**	**55,923**	**54,837**	**62,387**
Public and publicly guaranteed debt from:	20,009	19,733	18,978	18,145	18,606	28,027
Official creditors	10,672	8,130	4,919	4,447	4,916	7,174
Multilateral	7,870	6,729	3,867	3,426	3,843	6,123
of which: World Bank	2,965	2,610	1,093	1,145	1,564	3,441
Bilateral	2,802	1,401	1,053	1,021	1,074	1,051
Private creditors	9,337	11,604	14,059	13,698	13,690	20,853
Bondholders	9,311	11,604	14,059	13,698	13,690	20,853
Commercial banks and others	26	0	0	..	..	..
Private nonguaranteed debt from:	14,813	41,295	39,062	37,778	36,231	34,360
Bondholders	727	13,875	16,340	15,510	16,285	17,800
Commercial banks and others	14,086	27,420	22,723	22,268	19,946	16,560
Use of IMF credit	939	820	869	848	843	878
Net financial inflows						
Net debt inflows						
Use of IMF credit	..	..	..	..	..	..
Long-term	1,365	2,437	-3,347	-1,070	-1,036	7,266
Official creditors	-1,384	190	-3,265	-448	474	2,191
Multilateral	-528	315	-2,822	-431	419	2,283
of which: World Bank	119	-104	-1,516	51	423	1,877
Bilateral	-856	-125	-442	-16	55	-92
Private creditors	2,749	2,247	-83	-622	-1,510	5,075
Bondholders	1,764	-566	4,615	-1,077	812	8,461
Banks and others	985	2,813	-4,698	455	-2,322	-3,386
Short-term	1,608	690	930	1,304	-1,432	1,717
Net equity inflows						
Foreign direct investment	7,762	6,179	7,571	6,257	5,997	4,299
Portfolio equity	87	-307	-172	-442	-511	..
Debt ratios						
External debt stocks to exports (%)	105	157	125	115	112	154
External debt stocks to GNI (%)	31	38	34	32	29	38
Debt service to exports (%)	17	18	21	12	12	14
Short-term to external debt stocks (%)	15	11	13	15	13	14
Multilateral to external debt stocks (%)	19	10	6	5	6	8
Reserves to external debt stocks (%)	101	87	92	88	103	99
Gross national income (GNI)	136,693	183,939	201,299	211,455	218,650	195,376

PHILIPPINES

(US$ million, unless otherwise indicated)

	2010	2016	2017	2018	2019	2020
Summary external debt data by debtor type						
Total external debt stocks	**65,350**	**74,742**	**73,098**	**78,961**	**83,617**	**98,480**
Use of IMF credit	1,290	1,127	1,193	1,165	1,159	1,207
Long-term external debt	53,548	59,090	57,630	61,727	65,250	83,064
Public and publicly guaranteed sector	45,086	35,760	36,495	38,348	41,727	56,220
Public sector	45,020	35,732	36,469	38,325	41,706	56,201
of which: General government	36,720	30,706	31,706	33,782	37,058	51,945
Private sector guaranteed by public sector	66	28	26	24	21	18
Private sector not guaranteed	8,462	23,330	21,136	23,379	23,524	26,844
Short-term external debt	10,512	14,526	14,275	16,068	17,208	14,209
Disbursements (long-term)	**10,928**	**5,886**	**6,487**	**9,867**	**11,351**	**20,985**
Public and publicly guaranteed sector	8,251	3,329	3,463	4,992	7,031	14,874
Public sector	8,251	3,329	3,463	4,992	7,031	14,874
of which: General government	8,032	2,982	3,410	4,934	6,194	14,818
Private sector guaranteed by public sector	0	0	0	0	0	0
Private sector not guaranteed	2,677	2,557	3,025	4,876	4,320	6,111
Principal repayments (long-term)	**8,341**	**7,811**	**8,244**	**6,238**	**7,363**	**6,372**
Public and publicly guaranteed sector	6,813	4,079	3,025	2,383	4,104	3,431
Public sector	6,809	4,041	3,022	2,380	4,101	3,428
of which: General government	5,238	3,290	2,828	2,202	2,706	2,911
Private sector guaranteed by public sector	4	39	3	3	3	3
Private sector not guaranteed	1,527	3,732	5,219	3,855	3,259	2,941
Interest payments (long-term)	**3,112**	**3,174**	**2,952**	**2,552**	**3,104**	**2,861**
Public and publicly guaranteed sector	2,977	2,430	2,236	2,288	2,308	2,182
Public sector	2,975	2,428	2,236	2,287	2,308	2,181
of which: General government	2,450	2,076	1,931	1,999	2,091	1,999
Private sector guaranteed by public sector	2	2	1	1	1	1
Private sector not guaranteed	135	744	716	264	795	679
Summary external debt stock by creditor type						
Long-term external debt stocks	**53,548**	**59,090**	**57,630**	**61,727**	**65,250**	**83,064**
Public and publicly guaranteed debt from:	45,086	35,760	36,495	38,348	41,727	56,220
Official creditors	23,209	18,585	19,078	20,047	21,527	29,218
Multilateral	8,372	10,487	11,014	12,056	13,173	19,648
of which: World Bank	2,738	4,672	5,132	5,842	6,456	8,100
Bilateral	14,837	8,098	8,063	7,990	8,355	9,569
Private creditors	21,877	17,175	17,417	18,301	20,199	27,002
Bondholders	20,590	16,460	16,713	17,632	19,077	26,058
Commercial banks and others	1,287	715	704	670	1,123	944
Private nonguaranteed debt from:	8,462	23,330	21,136	23,379	23,524	26,844
Bondholders	1,651	5,262	4,012	5,187	7,041	9,251
Commercial banks and others	6,811	18,067	17,123	18,192	16,483	17,593
Use of IMF credit	1,290	1,127	1,193	1,165	1,159	1,207
Net financial inflows						
Net debt inflows						
Use of IMF credit	..	..	..	..	..	..
Long-term	2,587	-1,925	-1,757	3,630	3,988	14,613
Official creditors	-447	-22	112	883	1,427	7,102
Multilateral	-180	321	481	1,043	1,148	6,368
of which: World Bank	52	10	443	709	615	1,641
Bilateral	-267	-343	-369	-160	279	734
Private creditors	3,035	-1,903	-1,868	2,747	2,561	7,511
Bondholders	1,700	-962	-879	2,932	2,898	6,738
Banks and others	1,335	-941	-989	-184	-338	773
Short-term	6,509	-573	-252	1,793	1,140	-3,000
Net equity inflows						
Foreign direct investment	-214	3,302	4,261	3,242	3,427	2,454
Portfolio equity	833	131	496	-1,031	1,764	-2,541
Debt ratios						
External debt stocks to exports (%)	107	90	75	77	77	109
External debt stocks to GNI (%)	28	21	20	21	20	25
Debt service to exports (%)	19	13	12	9	10	10
Short-term to external debt stocks (%)	16	19	20	20	21	14
Multilateral to external debt stocks (%)	13	14	15	15	16	20
Reserves to external debt stocks (%)	85	98	100	90	95	100
Gross national income (GNI)	231,747	354,012	364,719	383,817	414,552	389,324

ROMANIA

(US$ million, unless otherwise indicated)

	2010	2016	2017	2018	2019	2020
Summary external debt data by debtor type						
Total external debt stocks	**115,393**	**96,118**	**114,008**	**112,547**	**118,298**	**142,390**
Use of IMF credit	16,609	1,324	1,402	1,370	1,362	1,418
Long-term external debt	81,627	82,459	97,658	94,907	100,544	123,204
Public and publicly guaranteed sector	20,801	32,720	37,966	37,977	39,605	58,674
Public sector	20,131	32,713	37,958	37,970	39,599	58,667
of which: General government	18,153	32,049	37,345	37,499	39,238	58,385
Private sector guaranteed by public sector	670	7	8	7	7	7
Private sector not guaranteed	60,826	49,739	59,692	56,930	60,939	64,530
Short-term external debt	17,157	12,335	14,948	16,270	16,392	17,767
Disbursements (long-term)	**17,435**	**14,593**	**25,503**	**19,747**	**20,357**	**34,812**
Public and publicly guaranteed sector	5,623	3,695	3,891	5,955	5,764	18,150
Public sector	5,199	3,692	3,891	5,955	5,764	18,150
of which: General government	5,042	3,674	3,885	5,955	5,761	18,150
Private sector guaranteed by public sector	425	3	..	0	1	0
Private sector not guaranteed	11,812	10,898	21,613	13,793	14,593	16,662
Principal repayments (long-term)	**15,784**	**16,634**	**18,396**	**19,176**	**16,835**	**18,042**
Public and publicly guaranteed sector	2,150	2,736	2,287	4,516	3,569	2,985
Public sector	2,150	2,736	2,286	4,515	3,568	2,984
of which: General government	1,869	2,597	2,163	4,396	3,459	2,886
Private sector guaranteed by public sector	0	..	0	1	1	0
Private sector not guaranteed	13,633	13,898	16,110	14,659	13,265	15,057
Interest payments (long-term)	**2,180**	**1,846**	**1,896**	**2,091**	**2,151**	**2,077**
Public and publicly guaranteed sector	617	1,286	1,284	1,447	1,314	1,427
Public sector	609	1,286	1,284	1,447	1,314	1,427
of which: General government	561	1,280	1,279	1,442	1,308	1,424
Private sector guaranteed by public sector	8	0	0	0	0	0
Private sector not guaranteed	1,563	559	611	644	837	650
Summary external debt stock by creditor type						
Long-term external debt stocks	**81,627**	**82,459**	**97,658**	**94,907**	**100,544**	**123,204**
Public and publicly guaranteed debt from:	20,801	32,720	37,966	37,977	39,605	58,674
Official creditors	14,280	12,734	12,909	10,378	8,535	13,780
Multilateral	13,420	12,226	12,414	9,916	8,099	13,348
of which: World Bank	2,830	4,009	4,952	4,677	4,492	5,382
Bilateral	860	508	496	462	437	432
Private creditors	6,520	19,986	25,056	27,599	31,070	44,894
Bondholders	3,006	19,453	24,639	27,329	30,872	44,746
Commercial banks and others	3,514	533	417	270	198	148
Private nonguaranteed debt from:	60,826	49,739	59,692	56,930	60,939	64,530
Bondholders	0	164	207	634	2,182	4,111
Commercial banks and others	60,826	49,575	59,485	56,297	58,757	60,419
Use of IMF credit	16,609	1,324	1,402	1,370	1,362	1,418
Net financial inflows						
Net debt inflows						
Use of IMF credit	5,664	-134	..	..	..	..
Long-term	1,651	-2,041	7,107	572	3,522	16,770
Official creditors	3,460	-733	-1,340	-2,055	-1,660	4,162
Multilateral	3,375	-704	-1,308	-2,013	-1,629	4,189
of which: World Bank	-75	-247	457	-65	-97	425
Bilateral	84	-28	-32	-42	-31	-27
Private creditors	-1,808	-1,308	8,447	2,627	5,182	12,608
Bondholders	398	1,917	3,137	4,158	5,250	12,368
Banks and others	-2,207	-3,226	5,311	-1,531	-68	241
Short-term	1,174	-101	2,613	1,321	122	1,375
Net equity inflows						
Foreign direct investment	2,397	4,778	4,462	6,503	5,613	4,518
Portfolio equity	3	-459	-61	-479	-656	-522
Debt ratios						
External debt stocks to exports (%)	207	114	120	105	110	143
External debt stocks to GNI (%)	70	52	55	47	48	58
Debt service to exports (%)	33	22	22	20	18	20
Short-term to external debt stocks (%)	15	13	13	14	14	12
Multilateral to external debt stocks (%)	12	13	11	9	7	9
Reserves to external debt stocks (%)	38	38	35	34	31	32
Gross national income (GNI)	164,339	185,632	208,688	237,010	246,123	244,536

RUSSIAN FEDERATION

(US$ million, unless otherwise indicated)

	2010	2016	2017	2018	2019	2020
Summary external debt data by debtor type						
Total external debt stocks	**417,886**	**529,275**	**514,280**	**471,885**	**484,240**	**475,518**
Use of IMF credit	8,735	7,625	8,077	7,888	7,843	8,169
Long-term external debt	348,938	476,550	455,167	415,697	418,697	409,980
Public and publicly guaranteed sector	165,665	185,495	216,167	195,227	210,378	212,465
Public sector	165,665	185,495	216,167	195,227	210,378	212,465
of which: General government	34,346	38,106	54,267	54,627	78,818	84,160
Private sector guaranteed by public sector	..	..	..	..	..	..
Private sector not guaranteed	183,273	291,056	239,000	220,470	208,319	197,515
Short-term external debt	60,214	45,100	51,035	48,300	57,700	57,370
Disbursements (long-term)	**70,301**	**89,772**	**83,355**	**51,285**	**81,078**	**69,758**
Public and publicly guaranteed sector	49,805	20,007	50,928	32,406	48,137	40,977
Public sector	49,805	20,007	50,928	32,406	48,137	40,977
of which: General government	10,485	9,925	17,045	17,205	27,815	16,869
Private sector guaranteed by public sector	..	..	..	..	..	..
Private sector not guaranteed	20,496	69,765	32,427	18,878	32,941	28,780
Principal repayments (long-term)	**42,974**	**73,036**	**61,773**	**90,548**	**78,405**	**79,798**
Public and publicly guaranteed sector	30,001	46,662	20,535	53,051	32,975	39,763
Public sector	30,001	46,662	20,535	53,051	32,975	39,763
of which: General government	7,136	12,594	1,034	16,753	3,580	11,726
Private sector guaranteed by public sector	..	..	..	..	..	..
Private sector not guaranteed	12,973	26,374	41,238	37,497	45,430	40,035
Interest payments (long-term)	**12,291**	**20,121**	**19,009**	**19,051**	**17,259**	**17,327**
Public and publicly guaranteed sector	1,707	5,643	6,555	8,930	7,306	8,182
Public sector	1,707	5,643	6,555	8,930	7,306	8,182
of which: General government	873	1,250	1,658	2,763	1,923	3,436
Private sector guaranteed by public sector	..	..	..	..	..	..
Private sector not guaranteed	10,584	14,478	12,455	10,121	9,953	9,145
Summary external debt stock by creditor type						
Long-term external debt stocks	**348,938**	**476,550**	**455,167**	**415,697**	**418,697**	**409,980**
Public and publicly guaranteed debt from:	165,665	185,495	216,167	195,227	210,378	212,465
Official creditors	7,637	2,145	1,176	966	772	610
Multilateral	3,087	744	617	476	353	261
of which: World Bank	2,618	646	551	428	315	236
Bilateral	4,550	1,402	559	489	420	350
Private creditors	158,028	183,349	214,991	194,261	209,606	211,855
Bondholders	25,510	39,185	61,081	64,595	91,825	98,235
Commercial banks and others	132,518	144,165	153,910	129,666	117,781	113,620
Private nonguaranteed debt from:	183,273	291,056	239,000	220,470	208,319	197,515
Bondholders	2,100	18,156	16,879	19,890	27,126	29,324
Commercial banks and others	181,173	272,900	222,121	200,580	181,193	168,191
Use of IMF credit	8,735	7,625	8,077	7,888	7,843	8,169
Net financial inflows						
Net debt inflows						
Use of IMF credit	..	..	..	..	..	..
Long-term	27,327	16,735	21,582	-39,264	2,674	-10,040
Official creditors	227	-330	-969	-210	-192	-161
Multilateral	-656	-133	-127	-140	-122	-91
of which: World Bank	-596	-85	-95	-123	-111	-79
Bilateral	883	-197	-842	-70	-70	-70
Private creditors	27,100	17,065	22,551	-39,053	2,865	-9,879
Bondholders	3,674	5,170	20,326	6,841	34,480	7,696
Banks and others	23,426	11,895	2,225	-45,894	-31,615	-17,575
Short-term	7,538	3,000	5,935	-2,735	9,400	-330
Net equity inflows						
Foreign direct investment	28,684	35,715	26,601	9,913	28,847	12,606
Portfolio equity	-4,885	-1,788	-7,940	-4,164	-4,320	-14,794
Debt ratios						
External debt stocks to exports (%)	87	142	113	84	90	112
External debt stocks to GNI (%)	28	43	34	29	30	33
Debt service to exports (%)	12	25	18	20	18	23
Short-term to external debt stocks (%)	14	9	10	10	12	12
Multilateral to external debt stocks (%)	1	0	0	0	0	0
Reserves to external debt stocks (%)	106	60	69	81	92	96
Gross national income (GNI)	1,477,813	1,241,290	1,532,146	1,616,937	1,633,928	1,448,705

RWANDA

(US$ million, unless otherwise indicated)

	2010	2016	2017	2018	2019	2020
Summary external debt data by debtor type						
Total external debt stocks	**1,233**	**4,319**	**5,076**	**5,681**	**6,515**	**8,193**
Use of IMF credit	133	203	291	308	306	520
Long-term external debt	1,086	3,889	4,479	5,019	5,866	7,295
Public and publicly guaranteed sector	759	2,353	2,833	3,249	3,929	5,122
Public sector	759	2,353	2,833	3,249	3,929	5,122
of which: General government	758	2,353	2,833	3,249	3,928	5,121
Private sector guaranteed by public sector	..	..	..	..	..	..
Private sector not guaranteed	327	1,536	1,645	1,769	1,937	2,173
Short-term external debt	14	227	307	354	343	378
Disbursements (long-term)	**182**	**775**	**718**	**852**	**1,044**	**1,368**
Public and publicly guaranteed sector	63	368	411	497	727	1,086
Public sector	63	368	411	497	727	1,086
of which: General government	63	368	411	497	727	1,086
Private sector guaranteed by public sector	..	..	..	..	..	..
Private sector not guaranteed	119	407	306	355	318	282
Principal repayments (long-term)	**41**	**148**	**155**	**155**	**185**	**102**
Public and publicly guaranteed sector	8	23	28	29	31	52
Public sector	8	23	28	29	31	52
of which: General government	8	23	28	29	31	52
Private sector guaranteed by public sector	..	..	..	..	..	..
Private sector not guaranteed	33	125	128	126	154	50
Interest payments (long-term)	**10**	**69**	**83**	**101**	**133**	**148**
Public and publicly guaranteed sector	6	42	46	51	56	61
Public sector	6	42	46	51	56	61
of which: General government	6	42	46	51	56	61
Private sector guaranteed by public sector	..	..	..	..	..	..
Private sector not guaranteed	4	27	38	50	78	87
Summary external debt stock by creditor type						
Long-term external debt stocks	**1,086**	**3,889**	**4,479**	**5,019**	**5,866**	**7,295**
Public and publicly guaranteed debt from:	759	2,353	2,833	3,249	3,929	5,122
Official creditors	759	1,953	2,433	2,849	3,465	4,377
Multilateral	639	1,646	2,081	2,467	2,979	3,737
of which: World Bank	259	1,049	1,404	1,610	1,897	2,432
Bilateral	120	308	353	382	486	640
Private creditors	..	400	400	400	464	745
Bondholders	..	400	400	400	421	475
Commercial banks and others	..	..	..	..	43	270
Private nonguaranteed debt from:	327	1,536	1,645	1,769	1,937	2,173
Bondholders	..	..	..	..	..	..
Commercial banks and others	327	1,536	1,645	1,769	1,937	2,173
Use of IMF credit	133	203	291	308	306	520
Net financial inflows						
Net debt inflows						
Use of IMF credit	0	98	73	24	0	195
Long-term	141	627	562	696	859	1,266
Official creditors	55	345	384	468	631	753
Multilateral	36	323	349	429	524	625
of which: World Bank	10	217	288	241	295	434
Bilateral	19	22	34	38	108	128
Private creditors	86	282	179	229	228	513
Bondholders	..	..	..	0	21	54
Banks and others	86	282	179	229	207	459
Short-term	4	215	80	48	-11	35
Net equity inflows						
Foreign direct investment	105	184	180	251	249	44
Portfolio equity	8	3	0	0	0	3
Debt ratios						
External debt stocks to exports (%)	172	283	264	276	288	422
External debt stocks to GNI (%)	20	51	57	61	65	81
Debt service to exports (%)	7	15	13	13	14	15
Short-term to external debt stocks (%)	1	5	6	6	5	5
Multilateral to external debt stocks (%)	52	38	41	43	46	46
Reserves to external debt stocks (%)	65	23	23	24	22	22
Gross national income (GNI)	6,070	8,452	8,962	9,293	10,008	10,097

SAMOA

(US$ million, unless otherwise indicated)

	2010	2016	2017	2018	2019	2020
Summary external debt data by debtor type						
Total external debt stocks	**325.1**	**417.5**	**443.1**	**427.5**	**408.6**	**437.3**
Use of IMF credit	26.0	27.4	27.4	24.3	21.0	43.5
Long-term external debt	299.1	390.1	415.7	403.2	387.6	393.8
Public and publicly guaranteed sector	299.1	390.1	415.7	403.2	387.6	393.8
Public sector	299.1	390.1	415.7	403.2	387.6	393.8
of which: General government	297.5	389.7	415.5	403.1	387.6	393.8
Private sector guaranteed by public sector	..	..	..	..	..	..
Private sector not guaranteed	..	..	..	..	..	..
Short-term external debt	0.0	0.0	0.0	0.0	0.0	0.0
Disbursements (long-term)	**78.9**	**14.3**	**21.0**	**22.0**	**9.3**	**3.1**
Public and publicly guaranteed sector	78.9	14.3	21.0	22.0	9.3	3.1
Public sector	78.9	14.3	21.0	22.0	9.3	3.1
of which: General government	78.9	14.3	21.0	22.0	9.3	3.1
Private sector guaranteed by public sector	..	..	..	..	..	..
Private sector not guaranteed	..	..	..	..	..	..
Principal repayments (long-term)	**7.2**	**15.6**	**18.3**	**21.9**	**21.3**	**18.1**
Public and publicly guaranteed sector	7.2	15.6	18.3	21.9	21.3	18.1
Public sector	7.2	15.6	18.3	21.9	21.3	18.1
of which: General government	7.1	15.4	18.1	21.7	21.3	18.1
Private sector guaranteed by public sector	..	..	..	..	..	..
Private sector not guaranteed	..	..	..	..	..	..
Interest payments (long-term)	**3.3**	**5.8**	**5.7**	**6.1**	**5.6**	**3.8**
Public and publicly guaranteed sector	3.3	5.8	5.7	6.1	5.6	3.8
Public sector	3.3	5.8	5.7	6.1	5.6	3.8
of which: General government	3.3	5.7	5.7	6.1	5.6	3.8
Private sector guaranteed by public sector	..	..	..	..	..	..
Private sector not guaranteed	..	..	..	..	..	..
Summary external debt stock by creditor type						
Long-term external debt stocks	**299.1**	**390.1**	**415.7**	**403.2**	**387.6**	**393.8**
Public and publicly guaranteed debt from:	299.1	390.1	415.7	403.2	387.6	393.8
Official creditors	299.1	390.1	415.7	403.2	387.6	393.8
Multilateral	219.2	203.7	215.0	208.1	205.8	206.1
of which: World Bank	99.3	92.8	103.4	104.9	110.3	114.6
Bilateral	79.9	186.4	200.7	195.1	181.8	187.8
Private creditors	..	..	..	..	..	..
Bondholders	..	..	..	..	..	..
Commercial banks and others	..	..	..	..	..	..
Private nonguaranteed debt from:	..	..	..	..	..	..
Bondholders	..	..	..	..	..	..
Commercial banks and others	..	..	..	..	..	..
Use of IMF credit	26.0	27.4	27.4	24.3	21.0	43.5
Net financial inflows						
Net debt inflows						
Use of IMF credit	..	-1.6	-1.6	-2.5	-3.2	21.0
Long-term	71.6	-1.3	2.8	0.1	-12.0	-14.9
Official creditors	71.6	-1.3	2.8	0.1	-12.0	-14.9
Multilateral	40.6	-4.3	-0.1	-2.0	-1.2	-7.7
of which: World Bank	19.9	-0.6	5.2	4.0	6.0	-0.1
Bilateral	31.1	3.0	2.9	2.1	-10.9	-7.3
Private creditors	..	..	..	..	..	..
Bondholders	..	..	..	..	..	..
Banks and others	..	..	..	..	..	..
Short-term	0.0	0.0	0.0	0.0	0.0	0.0
Net equity inflows						
Foreign direct investment	0.3	2.5	9.2	16.7	2.7	-0.8
Portfolio equity	0.0	0.0	0.0	0.0	0.7	..
Debt ratios						
External debt stocks to exports (%)	154.0	162.7	155.8	140.2	122.2	347.8
External debt stocks to GNI (%)	50.5	53.5	55.0	53.9	50.0	55.8
Debt service to exports (%)	5.0	9.0	9.0	10.0	9.1	18.7
Short-term to external debt stocks (%)	0.0	0.0	0.0	0.0	0.0	0.0
Multilateral to external debt stocks (%)	67.4	48.8	48.5	48.7	50.4	47.1
Reserves to external debt stocks (%)	53.2	21.3	27.9	38.0	43.4	63.4
Gross national income (GNI)	643.3	780.7	806.2	792.4	816.4	783.6

SÃO TOMÉ AND PRÍNCIPE

(US$ million, unless otherwise indicated)

	2010	2016	2017	2018	2019	2020
Summary external debt data by debtor type						
Total external debt stocks	**181.1**	**248.3**	**269.5**	**252.6**	**251.6**	**291.2**
Use of IMF credit	15.9	14.7	16.8	16.8	18.8	37.0
Long-term external debt	145.3	224.5	245.5	226.3	225.2	240.9
Public and publicly guaranteed sector	145.3	224.5	245.5	226.3	225.2	240.9
Public sector	140.3	220.3	241.2	222.1	220.6	236.3
of which: General government	140.3	220.3	241.2	222.1	220.6	236.3
Private sector guaranteed by public sector	5.0	4.2	4.2	4.2	4.6	4.6
Private sector not guaranteed	..	..	..	..	..	..
Short-term external debt	19.9	9.1	7.2	9.6	7.6	13.3
Disbursements (long-term)	**19.8**	**9.6**	**12.2**	**5.6**	**4.4**	**5.3**
Public and publicly guaranteed sector	19.8	9.6	12.2	5.6	4.4	5.3
Public sector	19.8	9.6	12.2	5.6	4.4	5.3
of which: General government	19.8	9.6	12.2	5.6	4.4	5.3
Private sector guaranteed by public sector	..	..	..	..	..	0.0
Private sector not guaranteed	..	..	..	..	..	..
Principal repayments (long-term)	**1.2**	**0.7**	**2.1**	**2.7**	**4.8**	**0.7**
Public and publicly guaranteed sector	1.2	0.7	2.1	2.7	4.8	0.7
Public sector	1.2	0.7	2.1	2.7	4.8	0.7
of which: General government	1.2	0.7	2.1	2.7	4.8	0.7
Private sector guaranteed by public sector	..	..	..	..	..	0.0
Private sector not guaranteed	..	..	..	..	..	..
Interest payments (long-term)	**0.3**	**1.1**	**1.1**	**1.3**	**3.4**	**1.0**
Public and publicly guaranteed sector	0.3	1.1	1.1	1.3	3.4	1.0
Public sector	0.3	1.1	1.1	1.3	3.4	1.0
of which: General government	0.3	1.1	1.1	1.3	3.4	1.0
Private sector guaranteed by public sector	..	..	..	..	..	0.0
Private sector not guaranteed	..	..	..	..	..	..
Summary external debt stock by creditor type						
Long-term external debt stocks	**145.3**	**224.5**	**245.5**	**226.3**	**225.2**	**240.9**
Public and publicly guaranteed debt from:	145.3	224.5	245.5	226.3	225.2	240.9
Official creditors	145.3	214.5	235.5	216.3	215.2	230.9
Multilateral	37.3	40.1	44.9	46.9	46.2	53.0
of which: World Bank	14.2	11.6	12.0	11.5	11.1	11.3
Bilateral	108.0	174.4	190.6	169.4	169.0	177.9
Private creditors	..	10.0	10.0	10.0	10.0	10.0
Bondholders	..	..	..	..	..	..
Commercial banks and others	..	10.0	10.0	10.0	10.0	10.0
Private nonguaranteed debt from:	..	..	..	..	..	..
Bondholders	..	..	..	..	..	..
Commercial banks and others	..	..	..	..	..	..
Use of IMF credit	15.9	14.7	16.8	16.8	18.8	37.0
Net financial inflows						
Net debt inflows						
Use of IMF credit	0.6	1.0	1.2	0.4	2.2	16.8
Long-term	18.6	8.8	10.1	2.9	-0.4	4.6
Official creditors	18.6	8.8	10.1	2.9	-0.4	4.6
Multilateral	1.1	2.9	2.9	2.9	-0.4	4.6
of which: World Bank	0.1	-0.3	-0.3	-0.3	-0.3	-0.3
Bilateral	17.4	5.9	7.2	..	0.0	0.0
Private creditors	..	..	..	..	..	..
Bondholders	..	..	..	..	..	..
Banks and others	..	..	..	..	..	..
Short-term	3.0	0.9	-2.1	2.4	0.1	0.2
Net equity inflows						
Foreign direct investment	50.6	23.3	32.9	22.7	20.8	47.1
Portfolio equity	0.0	-0.1	0.1	0.0	0.0	0.0
Debt ratios						
External debt stocks to exports (%)	690.9	241.4	284.3	257.1	331.7	522.3
External debt stocks to GNI (%)	91.8	71.7	72.0	61.3	59.1	61.8
Debt service to exports (%)	6.3	2.6	4.1	4.7	11.7	4.3
Short-term to external debt stocks (%)	11.0	3.6	2.7	3.8	3.0	4.6
Multilateral to external debt stocks (%)	20.6	16.2	16.7	18.6	18.3	18.2
Reserves to external debt stocks (%)	26.6	25.5	21.9	17.3	18.7	25.9
Gross national income (GNI)	197.2	346.4	374.5	412.3	425.9	471.5

SENEGAL

(US$ million, unless otherwise indicated)

	2010	2016	2017	2018	2019	2020
Summary external debt data by debtor type						
Total external debt stocks	**4,943**	**7,534**	**9,820**	**12,681**	**15,139**	**17,239**
Use of IMF credit	451	299	283	242	219	689
Long-term external debt	4,491	7,235	9,538	12,439	14,920	16,550
Public and publicly guaranteed sector	4,183	6,996	9,288	11,996	14,400	15,858
Public sector	4,183	6,996	9,288	11,996	14,400	15,858
of which: General government	4,179	6,996	9,288	11,996	14,400	15,858
Private sector guaranteed by public sector	..	..	..	..	..	..
Private sector not guaranteed	308	239	250	442	520	692
Short-term external debt	0	0	0	0	0	0
Disbursements (long-term)	**524**	**1,229**	**2,094**	**3,752**	**3,118**	**1,731**
Public and publicly guaranteed sector	441	1,096	1,929	3,356	3,041	1,560
Public sector	441	1,096	1,929	3,356	3,041	1,560
of which: General government	441	1,096	1,929	3,356	3,041	1,560
Private sector guaranteed by public sector	..	..	..	..	..	..
Private sector not guaranteed	83	133	165	396	78	172
Principal repayments (long-term)	**229**	**230**	**375**	**533**	**521**	**958**
Public and publicly guaranteed sector	84	145	195	366	521	958
Public sector	84	145	195	366	521	958
of which: General government	83	145	195	366	521	958
Private sector guaranteed by public sector	..	..	..	..	..	..
Private sector not guaranteed	144	86	180	167	..	..
Interest payments (long-term)	**75**	**155**	**298**	**303**	**378**	**378**
Public and publicly guaranteed sector	64	145	292	292	362	378
Public sector	64	145	292	292	362	378
of which: General government	63	145	292	292	362	378
Private sector guaranteed by public sector	..	..	..	..	..	..
Private sector not guaranteed	11	10	6	11	16	..
Summary external debt stock by creditor type						
Long-term external debt stocks	**4,491**	**7,235**	**9,538**	**12,439**	**14,920**	**16,550**
Public and publicly guaranteed debt from:	4,183	6,996	9,288	11,996	14,400	15,858
Official creditors	3,983	5,952	7,063	7,515	9,252	10,668
Multilateral	1,973	3,056	3,620	3,719	4,746	5,723
of which: World Bank	1,023	1,670	1,999	2,070	2,657	3,102
Bilateral	2,010	2,896	3,444	3,797	4,506	4,945
Private creditors	200	1,044	2,224	4,481	5,148	5,190
Bondholders	200	874	2,025	4,151	4,122	4,158
Commercial banks and others	0	170	199	330	1,026	1,031
Private nonguaranteed debt from:	308	239	250	442	520	692
Bondholders	..	..	..	..	..	..
Commercial banks and others	308	239	250	442	520	692
Use of IMF credit	451	299	283	242	219	689
Net financial inflows						
Net debt inflows						
Use of IMF credit	49	-36	-34	-34	-22	446
Long-term	295	998	1,719	3,220	2,597	774
Official creditors	358	949	629	664	1,819	785
Multilateral	204	368	314	208	1,070	644
of which: World Bank	110	124	224	123	604	281
Bilateral	155	581	315	456	749	140
Private creditors	-63	49	1,090	2,555	777	-11
Bondholders	..	..	1,100	2,181	0	-104
Banks and others	-63	49	-10	374	777	93
Short-term	0	0	0	0	0	0
Net equity inflows						
Foreign direct investment	273	272	368	439	1,065	1,481
Portfolio equity	23	25	13	15	..	..
Debt ratios						
External debt stocks to exports (%)	144	171	199	221	..	..
External debt stocks to GNI (%)	31	41	48	56	67	71
Debt service to exports (%)	9	10	14	15	..	..
Short-term to external debt stocks (%)	0	0	0	0	0	0
Multilateral to external debt stocks (%)	40	41	37	29	31	33
Reserves to external debt stocks (%)	41	..	..	..	..	..
Gross national income (GNI)	15,971	18,542	20,409	22,516	22,651	24,310

SERBIA

(US$ million, unless otherwise indicated)

	2010	2016	2017	2018	2019	2020
Summary external debt data by debtor type						
Total external debt stocks	**32,907**	**29,533**	**34,279**	**34,223**	**35,896**	**44,276**
Use of IMF credit	2,720	598	634	619	615	641
Long-term external debt	27,389	27,811	32,120	31,553	32,669	41,282
Public and publicly guaranteed sector	9,477	16,215	16,422	15,088	15,343	18,346
Public sector	9,476	16,084	16,308	15,088	15,343	18,346
of which: General government	7,762	14,879	15,140	14,183	14,467	17,464
Private sector guaranteed by public sector	1	131	114	0	..	..
Private sector not guaranteed	17,912	11,595	15,698	16,465	17,326	22,936
Short-term external debt	2,798	1,124	1,526	2,051	2,611	2,353
Disbursements (long-term)	**4,594**	**3,698**	**7,339**	**4,709**	**8,694**	**10,480**
Public and publicly guaranteed sector	1,365	1,207	1,439	1,502	3,125	4,183
Public sector	1,365	1,207	1,439	1,502	3,125	4,183
of which: General government	1,207	934	1,294	1,394	2,992	4,086
Private sector guaranteed by public sector	..	..	..	..	..	..
Private sector not guaranteed	3,230	2,492	5,899	3,207	5,569	6,297
Principal repayments (long-term)	**3,431**	**5,016**	**4,086**	**4,813**	**6,385**	**5,382**
Public and publicly guaranteed sector	351	1,030	2,195	2,501	2,743	2,221
Public sector	350	1,027	2,162	2,389	2,743	2,221
of which: General government	221	678	1,862	2,056	2,594	2,060
Private sector guaranteed by public sector	1	3	34	112	..	..
Private sector not guaranteed	3,081	3,986	1,891	2,312	3,643	3,162
Interest payments (long-term)	**759**	**917**	**869**	**908**	**912**	**815**
Public and publicly guaranteed sector	321	588	576	546	515	479
Public sector	321	582	571	542	515	479
of which: General government	233	536	542	522	502	467
Private sector guaranteed by public sector	0	6	5	4	..	..
Private sector not guaranteed	438	330	292	361	396	337
Summary external debt stock by creditor type						
Long-term external debt stocks	**27,389**	**27,811**	**32,120**	**31,553**	**32,669**	**41,282**
Public and publicly guaranteed debt from:	9,477	16,215	16,422	15,088	15,343	18,346
Official creditors	8,010	10,355	11,708	11,565	11,770	12,021
Multilateral	4,848	5,313	6,246	5,861	5,743	6,044
of which: World Bank	2,499	2,384	2,939	2,799	2,708	2,891
Bilateral	3,162	5,042	5,462	5,704	6,027	5,977
Private creditors	1,466	5,860	4,714	3,523	3,573	6,325
Bondholders	..	5,250	4,500	3,500	3,552	6,303
Commercial banks and others	1,466	610	214	23	22	21
Private nonguaranteed debt from:	17,912	11,595	15,698	16,465	17,326	22,936
Bondholders	165	1,206	2,825	2,752	3,336	5,809
Commercial banks and others	17,747	10,389	12,872	13,713	13,990	17,127
Use of IMF credit	2,720	598	634	619	615	641
Net financial inflows						
Net debt inflows						
Use of IMF credit	458	-16	..	..	..	..
Long-term	1,163	-1,318	3,252	-105	2,308	5,097
Official creditors	867	391	421	191	337	-369
Multilateral	708	114	206	-117	-9	-210
of which: World Bank	188	-56	226	-17	-38	-58
Bilateral	159	277	216	308	346	-159
Private creditors	295	-1,709	2,831	-295	1,971	5,467
Bondholders	..	166	775	-1,000	656	3,618
Banks and others	295	-1,874	2,056	705	1,315	1,849
Short-term	-442	378	300	624	529	-260
Net equity inflows						
Foreign direct investment	1,040	1,521	1,657	3,515	3,445	1,845
Portfolio equity	84	-14	-7	-28	-64	-10
Debt ratios						
External debt stocks to exports (%)	250	148	152	134	134	170
External debt stocks to GNI (%)	80	77	83	71	74	86
Debt service to exports (%)	33	30	22	22	27	24
Short-term to external debt stocks (%)	9	4	4	6	7	5
Multilateral to external debt stocks (%)	15	18	18	17	16	14
Reserves to external debt stocks (%)	39	34	32	35	38	33
Gross national income (GNI)	40,943	38,456	41,327	48,064	48,699	51,360

SIERRA LEONE

(US$ million, unless otherwise indicated)

	2010	2016	2017	2018	2019	2020
Summary external debt data by debtor type						
Total external debt stocks	**931.1**	**1,627.1**	**1,751.1**	**1,754.7**	**1,853.0**	**2,113.5**
Use of IMF credit	266.2	443.9	509.5	501.1	502.9	651.9
Long-term external debt	660.8	982.2	1,046.6	1,065.1	1,163.6	1,278.4
Public and publicly guaranteed sector	660.8	982.2	1,046.6	1,065.1	1,163.6	1,278.4
Public sector	660.8	982.2	1,046.6	1,065.1	1,163.6	1,278.4
of which: General government	660.8	982.2	1,046.6	1,065.1	1,163.6	1,276.5
Private sector guaranteed by public sector	..	..	..	..	..	..
Private sector not guaranteed	..	..	..	..	..	..
Short-term external debt	4.1	201.0	195.1	188.5	186.5	183.1
Disbursements (long-term)	**66.5**	**63.2**	**73.1**	**60.6**	**141.8**	**128.9**
Public and publicly guaranteed sector	66.5	63.2	73.1	60.6	141.8	128.9
Public sector	66.5	63.2	73.1	60.6	141.8	128.9
of which: General government	66.5	63.2	73.1	60.6	141.8	128.9
Private sector guaranteed by public sector	..	..	..	..	..	..
Private sector not guaranteed	..	..	..	..	..	..
Principal repayments (long-term)	**4.8**	**19.7**	**23.3**	**28.9**	**33.7**	**37.0**
Public and publicly guaranteed sector	4.8	19.7	23.3	28.9	33.7	37.0
Public sector	4.8	19.7	23.3	28.9	33.7	37.0
of which: General government	4.8	19.7	23.3	28.9	33.7	37.0
Private sector guaranteed by public sector	..	..	..	..	..	..
Private sector not guaranteed	..	..	..	..	..	..
Interest payments (long-term)	**4.0**	**12.4**	**13.1**	**6.4**	**9.8**	**6.9**
Public and publicly guaranteed sector	4.0	12.4	13.1	6.4	9.8	6.9
Public sector	4.0	12.4	13.1	6.4	9.8	6.9
of which: General government	4.0	12.4	13.1	6.4	9.8	6.9
Private sector guaranteed by public sector	..	..	..	..	..	..
Private sector not guaranteed	..	..	..	..	..	..
Summary external debt stock by creditor type						
Long-term external debt stocks	**660.8**	**982.2**	**1,046.6**	**1,065.1**	**1,163.6**	**1,278.4**
Public and publicly guaranteed debt from:	660.8	982.2	1,046.6	1,065.1	1,163.6	1,278.4
Official creditors	449.7	788.8	853.1	871.6	976.6	1,091.4
Multilateral	371.2	601.6	672.9	684.2	756.0	853.1
of which: World Bank	154.6	224.3	275.7	284.3	348.0	432.5
Bilateral	78.4	187.1	180.2	187.4	220.7	238.3
Private creditors	211.1	193.4	193.4	193.4	187.0	187.0
Bondholders	..	..	..	..	..	..
Commercial banks and others	211.1	193.4	193.4	193.4	187.0	187.0
Private nonguaranteed debt from:						
Bondholders	..	..	..	..	..	..
Commercial banks and others	..	..	..	..	..	..
Use of IMF credit	266.2	443.9	509.5	501.1	502.9	651.9
Net financial inflows						
Net debt inflows						
Use of IMF credit	40.7	66.8	38.1	3.6	4.7	123.9
Long-term	61.6	43.6	49.8	31.7	108.1	91.9
Official creditors	61.6	43.6	49.8	31.7	108.1	91.9
Multilateral	55.5	21.8	46.9	22.1	74.2	77.2
of which: World Bank	32.1	5.6	37.2	15.7	65.2	71.7
Bilateral	6.1	21.8	3.0	9.6	33.9	14.7
Private creditors	..	..	..	..	..	..
Bondholders	..	..	..	..	..	..
Banks and others	..	..	..	..	..	..
Short-term	-19.0	-12.9	-5.9	-6.6	-2.0	-3.4
Net equity inflows						
Foreign direct investment	225.3	121.5	390.2	215.1	301.5	348.7
Portfolio equity	0.1	..	..	..	..	..
Debt ratios						
External debt stocks to exports (%)	218.3	220.5	235.6	238.2	242.9	..
External debt stocks to GNI (%)	35.7	49.7	48.2	46.2	45.5	56.8
Debt service to exports (%)	2.7	5.1	7.7	8.2	8.9	..
Short-term to external debt stocks (%)	0.4	12.4	11.1	10.7	10.1	8.7
Multilateral to external debt stocks (%)	39.9	37.0	38.4	39.0	40.8	40.4
Reserves to external debt stocks (%)	43.9	30.6	31.4	28.6	28.6	33.5
Gross national income (GNI)	2,606.5	3,277.0	3,629.6	3,798.5	4,070.3	3,720.7

SOLOMON ISLANDS

(US$ million, unless otherwise indicated)

	2010	2016	2017	2018	2019	2020
Summary external debt data by debtor type						
Total external debt stocks	**230.8**	**263.8**	**376.7**	**323.5**	**350.5**	**428.9**
Use of IMF credit	24.9	23.6	21.0	17.1	15.0	25.3
Long-term external debt	201.9	205.6	327.8	263.4	299.3	376.8
Public and publicly guaranteed sector	125.3	86.7	96.5	96.0	98.1	124.0
Public sector	125.3	86.7	96.5	96.0	98.1	124.0
of which: General government	125.3	86.7	96.5	96.0	98.1	124.0
Private sector guaranteed by public sector	..	..	..	..	..	..
Private sector not guaranteed	76.6	118.9	231.3	167.4	201.3	252.8
Short-term external debt	4.0	34.7	27.9	43.0	36.2	26.8
Disbursements (long-term)	**36.8**	**38.4**	**177.0**	**36.8**	**18.0**	**95.3**
Public and publicly guaranteed sector	0.0	13.1	11.1	6.1	7.6	27.4
Public sector	0.0	13.1	11.1	6.1	7.6	27.4
of which: General government	0.0	13.1	11.1	6.1	7.6	27.4
Private sector guaranteed by public sector	..	..	..	..	..	..
Private sector not guaranteed	36.8	25.2	165.9	30.7	10.4	67.9
Principal repayments (long-term)	**17.5**	**13.2**	**17.1**	**29.5**	**9.8**	**5.7**
Public and publicly guaranteed sector	8.6	6.5	5.2	4.8	5.1	5.2
Public sector	8.6	6.5	5.2	4.8	5.1	5.2
of which: General government	8.6	6.5	5.2	4.8	5.1	5.2
Private sector guaranteed by public sector	..	..	..	..	..	..
Private sector not guaranteed	8.9	6.7	11.9	24.7	4.7	0.5
Interest payments (long-term)	**3.2**	**5.1**	**4.0**	**6.0**	**3.2**	**2.6**
Public and publicly guaranteed sector	1.7	1.1	1.1	1.1	1.1	1.1
Public sector	1.7	1.1	1.1	1.1	1.1	1.1
of which: General government	1.7	1.1	1.1	1.1	1.1	1.1
Private sector guaranteed by public sector	..	..	..	..	..	..
Private sector not guaranteed	1.5	4.0	3.0	4.9	2.1	1.5
Summary external debt stock by creditor type						
Long-term external debt stocks	**201.9**	**205.6**	**327.8**	**263.4**	**299.3**	**376.8**
Public and publicly guaranteed debt from:	125.3	86.7	96.5	96.0	98.1	124.0
Official creditors	125.2	86.7	96.5	96.0	98.1	124.0
Multilateral	105.6	75.9	86.8	87.5	90.7	117.8
of which: World Bank	41.7	33.6	36.1	36.6	38.5	47.0
Bilateral	19.6	10.8	9.7	8.5	7.4	6.3
Private creditors	0.1	..	..	..	..	..
Bondholders	..	..	..	..	..	..
Commercial banks and others	0.1	..	..	..	..	..
Private nonguaranteed debt from:	76.6	118.9	231.3	167.4	201.3	252.8
Bondholders	..	..	..	..	..	..
Commercial banks and others	76.6	118.9	231.3	167.4	201.3	252.8
Use of IMF credit	24.9	23.6	21.0	17.1	15.0	25.3
Net financial inflows						
Net debt inflows						
Use of IMF credit	9.5	-3.4	-3.8	-3.5	-2.0	9.4
Long-term	19.4	25.1	159.9	7.3	8.1	89.6
Official creditors	-8.4	6.6	6.0	1.3	2.5	22.2
Multilateral	-6.8	7.7	7.1	2.4	3.6	23.3
of which: World Bank	-1.2	3.5	0.5	1.4	2.2	7.4
Bilateral	-1.6	-1.1	-1.1	-1.1	-1.1	-1.1
Private creditors	27.8	18.5	154.0	6.0	5.7	67.4
Bondholders	..	..	..	..	..	..
Banks and others	27.8	18.5	154.0	6.0	5.7	67.4
Short-term	-1.0	13.0	-6.8	15.2	-6.9	-9.4
Net equity inflows						
Foreign direct investment	77.6	28.6	31.4	32.4	39.0	-2.7
Portfolio equity	..	..	0.0	0.0	0.0	0.0
Debt ratios						
External debt stocks to exports (%)	68.9	44.2	59.3	44.7	54.7	88.4
External debt stocks to GNI (%)	28.7	19.7	25.9	20.8	22.6	27.0
Debt service to exports (%)	6.2	3.8	4.0	5.6	2.6	1.9
Short-term to external debt stocks (%)	1.7	13.2	7.4	13.3	10.3	6.2
Multilateral to external debt stocks (%)	45.8	28.8	23.1	27.0	25.9	27.5
Reserves to external debt stocks (%)	115.2	184.4	144.2	181.2	152.7	154.1
Gross national income (GNI)	802.9	1,337.0	1,454.1	1,554.1	1,553.9	1,587.7

SOMALIA

(US$ million, unless otherwise indicated)

	2010	2016	2017	2018	2019	2020
Summary external debt data by debtor type						
Total external debt stocks	**2,934**	**2,745**	**2,834**	**5,558**	**5,621**	**4,660**
Use of IMF credit	244	212	225	220	219	444
Long-term external debt	1,879	1,744	1,787	2,080	2,077	2,639
Public and publicly guaranteed sector	1,879	1,744	1,787	2,080	2,077	2,639
Public sector	1,879	1,744	1,787	2,080	2,077	2,639
of which: General government	1,854	1,721	1,764	2,055	2,053	2,632
Private sector guaranteed by public sector	..	..	..	..	..	..
Private sector not guaranteed	..	..	..	..	..	..
Short-term external debt	811	788	821	3,259	3,325	1,577
Disbursements (long-term)	**0**	**0**	**0**	**0**	**0**	**0**
Public and publicly guaranteed sector	0	0	0	0	0	0
Public sector	0	0	0	0	0	0
of which: General government	0	0	0	0	0	0
Private sector guaranteed by public sector	..	..	..	..	..	..
Private sector not guaranteed	..	..	..	..	..	..
Principal repayments (long-term)	**0**	**0**	**0**	**0**	**0**	**350**
Public and publicly guaranteed sector	0	0	0	0	0	350
Public sector	0	0	0	0	0	350
of which: General government	0	0	0	0	0	333
Private sector guaranteed by public sector	..	..	..	..	..	..
Private sector not guaranteed	..	..	..	..	..	..
Interest payments (long-term)	**0**	**0**	**0**	**0**	**0**	**131**
Public and publicly guaranteed sector	0	0	0	0	0	131
Public sector	0	0	0	0	0	131
of which: General government	0	0	0	0	0	111
Private sector guaranteed by public sector	..	..	..	..	..	..
Private sector not guaranteed	..	..	..	..	..	..
Summary external debt stock by creditor type						
Long-term external debt stocks	**1,879**	**1,744**	**1,787**	**2,080**	**2,077**	**2,639**
Public and publicly guaranteed debt from:	1,879	1,744	1,787	2,080	2,077	2,639
Official creditors	1,879	1,744	1,787	2,080	2,077	2,639
Multilateral	773	698	725	716	714	373
of which: World Bank	443	404	420	413	411	138
Bilateral	1,106	1,046	1,062	1,363	1,363	2,265
Private creditors	..	..	..	..	..	..
Bondholders	..	..	..	..	..	..
Commercial banks and others	..	..	..	..	..	..
Private nonguaranteed debt from:	..	..	..	..	..	..
Bondholders	..	..	..	..	..	..
Commercial banks and others	..	..	..	..	..	..
Use of IMF credit	244	212	225	220	219	444
Net financial inflows						
Net debt inflows						
Use of IMF credit	..	..	..	..	..	203
Long-term	0	0	0	0	0	-350
Official creditors	0	0	0	0	0	-350
Multilateral	0	0	0	0	0	-350
of which: World Bank	0	0	0	0	..	-278
Bilateral	0	0	0	0	0	..
Private creditors	..	..	..	..	..	..
Bondholders	..	..	..	..	..	..
Banks and others	..	..	..	..	..	..
Short-term	0	0	0	0	0	0
Net equity inflows						
Foreign direct investment	112	330	369	408	447	464
Portfolio equity	..	..	..	..	..	..
Debt ratios						
External debt stocks to exports (%)	..	250	267	478	478	..
External debt stocks to GNI (%)	..	66	63	119	115	95
Debt service to exports (%)	..	0	0	0	0	..
Short-term to external debt stocks (%)	28	29	29	59	59	34
Multilateral to external debt stocks (%)	26	25	26	13	13	8
Reserves to external debt stocks (%)	..	..	..	..	..	..
Gross national income (GNI)	..	4,168	4,476	4,687	4,907	4,882

SOUTH AFRICA

(US$ million, unless otherwise indicated)

	2010	2016	2017	2018	2019	2020
Summary external debt data by debtor type						
Total external debt stocks	**108,429**	**143,967**	**174,921**	**174,094**	**185,357**	**170,767**
Use of IMF credit	2,750	2,400	2,543	2,483	2,469	6,966
Long-term external debt	83,949	111,776	139,480	134,857	148,348	136,013
Public and publicly guaranteed sector	36,311	69,601	90,539	89,092	101,975	99,363
Public sector	36,311	69,601	90,539	89,092	101,975	99,363
of which: General government	32,582	56,318	73,662	65,287	77,834	75,078
Private sector guaranteed by public sector	..	..	..	..	..	..
Private sector not guaranteed	47,638	42,175	48,942	45,765	46,373	36,649
Short-term external debt	21,730	29,791	32,898	36,754	34,540	27,788
Disbursements (long-term)	**12,112**	**18,740**	**30,177**	**22,433**	**21,972**	**13,308**
Public and publicly guaranteed sector	8,889	12,380	17,051	12,737	14,874	4,288
Public sector	8,889	12,380	17,051	12,737	14,874	4,288
of which: General government	8,052	11,227	13,115	4,055	11,336	1,303
Private sector guaranteed by public sector	..	..	..	..	..	..
Private sector not guaranteed	3,224	6,360	13,127	9,696	7,098	9,020
Principal repayments (long-term)	**3,473**	**8,048**	**8,632**	**20,951**	**15,527**	**21,747**
Public and publicly guaranteed sector	1,680	2,514	2,265	11,390	4,292	6,983
Public sector	1,680	2,514	2,265	11,390	4,292	6,983
of which: General government	186	1,919	1,610	10,265	931	4,206
Private sector guaranteed by public sector	..	..	..	..	..	..
Private sector not guaranteed	1,792	5,534	6,367	9,561	11,235	14,763
Interest payments (long-term)	**2,177**	**5,388**	**5,263**	**6,241**	**6,563**	**6,249**
Public and publicly guaranteed sector	1,558	3,176	3,265	4,308	4,281	4,670
Public sector	1,558	3,176	3,265	4,308	4,281	4,670
of which: General government	1,402	2,457	2,463	3,411	2,903	3,482
Private sector guaranteed by public sector	..	..	..	..	..	..
Private sector not guaranteed	618	2,213	1,998	1,933	2,282	1,579
Summary external debt stock by creditor type						
Long-term external debt stocks	**83,949**	**111,776**	**139,480**	**134,857**	**148,348**	**136,013**
Public and publicly guaranteed debt from:	36,311	69,601	90,539	89,092	101,975	99,363
Official creditors	1,219	4,659	7,053	6,722	8,029	10,160
Multilateral	1,130	4,175	5,466	4,794	4,870	5,859
of which: World Bank	384	2,343	2,686	2,277	2,239	2,002
Bilateral	80	483	1,588	1,927	3,160	4,301
Private creditors	35,092	64,943	83,485	82,370	93,945	89,203
Bondholders	30,676	58,658	75,193	69,412	83,262	79,651
Commercial banks and others	4,416	6,285	8,292	12,958	10,684	9,552
Private nonguaranteed debt from:	47,638	42,175	48,942	45,765	46,373	36,649
Bondholders	8,786	3,533	3,768	4,521	4,737	2,700
Commercial banks and others	38,852	38,642	45,174	41,244	41,636	33,949
Use of IMF credit	2,750	2,400	2,543	2,483	2,469	6,966
Net financial inflows						
Net debt inflows						
Use of IMF credit	..	..	..	..	..	4,251
Long-term	8,640	10,692	21,546	1,482	6,446	-8,439
Official creditors	874	458	1,981	350	1,166	2,116
Multilateral	873	370	930	-69	-53	1,019
of which: World Bank	363	324	230	-46	-90	-42
Bilateral	1	88	1,051	419	1,219	1,097
Private creditors	7,766	10,234	19,564	1,132	5,280	-10,555
Bondholders	6,496	9,727	11,044	-2,923	11,905	-5,717
Banks and others	1,270	507	8,521	4,055	-6,625	-4,838
Short-term	444	716	3,107	3,856	-2,214	-6,752
Net equity inflows						
Foreign direct investment	-4,194	364	-266	1,378	1,792	3,121
Portfolio equity	5,826	1,640	7,588	2,946	-4,289	-5,160
Debt ratios						
External debt stocks to exports (%)	96	148	160	148	164	170
External debt stocks to GNI (%)	30	50	52	49	54	58
Debt service to exports (%)	6	15	13	24	20	29
Short-term to external debt stocks (%)	20	21	19	21	19	16
Multilateral to external debt stocks (%)	1	3	3	3	3	3
Reserves to external debt stocks (%)	35	30	26	27	26	28
Gross national income (GNI)	367,345	288,167	339,071	356,649	341,523	296,206

SRI LANKA

(US$ million, unless otherwise indicated)

	2010	2016	2017	2018	2019	2020
Summary external debt data by debtor type						
Total external debt stocks	**21,684**	**46,661**	**50,766**	**52,920**	**56,118**	**56,342**
Use of IMF credit	1,920	1,086	1,329	1,545	1,864	1,927
Long-term external debt	17,349	38,163	41,426	43,194	45,812	46,019
Public and publicly guaranteed sector	16,430	30,114	32,624	34,355	36,986	37,167
Public sector	16,430	30,114	32,624	34,355	36,986	37,167
of which: General government	16,342	27,441	30,847	33,786	36,655	36,805
Private sector guaranteed by public sector	..	..	..	..	..	..
Private sector not guaranteed	919	8,049	8,802	8,839	8,826	8,852
Short-term external debt	2,416	7,413	8,011	8,181	8,442	8,396
Disbursements (long-term)	**3,091**	**4,606**	**5,338**	**7,256**	**7,071**	**3,035**
Public and publicly guaranteed sector	2,994	3,986	4,357	5,097	6,235	2,456
Public sector	2,994	3,986	4,357	5,097	6,235	2,456
of which: General government	2,994	3,806	4,247	5,016	6,184	2,394
Private sector guaranteed by public sector	..	..	..	..	..	..
Private sector not guaranteed	97	620	981	2,158	836	579
Principal repayments (long-term)	**727**	**1,702**	**2,713**	**5,523**	**4,431**	**3,498**
Public and publicly guaranteed sector	582	1,186	2,486	3,190	3,582	2,861
Public sector	582	1,186	2,486	3,190	3,582	2,861
of which: General government	574	1,048	1,477	1,902	3,294	2,823
Private sector guaranteed by public sector	..	..	..	..	..	..
Private sector not guaranteed	145	516	227	2,333	849	636
Interest payments (long-term)	**616**	**990**	**1,030**	**1,546**	**1,542**	**1,590**
Public and publicly guaranteed sector	596	924	970	1,247	1,384	1,492
Public sector	596	924	970	1,247	1,384	1,492
of which: General government	595	786	852	1,153	1,365	1,489
Private sector guaranteed by public sector	..	..	..	..	..	..
Private sector not guaranteed	20	65	59	300	159	97
Summary external debt stock by creditor type						
Long-term external debt stocks	**17,349**	**38,163**	**41,426**	**43,194**	**45,812**	**46,019**
Public and publicly guaranteed debt from:	16,430	30,114	32,624	34,355	36,986	37,167
Official creditors	13,400	17,604	18,817	18,952	19,396	20,342
Multilateral	6,089	7,186	7,853	8,060	8,254	9,135
of which: World Bank	2,531	2,970	3,244	3,210	3,226	3,492
Bilateral	7,311	10,418	10,964	10,892	11,142	11,207
Private creditors	3,029	12,511	13,807	15,403	17,590	16,826
Bondholders	2,000	10,150	11,150	12,400	15,050	14,050
Commercial banks and others	1,029	2,361	2,657	3,003	2,540	2,776
Private nonguaranteed debt from:	919	8,049	8,802	8,839	8,826	8,852
Bondholders	0	362	362	262	175	0
Commercial banks and others	919	7,687	8,440	8,577	8,651	8,852
Use of IMF credit	1,920	1,086	1,329	1,545	1,864	1,927
Net financial inflows						
Net debt inflows						
Use of IMF credit	597	-122	174	252	327	-14
Long-term	2,364	2,904	2,625	1,733	2,640	-463
Official creditors	1,314	623	644	289	457	425
Multilateral	299	452	340	343	228	662
of which: World Bank	83	270	118	34	33	153
Bilateral	1,015	171	304	-54	229	-237
Private creditors	1,049	2,281	1,980	1,444	2,183	-888
Bondholders	1,000	1,558	1,000	1,150	2,563	-1,175
Banks and others	49	723	980	294	-380	287
Short-term	-1,138	-234	490	166	251	-55
Net equity inflows						
Foreign direct investment	240	710	532	463	370	211
Portfolio equity	-1,049	24	359	-4	-4	-217
Debt ratios						
External debt stocks to exports (%)	190	266	264	258	285	424
External debt stocks to GNI (%)	39	58	60	62	69	72
Debt service to exports (%)	12	19	22	36	32	39
Short-term to external debt stocks (%)	11	16	16	15	15	15
Multilateral to external debt stocks (%)	28	15	15	15	15	16
Reserves to external debt stocks (%)	31	11	14	12	12	9
Gross national income (GNI)	56,109	80,205	85,107	85,556	81,558	78,523

ST. LUCIA

(US$ million, unless otherwise indicated)

	2010	2016	2017	2018	2019	2020
Summary external debt data by debtor type						
Total external debt stocks	**584.8**	**543.7**	**621.9**	**615.5**	**638.9**	**733.8**
Use of IMF credit	33.0	29.8	28.5	24.8	21.7	52.4
Long-term external debt	326.4	432.4	489.6	499.5	542.2	603.6
Public and publicly guaranteed sector	326.4	432.4	489.6	499.5	542.2	603.6
Public sector	308.8	428.3	486.8	498.1	542.1	603.6
of which: General government	296.4	419.8	475.8	487.5	525.4	580.2
Private sector guaranteed by public sector	17.7	4.1	2.8	1.4	0.1	0.0
Private sector not guaranteed	..	..	..	..	..	..
Short-term external debt	225.3	81.5	103.8	91.1	75.0	77.9
Disbursements (long-term)	**36.4**	**11.5**	**16.6**	**10.8**	**48.2**	**94.3**
Public and publicly guaranteed sector	36.4	11.5	16.6	10.8	48.2	94.3
Public sector	32.7	11.5	16.6	10.8	48.2	94.3
of which: General government	32.7	10.7	12.7	9.8	40.9	86.1
Private sector guaranteed by public sector	3.7	0.0	0.0	0.0	0.0	..
Private sector not guaranteed	..	..	..	..	..	..
Principal repayments (long-term)	**30.5**	**24.5**	**19.0**	**19.1**	**19.8**	**17.7**
Public and publicly guaranteed sector	30.5	24.5	19.0	19.1	19.8	17.7
Public sector	28.0	22.4	17.6	17.8	18.5	17.5
of which: General government	25.4	21.3	16.3	16.5	17.2	16.1
Private sector guaranteed by public sector	2.4	2.1	1.4	1.3	1.3	0.1
Private sector not guaranteed	..	..	..	..	..	..
Interest payments (long-term)	**10.8**	**19.8**	**23.4**	**24.9**	**26.1**	**24.7**
Public and publicly guaranteed sector	10.8	19.8	23.4	24.9	26.1	24.7
Public sector	10.2	19.6	23.2	24.8	26.1	24.7
of which: General government	9.7	19.3	22.8	24.4	25.7	24.2
Private sector guaranteed by public sector	0.6	0.3	0.2	0.2	0.0	0.0
Private sector not guaranteed	..	..	..	..	..	..
Summary external debt stock by creditor type						
Long-term external debt stocks	**326.4**	**432.4**	**489.6**	**499.5**	**542.2**	**603.6**
Public and publicly guaranteed debt from:	326.4	432.4	489.6	499.5	542.2	603.6
Official creditors	263.2	249.5	253.0	242.6	270.7	351.2
Multilateral	242.5	212.5	218.2	211.3	222.7	277.9
of which: World Bank	80.3	79.5	85.6	85.6	86.6	108.3
Bilateral	20.7	37.0	34.7	31.3	48.0	73.4
Private creditors	63.2	182.9	236.6	256.9	271.5	252.4
Bondholders	63.2	182.9	236.6	256.9	271.5	252.4
Commercial banks and others	..	..	..	..	..	..
Private nonguaranteed debt from:	..	..	..	..	..	..
Bondholders	..	..	..	..	..	..
Commercial banks and others	..	..	..	..	..	..
Use of IMF credit	33.0	29.8	28.5	24.8	21.7	52.4
Net financial inflows						
Net debt inflows						
Use of IMF credit	0.0	-2.7	-3.0	-3.0	-3.0	28.7
Long-term	6.0	-13.0	-2.4	-8.3	28.4	76.6
Official creditors	17.9	-7.6	-1.8	-8.1	28.6	76.8
Multilateral	20.2	-4.7	1.2	-4.9	11.9	51.5
of which: World Bank	11.8	0.4	1.7	2.0	1.4	18.1
Bilateral	-2.3	-3.0	-3.0	-3.2	16.7	25.2
Private creditors	-11.9	-5.4	-0.6	-0.2	-0.2	-0.2
Bondholders	-11.9	-5.4	-0.6	-0.2	-0.2	-0.2
Banks and others	..	..	..	..	..	..
Short-term	138.0	4.8	22.3	-12.7	-16.1	2.9
Net equity inflows						
Foreign direct investment	67.9	149.1	49.0	44.7	42.2	10.3
Portfolio equity	..	0.5	0.5	3.3	0.1	0.1
Debt ratios						
External debt stocks to exports (%)	93.3	55.6	55.7	49.1	50.3	150.4
External debt stocks to GNI (%)	40.4	31.0	32.9	31.5	31.8	45.7
Debt service to exports (%)	7.1	5.0	4.3	4.0	4.1	9.2
Short-term to external debt stocks (%)	38.5	15.0	16.7	14.8	11.7	10.6
Multilateral to external debt stocks (%)	41.5	39.1	35.1	34.3	34.9	37.9
Reserves to external debt stocks (%)	35.3	56.2	51.7	46.4	40.8	31.5
Gross national income (GNI)	1,447.2	1,751.4	1,892.3	1,953.5	2,008.0	1,605.1

ST. VINCENT AND THE GRENADINES

(US$ million, unless otherwise indicated)

	2010	2016	2017	2018	2019	2020
Summary external debt data by debtor type						
Total external debt stocks	**295.9**	**333.5**	**335.4**	**323.3**	**351.7**	**406.3**
Use of IMF credit	17.9	22.9	21.9	18.0	15.4	31.3
Long-term external debt	278.0	306.5	313.2	305.4	336.3	375.0
Public and publicly guaranteed sector	278.0	306.5	313.2	305.4	336.3	375.0
Public sector	278.0	306.5	313.2	305.4	336.3	375.0
of which: General government	260.7	299.3	306.6	299.0	330.8	369.3
Private sector guaranteed by public sector	..	..	..	..	..	..
Private sector not guaranteed	..	..	..	..	..	..
Short-term external debt	0.0	4.1	0.3	0.0	0.0	0.0
Disbursements (long-term)	**78.1**	**13.3**	**31.0**	**23.3**	**59.0**	**60.5**
Public and publicly guaranteed sector	78.1	13.3	31.0	23.3	59.0	60.5
Public sector	78.1	13.3	31.0	23.3	59.0	60.5
of which: General government	78.1	12.7	29.7	20.9	57.5	59.9
Private sector guaranteed by public sector	..	..	..	..	..	..
Private sector not guaranteed	..	..	..	..	..	..
Principal repayments (long-term)	**26.2**	**24.6**	**26.3**	**30.3**	**27.9**	**24.4**
Public and publicly guaranteed sector	26.2	24.6	26.3	30.3	27.9	24.4
Public sector	26.2	24.6	26.3	30.3	27.9	24.4
of which: General government	24.3	22.7	24.4	27.8	25.5	24.0
Private sector guaranteed by public sector	..	..	..	..	..	..
Private sector not guaranteed	..	..	..	..	..	..
Interest payments (long-term)	**10.0**	**6.0**	**6.2**	**7.1**	**8.2**	**7.2**
Public and publicly guaranteed sector	10.0	6.0	6.2	7.1	8.2	7.2
Public sector	10.0	6.0	6.2	7.1	8.2	7.2
of which: General government	9.0	5.7	6.0	6.7	8.0	7.1
Private sector guaranteed by public sector	..	..	..	..	..	..
Private sector not guaranteed	..	..	..	..	..	..
Summary external debt stock by creditor type						
Long-term external debt stocks	**278.0**	**306.5**	**313.2**	**305.4**	**336.3**	**375.0**
Public and publicly guaranteed debt from:	278.0	306.5	313.2	305.4	336.3	375.0
Official creditors	229.2	299.2	298.9	294.9	328.4	371.0
Multilateral	211.0	258.6	250.5	241.1	271.2	313.4
of which: World Bank	26.5	31.5	32.7	31.8	69.1	117.1
Bilateral	18.2	40.6	48.5	53.8	57.2	57.6
Private creditors	48.7	7.3	14.3	10.5	7.9	4.0
Bondholders	..	..	10.4	9.1	7.9	4.0
Commercial banks and others	48.7	7.3	3.9	1.3	0.0	0.0
Private nonguaranteed debt from:	..	..	..	..	..	..
Bondholders	..	..	..	..	..	..
Commercial banks and others	..	..	..	..	..	..
Use of IMF credit	17.9	22.9	21.9	18.0	15.4	31.3
Net financial inflows						
Net debt inflows						
Use of IMF credit	..	-1.3	-2.3	-3.5	-2.5	14.8
Long-term	51.9	-11.3	4.6	-7.0	31.1	36.1
Official creditors	63.0	-8.0	-2.3	-3.2	33.7	40.0
Multilateral	66.7	-6.1	-10.0	-8.5	30.3	39.6
of which: World Bank	3.1	0.5	-0.5	-0.2	37.5	45.5
Bilateral	-3.7	-1.8	7.7	5.3	3.4	0.5
Private creditors	-11.1	-3.4	7.0	-3.8	-2.6	-3.9
Bondholders	..	..	10.4	-1.2	-1.2	-3.9
Banks and others	-11.1	-3.4	-3.4	-2.6	-1.3	..
Short-term	0.0	0.0	0.0	0.0	0.0	0.0
Net equity inflows						
Foreign direct investment	63.1	95.8	143.8	100.3	92.4	64.7
Portfolio equity	..	-0.8	-0.1	-0.1	-0.4	-0.4
Debt ratios						
External debt stocks to exports (%)	151.1	109.5	111.4	100.1	106.5	234.3
External debt stocks to GNI (%)	44.2	43.4	42.5	39.9	43.0	50.0
Debt service to exports (%)	18.5	10.5	11.6	12.7	11.7	19.1
Short-term to external debt stocks (%)	0.0	1.2	0.1	0.0	0.0	0.0
Multilateral to external debt stocks (%)	71.3	77.5	74.7	74.6	77.1	77.1
Reserves to external debt stocks (%)	38.1	57.6	54.3	52.4	55.0	50.5
Gross national income (GNI)	668.9	769.3	788.5	809.8	817.9	812.0

SUDAN

(US$ million, unless otherwise indicated)

	2010	2016	2017	2018	2019	2020
Summary external debt data by debtor type						
Total external debt stocks	**22,323**	**21,092**	**21,701**	**21,529**	**22,264**	**22,954**
Use of IMF credit	664	531	555	542	528	548
Long-term external debt	14,481	15,506	15,806	15,579	16,309	16,584
Public and publicly guaranteed sector	14,481	15,506	15,806	15,579	16,309	16,584
Public sector	14,481	15,506	15,806	15,579	16,309	16,584
of which: General government	14,447	15,485	15,785	15,558	16,289	16,564
Private sector guaranteed by public sector	..	..	..	..	..	..
Private sector not guaranteed	..	..	..	..	..	..
Short-term external debt	7,179	5,055	5,340	5,408	5,427	5,822
Disbursements (long-term)	**935**	**134**	**89**	**62**	**853**	**0**
Public and publicly guaranteed sector	935	134	89	62	853	0
Public sector	935	134	89	62	853	0
of which: General government	935	134	89	62	853	0
Private sector guaranteed by public sector	..	..	..	..	..	..
Private sector not guaranteed	..	..	..	..	..	..
Principal repayments (long-term)	**400**	**224**	**139**	**159**	**139**	**111**
Public and publicly guaranteed sector	400	224	139	159	139	111
Public sector	400	224	139	159	139	111
of which: General government	400	224	139	159	139	111
Private sector guaranteed by public sector	..	..	..	..	..	..
Private sector not guaranteed	..	..	..	..	..	..
Interest payments (long-term)	**84**	**59**	**86**	**50**	**39**	**31**
Public and publicly guaranteed sector	84	59	86	50	39	31
Public sector	84	59	86	50	39	31
of which: General government	84	59	86	50	39	31
Private sector guaranteed by public sector	..	..	..	..	..	..
Private sector not guaranteed	..	..	..	..	..	..
Summary external debt stock by creditor type						
Long-term external debt stocks	**14,481**	**15,506**	**15,806**	**15,579**	**16,309**	**16,584**
Public and publicly guaranteed debt from:	14,481	15,506	15,806	15,579	16,309	16,584
Official creditors	11,835	10,969	11,190	10,982	11,679	11,757
Multilateral	3,378	3,338	3,455	3,411	3,672	3,731
of which: World Bank	1,290	1,180	1,225	1,206	1,201	1,234
Bilateral	8,457	7,631	7,734	7,571	8,007	8,025
Private creditors	2,645	4,537	4,616	4,597	4,630	4,828
Bondholders	..	..	..	..	..	..
Commercial banks and others	2,645	4,537	4,616	4,597	4,630	4,828
Private nonguaranteed debt from:	..	..	..	..	..	..
Bondholders	..	..	..	..	..	..
Commercial banks and others	..	..	..	..	..	..
Use of IMF credit	664	531	555	542	528	548
Net financial inflows						
Net debt inflows						
Use of IMF credit	-6	-10	-7	..	-11	-3
Long-term	535	-90	-50	-96	714	-111
Official creditors	535	-90	-50	-96	714	-111
Multilateral	63	39	2	1	268	-21
of which: World Bank	0	0	0	0	..	0
Bilateral	472	-128	-52	-98	445	-90
Private creditors	..	..	0	0	0	0
Bondholders	..	..	..	..	..	..
Banks and others	..	..	0	0	0	0
Short-term	251	-21	60	51	-78	63
Net equity inflows						
Foreign direct investment	2,064	1,064	1,065	1,136	825	717
Portfolio equity	7	..	..	0	0	..
Debt ratios						
External debt stocks to exports (%)	189	455	369	420	427	..
External debt stocks to GNI (%)	34	40	49	64	73	94
Debt service to exports (%)	4	6	4	4	4	..
Short-term to external debt stocks (%)	32	24	25	25	24	25
Multilateral to external debt stocks (%)	15	16	16	16	16	16
Reserves to external debt stocks (%)	5	1	1	..	..	..
Gross national income (GNI)	64,963	52,335	44,408	33,820	30,630	24,416

SYRIAN ARAB REPUBLIC

(US$ million, unless otherwise indicated)

	2010	2016	2017	2018	2019	2020
Summary external debt data by debtor type						
Total external debt stocks	**5,277**	**4,368**	**4,604**	**4,584**	**4,590**	**4,763**
Use of IMF credit	430	375	398	388	386	402
Long-term external debt	4,284	3,497	3,654	3,647	3,635	3,751
Public and publicly guaranteed sector	4,284	3,497	3,654	3,647	3,635	3,751
Public sector	4,284	3,497	3,654	3,647	3,635	3,751
of which: General government	3,708	3,013	3,144	3,150	3,142	3,240
Private sector guaranteed by public sector	..	..	..	..	..	..
Private sector not guaranteed	..	..	..	..	..	..
Short-term external debt	562	495	553	548	569	610
Disbursements (long-term)	**286**	**0**	**0**	**60**	**0**	**0**
Public and publicly guaranteed sector	286	0	0	60	0	0
Public sector	286	0	0	60	0	0
of which: General government	263	0	0	60	0	0
Private sector guaranteed by public sector	..	..	..	..	..	..
Private sector not guaranteed	..	..	..	..	..	..
Principal repayments (long-term)	**509**	**0**	**0**	**19**	**1**	**0**
Public and publicly guaranteed sector	509	0	0	19	1	0
Public sector	509	0	0	19	1	0
of which: General government	451	0	0	17	..	0
Private sector guaranteed by public sector	..	..	..	..	..	..
Private sector not guaranteed	..	..	..	..	..	..
Interest payments (long-term)	**111**	**0**	**0**	**1**	**0**	**0**
Public and publicly guaranteed sector	111	0	0	1	0	0
Public sector	111	0	0	1	0	0
of which: General government	94	0	0	1	..	0
Private sector guaranteed by public sector	..	..	..	..	..	..
Private sector not guaranteed	..	..	..	..	..	..
Summary external debt stock by creditor type						
Long-term external debt stocks	**4,284**	**3,497**	**3,654**	**3,647**	**3,635**	**3,751**
Public and publicly guaranteed debt from:	4,284	3,497	3,654	3,647	3,635	3,751
Official creditors	4,261	3,479	3,635	3,630	3,619	3,734
Multilateral	1,698	1,403	1,512	1,472	1,459	1,529
of which: World Bank	15	14	14	14	14	14
Bilateral	2,563	2,076	2,123	2,158	2,160	2,205
Private creditors	23	18	19	17	16	17
Bondholders	..	..	..	..	..	..
Commercial banks and others	23	18	19	17	16	17
Private nonguaranteed debt from:	..	..	..	..	..	..
Bondholders	..	..	..	..	..	..
Commercial banks and others	..	..	..	..	..	..
Use of IMF credit	430	375	398	388	386	402
Net financial inflows						
Net debt inflows						
Use of IMF credit	..	..	..	..	..	..
Long-term	-222	0	0	41	-1	0
Official creditors	-220	0	0	43	0	0
Multilateral	87	0	0	1	0	0
of which: World Bank	-1	0	0	0	..	0
Bilateral	-307	0	0	41	0	0
Private creditors	-2	0	0	-2	-1	0
Bondholders	..	..	..	..	..	..
Banks and others	-2	0	0	-2	-1	0
Short-term	-209	-25	0	1	-1	2
Net equity inflows						
Foreign direct investment	1,469	..	..	..	..	..
Portfolio equity	..	..	..	..	..	..
Debt ratios						
External debt stocks to exports (%)	26	..	..	..	..	..
External debt stocks to GNI (%)	..	..	..	..	..	..
Debt service to exports (%)	3	..	..	..	..	..
Short-term to external debt stocks (%)	11	11	12	12	12	13
Multilateral to external debt stocks (%)	32	32	33	32	32	32
Reserves to external debt stocks (%)	369	..	..	..	..	..
Gross national income (GNI)	..	..	..	..	..	..

TAJIKISTAN

(US$ million, unless otherwise indicated)

	2010	2016	2017	2018	2019	2020
Summary external debt data by debtor type						
Total external debt stocks	**3,561**	**5,181**	**5,622**	**6,089**	**6,642**	**6,798**
Use of IMF credit	227	217	204	170	144	330
Long-term external debt	2,733	4,150	4,672	5,037	5,139	5,351
Public and publicly guaranteed sector	1,806	2,169	2,825	2,848	2,842	3,125
Public sector	1,806	2,169	2,825	2,848	2,842	3,125
of which: General government	1,793	2,164	2,821	2,842	2,836	3,116
Private sector guaranteed by public sector	..	..	..	..	..	..
Private sector not guaranteed	927	1,981	1,847	2,190	2,298	2,226
Short-term external debt	601	814	745	881	1,359	1,117
Disbursements (long-term)	**924**	**729**	**975**	**540**	**465**	**530**
Public and publicly guaranteed sector	251	225	708	184	133	321
Public sector	251	225	708	184	133	321
of which: General government	251	222	708	182	132	318
Private sector guaranteed by public sector	..	..	..	..	..	..
Private sector not guaranteed	673	505	267	356	332	209
Principal repayments (long-term)	**631**	**487**	**595**	**402**	**383**	**726**
Public and publicly guaranteed sector	37	113	112	128	129	106
Public sector	37	113	112	128	129	106
of which: General government	35	111	112	127	129	105
Private sector guaranteed by public sector	..	..	..	..	..	..
Private sector not guaranteed	593	374	482	274	254	620
Interest payments (long-term)	**54**	**108**	**60**	**121**	**108**	**153**
Public and publicly guaranteed sector	23	35	38	72	75	62
Public sector	23	35	38	72	75	62
of which: General government	23	35	37	72	75	62
Private sector guaranteed by public sector	..	..	..	..	..	..
Private sector not guaranteed	31	73	22	49	33	91
Summary external debt stock by creditor type						
Long-term external debt stocks	**2,733**	**4,150**	**4,672**	**5,037**	**5,139**	**5,351**
Public and publicly guaranteed debt from:	1,806	2,169	2,825	2,848	2,842	3,125
Official creditors	1,800	2,147	2,301	2,325	2,319	2,600
Multilateral	943	881	969	1,015	1,039	1,260
of which: World Bank	377	305	326	333	342	356
Bilateral	856	1,267	1,332	1,309	1,280	1,341
Private creditors	6	21	524	523	522	525
Bondholders	..	..	500	500	500	500
Commercial banks and others	6	21	24	23	22	25
Private nonguaranteed debt from:	927	1,981	1,847	2,190	2,298	2,226
Bondholders	..	..	..	..	..	..
Commercial banks and others	927	1,981	1,847	2,190	2,298	2,226
Use of IMF credit	227	217	204	170	144	330
Net financial inflows						
Net debt inflows						
Use of IMF credit	60	-20	-25	-30	-25	174
Long-term	294	243	380	138	83	-196
Official creditors	215	112	96	56	4	216
Multilateral	131	-6	46	65	28	185
of which: World Bank	11	-1	3	15	10	0
Bilateral	83	119	49	-9	-24	30
Private creditors	79	130	284	82	79	-412
Bondholders	..	..	500	..	..	..
Banks and others	79	130	-216	82	79	-412
Short-term	527	-147	-69	136	478	-242
Net equity inflows						
Foreign direct investment	82	108	68	142	104	23
Portfolio equity	7	0	0	0	-73	0
Debt ratios						
External debt stocks to exports (%)	158	230	208	229	230	230
External debt stocks to GNI (%)	51	64	65	68	69	71
Debt service to exports (%)	31	28	26	22	19	31
Short-term to external debt stocks (%)	17	16	13	14	20	16
Multilateral to external debt stocks (%)	26	17	17	17	16	19
Reserves to external debt stocks (%)	9	2	11	6	8	..
Gross national income (GNI)	6,970	8,082	8,637	8,991	9,631	9,558

TANZANIA

(US$ million, unless otherwise indicated)

	2010	2016	2017	2018	2019	2020
Summary external debt data by debtor type						
Total external debt stocks	**8,937**	**19,436**	**21,418**	**22,352**	**24,164**	**25,538**
Use of IMF credit	647	515	459	364	301	274
Long-term external debt	6,922	16,443	18,341	19,405	21,071	22,110
Public and publicly guaranteed sector	5,698	13,091	14,551	15,300	16,843	17,619
Public sector	5,698	13,091	14,551	15,300	16,843	17,619
of which: General government	5,631	13,060	14,517	15,267	16,811	17,585
Private sector guaranteed by public sector	..	..	..	..	..	..
Private sector not guaranteed	1,224	3,351	3,791	4,105	4,228	4,491
Short-term external debt	1,368	2,479	2,618	2,582	2,792	3,153
Disbursements (long-term)	**1,347**	**1,129**	**1,728**	**1,684**	**2,387**	**1,191**
Public and publicly guaranteed sector	1,131	1,094	1,659	1,601	2,360	1,169
Public sector	1,131	1,094	1,659	1,601	2,360	1,169
of which: General government	1,131	1,094	1,659	1,601	2,360	1,169
Private sector guaranteed by public sector	..	..	..	..	..	..
Private sector not guaranteed	216	36	69	83	27	21
Principal repayments (long-term)	**132**	**412**	**453**	**639**	**783**	**865**
Public and publicly guaranteed sector	52	389	451	618	763	850
Public sector	52	389	451	618	763	850
of which: General government	52	389	451	618	763	850
Private sector guaranteed by public sector	..	..	..	..	..	..
Private sector not guaranteed	79	23	3	20	20	15
Interest payments (long-term)	**51**	**246**	**254**	**309**	**381**	**350**
Public and publicly guaranteed sector	33	227	250	301	375	348
Public sector	33	227	250	301	375	348
of which: General government	33	227	250	301	375	348
Private sector guaranteed by public sector	..	..	..	..	..	..
Private sector not guaranteed	17	19	4	8	6	2
Summary external debt stock by creditor type						
Long-term external debt stocks	**6,922**	**16,443**	**18,341**	**19,405**	**21,071**	**22,110**
Public and publicly guaranteed debt from:	5,698	13,091	14,551	15,300	16,843	17,619
Official creditors	5,563	11,802	13,047	13,633	14,275	15,294
Multilateral	4,412	7,750	8,866	9,385	10,088	11,176
of which: World Bank	3,248	5,621	6,467	6,815	7,341	8,148
Bilateral	1,152	4,052	4,182	4,248	4,187	4,118
Private creditors	135	1,289	1,503	1,667	2,569	2,325
Bondholders	..	..	..	..	..	..
Commercial banks and others	135	1,289	1,503	1,667	2,569	2,325
Private nonguaranteed debt from:	1,224	3,351	3,791	4,105	4,228	4,491
Bondholders	..	..	..	..	..	..
Commercial banks and others	1,224	3,351	3,791	4,105	4,228	4,491
Use of IMF credit	647	515	459	364	301	274
Net financial inflows						
Net debt inflows						
Use of IMF credit	30	-62	-84	-85	-61	-37
Long-term	1,216	717	1,275	1,045	1,604	326
Official creditors	1,071	955	1,034	804	691	589
Multilateral	856	531	738	711	748	737
of which: World Bank	691	398	519	517	568	488
Bilateral	215	424	296	93	-56	-148
Private creditors	145	-238	241	241	913	-263
Bondholders	..	..	..	..	..	..
Banks and others	145	-238	241	241	913	-263
Short-term	-53	193	-19	-236	16	-7
Net equity inflows						
Foreign direct investment	1,038	631	824	478	629	685
Portfolio equity	3	4	4	1	4	..
Debt ratios						
External debt stocks to exports (%)	137	227	267	259	245	295
External debt stocks to GNI (%)	28	40	41	40	39	41
Debt service to exports (%)	3	9	10	12	13	15
Short-term to external debt stocks (%)	15	13	12	12	12	12
Multilateral to external debt stocks (%)	49	40	41	42	42	44
Reserves to external debt stocks (%)	44	22	27	23	..	..
Gross national income (GNI)	31,437	48,664	52,107	56,211	61,908	61,909

THAILAND

(US$ million, unless otherwise indicated)

	2010	2016	2017	2018	2019	2020
Summary external debt data by debtor type						
Total external debt stocks	**106,358**	**139,220**	**161,647**	**172,494**	**179,773**	**204,147**
Use of IMF credit	1,494	1,304	1,382	1,349	1,342	1,397
Long-term external debt	54,207	83,454	91,528	107,740	118,649	127,935
Public and publicly guaranteed sector	15,929	23,169	29,521	35,878	39,207	39,540
Public sector	15,929	23,169	29,521	35,878	39,207	39,540
of which: General government	10,456	20,363	26,552	32,831	36,480	36,528
Private sector guaranteed by public sector	..	..	..	..	..	..
Private sector not guaranteed	38,278	60,285	62,007	71,862	79,442	88,395
Short-term external debt	50,657	54,462	68,738	63,405	59,782	74,814
Disbursements (long-term)	**16,838**	**16,799**	**21,092**	**40,537**	**28,259**	**24,053**
Public and publicly guaranteed sector	5,240	1,133	6,600	7,189	4,211	542
Public sector	5,240	1,133	6,600	7,189	4,211	542
of which: General government	4,748	1,113	6,324	6,886	3,874	192
Private sector guaranteed by public sector	..	..	..	..	..	..
Private sector not guaranteed	11,597	15,666	14,492	33,348	24,049	23,512
Principal repayments (long-term)	**9,386**	**12,332**	**13,452**	**16,891**	**24,927**	**14,602**
Public and publicly guaranteed sector	803	482	396	913	941	379
Public sector	803	482	396	913	941	379
of which: General government	199	196	194	645	251	240
Private sector guaranteed by public sector	..	..	..	..	..	..
Private sector not guaranteed	8,582	11,850	13,056	15,979	23,986	14,223
Interest payments (long-term)	**1,076**	**1,530**	**818**	**1,162**	**1,605**	**1,568**
Public and publicly guaranteed sector	199	309	389	695	1,024	997
Public sector	199	309	389	695	1,024	997
of which: General government	81	250	340	638	951	940
Private sector guaranteed by public sector	..	..	..	..	..	..
Private sector not guaranteed	877	1,221	429	467	581	571
Summary external debt stock by creditor type						
Long-term external debt stocks	**54,207**	**83,454**	**91,528**	**107,740**	**118,649**	**127,935**
Public and publicly guaranteed debt from:	15,929	23,169	29,521	35,878	39,207	39,540
Official creditors	6,881	5,483	5,592	5,094	4,445	4,428
Multilateral	187	1,304	1,261	1,313	1,191	1,068
of which: World Bank	128	1,032	1,025	1,018	927	837
Bilateral	6,693	4,179	4,331	3,781	3,254	3,359
Private creditors	9,048	17,686	23,929	30,783	34,762	35,112
Bondholders	8,004	17,685	23,929	30,783	34,762	35,112
Commercial banks and others	1,045	1	0	0	..	..
Private nonguaranteed debt from:	38,278	60,285	62,007	71,862	79,442	88,395
Bondholders	4,265	9,188	10,043	12,723	13,193	15,840
Commercial banks and others	34,012	51,097	51,964	59,139	66,249	72,555
Use of IMF credit	1,494	1,304	1,382	1,349	1,342	1,397
Net financial inflows						
Net debt inflows						
Use of IMF credit	..	..	..	..	..	..
Long-term	7,452	4,467	7,640	23,646	3,333	9,451
Official creditors	-375	-31	-39	-579	-709	-187
Multilateral	-21	-40	-43	52	-122	-122
of which: World Bank	-5	-7	-7	-7	-90	-90
Bilateral	-353	9	4	-630	-587	-65
Private creditors	7,827	4,498	7,679	24,224	4,042	9,638
Bondholders	4,470	985	7,099	9,538	4,449	2,950
Banks and others	3,356	3,513	580	14,686	-407	6,688
Short-term	17,379	1,886	14,276	-5,333	-3,623	15,032
Net equity inflows						
Foreign direct investment	15,305	4,327	9,059	13,453	5,350	-5,572
Portfolio equity	2,398	-786	598	-7,101	56	-8,019
Debt ratios						
External debt stocks to exports (%)	46	49	52	51	54	76
External debt stocks to GNI (%)	33	35	37	36	34	42
Debt service to exports (%)	5	5	5	6	8	6
Short-term to external debt stocks (%)	48	39	43	37	33	37
Multilateral to external debt stocks (%)	0	1	1	1	1	1
Reserves to external debt stocks (%)	158	119	121	116	121	122
Gross national income (GNI)	326,815	393,949	435,913	482,065	524,214	487,772

TIMOR-LESTE

(US$ million, unless otherwise indicated)

	2010	2016	2017	2018	2019	2020
Summary external debt data by debtor type						
Total external debt stocks	..	**80.9**	**124.5**	**158.1**	**203.4**	**231.8**
Use of IMF credit	..	10.4	11.0	10.7	10.7	11.1
Long-term external debt	..	70.5	110.5	144.7	191.2	220.2
Public and publicly guaranteed sector	..	70.5	110.5	144.7	191.2	220.2
Public sector	..	70.5	110.5	144.7	191.2	220.2
of which: General government	..	70.5	110.5	144.7	191.2	220.2
Private sector guaranteed by public sector	..	..	..	..	..	..
Private sector not guaranteed	..	..	..	..	..	..
Short-term external debt	..	0.0	3.0	2.6	1.5	0.4
Disbursements (long-term)	..	**25.1**	**35.7**	**40.0**	**49.7**	**30.1**
Public and publicly guaranteed sector	..	25.1	35.7	40.0	49.7	30.1
Public sector	..	25.1	35.7	40.0	49.7	30.1
of which: General government	..	25.1	35.7	40.0	49.7	30.1
Private sector guaranteed by public sector	..	..	..	..	..	..
Private sector not guaranteed	..	..	..	..	..	..
Principal repayments (long-term)	..	**0.0**	**0.3**	**0.7**	**3.3**	**3.9**
Public and publicly guaranteed sector	..	0.0	0.3	0.7	3.3	3.9
Public sector	..	0.0	0.3	0.7	3.3	3.9
of which: General government	..	0.0	0.3	0.7	3.3	3.9
Private sector guaranteed by public sector	..	..	..	..	..	..
Private sector not guaranteed	..	..	..	..	..	..
Interest payments (long-term)	..	**0.8**	**1.5**	**2.5**	**3.8**	**4.1**
Public and publicly guaranteed sector	..	0.8	1.5	2.5	3.8	4.1
Public sector	..	0.8	1.5	2.5	3.8	4.1
of which: General government	..	0.8	1.5	2.5	3.8	4.1
Private sector guaranteed by public sector	..	..	..	..	..	..
Private sector not guaranteed	..	..	..	..	..	..
Summary external debt stock by creditor type						
Long-term external debt stocks	..	**70.5**	**110.5**	**144.7**	**191.2**	**220.2**
Public and publicly guaranteed debt from:	..	70.5	110.5	144.7	191.2	220.2
Official creditors	..	70.5	110.5	144.7	191.2	220.2
Multilateral	..	68.1	101.4	131.5	166.3	189.4
of which: World Bank	..	15.6	27.0	33.5	43.2	47.6
Bilateral	..	2.4	9.1	13.2	24.9	30.9
Private creditors	..	..	..	..	..	..
Bondholders	..	..	..	..	..	..
Commercial banks and others	..	..	..	..	..	..
Private nonguaranteed debt from:	..	..	..	..	..	..
Bondholders	..	..	..	..	..	..
Commercial banks and others	..	..	..	..	..	..
Use of IMF credit	..	10.4	11.0	10.7	10.7	11.1
Net financial inflows						
Net debt inflows						
Use of IMF credit	..	..	..	..	..	..
Long-term	..	25.1	35.5	39.3	46.4	26.2
Official creditors	..	25.1	35.5	39.3	46.4	26.2
Multilateral	..	25.1	28.7	35.4	34.9	21.7
of which: World Bank	..	5.6	11.4	7.5	9.7	4.1
Bilateral	..	..	6.7	3.9	11.5	4.5
Private creditors	..	..	..	..	..	..
Bondholders	..	..	..	..	..	..
Banks and others	..	..	..	..	..	..
Short-term	0.0	-60.3	3.0	-0.4	-1.1	-1.1
Net equity inflows						
Foreign direct investment	28.5	5.5	6.7	47.9	74.6	72.4
Portfolio equity	0.0	..	0.0	0.0	0.0	0.0
Debt ratios						
External debt stocks to exports (%)	..	12.3	14.2	15.7	15.5	30.9
External debt stocks to GNI (%)	..	3.6	5.5	7.1	7.5	9.5
Debt service to exports (%)	..	0.1	0.2	0.3	0.5	1.1
Short-term to external debt stocks (%)	0.0	0.0	2.4	1.6	0.7	0.2
Multilateral to external debt stocks (%)	0.0	84.2	81.4	83.2	81.8	81.7
Reserves to external debt stocks (%)	..	347.3	437.2	426.4	322.6	283.2
Gross national income (GNI)	3,325.1	2,230.6	2,272.1	2,239.7	2,701.0	2,438.0

TOGO

(US$ million, unless otherwise indicated)

	2010	2016	2017	2018	2019	2020
Summary external debt data by debtor type						
Total external debt stocks	**1,279**	**1,216**	**1,646**	**1,720**	**2,010**	**2,546**
Use of IMF credit	241	171	226	266	319	459
Long-term external debt	999	987	1,152	1,175	1,367	1,767
Public and publicly guaranteed sector	999	987	1,152	1,175	1,367	1,767
Public sector	999	987	1,152	1,175	1,367	1,767
of which: General government	990	983	1,148	1,172	1,364	1,764
Private sector guaranteed by public sector	..	..	..	..	..	..
Private sector not guaranteed	..	..	..	..	..	..
Short-term external debt	39	58	268	278	324	320
Disbursements (long-term)	**91**	**223**	**152**	**115**	**266**	**353**
Public and publicly guaranteed sector	91	223	152	115	266	353
Public sector	91	223	152	115	266	353
of which: General government	91	223	152	115	266	353
Private sector guaranteed by public sector	..	..	..	..	..	..
Private sector not guaranteed	..	..	..	..	..	..
Principal repayments (long-term)	**28**	**42**	**52**	**57**	**62**	**54**
Public and publicly guaranteed sector	28	42	52	57	62	54
Public sector	28	42	52	57	62	54
of which: General government	28	41	51	57	62	54
Private sector guaranteed by public sector	..	..	..	..	..	..
Private sector not guaranteed	..	..	..	..	..	..
Interest payments (long-term)	**8**	**23**	**23**	**26**	**26**	**32**
Public and publicly guaranteed sector	8	23	23	26	26	32
Public sector	8	23	23	26	26	32
of which: General government	8	23	23	26	26	32
Private sector guaranteed by public sector	..	..	..	..	..	..
Private sector not guaranteed	..	..	..	..	..	..
Summary external debt stock by creditor type						
Long-term external debt stocks	**999**	**987**	**1,152**	**1,175**	**1,367**	**1,767**
Public and publicly guaranteed debt from:	999	987	1,152	1,175	1,367	1,767
Official creditors	999	967	1,141	1,172	1,251	1,458
Multilateral	852	420	526	551	646	823
of which: World Bank	554	39	50	66	165	205
Bilateral	147	547	614	620	604	635
Private creditors	..	20	11	4	116	309
Bondholders	..	..	..	..	..	..
Commercial banks and others	..	20	11	4	116	309
Private nonguaranteed debt from:	..	..	..	..	..	..
Bondholders	..	..	..	..	..	..
Commercial banks and others	..	..	..	..	..	..
Use of IMF credit	241	171	226	266	319	459
Net financial inflows						
Net debt inflows						
Use of IMF credit	44	-24	43	46	54	123
Long-term	63	181	101	58	204	299
Official creditors	63	192	111	65	92	131
Multilateral	26	85	62	44	102	126
of which: World Bank	-22	9	9	17	100	83
Bilateral	37	107	49	21	-10	5
Private creditors	..	-11	-10	-7	112	169
Bondholders	..	..	..	..	..	..
Banks and others	..	-11	-10	-7	112	169
Short-term	12	-5	210	10	46	-4
Net equity inflows						
Foreign direct investment	78	28	-87	-88	371	639
Portfolio equity	5	-3	-89	-184	-180	..
Debt ratios						
External debt stocks to exports (%)	92	66	89	88	104	..
External debt stocks to GNI (%)	38	20	26	24	28	34
Debt service to exports (%)	3	5	6	6	6	..
Short-term to external debt stocks (%)	3	5	16	16	16	13
Multilateral to external debt stocks (%)	67	35	32	32	32	32
Reserves to external debt stocks (%)	56	..	..	..	..	..
Gross national income (GNI)	3,406	6,075	6,400	7,132	7,243	7,591

TONGA

(US$ million, unless otherwise indicated)

	2010	2016	2017	2018	2019	2020
Summary external debt data by debtor type						
Total external debt stocks	**153.7**	**174.4**	**193.1**	**186.8**	**186.5**	**194.3**
Use of IMF credit	10.1	8.8	9.4	9.2	9.1	9.5
Long-term external debt	143.5	165.6	183.7	177.7	177.4	184.8
Public and publicly guaranteed sector	143.5	165.6	183.7	177.7	177.4	184.8
Public sector	143.5	165.6	183.7	177.7	177.4	184.8
of which: General government	143.5	165.6	183.7	177.7	177.4	184.8
Private sector guaranteed by public sector	..	..	..	..	..	..
Private sector not guaranteed	..	..	..	..	..	..
Short-term external debt	0.0	0.0	0.0	0.0	0.0	0.0
Disbursements (long-term)	**40.9**	**7.1**	**10.1**	**7.3**	**4.9**	**1.2**
Public and publicly guaranteed sector	40.9	7.1	10.1	7.3	4.9	1.2
Public sector	40.9	7.1	10.1	7.3	4.9	1.2
of which: General government	40.9	7.1	10.1	7.3	4.9	1.2
Private sector guaranteed by public sector	..	..	..	..	..	..
Private sector not guaranteed	..	..	..	..	..	..
Principal repayments (long-term)	**2.7**	**3.5**	**2.8**	**6.2**	**2.7**	**4.7**
Public and publicly guaranteed sector	2.7	3.5	2.8	6.2	2.7	4.7
Public sector	2.7	3.5	2.8	6.2	2.7	4.7
of which: General government	2.7	3.5	2.8	6.2	2.7	4.7
Private sector guaranteed by public sector	..	..	..	..	..	..
Private sector not guaranteed	..	..	..	..	..	..
Interest payments (long-term)	**2.4**	**2.7**	**2.7**	**4.1**	**2.7**	**1.3**
Public and publicly guaranteed sector	2.4	2.7	2.7	4.1	2.7	1.3
Public sector	2.4	2.7	2.7	4.1	2.7	1.3
of which: General government	2.4	2.7	2.7	4.1	2.7	1.3
Private sector guaranteed by public sector	..	..	..	..	..	..
Private sector not guaranteed	..	..	..	..	..	..
Summary external debt stock by creditor type						
Long-term external debt stocks	**143.5**	**165.6**	**183.7**	**177.7**	**177.4**	**184.8**
Public and publicly guaranteed debt from:	143.5	165.6	183.7	177.7	177.4	184.8
Official creditors	142.4	165.6	183.7	177.7	177.4	184.8
Multilateral	70.8	60.4	71.4	74.1	75.8	77.2
of which: World Bank	23.6	29.1	37.2	39.1	42.9	45.0
Bilateral	71.7	105.2	112.3	103.6	101.6	107.6
Private creditors	1.1	..	..	..	..	..
Bondholders	..	..	..	..	..	..
Commercial banks and others	1.1	..	..	..	..	..
Private nonguaranteed debt from:	..	..	..	..	..	..
Bondholders	..	..	..	..	..	..
Commercial banks and others	..	..	..	..	..	..
Use of IMF credit	10.1	8.8	9.4	9.2	9.1	9.5
Net financial inflows						
Net debt inflows						
Use of IMF credit	..	..	..	..	..	..
Long-term	38.2	3.6	7.3	1.2	2.2	-3.5
Official creditors	38.1	3.6	7.3	1.2	2.2	-3.5
Multilateral	-1.0	4.2	7.3	4.4	2.2	-1.5
of which: World Bank	0.8	3.5	6.2	2.8	4.1	0.3
Bilateral	39.1	-0.6	..	-3.2	..	-2.0
Private creditors	0.1	..	..	..	..	..
Bondholders	..	..	..	..	..	..
Banks and others	0.1	..	..	..	..	..
Short-term	0.0	0.0	0.0	0.0	0.0	0.0
Net equity inflows						
Foreign direct investment	4.5	6.8	-2.6	19.1	2.0	3.5
Portfolio equity	..	0.0	0.0	0.0	0.0	0.0
Debt ratios						
External debt stocks to exports (%)	283.9	142.8	138.3	120.0	111.1	129.8
External debt stocks to GNI (%)	40.6	41.3	40.3	36.0	34.7	..
Debt service to exports (%)	9.3	5.1	4.0	6.6	3.3	4.0
Short-term to external debt stocks (%)	0.0	0.0	0.0	0.0	0.0	0.0
Multilateral to external debt stocks (%)	46.1	34.6	37.0	39.6	40.6	39.7
Reserves to external debt stocks (%)	68.0	101.2	102.8	115.2	117.1	153.9
Gross national income (GNI)	378.8	422.8	478.6	518.9	537.7	..

TUNISIA

(US$ million, unless otherwise indicated)

	2010	2016	2017	2018	2019	2020
Summary external debt data by debtor type						
Total external debt stocks	**22,666**	**28,827**	**33,501**	**35,033**	**39,381**	**41,038**
Use of IMF credit	420	1,987	2,105	2,280	2,132	2,824
Long-term external debt	17,267	20,146	23,937	24,659	25,818	27,582
Public and publicly guaranteed sector	14,865	18,643	22,296	22,577	23,750	25,695
Public sector	14,596	18,375	21,997	22,332	23,547	25,507
of which: General government	11,367	14,577	15,418	15,890	16,855	18,585
Private sector guaranteed by public sector	269	268	299	245	203	188
Private sector not guaranteed	2,402	1,503	1,641	2,082	2,067	1,888
Short-term external debt	4,979	6,694	7,458	8,093	11,431	10,632
Disbursements (long-term)	**1,671**	**2,363**	**4,413**	**2,617**	**3,743**	**2,428**
Public and publicly guaranteed sector	1,574	1,949	3,899	2,375	3,321	2,297
Public sector	1,504	1,916	3,851	2,375	3,321	2,297
of which: General government	867	1,515	1,128	1,736	2,251	1,848
Private sector guaranteed by public sector	70	33	47	..	..	1
Private sector not guaranteed	97	414	514	242	422	130
Principal repayments (long-term)	**1,631**	**1,410**	**2,046**	**1,718**	**1,931**	**2,160**
Public and publicly guaranteed sector	1,411	1,194	1,778	1,399	1,931	1,813
Public sector	1,387	1,154	1,726	1,358	1,894	1,781
of which: General government	1,107	653	1,278	795	1,153	1,118
Private sector guaranteed by public sector	24	40	52	42	37	32
Private sector not guaranteed	220	216	268	319	..	346
Interest payments (long-term)	**672**	**505**	**514**	**603**	**666**	**659**
Public and publicly guaranteed sector	548	464	456	550	573	583
Public sector	539	458	451	545	569	581
of which: General government	435	356	334	353	393	420
Private sector guaranteed by public sector	9	6	5	4	4	3
Private sector not guaranteed	124	41	58	53	94	76
Summary external debt stock by creditor type						
Long-term external debt stocks	**17,267**	**20,146**	**23,937**	**24,659**	**25,818**	**27,582**
Public and publicly guaranteed debt from:	14,865	18,643	22,296	22,577	23,750	25,695
Official creditors	10,389	12,641	14,754	14,606	15,824	18,191
Multilateral	6,985	9,229	11,014	10,996	11,291	12,765
of which: World Bank	1,399	2,447	3,275	3,515	3,489	4,196
Bilateral	3,404	3,413	3,740	3,610	4,533	5,425
Private creditors	4,476	6,002	7,542	7,971	7,926	7,504
Bondholders	3,819	5,268	6,705	7,239	7,278	6,877
Commercial banks and others	657	734	837	732	648	626
Private nonguaranteed debt from:	2,402	1,503	1,641	2,082	2,067	1,888
Bondholders	..	..	..	..	..	..
Commercial banks and others	2,402	1,503	1,641	2,082	2,067	1,888
Use of IMF credit	420	1,987	2,105	2,280	2,132	2,824
Net financial inflows						
Net debt inflows						
Use of IMF credit	..	282	0	228	-135	583
Long-term	40	954	2,367	899	1,811	268
Official creditors	634	339	845	464	1,415	1,261
Multilateral	566	320	810	504	466	641
of which: World Bank	74	20	581	486	31	410
Bilateral	68	19	35	-40	949	620
Private creditors	-594	615	1,521	435	396	-993
Bondholders	..	500	1,260	591	49	-707
Banks and others	-594	115	262	-156	347	-287
Short-term	144	119	764	635	3,338	-799
Net equity inflows						
Foreign direct investment	1,339	631	815	998	817	600
Portfolio equity	-26	-57	-64	-41	13	-31
Debt ratios						
External debt stocks to exports (%)	100	166	186	176	200	247
External debt stocks to GNI (%)	54	71	87	91	105	107
Debt service to exports (%)	11	12	17	15	16	20
Short-term to external debt stocks (%)	22	23	22	23	29	26
Multilateral to external debt stocks (%)	31	32	33	31	29	31
Reserves to external debt stocks (%)	42	20	17	15	19	23
Gross national income (GNI)	41,984	40,618	38,573	38,407	37,479	38,196

TURKEY

(US$ million, unless otherwise indicated)

	2010	2016	2017	2018	2019	2020
Summary external debt data by debtor type						
Total external debt stocks	**300,869**	**409,421**	**456,562**	**445,973**	**440,773**	**435,889**
Use of IMF credit	7,277	1,440	1,526	1,490	1,481	1,543
Long-term external debt	216,361	306,738	335,174	327,989	316,189	295,908
Public and publicly guaranteed sector	93,281	107,727	117,843	121,211	124,923	132,392
Public sector	92,987	107,375	117,497	120,925	124,679	132,181
of which: General government	76,686	84,350	92,236	93,203	99,590	106,563
Private sector guaranteed by public sector	293	352	346	286	244	210
Private sector not guaranteed	123,080	199,011	217,331	206,778	191,267	163,517
Short-term external debt	77,232	101,243	119,863	116,494	123,102	138,438
Disbursements (long-term)	**48,832**	**81,760**	**88,318**	**68,568**	**58,895**	**58,061**
Public and publicly guaranteed sector	14,793	14,324	17,579	15,844	17,226	16,392
Public sector	14,664	14,324	17,579	15,844	17,226	16,392
of which: General government	13,305	7,142	12,046	9,467	13,423	10,821
Private sector guaranteed by public sector	128	..	0	0	0	..
Private sector not guaranteed	34,039	67,436	70,739	52,725	41,669	41,669
Principal repayments (long-term)	**45,503**	**61,603**	**69,197**	**67,974**	**69,212**	**68,665**
Public and publicly guaranteed sector	6,027	8,437	11,339	10,822	12,899	12,362
Public sector	6,023	8,393	11,288	10,777	12,862	12,310
of which: General government	5,329	5,010	7,595	7,387	6,614	6,632
Private sector guaranteed by public sector	4	45	51	45	37	52
Private sector not guaranteed	39,476	53,166	57,858	57,152	56,313	56,303
Interest payments (long-term)	**8,869**	**10,934**	**12,098**	**11,523**	**12,621**	**12,675**
Public and publicly guaranteed sector	4,692	4,499	4,875	4,876	5,492	5,651
Public sector	4,690	4,495	4,871	4,872	5,488	5,648
of which: General government	4,048	4,001	4,284	4,290	4,579	4,881
Private sector guaranteed by public sector	2	4	4	4	4	3
Private sector not guaranteed	4,177	6,435	7,223	6,647	7,129	7,024
Summary external debt stock by creditor type						
Long-term external debt stocks	**216,361**	**306,738**	**335,174**	**327,989**	**316,189**	**295,908**
Public and publicly guaranteed debt from:	93,281	107,727	117,843	121,211	124,923	132,392
Official creditors	26,929	30,880	34,596	34,503	34,252	34,710
Multilateral	19,924	25,593	28,505	28,269	26,845	27,689
of which: World Bank	11,605	10,860	12,039	11,685	11,362	11,925
Bilateral	7,005	5,287	6,091	6,233	7,407	7,021
Private creditors	66,352	76,848	83,247	86,709	90,670	97,682
Bondholders	45,774	67,141	74,436	77,326	82,205	88,291
Commercial banks and others	20,578	9,706	8,811	9,383	8,466	9,391
Private nonguaranteed debt from:	123,080	199,011	217,331	206,778	191,267	163,517
Bondholders	6,202	34,475	41,602	38,894	38,373	37,131
Commercial banks and others	116,878	164,536	175,729	167,884	152,893	126,386
Use of IMF credit	7,277	1,440	1,526	1,490	1,481	1,543
Net financial inflows						
Net debt inflows						
Use of IMF credit	-2,171	..	..	..	..	..
Long-term	3,328	20,157	19,121	594	-10,317	-10,605
Official creditors	4,030	765	925	941	148	-1,508
Multilateral	3,831	1,080	461	745	-1,024	-823
of which: World Bank	2,088	-644	185	5	-172	-99
Bilateral	199	-314	464	196	1,172	-685
Private creditors	-702	19,391	18,196	-347	-10,465	-9,097
Bondholders	5,970	4,307	9,466	1,753	3,102	579
Banks and others	-6,672	15,085	8,730	-2,100	-13,567	-9,676
Short-term	28,255	-3,889	18,620	-3,369	6,608	15,336
Net equity inflows						
Foreign direct investment	8,715	10,848	10,175	12,144	10,488	8,687
Portfolio equity	3,468	823	2,971	-1,131	406	-4,255
Debt ratios						
External debt stocks to exports (%)	185	200	201	183	175	207
External debt stocks to GNI (%)	39	48	54	58	59	61
Debt service to exports (%)	37	37	38	35	34	41
Short-term to external debt stocks (%)	26	25	26	26	28	32
Multilateral to external debt stocks (%)	7	6	6	6	6	6
Reserves to external debt stocks (%)	27	22	18	16	18	11
Gross national income (GNI)	770,477	860,511	847,900	766,430	748,585	711,418

TURKMENISTAN

(US$ million, unless otherwise indicated)

	2010	2016	2017	2018	2019	2020
Summary external debt data by debtor type						
Total external debt stocks	**1,682**	**8,167**	**8,650**	**8,160**	**6,516**	**5,636**
Use of IMF credit	108	94	99	97	97	101
Long-term external debt	1,520	7,920	8,135	7,757	6,419	5,394
Public and publicly guaranteed sector	1,513	7,892	8,088	7,722	6,376	5,342
Public sector	1,513	7,892	8,088	7,722	6,376	5,342
of which: General government	147	1,009	1,313	1,528	1,629	1,821
Private sector guaranteed by public sector	..	..	..	..	..	..
Private sector not guaranteed	7	29	47	35	43	51
Short-term external debt	54	153	416	306	0	142
Disbursements (long-term)	**1,051**	**2,238**	**1,530**	**1,095**	**518**	**747**
Public and publicly guaranteed sector	1,044	2,232	1,501	1,089	498	729
Public sector	1,044	2,232	1,501	1,089	498	729
of which: General government	3	680	290	305	315	345
Private sector guaranteed by public sector	..	..	..	..	..	..
Private sector not guaranteed	8	6	29	7	20	18
Principal repayments (long-term)	**148**	**1,194**	**1,381**	**1,460**	**1,804**	**1,850**
Public and publicly guaranteed sector	135	1,178	1,366	1,437	1,793	1,839
Public sector	135	1,178	1,366	1,437	1,793	1,839
of which: General government	18	13	15	83	165	188
Private sector guaranteed by public sector	..	..	..	..	..	..
Private sector not guaranteed	13	16	15	23	12	11
Interest payments (long-term)	**50**	**319**	**339**	**364**	**355**	**240**
Public and publicly guaranteed sector	50	319	339	363	354	239
Public sector	50	319	339	363	354	239
of which: General government	3	6	20	47	63	69
Private sector guaranteed by public sector	..	..	..	..	..	..
Private sector not guaranteed	0	0	1	1	1	1
Summary external debt stock by creditor type						
Long-term external debt stocks	**1,520**	**7,920**	**8,135**	**7,757**	**6,419**	**5,394**
Public and publicly guaranteed debt from:	1,513	7,892	8,088	7,722	6,376	5,342
Official creditors	1,513	7,892	7,871	7,356	5,875	4,726
Multilateral	06	430	441	432	471	673
of which: World Bank	11	1	0	..	..	..
Bilateral	1,417	7,462	7,429	6,924	5,404	4,053
Private creditors	0	0	217	367	501	616
Bondholders	..	..	..	..	..	..
Commercial banks and others	0	0	217	367	501	616
Private nonguaranteed debt from:	7	29	47	35	43	51
Bondholders	..	..	..	..	..	..
Commercial banks and others	7	29	47	35	43	51
Use of IMF credit	108	94	99	97	97	101
Net financial inflows						
Net debt inflows						
Use of IMF credit	..	..	..	..	..	..
Long-term	903	1,043	149	-364	-1,287	-1,103
Official creditors	924	1,054	-76	-507	-1,433	-1,197
Multilateral	-2	98	10	-9	88	202
of which: World Bank	-1	-2	-1	..	..	..
Bilateral	926	956	-86	-498	-1,521	-1,399
Private creditors	-21	-11	225	142	147	94
Bondholders	..	..	..	..	..	..
Banks and others	-21	-11	225	142	147	94
Short-term	-30	153	263	-110	-306	142
Net equity inflows						
Foreign direct investment	3,632	2,243	2,086	1,997	2,129	1,169
Portfolio equity	..	..	..	..	..	..
Debt ratios						
External debt stocks to exports (%)	..	..	..	..	..	..
External debt stocks to GNI (%)	8	23	24	21	15	..
Debt service to exports (%)	..	..	..	..	..	..
Short-term to external debt stocks (%)	3	2	5	4	0	3
Multilateral to external debt stocks (%)	6	5	5	5	7	12
Reserves to external debt stocks (%)	..	..	..	..	..	..
Gross national income (GNI)	20,689	35,226	36,352	39,044	43,576	..

UGANDA

(US$ million, unless otherwise indicated)

	2010	2016	2017	2018	2019	2020
Summary external debt data by debtor type						
Total external debt stocks	**2,975**	**10,086**	**11,673**	**12,315**	**13,971**	**17,207**
Use of IMF credit	275	233	246	241	239	769
Long-term external debt	2,673	9,352	10,953	11,566	12,780	15,246
Public and publicly guaranteed sector	2,673	5,446	6,890	7,701	8,638	11,335
Public sector	2,668	5,442	6,886	7,697	8,634	11,332
of which: General government	2,667	5,441	6,885	7,696	8,634	11,326
Private sector guaranteed by public sector	5	4	4	4	3	3
Private sector not guaranteed	..	3,906	4,064	3,865	4,142	3,911
Short-term external debt	26	502	473	509	952	1,191
Disbursements (long-term)	**489**	**936**	**1,568**	**1,167**	**1,411**	**2,486**
Public and publicly guaranteed sector	489	785	1,259	1,167	1,134	2,486
Public sector	489	785	1,259	1,167	1,134	2,486
of which: General government	489	785	1,259	1,167	1,134	2,481
Private sector guaranteed by public sector	0	..	..	..	..	..
Private sector not guaranteed	..	151	309	..	277	..
Principal repayments (long-term)	**40**	**779**	**97**	**422**	**166**	**402**
Public and publicly guaranteed sector	40	46	97	224	166	171
Public sector	40	46	97	224	166	171
of which: General government	40	46	97	224	166	171
Private sector guaranteed by public sector	..	0	0	..	0	0
Private sector not guaranteed	..	733	..	199	..	231
Interest payments (long-term)	**21**	**57**	**80**	**98**	**115**	**266**
Public and publicly guaranteed sector	21	55	80	98	115	141
Public sector	21	55	80	98	115	141
of which: General government	21	55	80	98	115	141
Private sector guaranteed by public sector	..	..	..	..	..	..
Private sector not guaranteed	..	1	..	..	..	125
Summary external debt stock by creditor type						
Long-term external debt stocks	**2,673**	**9,352**	**10,953**	**11,566**	**12,780**	**15,246**
Public and publicly guaranteed debt from:	2,673	5,446	6,890	7,701	8,638	11,335
Official creditors	2,673	5,445	6,881	7,650	8,555	10,816
Multilateral	2,416	4,077	4,867	5,039	5,654	7,215
of which: World Bank	1,682	2,576	2,980	3,095	3,443	4,300
Bilateral	257	1,368	2,014	2,612	2,901	3,601
Private creditors	0	1	8	50	83	519
Bondholders	..	..	..	..	..	..
Commercial banks and others	0	1	8	50	83	519
Private nonguaranteed debt from:	..	3,906	4,064	3,865	4,142	3,911
Bondholders	..	..	..	..	..	..
Commercial banks and others	..	3,906	4,064	3,865	4,142	3,911
Use of IMF credit	275	233	246	241	239	769
Net financial inflows						
Net debt inflows						
Use of IMF credit	0	0	..	..	..	503
Long-term	449	157	1,471	745	1,245	2,084
Official creditors	450	738	1,155	900	934	1,911
Multilateral	424	338	538	285	640	1,291
of which: World Bank	326	163	245	190	366	689
Bilateral	26	400	617	615	294	620
Private creditors	0	-581	316	-155	311	173
Bondholders	..	..	..	..	..	..
Banks and others	0	-581	316	-155	311	173
Short-term	-209	-52	-29	36	443	240
Net equity inflows						
Foreign direct investment	248	396	708	710	955	652
Portfolio equity	-70	16	15	66	15	4
Debt ratios						
External debt stocks to exports (%)	84	208	227	217	226	304
External debt stocks to GNI (%)	11	35	39	39	41	47
Debt service to exports (%)	2	17	4	9	5	12
Short-term to external debt stocks (%)	1	5	4	4	7	7
Multilateral to external debt stocks (%)	81	40	42	41	40	42
Reserves to external debt stocks (%)	91	31	32	27	..	..
Gross national income (GNI)	26,231	28,567	30,021	31,986	34,254	36,758

UKRAINE

(US$ million, unless otherwise indicated)

	2010	2016	2017	2018	2019	2020
Summary external debt data by debtor type						
Total external debt stocks	**124,527**	**115,004**	**122,700**	**121,091**	**123,921**	**129,899**
Use of IMF credit	16,262	13,075	14,001	12,997	11,328	12,824
Long-term external debt	81,001	81,706	86,439	87,403	90,568	92,997
Public and publicly guaranteed sector	25,327	33,104	36,068	36,207	38,475	41,519
Public sector	25,327	33,104	36,068	36,207	38,475	41,519
of which: General government	24,815	31,049	33,718	35,469	35,589	38,482
Private sector guaranteed by public sector	..	..	..	..	..	..
Private sector not guaranteed	55,674	48,602	50,371	51,197	52,093	51,478
Short-term external debt	27,264	20,223	22,259	20,690	22,025	24,078
Disbursements (long-term)	**32,240**	**5,019**	**8,175**	**9,488**	**12,525**	**15,718**
Public and publicly guaranteed sector	7,969	2,750	5,757	4,051	5,363	4,987
Public sector	7,969	2,750	5,757	4,051	5,363	4,987
of which: General government	7,935	2,679	5,446	3,711	3,061	4,826
Private sector guaranteed by public sector	..	..	..	..	..	..
Private sector not guaranteed	24,272	2,268	2,418	5,437	7,163	10,731
Principal repayments (long-term)	**22,885**	**8,608**	**8,507**	**8,846**	**8,275**	**12,664**
Public and publicly guaranteed sector	1,446	1,898	3,456	3,603	3,000	4,912
Public sector	1,446	1,898	3,456	3,603	3,000	4,912
of which: General government	1,165	1,882	3,439	1,657	2,851	4,886
Private sector guaranteed by public sector	..	..	..	..	..	..
Private sector not guaranteed	21,439	6,710	5,051	5,243	5,275	7,753
Interest payments (long-term)	**3,532**	**3,116**	**2,975**	**2,809**	**3,171**	**3,615**
Public and publicly guaranteed sector	594	1,435	1,502	1,464	1,683	1,852
Public sector	594	1,435	1,502	1,464	1,683	1,852
of which: General government	552	1,286	1,347	1,436	1,652	1,692
Private sector guaranteed by public sector	..	..	..	..	..	..
Private sector not guaranteed	2,938	1,681	1,473	1,345	1,488	1,763
Summary external debt stock by creditor type						
Long-term external debt stocks	**81,001**	**81,706**	**86,439**	**87,403**	**90,568**	**92,997**
Public and publicly guaranteed debt from:	25,327	33,104	36,068	36,207	38,475	41,519
Official creditors	14,961	12,304	13,833	12,978	12,420	13,971
Multilateral	13,560	10,992	12,241	11,406	10,793	12,429
of which: World Bank	3,212	5,510	5,362	5,335	5,360	5,741
Bilateral	1,400	1,312	1,592	1,573	1,627	1,541
Private creditors	10,366	20,800	22,235	23,228	26,054	27,548
Bondholders	9,058	20,643	22,067	22,467	24,485	25,553
Commercial banks and others	1,308	156	167	761	1,569	1,996
Private nonguaranteed debt from:	55,674	48,602	50,371	51,197	52,093	51,478
Bondholders	4,313	3,831	4,419	4,519	4,489	4,405
Commercial banks and others	51,361	44,771	45,952	46,678	47,604	47,073
Use of IMF credit	16,262	13,075	14,001	12,997	11,328	12,824
Net financial inflows						
Net debt inflows						
Use of IMF credit	3,433	995	146	-689	-1,593	992
Long-term	9,355	-3,589	-332	642	4,251	3,053
Official creditors	3,767	-431	878	-575	-462	369
Multilateral	3,915	-761	643	-570	-506	509
of which: World Bank	-85	-80	-149	-27	25	381
Bilateral	-149	330	235	-5	43	-140
Private creditors	5,589	-3,158	-1,210	1,217	4,713	2,685
Bondholders	2,193	541	1,589	-275	2,551	-146
Banks and others	3,396	-3,699	-2,799	1,492	2,162	2,830
Short-term	6,370	-974	1,114	-2,088	1,191	1,095
Net equity inflows						
Foreign direct investment	5,550	4,076	3,025	4,069	4,909	272
Portfolio equity	290	69	110	-9	49	173
Debt ratios						
External debt stocks to exports (%)	177	217	194	170	161	178
External debt stocks to GNI (%)	93	124	107	90	78	82
Debt service to exports (%)	38	23	21	21	18	25
Short-term to external debt stocks (%)	22	18	18	17	18	19
Multilateral to external debt stocks (%)	11	10	10	9	9	10
Reserves to external debt stocks (%)	27	13	14	16	19	21
Gross national income (GNI)	134,004	92,422	114,760	134,253	158,544	157,996

UZBEKISTAN

(US$ million, unless otherwise indicated)

	2010	2016	2017	2018	2019	2020
Summary external debt data by debtor type						
Total external debt stocks	**7,981**	**15,494**	**16,692**	**17,736**	**22,407**	**32,174**
Use of IMF credit	405	353	374	365	363	775
Long-term external debt	7,154	14,751	15,578	16,473	21,369	29,010
Public and publicly guaranteed sector	3,423	6,603	7,544	9,412	12,790	17,064
Public sector	3,419	6,603	7,544	9,412	12,790	17,064
of which: General government	2,534	4,311	5,085	6,768	10,117	14,044
Private sector guaranteed by public sector	4	..	..	..	..	..
Private sector not guaranteed	3,730	8,149	8,035	7,061	8,579	11,946
Short-term external debt	423	389	740	897	674	2,389
Disbursements (long-term)	**1,191**	**2,899**	**2,099**	**2,620**	**6,650**	**9,847**
Public and publicly guaranteed sector	455	1,399	1,118	2,291	3,803	4,624
Public sector	455	1,399	1,118	2,291	3,803	4,624
of which: General government	258	663	831	1,912	3,581	4,020
Private sector guaranteed by public sector	..	..	..	..	..	..
Private sector not guaranteed	736	1,501	981	330	2,846	5,223
Principal repayments (long-term)	**493**	**1,006**	**1,436**	**691**	**1,951**	**2,607**
Public and publicly guaranteed sector	370	341	341	383	429	594
Public sector	368	341	341	383	429	594
of which: General government	165	209	178	198	233	290
Private sector guaranteed by public sector	2	..	..	..	..	..
Private sector not guaranteed	123	665	1,095	309	1,521	2,013
Interest payments (long-term)	**118**	**354**	**449**	**285**	**670**	**700**
Public and publicly guaranteed sector	63	91	118	144	258	303
Public sector	63	91	118	144	258	303
of which: General government	47	49	68	95	196	242
Private sector guaranteed by public sector	0	..	..	..	..	..
Private sector not guaranteed	55	262	331	141	412	397
Summary external debt stock by creditor type						
Long-term external debt stocks	**7,154**	**14,751**	**15,578**	**16,473**	**21,369**	**29,010**
Public and publicly guaranteed debt from:	3,423	6,603	7,544	9,412	12,790	17,064
Official creditors	3,197	6,333	7,262	9,213	11,559	14,558
Multilateral	1,210	3,367	3,893	5,441	7,049	9,246
of which: World Bank	373	779	910	1,907	2,723	3,734
Bilateral	1,987	2,967	3,369	3,772	4,511	5,312
Private creditors	226	269	281	199	1,231	2,506
Bondholders	..	..	..	..	1,000	2,048
Commercial banks and others	226	269	281	199	231	458
Private nonguaranteed debt from:	3,730	8,149	8,035	7,061	8,579	11,946
Bondholders	..	..	..	..	300	600
Commercial banks and others	3,730	8,149	8,035	7,061	8,279	11,346
Use of IMF credit	405	353	374	365	363	775
Net financial inflows						
Net debt inflows						
Use of IMF credit	..	..	..	..	..	384
Long-term	698	1,893	662	1,929	4,699	7,240
Official creditors	184	1,034	800	1,980	2,338	2,764
Multilateral	110	361	460	1,580	1,616	2,134
of which: World Bank	5	196	101	1,013	820	978
Bilateral	74	673	340	400	722	630
Private creditors	514	859	-138	-51	2,361	4,477
Bondholders	..	..	..	..	1,300	1,348
Banks and others	514	859	-138	-51	1,061	3,129
Short-term	-120	228	351	157	-232	1,714
Net equity inflows						
Foreign direct investment	1,487	1,129	1,914	639	2,148	1,463
Portfolio equity	1	2	3	13	29	32
Debt ratios						
External debt stocks to exports (%)	61	121	111	102	112	200
External debt stocks to GNI (%)	17	19	28	34	38	56
Debt service to exports (%)	5	11	13	6	13	21
Short-term to external debt stocks (%)	5	3	4	5	3	7
Multilateral to external debt stocks (%)	15	22	23	31	31	29
Reserves to external debt stocks (%)	..	91	84	70	57	46
Gross national income (GNI)	47,535	82,632	60,373	51,900	58,465	57,466

VANUATU

(US$ million, unless otherwise indicated)

	2010	2016	2017	2018	2019	2020
Summary external debt data by debtor type						
Total external debt stocks	**177.7**	**293.4**	**401.4**	**402.2**	**420.6**	**427.2**
Use of IMF credit	25.1	44.7	47.4	43.3	37.2	34.4
Long-term external debt	102.6	210.9	287.6	313.8	341.3	354.4
Public and publicly guaranteed sector	102.6	210.9	287.6	313.8	341.3	354.4
Public sector	102.6	210.9	287.6	313.8	341.3	354.4
of which: General government	102.1	210.7	287.4	313.8	341.3	354.4
Private sector guaranteed by public sector	..	..	..	..	..	..
Private sector not guaranteed	..	..	..	..	..	..
Short-term external debt	50.0	37.8	66.4	45.1	42.1	38.4
Disbursements (long-term)	**3.3**	**53.2**	**68.7**	**46.4**	**41.8**	**7.5**
Public and publicly guaranteed sector	3.3	53.2	68.7	46.4	41.8	7.5
Public sector	3.3	53.2	68.7	46.4	41.8	7.5
of which: General government	3.3	53.2	68.7	46.4	41.8	7.5
Private sector guaranteed by public sector	..	..	..	..	..	..
Private sector not guaranteed	..	..	..	..	..	..
Principal repayments (long-term)	**3.6**	**4.9**	**5.0**	**12.0**	**12.5**	**12.8**
Public and publicly guaranteed sector	3.6	4.9	5.0	12.0	12.5	12.8
Public sector	3.6	4.9	5.0	12.0	12.5	12.8
of which: General government	3.5	4.9	5.0	11.8	12.5	12.8
Private sector guaranteed by public sector	..	..	..	..	..	..
Private sector not guaranteed	..	..	..	..	..	..
Interest payments (long-term)	**1.6**	**3.2**	**3.5**	**4.2**	**4.0**	**4.1**
Public and publicly guaranteed sector	1.6	3.2	3.5	4.2	4.0	4.1
Public sector	1.6	3.2	3.5	4.2	4.0	4.1
of which: General government	1.6	3.2	3.5	4.2	4.0	4.1
Private sector guaranteed by public sector	..	..	..	..	..	..
Private sector not guaranteed	..	..	..	..	..	..
Summary external debt stock by creditor type						
Long-term external debt stocks	**102.6**	**210.9**	**287.6**	**313.8**	**341.3**	**354.4**
Public and publicly guaranteed debt from:	102.6	210.9	287.6	313.8	341.3	354.4
Official creditors	102.6	210.9	287.6	313.8	341.3	354.4
Multilateral	68.8	53.7	76.1	101.8	135.0	145.2
of which: World Bank	11.7	12.2	29.1	54.7	83.0	91.6
Bilateral	33.8	157.2	211.5	212.0	206.3	209.1
Private creditors	..	..	..	..	..	..
Bondholders	..	..	..	..	..	..
Commercial banks and others	..	..	..	..	..	..
Private nonguaranteed debt from:	..	..	..	..	..	..
Bondholders	..	..	..	..	..	..
Commercial banks and others	..	..	..	..	..	..
Use of IMF credit	25.1	44.7	47.4	43.3	37.2	34.4
Net financial inflows						
Net debt inflows						
Use of IMF credit	..	0.0	0.0	-3.0	-5.9	-4.1
Long-term	-0.3	48.3	63.7	34.4	29.4	-5.3
Official creditors	-0.3	48.3	63.7	34.4	29.4	-5.3
Multilateral	-3.3	6.1	19.6	27.1	33.5	4.4
of which: World Bank	-0.5	3.4	15.8	26.8	28.7	5.0
Bilateral	3.0	42.1	44.0	7.2	-4.2	-9.7
Private creditors	..	..	..	..	..	..
Bondholders	..	..	..	..	..	..
Banks and others	..	..	..	..	..	..
Short-term	21.0	-0.9	28.6	-21.3	-3.1	-3.7
Net equity inflows						
Foreign direct investment	50.6	43.5	34.2	34.0	24.3	23.5
Portfolio equity	..	0.7	0.4	0.8	0.5	0.5
Debt ratios						
External debt stocks to exports (%)	48.9	71.2	92.8	81.1	86.2	161.4
External debt stocks to GNI (%)	27.4	37.8	46.2	43.6	42.7	50.6
Debt service to exports (%)	1.6	2.1	2.3	4.1	4.8	8.2
Short-term to external debt stocks (%)	28.1	12.9	16.6	11.2	10.0	9.0
Multilateral to external debt stocks (%)	38.7	18.3	19.0	25.3	32.1	34.0
Reserves to external debt stocks (%)	90.8	91.1	98.4	104.6	121.6	143.6
Gross national income (GNI)	649.2	775.7	869.5	922.6	984.4	844.7

VENEZUELA, RB

(US$ million, unless otherwise indicated)

	2010	2016	2017	2018	2019	2020
Summary external debt data by debtor type						
Total external debt stocks	**116,529**	**175,795**	**176,106**	**182,938**	**185,598**	**189,306**
Use of IMF credit	3,917	3,419	3,622	3,537	3,517	3,663
Long-term external debt	88,557	128,635	128,288	128,318	127,629	127,071
Public and publicly guaranteed sector	52,275	70,905	70,558	70,588	69,899	69,341
Public sector	52,275	70,905	70,558	70,588	69,899	69,341
of which: General government	37,070	46,347	46,000	46,030	45,341	44,783
Private sector guaranteed by public sector	..	..	..	..	..	..
Private sector not guaranteed	36,282	57,730	57,730	57,730	57,730	57,730
Short-term external debt	24,055	43,741	44,196	51,083	54,452	58,572
Disbursements (long-term)	**25,860**	**6,171**	**153**	**3,464**	**13**	**0**
Public and publicly guaranteed sector	9,718	6,171	153	3,464	13	0
Public sector	9,718	6,171	153	3,464	13	0
of which: General government	4,293	6,171	153	3,464	13	0
Private sector guaranteed by public sector	..	..	..	..	..	..
Private sector not guaranteed	16,143	..	..	..	..	0
Principal repayments (long-term)	**10,058**	**2,338**	**615**	**3,393**	**685**	**637**
Public and publicly guaranteed sector	885	2,338	615	3,393	685	637
Public sector	885	2,338	615	3,393	685	637
of which: General government	877	2,338	615	3,393	685	637
Private sector guaranteed by public sector	..	..	..	..	..	..
Private sector not guaranteed	9,174	..	..	..	..	..
Interest payments (long-term)	**6,273**	**2,641**	**2,741**	**199**	**436**	**279**
Public and publicly guaranteed sector	3,597	2,641	2,741	199	436	279
Public sector	3,597	2,641	2,741	199	436	279
of which: General government	2,786	2,641	2,741	199	436	279
Private sector guaranteed by public sector	..	..	..	..	..	..
Private sector not guaranteed	2,676	..	..	..	..	..
Summary external debt stock by creditor type						
Long-term external debt stocks	**88,557**	**128,635**	**128,288**	**128,318**	**127,629**	**127,071**
Public and publicly guaranteed debt from:	52,275	70,905	70,558	70,588	69,899	69,341
Official creditors	5,019	9,383	9,034	9,103	8,429	7,796
Multilateral	4,126	5,424	5,307	5,127	4,781	4,307
of which: World Bank	..	..	..	..	..	..
Bilateral	892	3,959	3,727	3,976	3,648	3,490
Private creditors	47,256	61,522	61,525	61,485	61,470	61,545
Bondholders	45,810	60,328	60,328	60,328	60,328	60,328
Commercial banks and others	1,446	1,195	1,197	1,158	1,142	1,217
Private nonguaranteed debt from:	36,282	57,730	57,730	57,730	57,730	57,730
Bondholders	8,067	12,744	12,744	12,744	12,744	12,744
Commercial banks and others	28,215	44,986	44,986	44,986	44,986	44,986
Use of IMF credit	3,917	3,419	3,622	3,537	3,517	3,663
Net financial inflows						
Net debt inflows						
Use of IMF credit	..	..	..	..	..	..
Long-term	15,802	3,833	-463	71	-672	-637
Official creditors	787	165	-353	71	-672	-637
Multilateral	830	130	-116	-177	-342	-472
of which: World Bank	..	..	..	..	..	..
Bilateral	-42	35	-237	248	-330	-165
Private creditors	15,015	3,669	-110	0	0	0
Bondholders	7,647	3,500	0	0	0	0
Banks and others	7,368	169	-110	0	0	0
Short-term	3,221	600	-458	3,296	0	0
Net equity inflows						
Foreign direct investment	117	446	-68	886	934	959
Portfolio equity	10	..	..	..	..	..
Debt ratios						
External debt stocks to exports (%)	165	600	..	..	..	..
External debt stocks to GNI (%)	30	..	..	..	..	..
Debt service to exports (%)	24	20	..	..	..	..
Short-term to external debt stocks (%)	21	25	25	28	29	31
Multilateral to external debt stocks (%)	4	3	3	3	3	2
Reserves to external debt stocks (%)	11	2	2	..	..	..
Gross national income (GNI)	388,341	..	..	..	..	..

VIETNAM

(US$ million, unless otherwise indicated)

	2010	2016	2017	2018	2019	2020
Summary external debt data by debtor type						
Total external debt stocks	**44,940**	**85,664**	**104,090**	**106,854**	**117,337**	**125,045**
Use of IMF credit	529	423	448	438	435	453
Long-term external debt	37,478	72,521	81,744	86,832	92,505	97,988
Public and publicly guaranteed sector	32,798	48,038	51,790	52,115	51,782	52,180
Public sector	32,798	47,842	51,620	51,970	51,662	52,086
of which: General government	26,995	33,256	36,159	36,738	36,671	36,957
Private sector guaranteed by public sector	..	196	170	145	120	94
Private sector not guaranteed	4,680	24,484	29,954	34,717	40,723	45,808
Short-term external debt	6,932	12,720	21,898	19,585	24,397	26,604
Disbursements (long-term)	**6,922**	**13,118**	**18,661**	**20,336**	**18,674**	**17,467**
Public and publicly guaranteed sector	5,637	4,464	4,270	3,210	2,404	2,265
Public sector	5,637	4,464	4,270	3,210	2,404	2,265
of which: General government	4,309	2,852	2,747	2,147	1,443	1,311
Private sector guaranteed by public sector	..	0	0	0	0	..
Private sector not guaranteed	1,285	8,654	14,391	17,126	16,271	15,202
Principal repayments (long-term)	**1,055**	**5,740**	**11,250**	**14,714**	**13,040**	**13,785**
Public and publicly guaranteed sector	1,055	2,530	2,329	2,587	2,775	3,667
Public sector	1,055	2,508	2,304	2,561	2,750	3,642
of which: General government	696	1,520	1,273	1,407	1,580	2,461
Private sector guaranteed by public sector	..	23	25	25	25	25
Private sector not guaranteed	..	3,210	8,920	12,127	10,265	10,118
Interest payments (long-term)	**707**	**1,412**	**2,059**	**2,721**	**2,678**	**1,870**
Public and publicly guaranteed sector	563	879	940	1,017	1,062	886
Public sector	563	874	935	1,011	1,056	883
of which: General government	382	505	527	574	597	524
Private sector guaranteed by public sector	..	5	5	5	6	3
Private sector not guaranteed	144	532	1,119	1,704	1,616	984
Summary external debt stock by creditor type						
Long-term external debt stocks	**37,478**	**72,521**	**81,744**	**86,832**	**92,505**	**97,988**
Public and publicly guaranteed debt from:	32,798	48,038	51,790	52,115	51,782	52,180
Official creditors	27,313	40,199	44,617	45,735	46,076	47,805
Multilateral	12,573	21,167	23,285	23,717	24,066	25,337
of which: World Bank	7,743	13,110	14,683	14,968	15,327	16,378
Bilateral	14,741	19,032	21,332	22,017	22,010	22,468
Private creditors	5,485	7,839	7,173	6,380	5,706	4,376
Bondholders	2,020	1,521	1,516	1,511	1,506	756
Commercial banks and others	3,465	6,318	5,657	4,869	4,199	3,620
Private nonguaranteed debt from:	4,680	24,484	29,954	34,717	40,723	45,808
Bondholders	..	235	235	35	1,014	1,094
Commercial banks and others	4,680	24,248	29,718	34,682	39,709	44,714
Use of IMF credit	529	423	448	438	435	453
Net financial inflows						
Net debt inflows						
Use of IMF credit	-38	..	..	..	..	..
Long-term	5,867	7,378	7,411	5,622	5,635	3,682
Official creditors	2,973	2,858	2,691	1,392	294	-35
Multilateral	1,953	1,443	1,145	839	458	491
of which: World Bank	1,543	830	885	592	443	499
Bilateral	1,020	1,415	1,545	553	-164	-526
Private creditors	2,894	4,520	4,720	4,230	5,341	3,717
Bondholders	981	-411	-5	-205	974	-671
Banks and others	1,912	4,931	4,725	4,435	4,367	4,388
Short-term	2,149	729	9,178	-2,313	4,812	2,207
Net equity inflows						
Foreign direct investment	7,101	8,820	8,418	13,977	11,980	13,212
Portfolio equity	2,383	..	..	..	..	..
Debt ratios						
External debt stocks to exports (%)	56	45	45	41	41	43
External debt stocks to GNI (%)	40	44	50	46	48	49
Debt service to exports (%)	2	4	6	7	6	6
Short-term to external debt stocks (%)	15	15	21	18	21	21
Multilateral to external debt stocks (%)	28	25	22	22	21	20
Reserves to external debt stocks (%)	28	43	47	52	67	76
Gross national income (GNI)	111,513	196,687	207,929	230,004	246,721	256,921

YEMEN, REPUBLIC OF

(US$ million, unless otherwise indicated)

	2010	2016	2017	2018	2019	2020
Summary external debt data by debtor type						
Total external debt stocks	**6,504**	**7,063**	**7,193**	**7,037**	**7,055**	**7,121**
Use of IMF credit	436	497	508	469	440	410
Long-term external debt	5,945	6,322	6,317	6,205	6,188	6,251
Public and publicly guaranteed sector	5,945	6,322	6,317	6,205	6,188	6,251
Public sector	5,945	6,322	6,317	6,205	6,188	6,251
of which: General government	5,945	5,322	5,317	5,205	5,188	5,251
Private sector guaranteed by public sector	..	..	..	..	..	..
Private sector not guaranteed	..	..	..	..	..	..
Short-term external debt	124	243	368	362	427	460
Disbursements (long-term)	**297**	**24**	**4**	**19**	**66**	**38**
Public and publicly guaranteed sector	297	24	4	19	66	38
Public sector	297	24	4	19	66	38
of which: General government	297	24	4	19	66	38
Private sector guaranteed by public sector	..	..	..	..	..	..
Private sector not guaranteed	..	..	..	..	..	..
Principal repayments (long-term)	**155**	**98**	**66**	**71**	**72**	**75**
Public and publicly guaranteed sector	155	98	66	71	72	75
Public sector	155	98	66	71	72	75
of which: General government	155	98	66	71	72	75
Private sector guaranteed by public sector	..	..	..	..	..	..
Private sector not guaranteed	..	..	..	..	..	..
Interest payments (long-term)	**74**	**31**	**13**	**13**	**12**	**11**
Public and publicly guaranteed sector	74	31	13	13	12	11
Public sector	74	31	13	13	12	11
of which: General government	74	28	13	13	12	11
Private sector guaranteed by public sector	..	..	..	..	..	..
Private sector not guaranteed	..	..	..	..	..	..
Summary external debt stock by creditor type						
Long-term external debt stocks	**5,945**	**6,322**	**6,317**	**6,205**	**6,188**	**6,251**
Public and publicly guaranteed debt from:	5,945	6,322	6,317	6,205	6,188	6,251
Official creditors	5,941	6,322	6,317	6,205	6,188	6,251
Multilateral	3,294	3,039	3,110	3,004	2,987	3,027
of which: World Bank	2,180	1,668	1,695	1,586	1,505	1,488
Bilateral	2,647	3,283	3,207	3,201	3,201	3,224
Private creditors	3	..	..	..	..	..
Bondholders	..	..	..	..	..	..
Commercial banks and others	3	..	..	..	..	..
Private nonguaranteed debt from:	..	..	..	..	..	..
Bondholders	..	..	..	..	..	..
Commercial banks and others	..	..	..	..	..	..
Use of IMF credit	436	497	508	469	440	410
Net financial inflows						
Net debt inflows						
Use of IMF credit	26	-10	-18	-27	-26	-47
Long-term	143	-74	-62	-52	-7	-38
Official creditors	144	-74	-62	-52	-7	-38
Multilateral	159	-72	-62	-51	-7	-38
of which: World Bank	28	-64	-66	-71	-72	-75
Bilateral	-15	-2	0	0	0	0
Private creditors	-1	..	..	..	..	..
Bondholders	..	..	..	..	..	..
Banks and others	-1	..	..	..	..	..
Short-term	-390	-109	50	-82	36	1
Net equity inflows						
Foreign direct investment	43	-561	-270	-282	-371	..
Portfolio equity	0	0	..	..	..	..
Debt ratios						
External debt stocks to exports (%)	70	738	..	..	..	..
External debt stocks to GNI (%)	22	23	27	30	..	..
Debt service to exports (%)	3	15	..	..	..	..
Short-term to external debt stocks (%)	2	3	5	5	6	6
Multilateral to external debt stocks (%)	51	43	43	43	42	43
Reserves to external debt stocks (%)	90	..	..	..	..	..
Gross national income (GNI)	29,088	30,870	26,696	23,469	..	..

ZAMBIA

(US$ million, unless otherwise indicated)

	2010	2016	2017	2018	2019	2020
Summary external debt data by debtor type						
Total external debt stocks	**4,253**	**15,221**	**22,954**	**23,526**	**27,726**	**30,046**
Use of IMF credit	1,117	813	794	715	667	678
Long-term external debt	1,986	13,646	21,260	22,189	26,224	28,690
Public and publicly guaranteed sector	1,192	7,060	8,786	9,888	11,017	12,245
Public sector	1,192	7,060	8,786	9,888	11,017	12,245
of which: General government	1,141	7,039	8,765	9,871	11,003	12,234
Private sector guaranteed by public sector	..	0	0	0	0	..
Private sector not guaranteed	794	6,586	12,474	12,301	15,208	16,445
Short-term external debt	1,150	762	901	623	835	677
Disbursements (long-term)	**177**	**3,768**	**7,857**	**4,884**	**5,501**	**5,863**
Public and publicly guaranteed sector	150	798	1,754	1,456	1,630	1,349
Public sector	150	798	1,754	1,456	1,630	1,349
of which: General government	150	798	1,754	1,455	1,630	1,349
Private sector guaranteed by public sector	..	0	0	0	..	..
Private sector not guaranteed	27	2,970	6,103	3,428	3,871	4,513
Principal repayments (long-term)	**86**	**209**	**367**	**667**	**1,758**	**3,103**
Public and publicly guaranteed sector	47	146	152	282	480	299
Public sector	47	146	152	282	480	299
of which: General government	41	143	148	279	477	296
Private sector guaranteed by public sector	..	0	0	0	0	..
Private sector not guaranteed	40	63	215	385	1,277	2,804
Interest payments (long-term)	**29**	**448**	**387**	**535**	**776**	**932**
Public and publicly guaranteed sector	11	326	341	444	442	298
Public sector	11	326	341	444	442	298
of which: General government	11	325	341	444	442	297
Private sector guaranteed by public sector	..	..	..	..	..	..
Private sector not guaranteed	18	122	45	91	334	635
Summary external debt stock by creditor type						
Long-term external debt stocks	**1,986**	**13,646**	**21,260**	**22,189**	**26,224**	**28,690**
Public and publicly guaranteed debt from:	1,192	7,060	8,786	9,888	11,017	12,245
Official creditors	1,189	3,764	4,227	4,670	5,614	6,540
Multilateral	924	1,408	1,622	1,818	2,113	2,498
of which: World Bank	430	760	894	1,003	1,108	1,296
Bilateral	265	2,356	2,606	2,851	3,501	4,042
Private creditors	2	3,297	4,558	5,219	5,403	5,705
Bondholders	..	3,000	3,000	3,000	3,000	3,000
Commercial banks and others	2	297	1,558	2,219	2,403	2,705
Private nonguaranteed debt from:	794	6,586	12,474	12,301	15,208	16,445
Bondholders	..	..	..	..	..	..
Commercial banks and others	794	6,586	12,474	12,301	15,208	16,445
Use of IMF credit	1,117	813	794	715	667	678
Net financial inflows						
Net debt inflows						
Use of IMF credit	55	-69	-66	-61	-44	-15
Long-term	90	3,558	7,490	4,217	3,743	2,759
Official creditors	105	621	340	510	963	756
Multilateral	71	156	133	234	303	308
of which: World Bank	30	86	86	132	112	139
Bilateral	35	465	207	275	660	448
Private creditors	-15	2,938	7,150	3,707	2,780	2,003
Bondholders	..	0	0	0	0	0
Banks and others	-15	2,938	7,150	3,707	2,780	2,003
Short-term	704	22	81	-225	196	-162
Net equity inflows						
Foreign direct investment	1,228	267	547	-502	-306	-201
Portfolio equity	101	3	-3	-5	-1	-1
Debt ratios						
External debt stocks to exports (%)	53	203	251	235	334	350
External debt stocks to GNI (%)	22	75	93	91	121	160
Debt service to exports (%)	2	10	9	13	31	47
Short-term to external debt stocks (%)	27	5	4	3	3	2
Multilateral to external debt stocks (%)	22	9	7	8	8	8
Reserves to external debt stocks (%)	49	15	9	7	5	4
Gross national income (GNI)	18,903	20,311	24,727	25,905	22,908	18,798

ZIMBABWE

(US$ million, unless otherwise indicated)

	2010	2016	2017	2018	2019	2020
Summary external debt data by debtor type						
Total external debt stocks	**6,763**	**11,465**	**12,510**	**12,620**	**12,245**	**12,741**
Use of IMF credit	529	455	482	471	468	488
Long-term external debt	4,405	7,869	8,302	8,765	8,255	8,401
Public and publicly guaranteed sector	3,800	4,228	4,320	4,287	4,366	4,577
Public sector	3,800	4,228	4,320	4,287	4,366	4,577
of which: General government	3,123	3,609	3,715	3,745	3,835	4,018
Private sector guaranteed by public sector	..	..	..	..	..	..
Private sector not guaranteed	605	3,640	3,983	4,478	3,889	3,825
Short-term external debt	1,829	3,141	3,726	3,384	3,521	3,852
Disbursements (long-term)	**847**	**1,132**	**815**	**980**	**972**	**906**
Public and publicly guaranteed sector	4	245	153	280	91	60
Public sector	4	245	153	280	91	60
of which: General government	4	245	153	280	91	60
Private sector guaranteed by public sector	..	..	..	..	..	..
Private sector not guaranteed	843	887	662	700	881	845
Principal repayments (long-term)	**338**	**988**	**384**	**281**	**1,214**	**930**
Public and publicly guaranteed sector	2	108	111	76	52	21
Public sector	2	108	111	76	52	21
of which: General government	1	41	61	26	42	21
Private sector guaranteed by public sector	..	..	..	..	..	..
Private sector not guaranteed	336	880	273	205	1,163	910
Interest payments (long-term)	**32**	**121**	**267**	**254**	**313**	**22**
Public and publicly guaranteed sector	14	44	27	14	13	17
Public sector	14	44	27	14	13	17
of which: General government	13	23	24	13	13	17
Private sector guaranteed by public sector	..	..	..	..	..	..
Private sector not guaranteed	18	78	240	240	301	5
Summary external debt stock by creditor type						
Long-term external debt stocks	**4,405**	**7,869**	**8,302**	**8,765**	**8,255**	**8,401**
Public and publicly guaranteed debt from:	3,800	4,228	4,320	4,287	4,366	4,577
Official creditors	3,351	3,815	3,885	3,869	3,954	4,146
Multilateral	1,614	1,557	1,414	1,213	1,207	1,245
of which: World Bank	976	885	907	896	890	910
Bilateral	1,738	2,258	2,471	2,656	2,746	2,901
Private creditors	448	413	435	418	412	431
Bondholders	0	0	0	0	0	0
Commercial banks and others	448	413	435	418	412	431
Private nonguaranteed debt from:	605	3,640	3,983	4,478	3,889	3,825
Bondholders	..	..	..	..	..	..
Commercial banks and others	605	3,640	3,983	4,478	3,889	3,825
Use of IMF credit	529	455	482	471	468	488
Net financial inflows						
Net debt inflows						
Use of IMF credit	-4	-87	..	..	..	..
Long-term	510	144	431	699	-243	-25
Official creditors	2	101	53	204	45	43
Multilateral	0	-69	-60	-41	0	2
of which: World Bank	0	-13	-5	0	-3	0
Bilateral	2	170	113	245	44	41
Private creditors	507	43	378	496	-287	-67
Bondholders	0	0	0	..	0	0
Banks and others	507	43	378	496	-287	-67
Short-term	160	31	452	-412	63	205
Net equity inflows						
Foreign direct investment	123	343	247	718	250	150
Portfolio equity	63	-80	-101	..	..	..
Debt ratios						
External debt stocks to exports (%)	185	268	253	243	232	242
External debt stocks to GNI (%)	64	61	67	66	74	77
Debt service to exports (%)	11	29	14	12	30	19
Short-term to external debt stocks (%)	27	27	30	27	29	30
Multilateral to external debt stocks (%)	24	14	11	10	10	10
Reserves to external debt stocks (%)	11	4	2	1	1	0
Gross national income (GNI)	10,614	18,773	18,628	19,212	16,635	16,495

APPENDIX
About the Data

User Guide to Tables

International Debt Statistics 2022 focuses on financial flows, trends in external debt, and other major financial indicators for low- and middle-income countries. This edition of *International Debt Statistics* (IDS) has been reconfigured to offer a more condensed presentation of the principal indicators. The longer version of the report will be found in the online tables.

Tables

Aggregate Tables

The aggregate tables are labeled by region name. Data are shown for all low- and middle-income countries and six regional groups (East Asia and Pacific, Europe and Central Asia, Latin America and the Caribbean, Middle East and North Africa, South Asia, and Sub-Saharan Africa).

Country Tables

Country tables are labeled by country name and ordered alphabetically. Data are shown for 123 low- and middle-income countries that report public and publicly guaranteed external debt to the World Bank's Debtor Reporting System (DRS). The tables also include key debt ratios and the composition of external debt stocks and flows for each country.

Each table shows a time series with the most recent five years, as well as 2010 as a comparison year. Full time series data are available for all countries in the World Bank's Open Data website (https://datacatalog.worldbank.org/dataset/international-debt-statistics).

Statistics

The general cutoff date for countries to report data for this publication was end-August 2021. The economic aggregates presented in the tables are prepared for the convenience of users. Although debt ratios can give useful information about developments in a debt-servicing capacity, conclusions drawn from them will not be valid unless accompanied by careful economic evaluation.

The macroeconomic data provided are collected from national statistical organizations, which in some cases may be subject to a considerable margin of error. The usual care must be taken in interpreting the ratios, particularly for the most recent years, because figures may be preliminary and subject to revision.

Specific country notes describing the sources of information that are not provided by the country are summarized in the "Data Documentation" section. Unless otherwise specified, data on long-term public and publicly guaranteed external debt for 2020 are based on reports provided by the country.

More detailed information on data sources, methodology, and compilation is provided in the appendix at the back of this book.

Aggregate Measures for Income Groups and Regions

Aggregate measures for income groups and regions include the 123 low- and middle-income countries that report public and publicly guaranteed external debt to the World Bank's DRS, whenever data are available. The aggregate "All low- and middle-income countries" is the sum of data for 123 countries.

Classification of Countries

For operational and analytical purposes, the World Bank's main criterion for classifying countries is gross national income (GNI) per capita (calculated by the *World Bank Atlas* method). Every country is classified as low-income, middle-income, or high-income. Low- and middle-income countries are sometimes referred to as developing countries. The term is used for convenience; it is not intended to imply that all countries in the group are experiencing similar development or that other countries have reached a preferred or final stage of development. Because GNI per capita changes over time, the country composition of income groups may change from one edition of *International Debt Statistics* to the next. Once the classification is fixed for an edition, based on GNI per capita in the most recent year for which data are available, all historical data presented are based on the same country grouping.

Symbols

0 or 0.0 means zero or small enough that the number would round to zero at the displayed number of decimal places.

.. means that data are not available or that aggregates cannot be calculated because of missing data in the years shown.

$ indicates current U.S. dollars unless otherwise specified.

User Guide to IDS Online Tables and Database

The country tables that were previously available in the *International Debt Statistics* print edition is now available online. Using an automated query process, these reference tables will be updated based on the revisions to the International Debt Statistics database.

Users can access all the online tables, download the PDF version of the publication, and view the report as an eBook on ISSUU, as well as access the database and download the archived editions of the publication by going to http://data.worldbank.org/products/ids. You can also access all of the publications through the Debt Website at https://www.worldbank.org/en/programs/debt-statistics/publications.

How to Access IDS Online Country Tables

To access the IDS online tables, visit https://www.worldbank.org/en/programs/debt-statistics/ids and select from "Country," "Region," or "Topic." Click on "Analytical" to view the table with a select number of indicators as reported in the IDS publication, or "Standard" to view the tables with the full list of indicators available in the database. To access the DSSI debt service payments due table, visit https://www.worldbank.org/en/programs/debt-statistics/dssi and select "Monthly presentation" for monthly projections or "Annual presentation" for yearly projections.

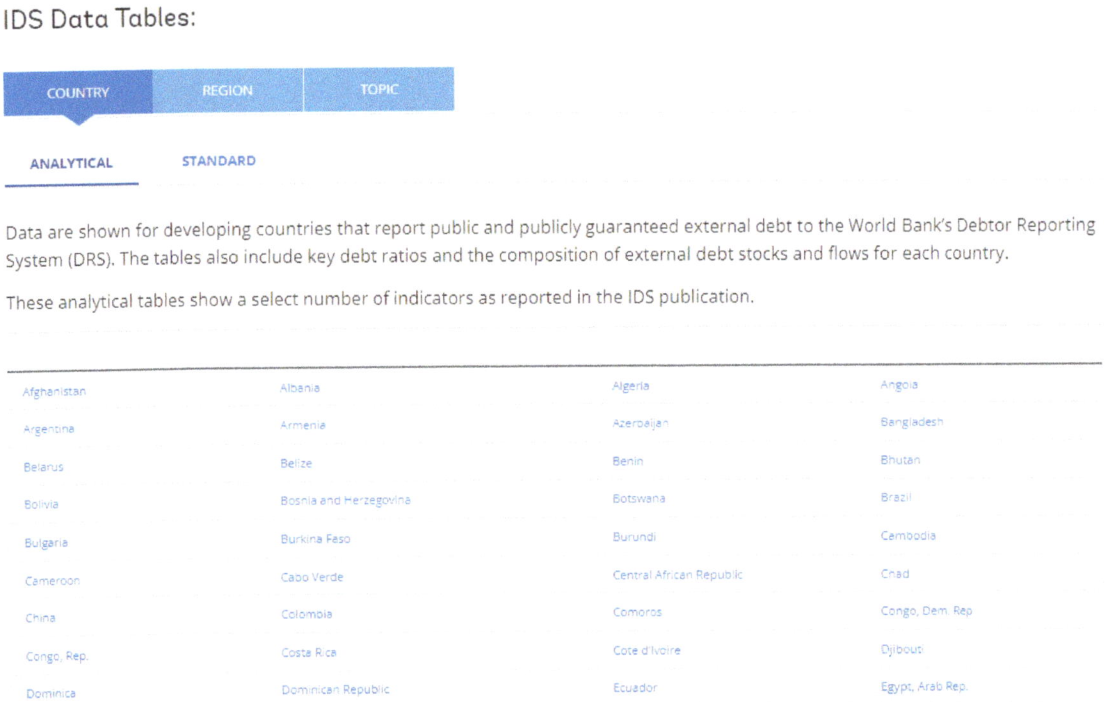

To access a specific country table directly without going through the above landing page, use the URL https://www.worldbank.org/en/programs/debt-statistics/ids and click on a country name to view the table. Similarly, to view the regional table, click on the "Region" tab and select one of the listed regions. The data can be filtered by Counterpart-Area (the creditor) and by Country (the debtor) using the drop-down filters.

International Debt Statistics

Data > Data Topics > Debt Data > Country Tables > Counterpart-Area: World; Country: Afghanistan

	2011	2012	2013	2014	2015	2016
Summary external debt data by debtor type						
Total External debt stocks	2,485.3	2,580.6	2,587.8	2,529.9	2,596.9	2,596.1
Use of IMF Credit	372.6	387.6	375.6	334.8	300.2	277.0
Long-term external debt	2,032.5	2,079.8	2,106.2	2,021.0	2,009.0	1,964.5
Public and publicly guaranteed sector	2,032.5	2,079.8	2,106.2	2,021.0	1,990.0	1,949.5
Public sector	2,032.5	2,079.8	2,106.2	2,021.0	1,990.0	1,949.5
of which: General Government	2,032.5	2,079.8	2,106.2	2,021.0	1,990.0	1,949.5
Private sector guaranteed by public sector	..	..	..	..	..	..
Private sector not guaranteed	..	..	..	..	19.0	15.0
Short-term external debt	80.3	113.2	105.9	174.1	287.8	354.6
Disbursements (long-term)	62.2	52.1	36.7	31.7	26.0	11.7
Public and publicly guaranteed sector	62.2	52.1	36.7	31.7	26.0	11.7
Public sector	62.2	52.1	36.7	31.7	26.0	11.7
of which: General Government	62.2	52.1	36.7	31.7	26.0	11.7
Private sector guaranteed by public sector	0.0	0.0	0.0	0.0	0.0	0.0
Private sector not guaranteed	0.0	0.0	0.0	0.0	0.0	0.0
Principal repayments (long-term)	0.9	1.6	4.2	12.1	23.8	26.8
Public and publicly guaranteed sector	0.9	1.6	4.2	12.1	18.7	22.7
Public sector	0.9	1.6	4.2	12.1	18.7	22.7
of which: General Government	0.9	1.6	4.2	12.1	18.7	22.7
Private sector guaranteed by public sector	..	..	..	..	..	..
Private sector not guaranteed	..	..	..	..	5.1	4.1
Interest payments (long-term)	8.9	8.3	7.5	9.1	9.9	8.4
Public and publicly guaranteed sector	8.9	8.3	7.5	9.1	8.7	7.5
Public sector	8.9	8.3	7.5	9.1	8.7	7.5
of which: General Government	8.9	8.3	7.5	9.1	8.7	7.5
Private sector guaranteed by public sector	..	..	..	..	..	..
Private sector not guaranteed	..	..	..	..	1.1	0.9

Indicators

The main indicator codes for each of the indicators online and in the publication are listed below. To view a specific indicator online, go to http://data.worldbank.org/indicator/ and add the indicator code at the end of the url; for example, to view a page for total debt stocks, this line should be in your browser: http://data.worldbank.org/indicator/DT.DOD.DECT.CD.

1. SUMMARY EXTERNAL DEBT DATA

External debt stocks	DT.DOD.DECT.CD
Long-term external debt	DT.DOD.DLXF.CD
Public and publicly guaranteed	DT.DOD.DPPG.CD
Private nonguaranteed	DT.DOD.DPNG.CD
Use of IMF credit	DT.DOD.DIMF.CD
Short-term debt	DT.DOD.DSTC.CD
interest arrears on long-term	DT.IXA.DPPG.CD
Memorandum items	
Principal arrears on long-term	DT.AXA.DPPG.CD
Long-term public sector debt	DT.DOD.DPPG.CD
Long-term private sector debt	DT.DOD.PRVS.CD
Public & publicly guaranteed commitments	DT.COM.DPPG.CD
External debt flows	
Disbursements	DT.DIS.DLTF.CD
Long-term external debt	DT.DIS.DLXF.CD
IMF purchases	DT.DIS.DIMF.CD
Principal repayments	DT.AMT.DLTF.CD
Long-term external debt	DT.AMT.DLXF.CD
IMF repurchases	DT.AMT.DIMF.CD
Net flows	DT.NFL.DECT.CD
Long-term external debt	DT.NFL.DLXF.CD
Short-term external debt	DT.NFL.DSTC.CD
Interest payments (INT)	DT.INT.DECT.CD
Long-term external debt	DT.INT.DLXF.CD
IMF charges	DT.INT.DIMF.CD
Short-term external debt	DT.INT.DSTC.CD

2. OTHER NON-DEBT RESOURCE FLOWS

Foreign direct investment (net equity inflows)	BX.KLT.DINV.CD.WD
Portfolio equity flows	BX.PEF.TOTL.CD.WD

3. CURRENCY COMPOSITION OF PUBLIC AND PUBLICLY GUARANTEED DEBT (%)

Euro	DT.CUR.EURO.ZS
Japanese yen	DT.CUR.JYEN.ZS
Pound sterling	DT.CUR.UKPS.ZS
Swiss franc	DT.CUR.SWFR.ZS
U.S. dollars	DT.CUR.USDL.ZS

4. AVERAGE TERMS OF NEW COMMITMENTS

Official creditors	
Interest (%)	DT.INR.OFFT
Maturity (years)	DT.MAT.OFFT
Grace period (years)	DT.GPA.OFFT
Private creditors	
Interest (%)	DT.INR.PRVT
Maturity (years)	DT.MAT.PRVT
Grace period (years)	DT.GPA.PRVT

5. MAJOR ECONOMIC AGGREGATES

Gross national income (GNI)	NY.GNP.MKTP.CD
Exports of goods, services, and primary income	BX.GSR.TOTL.CD
Personal transfers and compensation of employees	BX.TRF.PWKR.CD.DT
Imports of goods, services, and primary income	BM.GSR.TOTL.CD
Primary income on FDI (payments)	BX.KLT.DREM.CD.DT
International reserves	FI.RES.TOTL.CD

6. RATIOS

External debt stocks to exports (%)	DT.DOD.DECT.EX.ZS
External debt stocks to GNI (%)	DT.DOD.DECT.GN.ZS
Debt service to exports (%)	DOD.DECT.GN.ZS
Short-term to external debt stocks (%)	DT.DOD.DSTC.ZS
Multilateral to external debt stocks (%)	DT.DOD.MLAT.ZS
Reserves to external debt stocks (%)	FI.RES.TOTL.DT.ZS
Current account balance	BN.CAB.XOKA.CD
Reserves to imports (months)	FI.RES.TOTL.MO

7. LONG-TERM EXTERNAL DEBT			
Debt outstanding and disbursed	DT.DOD.DLXF.CD	**Interest payments**	DT.INT.DLXF.CD
Public and publicly guaranteed	DT.DOD.DPPG.CD	**Public and publicly guaranteed**	DT.INT.DPPG.CD
Official creditors	DT.DOD.OFFT.CD	Official creditors	DT.INT.OFFT.CD
Multilateral	DT.DOD.MLAT.CD	Multilateral	DT.INT.MLAT.CD
of which: IBRD	DT.DOD.MIBR.CD	of which: IBRD	DT.INT.MIBR.CD
IDA	DT.DOD.MIDA.CD	IDA	DT.INT.MIDA.CD
Bilateral	DT.DOD.BLAT.CD	Bilateral	DT.INT.BLAT.CD
Private creditors	DT.DOD.PRVT.CD	Private creditors	DT.INT.PRVT.CD
of which: Bonds	DT.DOD.PBND.CD	of which: Bonds	DT.INT.PBND.CD
Commercial banks	DT.DOD.PCBK.CD	Commercial banks	DT.INT.PCBK.CD
Private nonguaranteed	DT.DOD.DPNG.CD	Private nonguaranteed	DT.INT.DPNG.CD
of which: Bonds	DT.DOD.PNGB.CD	of which: Bonds	DT.INT.PNGB.CD
Disbursements	DT.DIS.DLXF.CD	**Principal repayments**	DT.AMT.DLXF.CD
Public and publicly guaranteed	DT.DIS.DPPG.CD	Public and publicly guaranteed	DT.AMT.DPPG.CD
Official creditors	DT.DIS.OFFT.CD	Official creditors	DT.AMT.OFFT.CD
Multilateral	DT.DIS.MLAT.CD	Multilateral	DT.AMT.MLAT.CD
of which: IBRD	DT.DIS.MIBR.CD	of which: IBRD	DT.AMT.MIBR.CD
IDA	DT.DIS.MIDA.CD	IDA	DT.AMT.MIDA.CD
Bilateral	DT.DIS.BLAT.CD	Bilateral	DT.AMT.BLAT.CD
Private creditors	DT.DIS.PRVT.CD	Private creditors	DT.AMT.PRVT.CD
of which: Bonds	DT.DIS.PBND.CD	of which: Bonds	DT.AMT.PBND.CD
Commercial banks	DT.DIS.PCBK.CD	Commercial banks	DT.AMT.PCBK.CD
Private nonguaranteed	DT.DIS.DPNG.CD	**Private nonguaranteed**	DT.AMT.DPNG.CD
of which: Bonds	DT.DIS.PNGB.CD	of which: Bonds	DT.AMT.PNGB.CD

8. DEBT STOCK-FLOW RECONCILATION	
Total change in external debt stocks	DT.DOD.DECT.CD.CG
Net flows on external debt	DT.NFL.DECT.CD

9. DEBT STOCK-FLOW RECONCILATION	
Total amount rescheduled	DT.DXR.DPPG.CD
Total amount forgiven	DT.DFR.DPPG.CD
Debt buyback	DT.DSB.DPPG.CD

10. CONTRACTUAL OBLIGATIONS ON OUTSTANDING LONG-TERM EXTERNAL DEBT	
Official creditors	
Principal	DT.AMT.OFFT.CD
Interest	DT.INT.OFFT.CD
Private creditors	
Principal	DT.AMT.PRVT.CD
Interest	DT.INT.PRVT.CD

How to Access the Database

DataBank (http://databank.worldbank.org) is an online web resource that provides simple and quick access to collections of time series data. It has advanced functions for selecting and displaying data, performing customized queries, downloading data, and creating charts and maps. Users can create dynamic, custom reports based on their selection of countries, indicators, and years. All these reports can be easily edited, shared, and embedded as widgets on websites or blogs. For more information, see http://databank.worldbank.org/help.

Actions

Click to share the table using either the embed code or the URL

Click to edit and revise the table in DataBank

Click to export all metadata to Excel

Click to export the table to Excel

Click to export the table and corresponding indicator metadata to PDF

Click to print the table and corresponding indicator metadata

Click to access the IDS Online Tables Help file

Data Sources and Methodology

Data Sources

Debtor reporting system

The principal sources of information for the tables in *International Debt Statistics 2022* are reports to the World Bank through the World Bank's Debtor Reporting System (DRS) from member countries that have received either International Bank for Reconstruction and Development (IBRD) loans or International Development Association (IDA) credits. The DRS has its origin in the World Bank's need to monitor and assess the financial position of its borrowers. Since 1951, borrowers have been required to provide statistics on their public external debt and private sector debt that benefit from a public guarantee. Reporting countries submit reports on the annual status, transactions, and terms of the long-term external debt of public agencies and that of private ones guaranteed by a public agency in the debtor country. The DRS maintains these records on a loan-by-loan basis. In 1973, coverage of the DRS was expanded to include private sector nonguaranteed borrowing, but for this category of debt, data are provided by borrowers in aggregate rather than loan by loan.

Data submitted to the DRS are processed in the World Bank External Debt (WBXD) system, along with additional information received from the African Development Bank, the Asian Development Bank, the Inter-American Development Bank (IDB), the International Monetary Fund (IMF), institutions of the World Bank Group (IBRD and IDA), and the European Bank for Reconstruction and Development (EBRD). The WBXD is an internal system of the World Bank. Among its outputs is the International Debt Statistics (IDS) database, from which the tables in this publication and online database are produced.

Data on exports and imports (on a balance of payments basis), international reserves, current account balances, foreign direct investment (FDI) on equity, portfolio equity flows, and primary income of FDI are drawn mainly from the IMF, supplemented by United Nations Conference on Trade and Development (UNCTAD) reports and country data. Balance of payments data are presented according to the sixth edition of the IMF's *Balance of Payments Manual* (BPM6). Official aid flows come from data collected and published by the Development Assistance Committee (DAC) of the Organisation for Economic Co-operation and Development (OECD). Short-term external debt data are as reported by debtor countries or are estimates based on the Bank for International Settlements (BIS) quarterly series of commercial banks' claims on low- and middle-income countries. For some countries, estimates were prepared by pooling creditor and debtor information. Data on the gross national income of most low- and middle-income countries are collected from national statistical organizations or Central Banks by visiting and resident World Bank missions.

Every effort has been made to ensure the accuracy and completeness of the external debt statistics. Coverage has been improved through the efforts of the reporting agencies and close collaboration between the Bank and our partners, Commonwealth Secretariat (COMSEC) and UNCTAD, which provide debt recording and reporting systems across the globe, as well as through the work of the World Bank missions, which visit member countries to gather data and to provide technical assistance on debt issues. Nevertheless, quality and coverage vary among debtors and may also vary for the same debtor from year to year. Data on long-term external debt reported by member countries are checked against, and supplemented by, data from several other sources. Among these sources are the statements and reports of several regional development banks, government lending agencies, and official government websites.

Methodology

Aggregations

Total debt stock and other aggregate measures are derived from the summation of loan-level data on stocks and flows after conversion to a common currency. Other tabulations are compiled using terms and conditions reported in the loan-level data, such as currency composition, cancellations, rescheduling of other liabilities into long-term public and publicly guaranteed external debt, and debt buybacks.

Aggregates for regional and income groups are based on the World Bank's operational classifications, which may differ from common geographic usage or income groups used by other organizations. Country classifications of DRS reporting countries in 2020 are shown in the country groups section. The same classification is used for all historical data shown in *International Debt Statistics* and the online tables and online database.

Currency conversion

Data on external obligations are normally reported to the World Bank in the currency of repayment and are converted into a common currency (U.S. dollars) using official exchange rates published by the IMF.

Commitments, disbursements, and debt service payments (flows) are converted to U.S. dollars at the annual average exchange rate for the year. Debt outstanding (disbursed and undisbursed) at the end of a given year (stock) is converted at the exchange rate in effect at the end of the relevant year. Consequently, year-to-year changes in debt outstanding and disbursed may not be equal to net flows (disbursements less principal repayments); similarly, changes in debt outstanding (including undisbursed debt) may not equal commitments less repayments. Discrepancies will be particularly significant when exchange rates have moved sharply during the year. Projected debt service is converted to U.S. dollars at rates in effect at the end of December 2020.

Beginning with 1991, all ruble debt owed to the former Soviet Union has been converted at a rate of US$1 = 0.6 ruble, except in cases where a bilateral agreement specifying a different conversion rate is in place. Adoption of this methodology does not constitute an endorsement by the World Bank staff of the appropriateness or validity of the exchange rate used. That matter must be resolved bilaterally between the Russian Federation and its debtor countries.

Starting with the 1988–89 edition of *World Debt Tables* (a predecessor of IDS), all data pertaining to IBRD loans from 1985 onward are recorded at their current market value. Starting with the 1991–92 edition, all data pertaining to Asian Development Bank loans from 1989 onward are recorded at their current market value. Starting with the 1998 edition, all data pertaining to African Development Bank and African Development Fund loans from 1997 onward are recorded at their current market value.

Debt stock and flow reconciliation

Because of currency conversions and the timing of transactions, there may be differences between the change in aggregate stocks from one period to the next and flows during the relevant period; changes in debt outstanding, including undisbursed amounts, will therefore differ from commitments less repayments.

Changes in the stock of debt from one period to the next can be attributed to five factors: the net flow of debt, the net change in interest arrears, the capitalization of interest, a reduction in debt resulting from debt forgiveness or other debt reduction mechanisms, and cross-currency valuation effects. Any residual difference in the change in stock not explained by one of those five factors may indicate inconsistencies in the reported data or specific phenomena prevailing in an individual country (for example, an incomplete historical series for all categories of debt). Starting in 1989, the IDS includes the debt stock reconciliation, but not all components are shown in the IDS print edition and online tables.

External debt restructuring

Starting in 1985, the WBXD includes information on the restructuring of debt by official creditors in the context of the Paris Club, restructuring by commercial creditors, debt swap operations, buybacks, and bond exchanges. It attempts to capture accurately the effect of debt restructuring on both external debt stocks and external debt flows, consistent with the terms on which the restructuring takes place. In the compilation and presentation of external debt data, a distinction is made between cash flows and imputed flows. According to this criterion, restructured service payments and the shift in liabilities from one financial instrument to another as a result of debt restructuring are considered to be imputed flows. Both cash flows and imputed flows are recorded separately in WBXD.

The imputed flows and stock changes associated with debt restructuring are included in the IDS tables and online database to complement the cash-basis transactions recorded in the main body of the data. Such data encompass information on the debt stock and debt flows restructured each year, the amount of principal forgiven (interest forgiven is shown as a memorandum item), and the amount of external debt stock reduced either by forgiveness or by a debt buyback operation. Changes in creditors and debtors that result from debt restructuring are also reflected. For example, when insured commercial credits are rescheduled, the creditor classification shifts from private to official (bilateral), reflecting the assumption of the assets by the official credit insurance agencies in the creditor country. The IDS data will show a reduction in the external debt owed to the original private creditors equal or similar to the amount of debt restructured and a corresponding increase in the debt owed to the new official creditor. Similarly on the debtor side, when a government accepts responsibility for the payment of restructured debt previously owed by a private enterprise, the relevant change in the debtor category will be reflected. Likewise, if short-term external debt is restructured into a long-term obligation, the stock of short-term external debt will decline and the stock of long-term external debt will rise by the amount of short-term debt restructured. In the event of a debt swap of long-term external debt (external debt to equity, external debt for nature, or external debt for development), the face value of the external debt swapped will be recorded as a decline in long-term external debt stock, but no flow transaction (principal repayment) will be recorded.

Projections of future disbursements and debt service payments

The WBXD system projects future disbursements and future debt service payments on the assumption that every existing loan commitment will be fully used and repaid in full.

Future disbursements

Disbursement projections are made using one of the following methods:

- *Specific schedules.* Debtor countries are requested to submit a schedule of future disbursements, if available, at the time each new loan is first reported.
- *Standard schedules.* In the absence of specific schedules, the WBXD system projects the future disbursement schedule according to the undisbursed balance of each loan at the end of the most recent reporting period.

These projected schedules are based on profiles derived from the disbursement pattern of comparable loans that fully disbursed. Thirty different profiles have been compiled corresponding to each category of creditor and, in the case of official creditors, for concessional and nonconcessional loans. Each profile is derived by applying regression analysis techniques to a body of data on actual disbursements for each fully disbursed loan in the WBXD database. The profiles are periodically updated to take into account the evolving pattern of disbursements observed for fully disbursed loans.

Future principal payments are generated by the WBXD system according to the repayment terms of each loan. Principal repayments (amortization) are based on the amount of the loan commitment. If the amortization schedule follows a set pattern (for example, equal semiannual payments), the WBXD system calculates repayments automatically using the loan commitment amount, the first and final payment dates, and the frequency of the payments. If future payments are irregular, the WBXD system requires a schedule.

Future interest payments are generated by the WBXD system according to the disbursed and outstanding balance of the loan at the beginning of the period. Using the interest rate specified in the loan contract, the first and final interest payment dates, and the frequency of payments, the WBXD system calculates the stream of future interest payments due. If interest payments are irregular, the WBXD system requires a schedule.

Future debt service payments are the sum of future principal and interest payments due on existing commitments, including the undisbursed portion. They do not include debt service payments that may become due as a result of new loans contracted in subsequent years, nor do they take into account the effect of any change to future debt service obligations resulting from actions such as prepayment or rescheduling or from cancellations that occurred after the most recent year-end data reported to the DRS.

Both projected disbursements and future debt service payments are converted into U.S. dollars using end-December 2020 exchange rates. Likewise, future interest payments on loans with a variable interest rate (for example, loans from commercial banks tied to the London Interbank Offered Rate [LIBOR]) are based on the interest rate prevailing at end-December 2020.

Treatment of arrears

The DRS collects information on arrears of both principal and interest. Principal in arrears is included in the amount of long-term external debt outstanding and is shown separately. Interest in arrears on long-term external debt and interest in arrears on the use of IMF credit are included as part of short-term external debt outstanding and are shown separately. Clearance of interest in arrears by repayment will be recorded as an interest payment in the relevant creditor category of the loan (or loans) on which the arrears were incurred, as a corresponding reduction in the level of short-term debt outstanding, and as a net reduction in interest arrears. Clearance of interest arrears through debt restructuring or forgiveness will be recorded as a reduction in the level of short-term debt outstanding and a net reduction in interest arrears. When interests are rescheduled, they will be capitalized: This change will be recorded as an increase in long-term debt outstanding equal to the amount of interest capitalized and the reduction in short-term debt outstanding noted previously.

External Debt and Its Components

This section describes the compilation of the major components of external debt included in the IDS tables and database and the relationship between them, as shown in figure A.1. Information about general methods of compiling external debt data is discussed in the previous section titled "Methodology." For concise definitions, see the glossary.

Total external debt

Total external debt shown in the IDS is the sum of long-term external debt, short-term debt, and IMF credit. It represents the total debt owed to nonresident creditors and is repayable in both foreign and domestic currency.

Short-term debt

Short-term debt is defined as external debt with an original maturity of one year or less. The DRS requires debtor countries to report only on their long-term external debt. However, to gain a comprehensive picture of total external obligations, the World Bank encourages debtor countries to voluntarily provide information on their short-term external obligations.

By its nature, short-term external debt is difficult to monitor: Loan-by-loan registration is normally impractical, and monitoring systems typically rely on information requested periodically by the Central Banks from the banking sector. The World Bank regards the debtor country as the authoritative source of information on its short-term debt. Unless otherwise specified in the country tables, the data for short-term debt are derived from the data provided by the quarterly external debt statistics database (see QEDS). BIS data on international bank lending is the second source of the short-term debt. These data are reported on the basis of residual maturity, but an estimate of short-term external liabilities by original maturity can be derived by deducting from claims due in one year those that, 12 months earlier, had a maturity of between one and two years. However, not all commercial banks report to the BIS in a way that allows the full maturity distribution to be determined, and the BIS data include liabilities only to banks within the BIS reporting area. Consequently, the results should be interpreted with caution.

The flow of short-term debt may be derived from the change in claims (stock) data in the BIS quarterly series over consecutive periods, but valuation adjustments resulting from exchange rate

Figure A.1. External Debt and Its Components

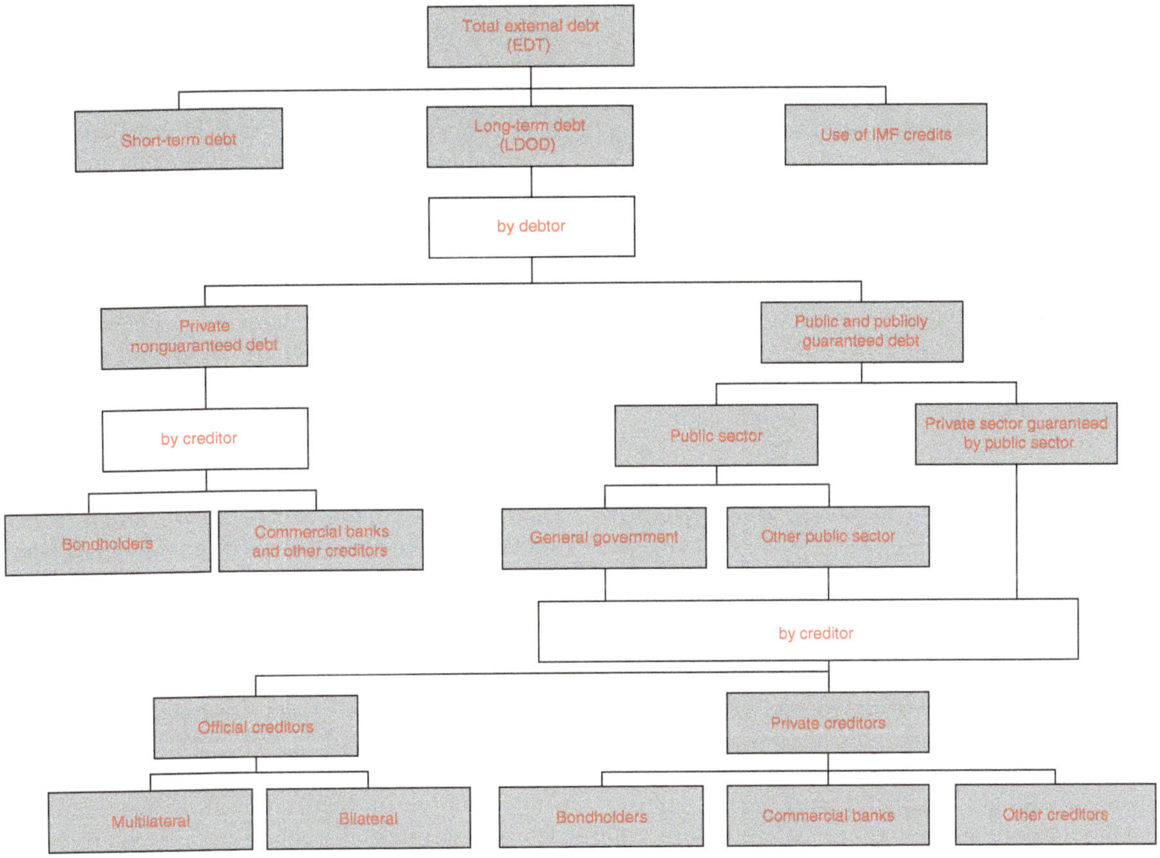

movements will affect the calculations, as will prepayment and refinancing of long-term maturities falling due. When short-term external debt has been rescheduled, lags in reporting and differences in the treatment of the rescheduled external debt by debtors and creditors may result in double counting.

Interest in arrears on long-term external debt and interest in arrears on the use of IMF credit are added to short-term debt and are separately identified.

Use of IMF credit

Data related to the operations of the IMF are provided by the IMF Treasurer's Department. They are converted from special drawing rights (SDR) into dollars using end-of-period exchange rates for stocks and average-over-the-period exchange rates for flows. IMF trust fund operations under the Enhanced Structural Adjustment Facility, Extended Fund Facility, Poverty Reduction and Growth Facility, and Structural Adjustment Facility (Enhanced Structural Adjustment Facility in 1999) are presented together with all of the IMF's special facilities (buffer stock, supplemental reserve, compensatory and contingency facilities, oil facilities, and other facilities). SDR allocations are also included in this category. According to the BPM6, SDR allocations are recorded as the incurrence of a debt liability of the member receiving them (because of a requirement to repay the allocation in certain circumstances, and also because interest accrues). This debt item was introduced for the first time in IDS 2013 with historical data starting in 1999.

Long-term debt

Long-term debt has an original maturity of more than one year. It comprises the obligations of both public and private debtors. Private nonguaranteed debt comprises the external obligations of private debtors that are not guaranteed for repayment by a public entity in the debtor country.

Public and publicly guaranteed debt comprises the external obligations of public debtors and has two components: (a) public debt, which is borrowing by the national government or agency, by a political subdivision or agency, or by autonomous public bodies, and (b) publicly guaranteed debt, which is borrowing by a private agency that is guaranteed for repayment by a public entity.

Private nonguaranteed debt

The DRS reporting requirements were expanded in 1973 to include long-term private nonguaranteed debt. Data are reported annually on an aggregate basis and include, for the reporting year, the total amount of disbursed and outstanding debt; the amount of disbursements, principal repayments, and interest payments; the principal and interest rescheduled; and the projected principal and interest payments for future years. The aggregate data are usually reported in U.S. dollars, and no information on the underlying currency composition is given.

DRS reporting countries recognize the importance of monitoring borrowing by their private sector, particularly when it constitutes a significant portion of total external debt, but many countries acknowledge the difficulty of this process. Detailed data are available only when countries have registration requirements for private nonguaranteed debt in place, most commonly in connection with exchange controls. When formal registration of private nonguaranteed debt is not mandatory, compilers must rely on balance of payments data and financial surveys.

The data on private nonguaranteed debt in this publication is as reported or as estimated for countries where this type of external debt is known to be significant. The estimation of private nonguaranteed debt is based on the national data on quarterly external debt statistics (QEDS) or IMF data. Flows are derived from the change in stock over consecutive periods and are adjusted for the effects of exchange rate movements (assuming the currency composition mirrors that of public and publicly guaranteed debt) and for any known debt restructuring. Principal repayments are estimated on the basis of the average maturity observed for loans to private sector borrowers in countries reporting to the DRS and on the basis of the stock of debt outstanding. Interest payments are estimated on the basis of the stock of debt outstanding and interest rates prevailing in international capital markets.

Balance of payments data provide a useful guideline in the estimation process: private nonguaranteed external debt may be derived as a residual between net long-term external borrowing recorded in the balance of payments and net long-term public and publicly guaranteed external debt reported to the DRS.

Public and publicly guaranteed debt

Data related to public and publicly guaranteed debt are reported to the DRS on a loan-by-loan basis. The data provide annual information on the disbursed and outstanding balance and the undisbursed balance of each loan, the cumulative disbursements, the principal and interest paid and principal and interest restructured in the reporting year, and the stock of any outstanding payment's arrears of principal and interest. Detailed information on the terms and conditions of each loan is also reported. Public debt and private debt publicly guaranteed are shown separately in this publication. Public sector debt is disaggregated by government and "other public" and further disaggregated by creditor type.

Official creditors

Official creditors include multilateral and bilateral lenders. In general, official creditors provide loans (and, in some cases, provide grants) to public bodies, although in some cases they may lend to other entities with a public guarantee.

Multilateral creditors are international financial institutions such as the World Bank, regional development banks, and other multilateral and intergovernmental agencies whose lending is administered on a multilateral basis. Funds administered by an international financial organization on behalf of a single donor government constitute bilateral loans (or grants). For lending by a number of multilateral creditors, the data presented in this publication are taken from the creditors' records. Such creditors include the African Development Bank, the Asian Development Bank, the IDB, IBRD, and IDA. (IBRD and IDA are institutions of the World Bank.)

Bilateral creditors are governments and their agencies, including Central Banks, aid agencies, official export credit agencies, and autonomous agencies such as the U.S. Department of Agriculture or the Federal Home Loan Bank. Member countries of the OECD Development Assistance Committee (DAC) and some other countries also report information on loans extended bilaterally or officially guaranteed to the Creditor Reporting System of the OECD.

Private creditors

Private creditors include commercial banks, bondholders, and other private creditors. This line includes only publicly guaranteed creditors. Nonguaranteed private creditors are shown separately.

Bonds include publicly issued or privately placed bonds.

Commercial bank loans are loans from private banks and other private financial institutions.

Credits of other private creditors include credits from manufacturers, exporters, and other suppliers of goods, plus bank credits covered by a guarantee of an export credit agency. This line is included in the online database but is not shown in the published tables. It can be obtained as the difference between (a) credits of total private creditors and (b) bonds and commercial bank loans.

Data Documentation

Country-Specific Notes on Debt

Country	Country Notes
Afghanistan	Short-term debt before 2015 is based on data from the BIS. Data include the effects of Paris Club debt restructuring agreements signed in 2010 and HIPC and MDRI debt relief. DSSI eligible and participating in 2020.
Angola	Long-term private nonguaranteed debt data are estimates based on Central Bank data and are not available before 2009. Short-term debt before 2012 is based on data from the BIS. DSSI eligible and participating in 2020.
Argentina	Long-term private nonguaranteed debt data before 2008 are World Bank staff estimates. Short-term debt before 2010 is based on data from the BIS. Long-term foreign direct investment debt is reported according to the BPM5 definition for entities with foreign ownership of 10 percent or more of the ordinary shares or voting power and excludes debt of fellow companies.
Azerbaijan	Long-term private nonguaranteed debt data are World Bank staff estimates based on the market data. Short-term debt is based on data from the BIS.
Bangladesh	Short-term debt before 2012 is based on data from the BIS. Long-term private nonguaranteed debt data from 2007 to 2018 are World Bank staff estimates based on reports provided by the country and are not available prior to 2007. DSSI eligible and not participating in 2020.
Belarus	Long-term private nonguaranteed debt data from 2014 are World Bank staff estimates based on reports provided by the country.
Belize	Long-term private nonguaranteed debt data from 2008 are based on Central Bank data. Long-term private nonguaranteed debt data for 2020 are based on reports provided by the country.
Benin	Short-term debt is based on data from the BIS. Data include the effects of Paris Club debt restructuring agreement and HIPC and MDRI debt relief. DSSI eligible and not participating in 2020.
Bhutan	Short-term debt is based on data from the BIS. DSSI eligible and not participating in 2020.
Bolivia	Long-term private nonguaranteed debt data are World Bank staff estimates based on reports provided by the country.
Bosnia and Herzegovina	With the release of 2020 data, long-term private nonguaranteed debt (PNG) data for the period 2011–2019 are revised. Since 2005, PNG data are World Bank staff estimates. Short-term debt is based on data from the BIS.
Botswana	Short-term debt is based on data from the BIS.
Bulgaria	Long-term private nonguaranteed debt data from 2020 reported by the country. The data may include long-term public and publicly guaranteed debt owed by the state-owned railway.

Country	Country Notes
Burkina Faso	Long-term private nonguaranteed debt data prior to 2018 are World Bank staff estimates based on reports provided by the country. Data include HIPC and MDRI debt relief. DSSI eligible and participating in 2020.
Burundi	Data include the effects of Paris Club debt restructuring agreement and HIPC and MDRI debt relief. DSSI eligible and participating in 2020.
Cabo Verde	DSSI eligible and participating in 2020.
Cambodia	Data include MDRI debt relief. DSSI eligible and not participating in 2020.
Cameroon	Short-term debt is based on data from the BIS. Data include the effects of HIPC and MDRI debt relief. DSSI eligible and participating in 2020.
Central African Republic	Short-term debt is based on data from the BIS. Data include the effects of HIPC and MDRI debt relief. DSSI eligible and participating, but with no deferred payments reported in 2020.
Chad	Short-term debt is based on data from the BIS. Data include the effects of Paris Club debt restructuring agreement and HIPC and MDRI debt relief. DSSI eligible and participating, but with no deferred payments reported in 2020.
China	Long-term public and publicly guaranteed and long-term private nonguaranteed debt data are World Bank staff estimates based on the aggregate reports provided by the country and market data.
Comoros	Data include the effects of Paris Club debt restructuring agreements signed in 2010 and 2013 and the HIPC debt relief. DSSI eligible and participating in 2020.
Congo, Democratic Republic of	Short-term debt is based on data from the BIS. Data include the effects of Paris Club debt restructuring agreement and HIPC and MDRI debt relief. DSSI eligible and participating in 2020.
Congo, Republic of	Short-term debt is based on data from the BIS. Data include the effects of Paris Club debt restructuring agreement and HIPC and MDRI debt relief. DSSI eligible and participating in 2020.
Costa Rica	Short-term debt before 2005 is based on data from the BIS.
Côte d'Ivoire	Long-term private nonguaranteed debt data are World Bank staff estimates. Short-term debt is based on data from the BIS. Data include the effects of Paris Club agreements signed in 2011 and 2012 and HIPC and MDRI debt relief. DSSI eligible and participating in 2020.
Djibouti	Short-term debt before 2017 is based on data from the BIS. Data include the effects of Paris Club debt restructuring agreement signed in 2008. DSSI eligible and participating in 2020.
Dominican Republic	Long-term private nonguaranteed debt data from 2018 are World Bank staff estimates based on reports provided by the country. Short-term debt before 2009 and 2014 onward is based on data from the BIS. Data include the effects of Paris Club debt restructuring agreement signed in 2005.
Dominica	DSSI eligible and participating in 2020.
El Salvador	Long-term private nonguaranteed debt data are World Bank staff estimates based on reports provided by the country.
Eritrea	Long-term public and publicly guaranteed debt data from 2010 are World Bank staff estimates. Short-term debt for 2020 is based on data from the BIS.
Eswatini	Short-term debt is based on data from the BIS.
Ethiopia	Short-term debt is based on data from the BIS. Data include the effects of HIPC and MDRI debt relief. DSSI eligible and participating in 2020.
Fiji	Long-term private nonguaranteed debt data for 2012 are World Bank staff estimates. Short-term debt is based on data from the BIS. DSSI eligible and participating in 2020.
Gabon	Long-term public and publicly guaranteed debt data before 2008 are World Bank staff estimates based on reports provided by the country. Short-term debt is based on data from the BIS. Data include the effects of Paris Club debt buyback agreement signed in 2007.
Gambia, The	Short-term debt is based on data from the BIS. Data include the effects of HIPC and MDRI debt relief. DSSI eligible and participating in 2020.
Ghana	Long-term public and publicly guaranteed debt data are World Bank staff estimates. Short-term debt is based on data from the BIS. Data include the effects of MDRI debt relief. DSSI eligible and not participating in 2020.

Country	Country Notes
Grenada	Short-term debt is based on data from the BIS. DSSI eligible and participating in 2020.
Guatemala	Long-term private nonguaranteed debt data are World Bank staff estimates based on market data. Short-term debt before 2012 is based on data from the BIS.
Guinea	Long-term public and publicly guaranteed debt data for 2016 are World Bank staff estimates. Short-term debt is based on data from the BIS. Data include the effects of Paris Club debt restructuring agreements signed in 2010 and 2012 and HIPC debt relief. DSSI eligible and participating in 2020.
Guinea-Bissau	Short-term debt before 2019 is based on data from the BIS. Data include the effects of Paris Club debt restructuring agreement and HIPC and MDRI debt relief. DSSI eligible and participating, but with no deferred payments reported in 2020.
Guyana	Long-term private nonguaranteed debt data after 2014 are World Bank staff estimates based on market data. Short-term debt is based on data from the BIS. Principal payment shown from 2012 include rice-for-oil deal. Data include the effects of HIPC and MDRI debt relief. DSSI eligible and not participating in 2020.
Haiti	Long-term private nonguaranteed debt data cover only IDB loans. Short-term debt is World Bank staff estimates based on Central Bank data. Data include the effects of Paris Club restructuring agreements signed in 2006 and 2009 and HIPC and MDRI debt relief. DSSI eligible and not participating in 2020.
Honduras	Data include the effects of HIPC and MDRI debt relief. DSSI eligible and not participating in 2020.
India	External debt data prior to 2003 are revised from fiscal year to calendar year. Long-term public and publicly guaranteed bonds include Foreign Institutional Investor (FII) debt as reported by the Reserve Bank of India.
Indonesia	Long-term private nonguaranteed debt data are World Bank staff estimates based on reports provided by the country.
Iran, Islamic Republic of	Short-term debt for 2020 is based on Central Bank data.
Jamaica	Short-term debt data for 2020 are based on reports provided by the country.
Jordan	Long-term private nonguaranteed debt data from 2001 are based on reports provided by the country. Short-term debt before 1999 is based on data from the BIS.
Kenya	Long-term private nonguaranteed debt data are World Bank staff estimates based on market data. Short-term debt is based on data from the BIS. DSSI eligible and participating, but with no deferred payments reported in 2020.
Kosovo	DSSI eligible and not participating in 2020.
Kyrgyz Republic	DSSI eligible and participating, but with no deferred payments reported in 2020.
Lao People's Democratic Republic	Long-term public and publicly guaranteed debt data for 2019 and 2020 are World Bank staff estimates. Long-term private nonguaranteed debt data are World Bank staff estimates. Short-term debt is based on data from the BIS. DSSI eligible and not participating in 2020.
Lebanon	Long-term private nonguaranteed debt data from 2008 to 2012 are World Bank staff estimates based on the 2013–2017 debt stock. Short-term debt before 2013 is based on data from the BIS.
Lesotho	Large interest payment was made during 2007 to a creditor country to settle a long-standing claim. Short-term debt is based on data from the BIS. DSSI eligible and participating in 2020.
Liberia	Long-term private nonguaranteed debt data are World Bank staff estimates based on market data. Data include the effects of Paris Club rescheduling agreements signed in 2008 and 2010 and HIPC and MDRI debt relief. DSSI eligible and participating, but with no deferred payments reported in 2020.
Madagascar	Long-term private nonguaranteed debt data after 2016 are World Bank staff estimates based on market data. Short-term debt from 2017 is based on data from the BIS. Data include the effects of HIPC and MDRI debt relief. DSSI eligible and participating in 2020.
Malawi	Short-term debt is based on data from the BIS. Data include the effects of Paris Club rescheduling agreement signed in 2006 and HIPC and MDRI debt relief. DSSI eligible and participating, but with no deferred payments reported in 2020.
Maldives	Long-term private nonguaranteed and short-term debt data from 2006 are World Bank staff estimates based on reports provided by the country. Short-term debt is based on data from the BIS. DSSI eligible and participating in 2020.
Mali	Short-term debt is based on data from the BIS. Data include the effects of HIPC and MDRI debt relief. DSSI eligible and participating in 2020.

Country	Country Notes
Mauritania	Short-term debt is based on data from the BIS. Data include the effects of MDRI debt relief. DSSI eligible and participating in 2020.
Mauritius	Long-term private nonguaranteed debt data from 2009 to 2010 and from 2017 to 2020 are based on reports provided by the country and do not include offshore liabilities, while data from 2011 to 2016 are World Bank staff estimates based on reports provided by the country. Short-term debt is based on reports provided by the country and includes offshore liabilities.
Moldova	DSSI eligible and not participating in 2020.
Mongolia	Long-term private nonguaranteed debt data before 2016 are World Bank staff estimates based on reports provided by the country. Short-term debt before 2008 is based on data from the BIS. DSSI eligible and not participating in 2020.
Montenegro	Long-term private nonguaranteed debt data for 2020, 2018, and 2017 are World Bank staff estimates and prior to 2017 are based on country reports. Short-term debt is based on data from the BIS and prior to 2018 is based on country reports.
Morocco	Short-term debt before 2009 is based on data from the BIS.
Mozambique	Long-term private nonguaranteed debt data before 2018 are World Bank staff estimates based on reports provided by the country. Short-term debt is based on data from the BIS. Data include HIPC and MDRI debt relief. DSSI eligible and participating in 2020.
Myanmar	Long-term public and publicly guaranteed debt data before 2018 are World Bank staff estimates based on the original terms of the loans. Long-term private nonguaranteed debt data are World Bank staff estimates based on the market data. DSSI eligible and participating in 2020.
Nepal	Long-term private nonguaranteed debt data are World Bank staff estimates based on reports provided by the country. DSSI eligible and participating in 2020.
Nicaragua	Short-term debt before 2007 is based on data from the BIS. Data include the effects of HIPC and MDRI debt relief. DSSI eligible and not participating in 2020.
Niger	Short-term debt is based on data from the BIS. Data include the effects of HIPC and MDRI debt relief. DSSI eligible and participating in 2020.
Nigeria	Long-term private nonguaranteed debt data from 2005 are estimates based on market data. DSSI eligible and not participating in 2020.
Pakistan	Debt rescheduling reflected in the DSSI is World Bank staff estimates using the partial reports from the country. Short-term debt before 2012 is based on data from the BIS. Long-term private nonguaranteed debt data from 2006 to 2015 are World Bank staff estimates based on reports provided by the country; 2020 debt flows of private nonguaranteed debt are World Bank staff estimates. DSSI eligible and participating in 2020.
Papua New Guinea	Short-term debt is based on data from the BIS. DSSI eligible and participating in 2020.
Peru	Long-term private nonguaranteed debt data are World Bank staff estimates based on reports provided by the country.
Philippines	Long-term private nonguaranteed debt data no longer include unregistered debt and are revised from 2005 based on reports provided by the country.
Russian Federation	Long-term public and publicly guaranteed and long-term private nonguaranteed debt data are World Bank staff estimates based on reports provided by the country.
Rwanda	Data include the effects of HIPC and MDRI debt relief. DSSI eligible and not participating in 2020.
Samoa	Short-term debt data are excluded, since BIS data include debt liabilities of offshore centers located in the country. BIS short-term debt data for 2018, 2019, and 2020 are $4.4 billion, $4.5 billion, and $3.9 billion, respectively. DSSI eligible and participating in 2020.
São Tomé and Príncipe	Short-term debt is based on data from the BIS. Data include HIPC and MDRI debt relief. DSSI eligible and participating in 2020.
Senegal	Short-term debt before 2009 is based on data from the BIS. DSSI eligible and participating in 2020.
Serbia	Beginning in 2006, data for Serbia exclude Montenegro. Long-term private nonguaranteed bonds debt data are estimates based on market data. Short-term debt is based on reports provided by the country.
Sierra Leone	Short-term debt before 2016 is based on data from the BIS. DSSI eligible and participating in 2020.
Solomon Islands	DSSI eligible and not participating in 2020.

Country	Country Notes
Somalia	Long-term public and publicly guaranteed debt data before 2018 are World Bank staff estimates based on the original terms of the loans. Beginning in 2018, data reflect the outstanding debt stock, principal, and interest arrears and include late interest/penalty amounts following the reconciliation exercise by the Government of Somalia with respective creditors. DSSI eligible and not participating in 2020.
South Africa	Long-term public and publicly guaranteed and long-term private nonguaranteed debt data before 2019 are World Bank staff estimates.
St. Lucia	Short-term debt before 2012 is based on data from the BIS. DSSI eligible and participating, but with no deferred payments reported in 2020.
St. Vincent and the Grenadines	Short-term debt data are excluded, since BIS data include debt liabilities of offshore centers located in the country. BIS short-term debt data for 2016, 2017, 2018, 2019, and 2020 are $806 million, $787 million, $532 million, $363 million, and $321 million, respectively. DSSI eligible and participating, but with no deferred payments reported in 2020.
Sudan	Long-term public and publicly guaranteed debt data exclude penalty interest that has accumulated over an extended period and is extensive. Short-term debt is based on data from the BIS.
Syrian Arab Republic	Long-term public and publicly guaranteed debt data are World Bank staff estimates. Short-term debt is based on data from the BIS.
Tajikistan	Short-term debt before 2015 is based on data from the BIS. Data include MDRI debt relief. DSSI eligible and participating in 2020.
Tanzania	Long-term public and publicly guaranteed debt data include debt liabilities of Zanzibar. Short-term debt is based on data from the BIS. Data include the effects of HIPC and MDRI debt relief. DSSI eligible and participating, but with no deferred payments reported in 2020.
Timor-Leste	Short-term debt is based on data from the BIS. DSSI eligible and not participating in 2020.
Togo	Short-term debt is based on data from the BIS. Data include the effects of Paris Club debt restructuring agreement and HIPC and MDRI debt relief. DSSI eligible and participating in 2020.
Tonga	DSSI eligible and participating in 2020.
Tunisia	Long-term private nonguaranteed debt data from 2008 to 2014 are estimates based on reports provided by the country.
Turkey	Long-term public and publicly guaranteed debt data include nonresident deposits made under the Dresdner Bank scheme, amounting to $8.2 million at end-2020.
Turkmenistan	Country resumed reporting of long-term public and publicly guaranteed debt from 2008 onward; time series have been revised. Long-term private nonguaranteed debt data (excluding bonds) cover only European Bank for Reconstruction and Development lending.
Uganda	Long-term private nonguaranteed debt data are World Bank staff estimates based on market data. Data include the effects of HIPC and MDRI debt relief. DSSI eligible and participating, but with no deferred payments reported in 2020.
Uzbekistan	Short-term debt before 2009 is based on data from the BIS. DSSI eligible and not participating in 2020.
Vanuatu	Long-term public and publicly guaranteed debt data for 2019 and 2020 are World Bank staff estimates. Short-term debt is based on data from the BIS. DSSI eligible and not participating in 2020.
Venezuela, República Bolivariana de	Country resumed reporting of long-term public and publicly guaranteed debt from 2016 onward; time series have been revised. Long-term private nonguaranteed debt and short- term debt data are World Bank staff estimates based on country reports. Venezuela, RB is unclassified according to the World Bank FY2022 income classification owing to lack of available data. Thus, Venezuela, RB has been excluded from the aggregate data.
Vietnam	Short-term debt before 2016 is based on data from the BIS.
Yemen, Republic of	Long-term public and publicly guaranteed debt data for 2019 and 2020 are World Bank staff estimates based on the original terms of the loans. Short-term debt is based on data from the BIS. DSSI eligible and participating in 2020, but country has not reported data.
Zambia	Long-term private nonguaranteed debt data before 2016 are World Bank staff estimates based on reports provided by the country. Short-term debt is based on data from the BIS. Data include the effects of HIPC and MDRI debt relief. DSSI eligible and participating in 2020.
Zimbabwe	Long-term private nonguaranteed debt data are World Bank staff estimates based on reports provided by the country. Data from 2001 include late interest fee owed to Paris Club and commercial creditors. Short-term debt is based on data from the BIS. Reserve Bank of Zimbabwe Assumed External Debt is not included in the data.

Sources of the Macroeconomic Indicators

The macroeconomic data are prepared by The World Bank from a variety of sources. Data on Personal Transfers and Compensation of Employees are prepared by World Bank staff based on IMF balance of payments statistics. Data on foreign direct investments and current account balance are prepared by World Bank staff based on IMF balance of payments statistics and UNCTAD's *World Investment Report*. Other macroeconomic data are from IMF balance of payments statistics.

Data on exports of goods, services, and primary income are based on countries' balance of payments statistics for the following countries:

Cameroon (2020)
Comoros (2020)
Dominica (2019–2020)
Gambia, The (2019–2020)
Grenada (2019–2020)
Iran, Islamic Rep. (2010–2020)
Jordan (2020)
Kenya (2020)
Kyrgyz Rep. (2020)
Liberia (2020)
Madagacar (2020)
Malawi (2020)
Mauritania (2020)
Papua New Guinea (2019–2020)
Peru (2020)
Rwanda (2020)
Samoa (2020)
St. Lucia (2019–2020)
St. Vincent and the Grenadines (2019–2020)
Tanzania (2020)
Uganda (2020)
Zimbabwe (2018–2020)

Data on imports of goods, services, and primary income are based on countries' balance of payments statistics for the following countries:

Cameroon (2020)
Comoros (2020)
Dominica (2019–2020)
Gambia, The (2019–2020)
Grenada (2019–2020)
Iran, Islamic Rep. (2010–2020)
Jordan (2020)
Kenya (2020)
Kyrgyz Rep. (2020)
Liberia (2020)
Madagacar (2020)
Malawi (2020)
Mauritania (2020)
Papua New Guinea (2019–2020)
Peru (2020)
Rwanda (2020)
Samoa (2020)
St. Lucia (2019–2020)
St. Vincent and the Grenadines (2019–2020)
Tanzania (2020)
Uganda (2020)
Zimbabwe (2018–2020)

Data on current account balance are based on countries' balance of payments statistics for the following countries:

Benin (2020)
Burkina Faso (2020)
Cameroon (2020)
Central African Rep. (2020)
Chad (2020)
Comoros (2020)
Congo, Rep. of (2020)
Côte d'Ivoire (2020)
Dominica (2019–2020)
Gabon (2020)
Gambia, The (2019–2020)
Grenada (2019–2020)
Guinea-Bissau (2020)
Guyana (2020)
Iran, Islamic Rep. (2010–2020)
Jordan (2020)
Kenya (2020)
Kyrgyz Rep. (2020)
Liberia (2020)
Madagascar, Rep. of (2020)
Malawi (2020)
Mali (2019–2020)
Mauritania (2020)
Myanmar (2020)
Niger (2020)
Papua New Guinea (2019–2020)
Peru (2020)
Rwanda (2020)
Samoa (2020)
Senegal (2019–2020)
Sierra Leone (2020)
Solomon Islands (2020)
Somalia (2020)
St. Lucia (2019–2020)
St. Vincent and the Grenadines (2019–2020)
Sudan (2020)
Tanzania (2020)
Togo (2020)
Uganda (2020)
Zimbabwe (2018–2020)

Data on personal transfers and compensation of employees are based on countries' balance of payments statistics for the following countries:

Dominica (2019–2020)
Grenada (2019–2020)
Jordan (2020)
Kyrgyz Rep. (2020)
Peru (2020)
Rwanda (2020)
St. Lucia (2019–2020)
St. Vincent and the Grenadines (2019–2020)
Tanzania (2020)
Uganda (2020)
Zimbabwe (2018–2020)

Data on primary income on foreign direct investment are based on countries' balance of payments statistics for the following countries:

Cameroon (2020)
Dominica (2019–2020)
Grenada (2019–2020)
Rwanda (2020)
St. Lucia (2019–2020)
St. Vincent and the Grenadines (2019–2020)
Sudan (2020)
Uganda (2020)

Data on foreign direct investment are based on countries' balance of payments statistics for the following countries:

Dominica (2019–2020)
Grenada (2019–2020)
Jamaica (2012–2020)
Jordan (2020)
Kyrgyz Rep. (2020)
Liberia (2020)
Myanmar (2020)
Peru (2020)
Rwanda (2020)
St. Lucia (2019–2020)
St. Vincent and the Grenadines (2019–2020)
Tanzania (2020)
Uganda (2020)
Zimbabwe (2018–2020)

Data on portfolio equity are based on countries' balance of payments statistics for the following countries:

China (2010–2020)
Dominica (2019–2020)
Grenada (2019–2020)
Rwanda (2020)
St. Lucia (2019–2020)
St. Vincent and the Grenadines (2019–2020)
Uganda (2020)

Country Groups

Regional Groups

East Asia and Pacific

Cambodia (A)
China (P)
Fiji (A)
Indonesia (A)
Lao PDR (E)
Mongolia (A)
Myanmar (A)
Papua New Guinea (A)
Philippines (A)
Samoa (A)
Solomon Islands (A)
Thailand (A)
Timor-Leste (A)
Tonga (A)
Vanuatu (E)
Vietnam (A)

Europe and Central Asia

Albania (A)
Armenia (A)
Azerbaijan (A)
Belarus (A)
Bosnia and Herzegovina[a] (A)
Bulgaria (A)
Georgia (A)
Kazakhstan (A)
Kosovo (A)
Kyrgyz Republic (A)
Moldova (A)
Montenegro (A)
North Macedonia (A)
Romania (A)
Russian Federation (P)
Serbia[a,b] (A)
Tajikistan (A)
Turkey (A)
Turkmenistan (A)
Ukraine (A)
Uzbekistan (A)

Latin America and the Caribbean

Argentina (A)
Belize (A)
Bolivia (A)
Brazil (A)
Colombia (A)
Costa Rica (A)
Dominica (A)
Dominican Republic (A)
Ecuador (A)
El Salvador (A)
Grenada (A)
Guatemala (A)
Guyana (A)
Haiti (A)
Honduras (A)
Jamaica (A)
Mexico (A)
Nicaragua (A)
Panama (A)
Paraguay (A)
Peru (A)
St. Lucia (A)
St. Vincent and the Grenadines (A)
Venezuela, RB (A)

Middle East and North Africa

Algeria (A)
Djibouti (A)
Egypt, Arab Rep. (A)
Iran, Islamic Rep. (A)
Jordan (A)
Lebanon (A)
Morocco (A)
Syrian Arab Republic (E)
Tunisia (A)
Yemen, Rep. (E)

South Asia

Afghanistan (A)
Bangladesh (A)
Bhutan (A)
India (A)
Maldives (A)
Nepal (A)
Pakistan (A)
Sri Lanka (A)

Sub-Saharan Africa

Angola (A)
Benin (A)
Botswana (A)
Burkina Faso (A)
Burundi (A)
Cabo Verde (A)
Cameroon (A)
Central African Republic (A)
Chad (P)
Comoros (A)
Congo, Dem. Rep. (A)
Congo, Rep. (A)
Côte d'Ivoire (A)
Eritrea (E)
Eswatini (A)
Ethiopia (A)
Gabon (A)
Gambia, The (A)
Ghana (E)
Guinea (A)
Guinea-Bissau (A)
Kenya (A)
Lesotho (A)
Liberia (A)
Madagascar (A)
Malawi (A)
Mali (A)
Mauritania (A)
Mauritius (A)
Mozambique (A)
Niger (A)
Nigeria (A)
Rwanda (A)
São Tomé and Príncipe (A)
Senegal (A)
Sierra Leone (A)
Somalia (A)
South Africa (A)
Sudan (P)
Tanzania (A)
Togo (A)
Uganda (A)
Zambia (A)
Zimbabwe (A)

Note: Letters in parenthesis indicate DRS reporters' status: (A) as reported, (P) preliminary, and (E) estimated. The status "as reported" indicates that the country was fully current in its reporting under the DRS and that World Bank staff are satisfied that the reported data give an adequate and fair representation of the country's total public debt. "Preliminary" data are based on reported or collected information, but because of incompleteness or other reasons, an element of staff estimation is included. "Estimated" data indicate that countries are not current in their reporting and that a significant element of staff estimation has been necessary in producing the data tables.

a. For Bosnia and Herzegovina, total debt before 1999, excluding IBRD and IMF obligations and short-term debt, is included under Serbia.

b. Data prior to 2006 include Montenegro.

Income Groups

Low-income countries

Afghanistan
Burkina Faso
Burundi
Central African Republic
Chad
Congo, Dem. Rep.
Eritrea
Ethiopia
Gambia, The
Guinea
Guinea-Bissau
Liberia
Madagascar
Malawi
Mali
Mozambique
Niger
Rwanda
Sierra Leone
Somalia
Sudan
Syrian Arab Republic
Togo
Uganda
Yemen, Rep.

Middle-income countries

Albania
Algeria
Angola
Argentina
Armenia
Azerbaijan
Bangladesh
Belarus
Belize
Benin
Bhutan
Bolivia
Bosnia and Herzegovina
Botswana
Brazil
Bulgaria
Cabo Verde
Cambodia
Cameroon
China
Colombia
Comoros
Congo, Rep.
Costa Rica
Côte d'Ivoire
Djibouti
Dominica
Dominican Republic
Ecuador
Egypt, Arab Rep.
El Salvador
Eswatini
Fiji
Gabon
Georgia
Ghana
Grenada
Guatemala
Guyana
Haiti
Honduras
India
Indonesia
Iran, Islamic Rep.
Jamaica
Jordan
Kazakhstan
Kenya
Kosovo
Kyrgyz Republic
Lao PDR
Lebanon
Lesotho
Maldives
Mauritania
Mauritius
Mexico
Moldova
Mongolia
Montenegro
Morocco
Myanmar
Nepal
Nicaragua
Nigeria
North Macedonia
Pakistan
Panama
Papua New Guinea
Paraguay
Peru
Philippines
Romania
Russian Federation
Samoa
São Tomé and Príncipe
Senegal
Serbia
Solomon Islands
South Africa
Sri Lanka
St. Lucia
St. Vincent and the Grenadines
Tajikistan
Tanzania
Thailand
Timor-Leste
Tonga
Tunisia
Turkey
Turkmenistan
Ukraine
Uzbekistan
Vanuatu
Vietnam
Zambia
Zimbabwe

Unclassified

Venezuela, RB

Note: Low-income countries are those with a GNI per capita of $1,045 or less in 2020. Middle-income countries are those with a GNI per capita equal to or more than $1,046 but equal to or less than $12,695. Italicized countries are IDA-only countries as of July 1, 2021; IDA-only excludes blend and IBRD countries. Venezuela, RB is unclassified according to the World Bank FY2022 income classification owing to a lack of available data. Thus, Venezuela, RB has been excluded from the aggregate data.

Glossary

Debtor Reporting System (DRS)

Bilateral official creditors are official agencies that make loans on behalf of one government to another government or to public (and, in some cases, private) borrowers in another country.

Bonds are debt instruments issued by public and publicly guaranteed or private debtors with durations of one year or longer. Bonds usually give the holder the unconditional right to fixed money income or contractually determined, variable money income.

Commitments of public and publicly guaranteed debt constitute the total amount of new long-term loans to public sector borrowers or borrowers with a public sector guarantee extended by official and private lenders and for which contracts were signed in the year specified.

Concessional debt conveys information about the borrower's receipt of aid from official lenders at concessional terms as defined by the World Bank, that is, loans with an original grant element of 35 percent or more. Loans from major regional development banks—African Development Bank, Asian Development Bank, and the Inter-American Development Bank—are classified as concessional according the World Bank classification.

Contractual obligations on outstanding long-term external debt are the anticipated debt service payments on long-term external debt contracted up to December 31 of the reporting year.

Debt buyback is the repurchase by a debtor of its own debt, either at a discount price or at par value. In the event of a buyback of long-term debt, the face value of the debt bought back will be recorded as a decline in stock outstanding of long-term debt, and the cash amount received by creditors will be recorded as a principal repayment. For example, if a country buys back long-term external debt of face value B at a price P, then long-term external debt will decline by B, and principal repayment will increase by P. The difference between the price at which the debt was bought back and the face value is recorded as a debt stock write-off (the related transactions are not separately identified in the International Debt Statistics [IDS] publication but are available in the online database).

Debt forgiveness grants include both debts canceled by agreement between debtor and creditor and reductions in the net present value of official nonconcessional loans resulting from concessional rescheduling or refinancing. Data are recorded on a disbursement basis and include debt forgiveness from bilateral and multilateral creditors.

Debt outstanding and disbursed is the value at year's end of long-term external debt owed by public and publicly guaranteed debtors and private nonguaranteed debtors.

Debt restructurings are revisions to debt service obligations agreed on by creditors and debtors. Such agreements change the amount and timing of future principal and interest payments.

Debt service to exports is the ratio of the sum of principal repayments and interest paid on total long-term debt (public and publicly guaranteed debt and private nonguaranteed debt) to the value of exports of goods and services and receipts of primary income from abroad.

Debt Service Suspension Initiative (DSSI) took effect on May 1, 2020, and allowed 73 eligible countries to apply for a temporary suspension of debt-service payments owed to official bilateral creditors. The suspension period, originally set to end on December 31, 2020, has been extended through December 2021.

Debt stock-flow reconciliation shows the indicators that affect the change in debt stocks from one period to the next.

Disbursements are drawings during the year specified on loan commitments contracted by the borrower.

Exports of goods, services, and primary income constitute the total value of exports of goods and services, and primary income.

External debt flows are debt-related transactions during the year specified. They include disbursements, principal repayments, and interest payments.

External debt stocks comprise public and publicly guaranteed long-term external debt, private nonguaranteed long-term external debt, use of IMF credit, and short-term external debt, including interest arrears on long-term debt.

External debt stocks to exports is the ratio of outstanding external debt to the value of exports of goods and services and receipts of primary income from abroad.

External debt stocks to GNI is the ratio of outstanding external debt to gross national income.

Foreign direct investment refers to direct investment equity flows in the reporting economy. It is the sum of equity capital, reinvestment earnings, and other capital. Direct investment is a category of cross-border investment associated with a resident in one economy having control or a significant degree of influence on the management of an enterprise that is resident in another economy. Ownership of 10 percent or more of the ordinary shares or voting stock is the criterion for determining the existence of a direct investment relationship.

Government sector debt consists of all external debt obligations of all levels of the departments, branches, agencies, foundations, institutes, non-market and non-profit institutions controlled by the government, and other publicly controlled organizations engaging in non-market activities.

Grace period is the time between the date on which a loan is committed and the date on which the first principal payment is due. The information presented in International Debt Statistics is the average grace period on all public and publicly guaranteed debt committed during the specified period.

Grants are legally binding commitments that obligate a specific value of funds available for disbursement for which there is no payment requirement. They include debt forgiveness grants and grants from bilateral and multilateral agencies (such as the International Development Association).

Gross national income (GNI) is the sum of value added by all resident producers, plus any product taxes (less subsidies) not included in the valuation of output, plus net receipts of primary income compensation of employees and property income from abroad. Yearly average exchange rates are used to convert GNI from local currency to U.S. dollars.

Heavily Indebted Poor Country (HIPC) Initiative is a program of the World Bank and the International Monetary Fund (IMF) to provide debt relief to qualifying countries with unsustainable debt burdens.

Imports of goods, services, and primary income constitute the total value of goods and services imported and income payable to nonresidents. Interest arrears on long-term debt are interest payments due but not paid, shown on a cumulative basis.

Interest arrears are due and payable immediately and are therefore regarded as short-term obligations. Thus, an increase in interest arrears on long-term debt will be recorded as an increase in short-term debt. Interest in arrears on the use of IMF credit is also considered to be part of short-term external debt.

Interest payments are the amounts of interest paid in foreign currency, goods, or services in the year specified.

Interest rate is the interest rate applicable to a loan commitment as specified in the loan contract. The information presented in International Debt Statistics is the average interest on all public and publicly guaranteed debt committed during the specified period.

IMF charges are the amounts of interest paid in foreign currency in the year specified for transactions with the IMF.

IMF purchases are the total drawings on the general resources account of the IMF during the year specified, excluding drawings in the reserve tranche.

IMF repurchases are the amounts of principal (amortization) paid in foreign currency in the year specified for transactions with the IMF.

International reserves constitute the sum of a country's monetary authority's holdings of special drawing rights, its reserve position in the IMF, its holdings of foreign exchange, and its holdings of gold (valued at year-end London prices).

Long-term external debt is debt that has an original or extended maturity of more than one year and that is owed to nonresidents by residents of an economy and is repayable in foreign currency, goods, or services.

Maturity is the date on which the final principal repayment on a loan is due. It is the sum of the grace and repayment periods. The information presented in International Debt Statistics is the average maturity on all public and publicly guaranteed debt committed during the specified period.

Multilateral Debt Relief Initiative (MDRI) is a program of the World Bank, the IMF, the Inter-American Development Bank, and the African Development Bank that provides additional debt relief to countries that have completed the HIPC process.

Multilateral official creditors are official agencies owned or governed by more than one country that provide loan financing. They include international financial institutions such as the World Bank, regional development banks, and other intergovernmental agencies.

Multilateral to external debt stocks is the ratio of the stock of debt owed to multilateral creditors to total external debt.

Net flows on external debt are disbursements on long-term external debt and IMF purchases minus principal repayments on long-term external debt and IMF repurchases. Up to 1984, this calculation included only long-term external debt and IMF flows. Since 1985, the calculation includes the change in stock of short-term debt (excluding interest arrears on long-term external debt).

Official creditors are governments or other bilateral public entities, such as export-import agencies, development agencies, and multilateral financial institutions, such as the World Bank and regional development banks.

Personal transfers and compensation of employees is the sum of personal transfers and compensation of employees. Personal transfers consist of all current transfers in cash or in kind made or received by resident households to or from nonresident households. Personal transfers thus include all current transfers between resident and nonresident individuals. Compensation of employees refers to the income of border, seasonal, and other short-term workers who are employed in an economy where they are not resident and of residents employed by nonresident entities.

Portfolio equity is the category of international investment that covers investment in equity securities. Equity securities include shares, stocks, participation, or similar documents (such as American Depositary Receipts) that usually denote ownership of equity.

Present value of debt outstanding is the nominal value of all future debt service obligations on existing debt discounted at prevailing market rates of interest. The interest rates used in this calculation are the Commercial Interest Reference Rates (CIRR) for each relevant currency compiled and published by the Organisation for Economic Co-operation and Development.

Primary income on FDI are payments of direct investment income (debit side), which consist of income on equity (dividends, branch profits, and reinvested earnings) and income on the intercompany debt (interest).

Principal arrears on long-term debt are principal repayments due but not paid on long-term external debt, shown on a cumulative basis.

Principal repayments are the amounts of principal (amortization) paid in foreign currency, goods, or services in the year specified with respect to long-term external debt.

Private creditors are bondholders, commercial banks, and other trade-related lenders.

Private nonguaranteed debt is debt owed by private sector borrowers to external creditors on loans that do not benefit from a public sector guarantee by the debtor country.

Public and publicly guaranteed debt outstanding and disbursed is the value of debt at year's end of public sector borrowers, or borrowers with a public sector guarantee, owed to official and private lenders.

Public and publicly guaranteed external debt comprises public debt (an external obligation of a public debtor, such as the national government or agency, a political subdivision or agency, or an autonomous public body) and publicly guaranteed external debt (an external obligation of a private debtor that is guaranteed for repayment by a public entity).

Public debt is an external obligation of a public debtor, including all levels of government, state-owned enterprises, public corporations, development banks, and any other autonomous public bodies of government.

Publicly guaranteed debt is an external obligation of a private debtor that is guaranteed for repayment by a public entity.

Reserves to external debt stocks is the ratio of international reserves to outstanding external debt.

Reserves to imports (months) is the ratio of international reserves to the value of imports of goods, services, and primary income in the year shown and is expressed in months:

$$\frac{\text{Reserves}}{\text{Imports}/12}$$

Short-term external debt has an original maturity of one year or less. Available data permit no distinction among public, publicly guaranteed, and private nonguaranteed short-term external debt.

Short-term to external debt stock ratio is the ratio of short-term external debt to total outstanding external debt.

Special Drawing Rights (SDRs) refer to an international reserve asset that was created by the IMF in 1969 to supplement its member countries' official reserves. The value of SDRs is based on a basket of four key international currencies: the U.S. dollar, the pound sterling, the Japanese yen, and the euro. In addition to playing a role as a supplementary reserve asset, SDRs serve as the unit of account for the IMF and some other international organizations.

Technical cooperation grants include (a) free-standing technical cooperation grants, which are intended to finance the transfer of technical and managerial skills or of technology for the purpose of building up general national capacity without reference to any specific investment projects, and (b) investment-related technical cooperation grants, which are aimed at strengthening the capacity to execute specific investment projects.

Total amount forgiven is the total amount of principal and interest due, principal and interest in arrears, and debt stock forgiven in the year specified.

Total amount rescheduled is the total amount of external debt rescheduled, including principal and interest due, principal and interest in arrears, charges, penalties, and debt stock in the year specified.

Total change in external debt stocks is the difference in the external debt stock between two consecutive years.

Use of IMF credit denotes members' drawings on the IMF other than amounts drawn against the country's reserve tranche position. Use of IMF credit includes purchases and drawings under Stand-By, Extended, Structural Adjustment, Enhanced Structural Adjustment, and Systemic Transformation Facility Arrangements as well as trust fund loans. SDR allocations are also included in this category.

www.ingramcontent.com/pod-product-compliance
Ingram Content Group UK Ltd.
Pitfield, Milton Keynes, MK11 3LW, UK
UKHW060419100426
469794UK00007B/22

9 781464 818004